SLAVERY'S MEDICINE

Early American Histories

Douglas Bradburn, John C. Coombs, and
S. Max Edelson, Editors

Slavery's Medicine

Illness and Labor in the British Plantation Caribbean

Claire E. Gherini

University of Virginia Press
Charlottesville and London

The University of Virginia Press is situated on the traditional lands of the Monacan Nation, and the Commonwealth of Virginia was and is home to many other Indigenous people. We pay our respect to all of them, past and present. We also honor the enslaved African and African American people who built the University of Virginia, and we recognize their descendants. We commit to fostering voices from these communities through our publications and to deepening our collective understanding of their histories and contributions.

University of Virginia Press
© 2025 by the Rector and Visitors of the University of Virginia
All rights reserved
Printed in the United States of America on acid-free paper

First published 2025

1 3 5 7 9 8 6 4 2

Library of Congress Cataloging-in-Publication Data
Names: Gherini, Claire, author
Title: Slavery's medicine : illness and labor in the British plantation Caribbean / Claire E. Gherini.
Description: Charlottesville : University of Virginia Press, 2025. | Series: Early American histories | Includes bibliographical references and index.
Identifiers: LCCN 2025001934 | ISBN 9780813952741 hardback | ISBN 9780813952758 paperback | ISBN 9780813952765 ebook
Subjects: LCSH: Medicine—West Indies, British—History—18th century | Enslaved persons—Health and hygiene—West Indies, British—History—18th century | Plantation workers—Health and hygiene—West Indies, British—History—18th century | West Indies, British—Social conditions—18th century | Great Britain—Colonies—America—History—18th century | BISAC: HISTORY / Caribbean & West Indies / Jamaica | HISTORY / Europe / Great Britain / Georgian Era (1714–1837)
Classification: LCC RA456.C27 G44 2025 | DDC 362.1086/2509729—dc23/eng/20250421
LC record available at https://lccn.loc.gov/2025001934

Cover art: Waeel quttene/shutterstock.com
Cover design: David Drummond

CONTENTS

	Acknowledgments	vii
	Notes on Sources and Methods	xi
	Introduction	1
1	Catastrophe's Threshold: Enslaved Sufferers, Speech, and the Negotiation of Incapacity	23
2	The New Business of Plantation Medicine	63
3	"All Lesser Matters Related to the Sick": Enslaved Healers and the Greater Work of Improvement Medicine	102
4	Uncontrolled Experiments	152
	Conclusion	183
	Notes	193
	Index	255

ACKNOWLEDGMENTS

After many years spent making this book, I hope to be able to express how deeply grateful I am for the generosity that so many people and institutions have shown to me.

I had the good fortune to work with excellent mentors at The Johns Hopkins University and the University of Texas at Austin. At UT, Carolyn Eastman nurtured my interest in the history of Early America. At every turn, she helped me navigate the process of becoming a PhD student and then a professional historian. Toby Ditz acculturated me to JHU and guided a seminar paper that became my first foray into healthcare and the plantation system. I remain in awe of Mary Fissell as an advisor and scholar. Amid a heavy load of her own and others' graduate students, she took me on as a student. She generously offered her time, thoughtful critique, and much-needed candor. I also owe a great deal to Philip D. Morgan, who shepherded this project's early stages and ensured that its scope remained manageable. As many have observed, Phil stressed that good history begins with iterative, empirical research. In marshalling the resources to ensure that I had the means to visit archives, Phil also made sure that there was room for the inevitable rabbit holes and wrong turns.

I have benefited from the extensive feedback of faculty and graduate students at JHU and the McNeil Center for Early American Studies. At Hopkins, I am grateful for the support, questions, and thoughtful critique I received from François Furstenberg, Katherine Arner, Joseph Adelman, Ian Beamish, Sara Damiano, Stephanie Gamble, Jonathan Gienapp, T. Cole Jones, Seth Stein LeJacq, Kathleen Murphy, Dexnell Peters, Nicholas Radburn, Jessica Rooney, Justin Roberts, David Schley, and Molly Warsh. A dissertation fellowship at the McNeil Center allowed me the time to write. My thinking was aided by Daniel Richter, Michelle and Roderick McDonald, and members of "the Room," especially Philippa Koch, Michael Blaakman, and Lindsay Van Tine.

Financial support for my dissertation research was provided by the Consortium for the History of Science, Technology, and Medicine; the American Antiquarian Society; the Virginia Historical Society;

Colonial Williamsburg; the Henry E. Huntington Library; the Library Company of Philadelphia; the John Carter Brown Library; the American Philosophical Society; the Charles Singleton Center for the Study of Premodern Europe at The Johns Hopkins University; the International Seminar on the History of the Atlantic World at Harvard University; the McNeil Center for Early American Studies; and the American Institute for the History of Pharmacy. Thank you as well to the research staff and directors of the libraries and archives whose collections form the basis for this book. Thank you especially to Jim Greene and Connie King at the Library Company of Philadelphia, Paul Erickson at the American Antiquarian Society, and Arlene Shaner at the New York Academy of Medicine.

When I moved to New York, colleagues at Fordham and beyond gave the professional advice and encouragement that helped to move this project to completion. Some of my largest thanks go to Kirsten Swinth, who provided invaluable professional guidance that helped me navigate the process of book publication as well as the twists and turns of the early career. Thank you as well to my other Fordham colleagues, especially Saul Cornell, Ebru Turan, David Meyers, Wolfgang Mueller, Thierry Riggone, Nick Paul, Sal Acosta, Julie Kim, Yuko Miki, Samantha Iyer, Wes Alcenat, Tyesha Maddox, Matthew Armstrong, Chris Dietrich, and Maryanne Kowaleski. An O'Connell Grant from the department of history and a Faculty Research Grant underwrote additional research in British archives. A Fordham Faculty Fellowship allowed me to take time off from teaching. With keen eyes for detail, Clare McCabe and Ian Gere gave valuable research assistance. Ongoing conversations with Nicholas Crawford have shaped this project significantly. During the loneliest days of the pandemic, he was a reliable Zoom writing companion. Our ongoing conversations about slavery, archives, and narrative continue to stimulate my thinking. Andrew Lipman has been an exceptional friend. When I came to the city, he welcomed me with open arms, introduced me to his social circles, and dragged me out of the apartment for fresh air and perspective.

A postdoctoral fellowship in the history of medicine at Cedars-Sinai Medical Center, generously endowed by Stephen and Sandra Joffe, facilitated the project's pivot from a dissertation on disease concepts and laboring populations in the British Atlantic to a study on healthcare, resistance, and plantation management in the British Caribbean. At Cedars-Sinai,

I received valuable mentorship on working in a medical research center from Leon Fine and Giddeon Manning and benefitted from the camaraderie and thoughts of Sari Siegel. Thank you as well to the faculty and students at the Department of the History of Science, Medicine, and Technology at UCLA for hosting me during my time in Los Angeles. I consider it my extremely good fortune to have met the wonderful Kirsten Moore-Sheeley. Over many years, she has read hundreds of messy pages, provided thoughtful feedback, and reassured me when I felt discouraged. Much of my thinking in this book has been shaped by our conversations.

As I was reaching the final stages, many colleagues read chapter drafts, book proposals, introductions, and more. David Schley, Justin Roberts, Matthew Crawford, Jim Sidbury, Carolyn Eastman, Brett Rushforth, Christopher Parsons, Ryan A. Kashanipour, and Paul Conrad provided feedback on chapter drafts and the introduction.

I am so thankful to have Benjamin Carp in my corner. He read the entire manuscript more than once and answered phone calls to talk to through problems and sticking points. I benefitted enormously from his careful eye, wise insights, and steady kindness. It has been a pleasure to think with him.

The final product was greatly enhanced by opportunities to share my research at conferences and smaller workshops and seminars. Portions of book chapters were presented at the Omohundro Institute of Early American History and Culture, the American Association for the History of Medicine, the North American Conference for British Studies, and the Society for the History of the Early American Republic. Thank you to Daniel Richter for inviting me to present at the McNeil Center's seminar on labor history in honor of Billy Smith. I thank Soraya de Chadarevian for inviting me to present my research on Black healers at UCLA's colloquium on the history science, medicine, and technology; Justin Roberts and the Lawrence D. Stokes Seminar at Dalhousie University; Nicole Eustace and the Atlantic History Workshop at New York University; Hannah Farber and Andrew Lipman and the participants of the Seminar on Early American History and Culture at Columbia University; and Blake McGready and Maddy Lafuse for inviting me to present at the Early American Research Seminar at CUNY Graduate Center.

I could not have asked for a better group of editors and production staff than I found at the University of Virginia Press. I am especially grateful to Nadine Zimmerli and the insightful reviewers she selected. Nadine believed in this project well before it was finished and her support, as well as line edits, made it that much easier to complete. Thank you as well to Wren Morgan Myers for ensuring that everything stayed on course.

Most of all I want to thank my family. My parents' support has been unwavering. They are exemplars of generosity, good humor, and curiosity. I thank as well my siblings, Sarah Gherini, Laurel Gherini, and William Kuntz. In addition to demystifying academia for me, Claire Smrekar has tirelessly checked in to offer her enthusiasm, love, and support. It is so easy to see why she is so beloved by her own students. For many years, Darren Schmidt has shown up to help out. He has been such an important person in my life and a wonderful source of support. Extended family—the Bells and the McDonalds especially—have hosted me on many occasions and given their good cheer along the way.

I dedicate this book to my parents.

NOTES ON SOURCES AND METHODS

I did not set out to write a labor history. When I first began this project, I aimed to tell stories about sickness, healing, and its negotiation at a more intimate scale than that offered by previous studies of medicine and plantation management, particularly Richard Sheridan's monumental *Doctors and Slaves*. I began first with correspondence related to the management of plantations, though discussions of illness occur infrequently in these records. While it is common for historians of plantation management to focus on particular regions or islands, as I sifted through this material it quickly became apparent that this study could not focus on a single region in the British Caribbean. There simply was not enough source material to differentiate among regions. The difference lay in the type of crop—the scale of sugar operations created more illness and encouraged particular arrangements for its management. So I ranged far and wide, examining records from multiple sugar plantations located across the British Caribbean, and some of the most extensive material came from Jamaica. These records include letters between absentee proprietors and their managers, rolls of enslaved people and their stations, and inventories of buildings. I also consulted prescriptive advice literature written for prospective plantation owners.

What I found surprised me. Instead of the confident voices of proprietors and medical men working in alignment with one another, I discovered that many different parties held their own convictions and pursued their own interests. Discussions of remedies and hospitals that appear in proprietor-attorney correspondence also revealed underlying intentions that I had not anticipated. Yes, these conversations reflected efforts to increase medical provision so as to improve enslaved people's health, albeit with the limited goal of extending their capacity for labor. But the correspondence also revealed that proprietors and attorneys were trying to wield greater control over the work and materials of healing itself. Numbers were one part of a larger story. Attorneys and proprietors also aimed to standardize diets and remedies; control the physical space where the sick would recuperate; set practitioners' pay; and constrain the mobility of healers and the sick. At a distance from the estate's daily operations, proprietors and attorneys tried to supersede enslaved people's customary autonomy to manage illness on their own terms, and they often challenged the ability of journeyman practitioners to set their rates of pay. Many of the conflicts I was seeing in these materials, I came to appreciate, were people's reactions to proprietors' and attorneys' efforts to upend long-standing customary arrangements.

The conflicts that emerged in these sources and other primary source materials were also a response to the novelty and difficulty of treating illness in large numbers, which required a delegated system of body management and created boundary disputes over different arenas of control. Parties who did not previously have sustained interactions with one another were now compelled into new working relationships. Doctors complained about their low pay and excessive responsibilities; managers bemoaned that enslaved healers did not heed their directions; the sick pushed back and tried to negotiate over the terms of their recovery; healers challenged managers and also used their position to wield power over other bondspeople. It was apparent that the demands of treating illness on such a large scale were forcing changes to the work of healing itself.

I realized that I was writing a labor history about the work involved in the management of illness en masse. To capture the work of treating the sick from the perspective of the many different parties, I pursued a research strategy that ranged across different types of sources. I also revisited old sources, such as plantation management records, and looked at them in new ways.

To understand the role of middling white men on plantations, I developed collective biographical profiles. Preliminary work on plantation business records indicated that plantation practitioners were not part of the elite but rather white immigrants who sought upward social mobility. To understand their working lives required looking in new places: I consulted the memoirs, diaries, and correspondence of overseers and plantation doctors and civil histories of the region. An unexpectedly revelatory set of texts included printed texts on tropical fevers, where members of the island's medical elite, located in garrisons and seaports, sometimes relayed practitioners' anecdotes about medical practice and medical conflict. Drawing on these materials, I compiled a prosopography of almost 150 medical practitioners in the Caribbean during the period under study—each practitioner's place of origin, death date, education, publications, and previous employment. I was expecting to find patterns—perhaps they shared a common religious affiliation or had passed through the same centers of medical education. I learned instead that many had experience in the British armed forces. At the same time, I also came to understand that the rich variety and oversupply of medical men *was* a major component of plantation medicine in the era of improvement.

Another important avenue of investigation led me to House of Commons Sessional Papers (HCSP), which contain testimony given on the floor of Parliament by planters, overseers, and plantation doctors on the conditions of slavery in West Indian colonies. This is some of the most richly detailed material on the activities, routines, and wages of medical men as well as colonists' arguments about why sickness abounded among enslaved people. Although these Parliamentary materials were created in 1788–92, it was clear in the actual testimony that they referred backward to earlier arrangements on plantations.

Hospital healers and yaws-house attendants formed the other group of people with a formally designated healing role on estates. Their interior lives and thoughts proved more elusive than those of medical men, but that did not mean I could not seek the answers to seemingly rudimentary yet revelatory questions. What did their work entail? What types of power did they amass through healing the sick? What did proprietors' efforts to reform body management do to healers' autonomy and authority?

As with the medical men, I began by creating a collective profile. I used lists of enslaved people from a particular estate (Mesopotamia in Jamaica). Mesopotamia's lists tracked the age, health, and occupations of the people enumerated within them over several decades. I chose Mesopotamia's records because their continuity over such a long span of time is exceptional. While plantation management texts generalized about enslaved healers, the Mesopotamia records enabled me to reconstruct the working lives and health of men and women healers with greater precision. These records were, however, far more recalcitrant than those I had employed for the medical men.

Moreover, like other documents produced by colonists about the enslaved, lists of enslaved people have their own form of tunnel vision.[1] They are part of the larger genre of records relating to slavery that enumerate. Such records are built around particular representational strategies that aim to reduce enslaved people to common qualities so as to facilitate enslaved people's exchange value as chattels. They are part of the enslaver's tools of commodification.[2] The Mesopotamia lists (and those from other estates) performed a similar type of abstraction. They provided to proprietors and attorneys a synoptic account of the estate's productive potential by reducing the quiddity of men, women, girls, and boys to their capacity for labor. They assign value and significance to enslaved people's lives according to their capacity to produce and reproduce while papering over relations of kinship, intimacy, and enmity. Although they represent that enslaved healers worked, they do not reveal how healers gained the knowledge that enabled that work. Nor do they explain how healers constituted their authority in relationship to others. They do not tell us much about what their work meant to them, to their families, to other people on the estate and elsewhere. The limitations of Mesopotamia's records are emblematic of the larger difficulties that arise in what Saidiya Hartman calls the "counter-histories of slavery," which often require using sources written for and by enslavers.[3]

One purpose for scholarship on slavery stems from the urgency to contest the perspective that enslaved people have no history or value beyond what colonists determined for them. The representational strategies that organize many of the records available to scholars, however, create silences that, in turn, challenge scholars' efforts to recover the inner worlds and tactical maneuvers of enslaved people. Records like Mesopotamia's lists of enslaved people (and others that deny enslaved people's capacity to think and respond) exemplify this problem, and they comprise a large portion of the materials with which scholars of slavery of the eighteenth-century British Caribbean work. Scholars who seek to learn something beyond the basic facts of enslaved people's lives are thus repeatedly confronted with the ethical and pragmatic challenges posed by these materials.

The historian Jennifer L. Morgan points a way forward. She contends that one must "foreground the speculative."[4] Speculation challenges the historical discipline's demand for "mountains of evidence" as a prerequisite for the claim that "Africans and African Americans actually possessed a history."[5] Yet as a practice, it is often at odds with the discipline's other demand—that scholars write with "the authority of the omniscient narrator's voice."[6] Thus, speculation also sets out the terms under which scholars write about enslaved people ethically and with complexity using scraps of disparate evidence rather than coherent and orderly archives. It recognizes the impossibility of fully reconstructing the many motivations and thoughts of the people whom the archives of slavery treat as objects rather than human agents. At the same time, it demands that we try.

Speculation goes hand in hand with triangulation. Triangulation involves bringing multiple points of view to the same subject. In the case of historical documents relating to slavery, it entails moving between what is stated in the document, what is left out, and bringing a wide reading of primary and secondary sources—especially what is known about enslaved people's political strategies—to bear on the interpretation of what enslaved people were trying to accomplish at any given moment.[7] Triangulation works especially well in instances in primary source material when managers and proprietors complained about enslaved people's actions. In those instances, the archive cracks open and one can apprehend that enslaved people registered the novelty of their circumstances and challenged them, responding with creativity. Indeed, working through plantation records reveals that managers' and proprietors' efforts to control the work of healing did not go uncontested. On the one hand, these sources illustrate how colonists attempted to place blame on enslaved people, whether patients or healers, for perpetuating illness and subverting discipline. On the other, they inadvertently reveal that these same groups struggled against plantation managerial staff and with one another.

Medical case histories are one type of record that is unusually rich with enslaved people's presence and actions. They appear in both manuscript and print. Accessing case histories is in some ways more difficult than the business records of plantation management. To be sure, the doctors who wrote them were noisy and good at self-promotion, but the British medical journals where many published their work were often short-lived. Major databases of printed material, such as Eighteenth-Century Collections Online, have not digitized many of them. To unearth these obscure, relatively inaccessible journals required visits to independent medical libraries and the archives of colleges of physicians.

Case histories are not typically understood as part of the archives of slavery. But the conventions of the case history genre mean that these writings are an especially good resource for reconstructing the many parties involved in healing and enslaved people's struggles for control. The author of a case history was expected to summarize the basic parameters of what had occurred and what he had observed, which give them a narrative quality.[8] Accounts include the patient's age, sex, demeanor, symptoms, and how the doctor treated the affliction. Their narratives often displayed verbosity and circuitous thinking—so their case histories also contain asides with further details about enslaved people's actions, expectations, and testimony. Practitioners often composed them during the time of their employment, often mere days or weeks after the event under discussion. This genre expected its authors to transform readers into "virtual witnesses" by including the many details of the event under discussion.[9] Practitioners mentioned, therefore, the myriad ways that enslaved people disrupted their work, which I read as enslaved people's efforts to bend this system of body management to their own needs. Reading these case histories cumulatively and seeing the same patterns across them reveals that medical men's claims for authority and control were aspirational rather than actual. Moreover, case histories provide a sense of what enslaved people wanted and did in response to doctors' and overseers' actions. These unique sources help to underpin my argument about the negotiated nature of medical authority and managers' interventions.

How can one use archival records to recover not just enslaved people's pushback but, in each instance, what enslaved people were trying to achieve either as individuals or collectively? What had proprietors' and attorneys' interventions disrupted? What previous arrangements or set of norms were enslaved people trying to reproduce? Managers, proprietors, and practitioners rarely took notice of enslaved people's motivations. They framed enslaved people's insistence on certain medicines or diets, or their flight from yaws houses and hot-houses to convalesce in quarters, as irksome disruptions. Here triangulating with secondary material pointed a path forward to speculating on what men and women wanted when they disrupted proprietors' and practitioners' plans.

The archives from the British plantation Caribbean are thinner for the period prior to 1750; therefore, it was challenging to understand what medicine and care looked like when enslaved people had much more autonomy. I have filled in the picture by reorienting my thinking geographically. To understand what managers and proprietors disrupted, I investigate the practices of healing and beliefs about illness that prevailed in enslaved people's quarters and other spaces outside of managers' purview. I benefited from scholarship on Obeah as well as on slavery in the Spanish and French Caribbean. These scholars have revealed that medicine intersected with a sacralized natural world and functioned as a way for enslaved people to mediate conflict and cement their ties to one another. Of course, enslaved people's engagement with this system of body management was not uniform. Still, it is possible to see enslaved people's responses to managers' intrusions not as an effort to preserve tradition for tradition's sake. Instead, these responses were sometimes expressions of affective ties or an attempt to re-create what Vincent Brown calls "idioms of belonging" that enslaved people performed when confronted with illness. Enslaved people tried to use hospitals and yaws houses as best as they could to survive, to reconfirm their relations with one another, to identify who belonged and who did not, and to reassert their interpretive authority and their autonomy to heal, often in defiance of how managers wanted these spaces to operate.

Proprietors and attorneys had sought a solution to the problem of illness in abstraction by thinking about sick individuals in aggregates—to them, enslaved people were a group whose illnesses would be treated and tracked collectively. Proprietors' actions generated quantitative records that allowed scholars to reveal the scope and volume of illness on sugar estates at different times and places. But as much as they illuminate, the numbers also obscure the social frictions that arose when proprietors and managers tried to impose their own terms for how the sick would recuperate. By thinking capaciously about the labor of healing and using a rich variety of sources from across the British plantation Caribbean, it becomes apparent that the varieties of people involved in healing extended beyond doctors and healers and that enslaved people contested proprietors' intrusions.

Introduction

———•◦•———

IN THE 1780s, William Chamberlaine, a plantation doctor in Jamaica, spent his days riding among the estates of his enslaver-clients. On a visit to one of the plantations on his list, he encountered the bookkeeper, John Edmonds. Bookkeepers were men in their early adolescence who lived on plantations and worked as overseers' apprentices.[1] As part of his training to become an overseer, Edmonds was responsible for creating some of the records that tracked the laboring capacity of the estate's enslaved people. Chamberlaine's first order of business was to consult Edmonds's hot-house book. This small book was kept in the plantation's hospital (known colloquially as a hot-house), where the enslaved sick were confined during their illnesses.[2]

Before Chamberlaine's arrival, Edmonds had visited the building and begun his daily responsibilities. He likely checked the hospital book and started to make the medicines that Chamberlaine had prescribed on an earlier visit. He almost certainly consulted the enslaved healer who maintained a consistent presence there.[3] Typically, this was an older woman, sometimes as much as twenty-five years senior to the adolescent bookkeeper, outranking him in age and experience. The healer would have given Edmonds an account of sufferers housed at the hospital and perhaps suggested remedies alongside those that Chamberlaine had prescribed.[4] Every day, enslaved people would have staggered to the building from their own quarters to petition the healer or Edmonds for admission to the hospital to obtain two elements critical to their survival—sustenance and a reprieve from work. Edmonds admitted few; when he did, he jotted down their names and described their afflictions with a single word each—sometimes a disease name, more often a symptom—in the hospital book. His entries condensed sufferers' accounts of their unusual sensations and pains, omitting from the record the immediate and remote events that had precipitated them. Edmonds also noted the remedies the healer administered to the sick. If and when they recuperated, Edmonds entered the date of their departure and completed the entry.

These records were a way for Edmonds to create a paper trail of his own activities. They also placed enslaved people into the estate's larger "paper panopticon," comprised not only of hospital books but also worklogs, lists of the sick, and inventories of enslaved people. Managers created these documents to track the work, strength, and illnesses of enslaved people, all with the goal of extracting additional labor value from them.[5] The medical arithmetic that underlay this type of accounting boosted managers' confidence in their ability to treat illness expeditiously for large numbers of people at once.[6]

The hot-house book was also useful for other medical workers on the estate. Chamberlaine made use of it. Doctors like him operated in a particular social and economic context: since absentee proprietors of sugar estates and their resident attorneys determined the doctors' compensation, their business was only viable if they could scale up their operations to service many plantations at a time and cut the duration of each visit to the bare minimum. The hot-house book was especially useful for facilitating such efficiencies. Because of these records, Chamberlaine generally did not consult the sick directly, nor did he spend much time with bookkeepers like Edmonds; instead, he scanned Edmonds's entries and scribbled down remedies.[7] Then he shut the hospital book, remounted his horse, and made his way to the next estate. Edmonds then read Chamberlaine's instructions to the healer, whom he expected to work as his auxiliary. Edmonds, the bookkeeper, did not interact much with the sick; Chamberlaine, the doctor, even less so. Instead, an enslaved healer ascertained illness, provided care, and administered the remedies that either she, Chamberlaine, or Edmonds would have prescribed. As she did so, she maneuvered among the rival demands of Edmonds and Chamberlaine as well as those of the sick and their family members.

The hot-house book—Chamberlaine's and Edmonds's interactions with it as well as the enslaved people whose thoughts, words, and actions were kept out of it—marked significant transformations in the ways that illness was experienced and managed on sugar estates in the British Caribbean. During the second half of the eighteenth century, absentee proprietors and their managerial staff (a category that includes estate attorneys who made purchasing decisions, overseers who managed day-to-day operations, as well as adolescent bookkeepers such as Edmonds)

INTRODUCTION

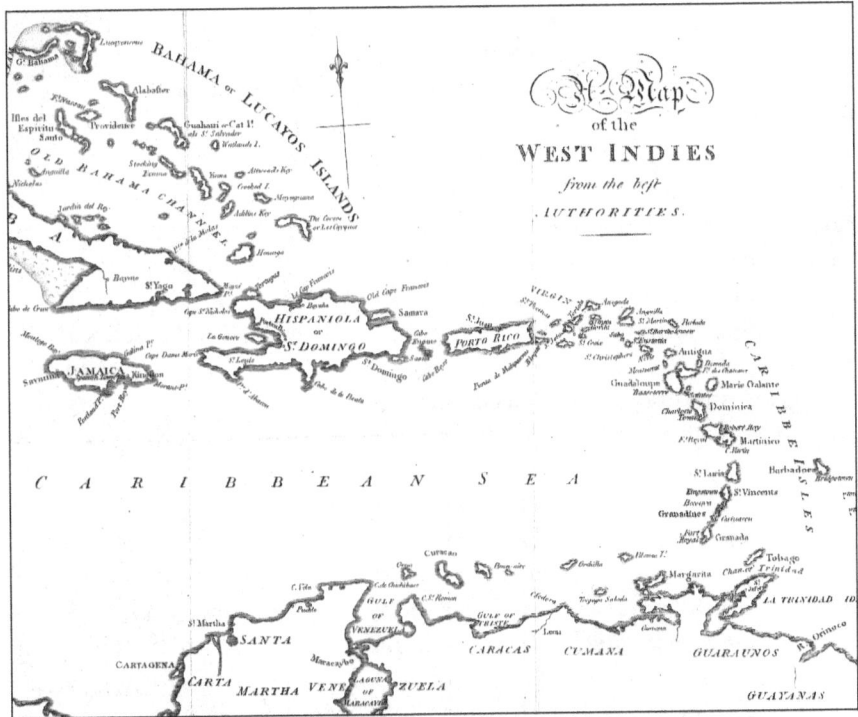

FIG. I. *A map of the West Indies from the best authorities.* London: I. Stockdale, Picadilly, 1799. (John Carter Brown Library).

tried to take control over how enslaved people healed and contributed to the labor of healing. Proprietors believed that making their estates more profitable required gaining better control over medicine and developing a program of body management that could treat a number of people for illness at the same time.

The ability to scale up the treatment of illness was especially necessary on sugar plantations, where the rates of mortality among the enslaved population were ghastly and significantly higher than on other types of estates. While plantation slavery enfeebled enslaved people everywhere, sugar wore people down and killed faster than other crops. Managers and proprietors pushed enslaved men and women to their physical limits, forcing enslaved people into a punishing existence that made them especially vulnerable to illness. The combination of proprietors' greed and sugar's demands meant that nearly every enslaved person spent a part of the year incapacitated in one way or another.[8] To uphold this brutal work regime, proprietors created another one to manage illness. At their direction, a bricolage of people and things coalesced around plantation sickhouses, forming a labor system of care and discipline that sustained the work in cane fields and boiling houses.

Slavery's Medicine is a new social and labor history of medicine and care on West Indian sugar plantations that charts transformations in the experience of illness and its management by foregrounding important changes in the work undertaken by a complex series of actors, Black and white, enslaved and free, elite and middling, in the labor of recuperating the sick and in the development of medical knowledge. This was a "hybrid system of exploitation" that used both free and enslaved labor to recover the sick to a laboring capacity.[9] In treating the history of medicine in slavery as a history of work, *Slavery's Medicine* asks how enslaved people's and middling whites' practices of interpreting illness, making remedies, and administering care were transformed by new methods in plantation management. Proprietors first pursued these strategies in the middle of the eighteenth century. They did so not as ameliorating paternalists, as they would later argue, but as businessmen and capitalists.[10] Looking at how the work of healing changed over time reveals a much more variegated landscape of healing than that of doctors and slaves.

Absentees and their attorneys targeted their interventions to the locations where enslaved people recuperated, the activities that people undertook in recovering the sick, and the medicines that sufferers consumed. They hired medical men like Chamberlaine; built spaces of medical confinement and surveillance, such as hospitals and yaws-houses (separate spaces reserved for the isolation and treatment of enslaved people afflicted with yaws); warehoused the sick within them; and stationed enslaved workers in these spaces as healers and guards. As they incentivized enslaved hospital healers to undermine the bodily autonomy of others, proprietors' interventions elevated some enslaved people at the expense of others, reshaping old hierarchies and creating new ones. Managers and proprietors also integrated new remedies into the therapeutic repertoire, purchasing imported pharmaceuticals as well as locally produced remedies on offer from enterprising practitioners. Finally, they made records about the sick and tracked the disbursement of medicines by hiring young men to their estates as bookkeepers and assigning these responsibilities to them. This assemblage formed a system of body management, one intended to make medical care more efficient, not only through the introduction of new materials and ideas but in the co-option and redeployment of enslaved people's medical knowledge and carework. As Chamberlaine rode away, he left behind an estate where healers and the sick had less autonomy to determine how they operated than they did fifty years earlier. These circumstances were novel. But they did not go uncontested.

Indeed, sufferers, enslaved healers, and families of the sick would continue to influence the spaces, materials, languages, and records that formed the rudiments of proprietors' system of body management, even as managers and proprietors tried to dictate from the top down. In addition to composing remedies, healers fetched and administered medicines that practitioners prescribed. Healers kept sick-houses orderly to support the viability of practitioners' experiments. Or they decided to forgo the administration of some medicines and foiled practitioners' trials. Sufferers refused to ingest imported pharmaceuticals without sugar to help them go down more easily. Their family members surreptitiously offered them familiar articles of dietary comfort that, in turn, undermined managers' efforts to standardize diets for the sick. Enslaved people petitioned for rest and nourishment and learned the languages, gestures, and words necessary to make a convincing case. Sufferers lingered in plantation hospitals rather than return to a brutalizing work regime that they understood would kill them. The sick and healers challenged adolescent bookkeepers. Enslaved people banded together to intimidate overseers and dissuade them from handing over the dead to doctors to dissect. Scholarship examining medicine's role in enslaved people's resistance to slavery has tended to focus on the use of medicine and medical ritual in collective, coordinated action against the plantation labor system.[11] Yet, as *Slavery's Medicine* contends, enslaved people's responses to proprietors' programs, although often improvised and carried out as individuals, are also part of the history of antislavery.

They are also part of the history of modern medicine. In recent years, scholars have convincingly argued that empire and the slavery were vital for the emergence of modern medicine. War-making and slave-trading created dependent, sickly populations and placed them together in a single space, thereby enabling doctors and medical students to observe, medicate, and dissect. In field hospitals, barracks, and slave ships, practitioners developed novel theories about disease distinctiveness, aggregated data, and developed explanations to account for how certain afflictions spread and became infectious.[12] Proprietors' innovations in plantation management also created the material conditions by which managers and practitioners prodded, observed, and aggregated information about the sick and their afflictions. Yet our understanding of modern medicine is incomplete without examining enslaved people's creative responses to these intrusions, which they pursued for myriad reasons: to etch out a modicum of comfort, gain power over others, form connections, and, above all, to survive.[13] A tidy global story of evolution, empiricism, and reform in medicine looks different from the perspective of a bedridden patient on a Jamaican plantation, seeking medicine, sugar, or simply rest, or an elderly healer arguing to a fifteen-year-old bookkeeper that the roots of the hog plum tree were a better cure for yaws than tartar emetic. It was not just the ambitions of medical men or proprietors that created modern medicine; it was also the wants and needs of enslaved people. Modern medicine was, in part, the creation of slaves themselves.

It is tempting to assume that proprietors increased their attention to illness only in the late eighteenth century and were acting to ameliorate slavery in response to the subsistence crises associated with the Revolutionary War era, the increase in the cost of African captives, as well as the rise of slave-trade abolitionism.[14] Proprietors did try to gain control over how enslaved women conceived, gave birth, and reared children in the last decades of the eighteenth century, as a way to stabilize an enslaved population that could not expand, naturally, on its own due to the ways that slavery brutalized enslaved women in particular.[15] Yet proprietors came to realize several decades earlier, independent of their concerns about slave-trade abolitionism, that they needed to standardize medicines and diets for the sick, minimize unpredictability in the costs of caring for the sick, and develop a program of body management that could treat a number of people for illness at the same time.

The capacity to manage large numbers of the sick first became urgent on sugar estates in the middle of the eighteenth century, when proprietors increased the size of their slaveholdings and decided that they needed to take a more systematic approach to the management of their estates. The number of men, women, and children that proprietors held in captivity presented a daunting amount of sickness with which to contend. Although these reforms might have occurred on plantations growing other types of crops, the ability to manage illness on an industrial scale was particularly relevant to sugar estates.

Sugar cultivation "favors economies of scale."[16] British planters grew wealthy by creating integrated plantations that combined cane fields with manufacturing facilities on a single estate, powered by large forces of enslaved people.[17] In terms of the number of people they held in bondage, sugar plantations were always larger than those that grew other types of crops. The creation of some of the largest slaveholdings across the Caribbean took place after midcentury. A sizeable number developed in Jamaica, where the island's economy was ruled by a few hundred sugar planters. Jamaica's Worthy Park plantation had 500 slaves; York had 449.[18] Each massive slaveholding in Jamaica and other islands came to form its own "center of population" in the island's hinterlands.[19] These agricultural behemoths represent extremes. On average, in the late eighteenth century, an enslaved sugar worker in Jamaica lived on a plantation with 154 enslaved people. Looking more broadly across the British Caribbean, enslaved people who lived on sugar estates were, on average, on slaveholdings with 100 people.[20] *Slavery's Medicine* argues that proprietors' actions and enslaved people's responses need to be understood in the context of the growth in the size of slaveholdings.

Numbers are nothing new to historians of plantation management. Until very recently, most scholarship on medicine in the sugar plantation complex has focused on the diseases that plagued enslaved people and analyzed rates of mortality and morbidity.[21] This scholarship shows seasonal fluctuations in sickliness and death and reveals that some periods of slavery were more brutal than others. This literature has shown that efforts to improve slavery did not meaningfully alter the brutality or brevity of enslaved people's lives.[22] A focus on variations in rates of attrition are important. Yet this fixation on numbers to the exclusion of all else replicates the methods of quantification and enumeration that enslavers had used, and therefore runs the risk of abstracting the emotional and fleshy experiences of illness and death into bloodless accounts of decrease and loss. To borrow a metaphor from scholars of urban history, looking at the numbers alone is a bit like looking at a map to understand a city. It reveals much about the shape of things but not the relationships and struggles within that shape. *Slavery's Medicine* seeks to recapture the history of healing at a more intimate scale so as to excavate the ways enslaved people reckoned with proprietors' and managers' actions. To do so is to escape the prison of numbers and reconstruct enslaved people as individuals: their interests, vices, and strategies, as well as their antagonisms with and connections to others—in short, the thoughts and actions that made them human.

Looking at enslaved people's changing experiences of illness requires better periodizing proprietors' efforts to gain greater control over medicine and care. Their efforts were part of a larger agricultural improvement movement that first took hold in the plantation Caribbean in the middle of the eighteenth century.[23] Sugar plantations were intricate and sophisticated enterprises. As scholars of agricultural improvement and the plantation enlightenment have demonstrated, adherents of this movement sought to make plantations more productive by making them more efficient. They focused their efforts on improving agricultural techniques—such as manuring and intercropping techniques—as a way to simultaneously ameliorate enslaved people's labor burdens and increase productivity. Proprietors and managers believed they could simultaneously rationalize the production of cane and soften the effects of slavery. Simultaneously, they implemented complex managerial hierarchies, diversified the labor force, and developed sophisticated systems of recordkeeping that allowed them to judge the effects of their experiments and lay down principles of management that would direct their future actions.[24] Collectively these strategies allowed proprietors to derive greater labor value from the people they held in bondage. Just as proprietors sought to rationalize the production of sugarcane, they also, as *Slavery's Medicine* contends, believed that they could take a more systematic approach to the management of illness.

When proprietors surveyed how estates were run, they saw opportunities to exercise more control over medicine and care, standardize remedies, and impose more uniformity in the treatment of illness. Few letters, diaries, and plantation management guides from the seventeenth and first half of the eighteenth centuries discussed sick-houses, the appointment of enslaved people to healing stations, remedies, surgical tools, and measuring instruments. Only sugar barons—that is, plantation owners with massive plantation operations—employed doctors as salaried members of their estates. Yet, by the end of the Seven Years' War, these materials and personnel had become as essential to good plantation management (and proprietors' and managers' control) as agricultural implements, imported rations, textiles, account books, manacles, whips, and chains. These implements were made as economic calculations that proprietors decided would make medicine's costs more predictable. Above all, proprietors wanted to make medicine more efficient.

The medical system that developed under proprietors' direction, as *Slavery's Medicine* reveals, was a modern, innovative, and adaptive one. I call the system of body management that proprietors developed "plantation medicine." This health care system was meant to sustain enslaved people's working capacity with a bare minimum of expenditure. It engaged in practices of abstraction that also prevailed on the "floating factory" of the slave ship and the "factory-like" and "industrial" production regime in the fields, where individual Africans with pasts, particular bodies, and connections to others were transformed into fungible units of manpower.[25]

Edmonds's entries in the hot-house book, for example, transformed the sick from a group of individuals into a series of cases—bodies to be counted, symptoms to be studied, and remedies to be tracked—and encouraged medical practitioners, such as Chamberlaine, to see them that way as well. These processes of aggregation, standardization, and abstraction were at the heart of this system. The hot-house book allowed managers and doctors to condense information about individuals' illness into standardized units of information—name and symptom or disease—that would be addressed by standardized remedies. Such compression streamlined the treatment of illness by reducing the amount of attention given to each person's case and minimizing the particulars of their afflictions. Plantation managers used hospital books for a number of functions: they tracked the prevalence of particular complaints and the consumption of medicines to remedy them. By studying this information serially, they could identify which medicines worked best; for instance, Edmonds concluded that cowhage was particularly efficacious in treating worms.[26] This new modern system of body management transformed its suffering subjects into objects for the study of disease and remedies, with deliberate indifference to the sick's physiological individuality and social personhood.

To render the enslaved sick "interchangeable," proprietors relied on the labor of others to coerce the enslaved sick into new social relationships, drugs, and edifices.[27] As *Slavery's Medicine* argues, many interests, accommodations, and antagonisms shaped the enslaved experience of sickness. *Slavery's Medicine* therefore revises what we know about the social and labor relations of the more familiar people involved in the management of illness—ordinary doctors and healers—and it also discusses four additional groups of players: proprietors and attorneys, overseers, the sick and their families, and plantation management writers. The how-to texts of plantation management authors nurtured an optimism among managers that it was within their capacity to select and make medicines themselves. These groups all mediated the experience of illness in the second half of the eighteenth century. *Slavery's Medicine* asks how proprietors and attorneys tried to change the work of healing. It highlights the ways that proprietors and attorneys had to reshape and temper their plans, due to middling whites' pursuit of their own interests and enslaved people's accommodations, acts of resistance, and outright refusals.

Efforts to develop a scheme to treat and tend to many patients at once changed the work of healing itself. Absentees and the attorneys who counseled them believed that body management should be organized around a hierarchical division of labor; they also purchased new materials that would allow them to treat the sick in large numbers. Medical work on West Indian plantations came to resemble the organization of labor in hospitals of the British metropole and the armed forces: white men, such as Edmonds and Chamberlaine, interpreted symptoms and ordered cures, while (enslaved) women administered the medicines and performed more menial forms of carework.

This new configuration challenged established hierarchies of decision-making and expertise on estates. It created boundary disputes among healers, doctors, and managers. Many of the conflicts that ensued concerned medical remedies. Traditionally, enslaved healers (many of whom were women) wielded great power and authority to diagnose and administer remedies. The roots of their power ran deep.[28] During the era of improvement, managers continued to hold African and Afro-Caribbean healers' counsel in high regard. Yet they also subjected healers' remedies to greater scrutiny, and they sought to arrogate for themselves the existing practices and conventions of care that enslaved people had laid down.[29] Proprietors sought as well to integrate manufactured medicines purchased from abroad and local remedies ordered from practitioners into existing therapeutic practices. Healers thus found themselves contending with orders to impose new, alien remedies onto others. They were forced to mediate between managers' and the sick's beliefs about what materials best supported health. The men in this program also struggled with one another over decision-making. To be sure, medical practitioners like Chamberlaine became a more regular presence on estates. But they did not outrank overseers and attorneys. Many colonists, as well as most absentees, regarded medical men's ideas, decisions, and remedies as subordinate.

In their efforts to treat the enslaved sick in large numbers, quickly, and with as few resources as possible, proprietors, overseers, doctors, and attorneys were aided by developments overseas. In Britain, a robust pharmaceutical industry promoted the idea that good health was both a matter of public necessity and within the means of ordinary consumers to attain.[30] Merchant-druggists selling commercial pharmaceuticals promoted the idea in their packaging and marketing materials that "anybody, whether free or unfree, old or young, poor or rich, suffering from a certain ailment," could find relief "with a similar pill or tincture from a laboratory in London."[31] Imported pharmaceuticals, which offered the possibility of healing the sick in large numbers irrespective of the sick's race, gender, or station, would come to have a more prominent place on estates. Indeed, the incorporation of commercial pharmaceuticals and diets that addressed particular illnesses rather than particular people was foundational to efforts to make treatments for illness more uniform. Instead of calibrating care to the individual and listening to the patient-person, practitioners and managers employed medicines and diets that they believed would target the specific disease or cluster of symptoms. The premise of these medicines—known as specifics—was that they had the same effects from person to person.[32] Unfree labor regimes across the British Empire increasingly incorporated imported pharmaceutical medicines. Commercial medicines that targeted specific diseases encouraged the managers in charge of dependent populations, including those who managed enslaved people, to imagine bodies as interchangeable.[33]

The premises about bodies that underwrote imported pharmaceuticals contravened medical orthodoxy and vernacular practice. Traditionally, colonists believed people each possessed their own "idiosyncratic constitution."[34] A person's sex, age, strength, location, diet, station, and emotions were supposed to have molded their body into its particular form. Traditional medical practice maintained that it was necessary to calibrate treatments to a person's physiologically distinctive body, which meant that practitioners could adjust medicines and courses of therapeutic action as the distemper or condition changed its form.[35] Yet in the rough-and-ready world of sugar estates, where illness represented lost labor value, proprietors and managers treated enslaved people's bodies as fungible. This was a matter of pragmatic calculation that discarded older norms governing diagnosis and treatment.

Practitioners treated bodies as interchangeable therapeutically as well as socially through a process of isolation. Enslaved sufferers often rejected the new medicines that proprietors and managers sought to impose on them from above. To circumvent sufferers' and their kin's protests, managers temporarily separated enslaved sufferers from larger webs of affinity by sequestering the sick in hospitals and sick-houses. Separating the sick from the healthy also limited contagion, of course. Additionally, keeping the sick in one place instead of the sick's individual houses saved the healers and practitioners from trekking throughout the estate. Yet the sequestration of sufferers was also a principal goal of the new hospital system. To be sure, managers and proprietors did not achieve the total alienation of the sick. Enslaved people continued to express affinity through surreptitious gestures of care, and the enslaved sick bargained with managers over the terms of their recovery. All the same, by keeping many of the sick locked away, managers made illness into an alienating event.

Achieving uniformity and standardizing treatments was a bumpy process. A veritable cornucopia of ideas and advice moved through local circuits of exchange and the transatlantic information economy, alongside a world swirling with commercial pharmaceuticals and homemade remedies. The sheer abundance of information and commodities stymied efforts to create uniformity and develop standard practices. Managers struggled to reconcile timeworn therapeutic traditions, which they learned about from one another and from enslaved healers, with new information and materials coming from outside—from their proprietor-employers, overseas druggists, and the practitioners who made regular visits to the estate. A neighbor's, doctor's, or merchant's endorsement of a drug or remedy did not necessarily make it viable, safe, and efficacious. Verifying a remedy therefore became a requisite component of good plantation management. Managers had to learn how people, pressed to their human limits, could be recuperated cheaply. The aggregation of people into hospitals and hospital books engendered experiments about how best to cure illnesses. Sometimes the scale of experiments on enslaved people rivaled what occurred in British voluntary hospitals.[36]

Enslaved labor was vital to the quest to standardize remedies. A trial could only work so long as experimental subjects consumed the remedy in question, without corruption from other substances that were not part of the experiment. Healers' disciplinary work to keep sick-houses in order and administer cures generated the credibility for managers' (and practitioners') medical truth-claims. Managers could argue, under such conditions, that certain substances were particularly efficacious and worked universally because they had been vetted in a controlled space.

As they routinized medicine, proprietors imagined that the people they employed and held in bondage would work in harmony with one another, moving predictably, almost like gears in a machine. Indeed, machine metaphors were popular among plantation owners. The Antiguan enslaver and advice writer Samuel Martin advised readers to conceive of the sugar plantation as a "well-constructed machine, composed of various wheels, turning different ways, and yet all contributing to the great end proposed."[37] The salience of the machine metaphor lay in its ability to cast enslaved people as objects driven by the laws of physics rather than human will.

But "human beings are not drive gears and human institutions are not steam engines," as Edmund Morgan and Marie Morgan write.[38] It would therefore be a mistake to consider this new program of body management as a mechanistic system where proprietors achieved efficiency through greater control. Proprietors' ability to make medical care more efficient by treating the sick as interchangeable was incomplete, because they required enslaved people not just for their work but also for their expertise, their botanical knowledge, and their relationships with others. This was, moreover, a delegated system of body management that involved overseers and journeymen practitioners as well. Under these circumstances, enslaved people resisted and aligned with doctors or overseers as warranted, to thereby shape the system's ultimate form. They refused to accept slavery's governing logic—that enslaved people and their bodies were fungible.

Conflicts arose over the types of remedies employed in restoring the sick. Many other tensions about health concerned time—most especially how long it ought to take to recuperate the sick from illness. In erecting spaces for the control of the sick, proprietors believed that they were better able to impose their own expectations on the duration of illness and the amount of rest one needed to recuperate. Proprietors envisioned the people they held in captivity as both capital and manpower—and they sought to extend their working capacity over a time horizon of many years rather than several seasons.[39] They believed their white overseers ought to hold the same view, and they imagined that their white subordinates and enslaved healers would work in lockstep with one another and in accordance with absentees' expectations. But proprietors who were able to achieve forced synchronization in the field could not as easily do the same in hospitals and yaws huts. Medicine in the era of improvement was rarely orderly, because the players' divergent ambitions to either get ahead or stay alive and protect their innermost circles were often at odds with one another and with enslavers' intentions. Overseers, for instance, often warped plantation medicine into a system with even shorter time horizons than those demanded by absentees. Managers faced productivity quotas but knew that purchases of new slaves would be the plantation owners' responsibility. They tried to make stays in hospitals as unpleasant as possible, therefore, so as to motivate the sick to get back to work for the immediate cultivation cycle. The impact of this speedup would be a greater death rate, but the managers would be off the hook.

Although doctors like Chamberlaine understood that their business was only viable so long as they could address the needs of many plantations at a time, the behavior of absentees and managers also incentivized practitioners to spend as little time with the sick as possible. Attorneys cut plantation practitioners' salaries to the bone, forcing them into working conditions that required them to take on many estates, which limited the amount of time they spent with the sick. As Chamberlaine's visit reveals, hot-house books functioned as a recordkeeping device as well as a communications technology. Their brief entries bridged the gap between the paltry pay afforded to plantation practitioners and the demands that absentees and managers made on their time. These records informed doctors like Chamberlaine of enslaved people's illnesses. Simultaneously, they ensured that people like Chamberlaine did not have to speak with the hospital healer, much less the sick. Plantation doctors thus developed their own version of short-termism and prescribed medicines according to the symptom rather than the story that a patient might tell.

Enslaved people's bonds of affinity created time-consuming frictions that managers sought to circumvent. The reorganization of the work of healing was meant to exclude family members and outside parties from assisting the sick, so as to keep outside interference at bay. Limiting outsiders was one of the ways that managers tried to enforce short time-horizons for recovery. They believed that this arrangement would better control people who were absent from work.

Yet managers attempted to impose these changes in a Black world. Enslaved people developed creative ways to affirm their ties to one another *within* as well as *outside* of this system of body management. For enslaved sufferers, strength came in numbers. The sick and their families pushed to be met on their terms: to have managerial staff listen to accounts of their ailments and to take into consideration the lengthy nature of their complaints. When they pressured an overseer, plantation doctor, or even a hospital healer to let the sick into the hospital for much-needed rest and sustenance, when they crowded around a doctor to make sure that he knew he was under scrutiny, and when they covertly refused to administer a harsh medicine or to respond to a doctor's inquiries, bondspeople reinforced their solidarities with one another across the lines of rank and status. Such expressions of affinity occurred as much through enslaved people's engagement with this system as in their avoidance of it. Although hospitals were designed to isolate the sick from the estate's larger social world, far more people clamored to be part of the decision-making process than proprietors intended.

Managers and practitioners also attempted to reduce the amount of talk and negotiation involved in the process of recuperation, primarily as a matter of expediency. In times of illness, one's ability to speak about unusual pains and sensations is fundamental to claiming one's personhood. Yet managers rarely expressed interest in the unusual and uncomfortable sensations that brought sufferers to the hospital, beyond whether they were severe enough to warrant time away from work. They often saw little value in documenting enslaved affliction or its uncertain origins extensively. The hot-house book and hospitals were valuable because they limited communications. The hospital books facilitated the exchange of information between middling white managers and people like Chamberlaine *about* the sick. Hospitals, meanwhile, limited communications *among* enslaved people and the kin who cared about them.

The compression of enslaved people's testimony in official records is visible in the ways that people like Edmonds and Chamberlaine made and exchanged knowledge about particular remedies. Like previous generations of colonists, Edmonds and Chamberlaine had learned much of what they knew by speaking with enslaved healers. Yet unlike their predecessors, Edmonds and other managers did not narrate the discovery of the efficacy of different medical simples as a heroic process of speaking to and translating from enslaved people. When the adolescent Edmonds tried to impress Chamberlaine with what he had learned—that cowhage, a plant, was an effective worm medicine—he did not cite the enslaved healer or the sufferers locked up in the hot-house. Instead, he explained that he had drawn conclusions about cowhage's efficacy from the numbers in the hospital book. The bookkeeper came to know about how fast cowhage worked and its universal application at several degrees' remove from the sick who struggled with worms; he drew his conclusions by looking at sufferers serially—as a series of numbers.

And yet, enslaved people spoke back and pushed to be heard. Healers, overseers, practitioners, and the sick did not speak the same languages of affliction; therefore, everyone involved had to learn to communicate with one another in ways that advanced their respective interests. To decide that a particular set of physical sensations or visible symptoms constituted a definitive symptomology of a particular disease and to assign a name to this illness was an act of epistemological control. "Naming—the way cultures come to refer to objects, whether animate or inanimate—is a deeply social process," as well as an expression of power.[40] To gain admission to plantation hospitals, therefore, enslaved patients had to speak colonists' languages of affliction. At the same time, managers also had to decipher and learn how enslaved people expressed their own symptoms and sensations. Any manager who might dispatch a healer to forage for particular ingredients, moreover, would have to use terms from the Afro-Caribbean botanical vocabulary. Efforts to reform the way enslaved people recovered from illness did not result only in the construction of new buildings or the application of new remedies. They birthed multiple modes of speech, silence, and selective listening among enslaved people, managers, and doctors as they bargained with one another over the terms of medical work and illness. Resistance thus took many forms. Enslaved people insisted on being heard, both at the hospital's threshold and beyond. Such clamoring complicates broader narratives from the history of medicine about the silencing of the sick due to the increasing authority of practitioners and the medicalization of transient, acute, or chronic pains and sensations.[41]

Indeed, because of this system's novelty, enslaved people constantly negotiated the terms of their work and illness with managers, and managers bargained with their absentee employers over compensation and their customary obligations to one another. Thus, much of the players' work involved gatekeeping and brokering. In the process, many became intermediaries among the enslaved, absentees, and those in between. Tensions arose from the rival expectations that different communities imposed upon these intermediaries. But so too did collaborations among different members of plantation communities. This system of body management materialized in the disjuncture that developed among people's disparate goals.

Enslaved people's pushback was not monolithic. Proprietors' and attorneys' interventions sometimes deepened cleavages among enslaved people. Enslaved healers occupied positions of status and leadership within the enslaved community. But they also lived along thin margins, and they were members of smaller kin groups whose integrity they sought to protect. Sometimes they aligned with overseers and undermined the bodily autonomy of their fellow enslaved people. Just as often, they refused medical men's interventions or overseers' demands because healers had ties to the people they were supposed to oppress.

How should we understand the place of this system of body management within the larger history of medicine in the British medical world? And within the histories of mercantile capitalism? The widespread adoption of medical specifics and the associated assumption that medicines should target individual diseases rather than individual people appeared backward to some colonists, a criticism that some scholars of plantation management have echoed. The Kingston physician Thomas Dancer, for instance, lambasted plantation practitioners' indifference to the particularities of individual sufferers' bodies; he scorned practitioners who were unwilling to tailor each sufferer's diet according to his or her constitution.[42] Edward Long, an absentee proprietor, was trying to save the plantation system by advocating for its reform; he bemoaned the rudimentary nature of knowledge-making on West Indian estates.[43] There is some truth to these criticisms. Managers and practitioners prioritized expediency, which led them to treat symptoms on the spot rather than investigate a disorder's deep, underlying causes.

Many scholars of plantation management have also depicted proprietors' medical interventions as primitive. Such characterizations come from scholarship studying proprietors' efforts to ameliorate slavery in the early nineteenth century. Since proprietors' interventions did little to improve rates of reproduction and even less to reduce mortality, some scholars conclude that proprietors' medicine was regressive. To fill out the picture provided by the abysmal rates of mortality and morbidity, they note the shabby hospitals, the varied qualifications of practitioners coming to the region, the absence of any local system for licensing and credentialing, the deleterious effects of imported pharmaceuticals, and the practitioners hidebound to medical ideas rooted in classical theories.[44]

That perspective clashes with another argument advanced by many historians of West Indian plantation management, who have long contended that sugar plantation slavery was modern because its management had all the hallmarks of modern systems of industrial production that treated its laborers as commensurate with one another. These scholars point to managers' treatment of enslaved people as interchangeable units of manpower and the discipline of enslaved people into an industrial time consciousness. They also argue that enslaved people's creative adaptations to social dislocation and horrific violence were part of the process of modernization on estates.[45]

The characterization of Caribbean slavery as a modern labor regime (as opposed to one organized around feudal social relationships) is linked to historians' questions about the relationship between slavery, capitalism, and industrialization. Responding to Eric Williams's provocative thesis that linked West Indian slavery to the development of British industrial capitalism, scholars since the 1970s have tracked rates of productivity, profitability, as well as new forms of labor management that made sugar production "factory-like." This literature shows the strategies that enslavers used to render West Indian sugar plantation slavery into a brutal yet highly lucrative system.

For many of these scholars, West Indian slavery was not a form of labor antecedent to industrial capitalism but shared many features with it. Although gang-labor and integrated plantations had been features of English sugar production since the middle of the seventeenth century, many scholars of plantation management argue that the developments that made plantations even more industrial-like and brutal emerged in the eighteenth century and facilitated managers' increasing control. Proprietors and attorneys adopted a number of different labor practices from the British agricultural improvement movement to reduce waste, capture efficiencies of scale, and drive enslaved people to ever-greater levels of productivity.[46] The diversification of the enslaved labor force and the creation of specialized classes of male craftsmen meant that estates no longer had to rely on salaried artisans and could avoid downtime in the production cycle. The use of jobbing gangs allowed managers to solve bottlenecks in production.[47] Some adaptations, such as the creation of worklogs, allowed for greater surveillance and time-discipline in the field.[48] The creation of a class of experienced resident overseers and attorneys with extensive experience managing particular types of crops allowed absenteeism to flourish without loss of productivity.[49] All of these technological and managerial adaptations were intended to bring about gains in efficiency, productivity, and profitability, and nearly all of them concerned how enslaved people worked.

Scholars examining West Indian slavery through the lens of gender have broadened our understanding of the intertwinement of slavery and capitalism, expanding the sites of analysis from the fields and attorneys' ledgers to women's bodies. Enslaved women shouldered the burdens of "reproducing the next generation of the enslaved from their own bodies" while also laboring for others. Their work facilitated the integration of plantations into larger systems of capitalist exchange.[50] The late eighteenth century emerges as an important pivot point—proprietors attempted to "rationalize" reproduction, largely in response to the possibility of the abolition of the Atlantic slave trade.[51] Together, scholars of gender and plantation management have drawn our attention to the variety of sites on sugar estates that proprietors targeted in their efforts to rationalize the processes of production and make estates more efficient. Both see the eighteenth century as a crucial period for the creation of a systematized approach to the management of estates as well as new forms of resistance that enslaved people developed in response to proprietors' efforts to gain greater control over enslaved people's working and domestic lives. We now understand the brutal eighteenth-century history of the laboring and the reproductive body.

Yet our understanding of the rationalization of the sick-body demands greater attention. *Slavery's Medicine* shows that the work of healing as well as illness itself were just as subject to rationalization as any other activity on estates. It is tempting to interpret proprietors as merely increasing items of medical provision, including medical counsel, as a way to soften plantation agriculture's murderous blows. Yet their interventions were made in order to delimit how long the enslaved sick remained away from work as well as the work of healing itself. They thought in a timeline of cultivation cycles rather than decades. Proprietors were not concerned with augmenting enslaved people's health over the long term. Instead, they used medicine to recuperate the sick to a bare minimum capacity so as to acquire more days of work. At the same time, they also used hospitals to create uniformity in the management of illness. When they built sick-houses and hired medical men, this was a means to gain control and to standardize drugs, dietaries, and the amount of time the sick would require to rest. Appointing enslaved women as healers allowed them to appropriate the knowledge of women who had survived into old age. All of these activities made the costs of care more predictable and were intended to minimize economic risk. Proprietors' involvement in medicine was part of the integration of West Indian plantations into a system of mercantile capitalism.

Managers and practitioners operated in a system of racial capitalism that generated enormous wealth for Europeans by assigning the most brutalizing work to people of African heritage.[52] *Slavery's Medicine* does not trace development of theoretical ideas about race by elite scientists and medical men, a topic already covered in many excellent studies.[53] Instead, in thinking about how medicine operated in a system of racial capitalism, this book explores what might be understood as the racialized practices of disregard. Though they adopted commercial pharmaceuticals that operated on the principle that bodies were interchangeable, colonists and practitioners continued to understand bodies as particular. They maintained that gender, work/station, diet, age, and, above all, a person's acclimatization (or seasoning) made each person's body distinctive. That premise guided how they contended with illness among themselves. When they took commercial pharmaceuticals or remedies that targeted distinctive diseases, colonists expected their own doctors to tailor remedies to fit their unique constitutions. As consumers, they also used the same habits of thought. Depending on what they thought their particular constitutions could handle or needed, they stayed away from some remedies or adjusted the doses of different commercial medicines to suit their particular bodies.

Enslaved people rarely received the same level of concern regarding the niceties of their individual bodies. One of the defining features of medicine under slavery, *Slavery's Medicine* shows, was that practitioners and managers often overlooked important markers of constitutional difference in the treatment of enslaved people's illnesses, but they did not need to develop racial theories to explain why they operated in this manner. In fact, disregarding a sufferer's constitutional particularity was a way to enact racial and class hierarchies. Individual managers and practitioners noticed bodily differences among individual enslaved people—that sex, age, strength, and station affected one's health and vulnerability to illness. Simultaneously, they generalized about the physiological effects of slavery, concluding that punishing working lives and recurrent dietary privation might make certain courses of medicine unsuitable or harmful for enslaved people, especially those who labored in the field. Yet, practitioners pressed on, prescribing according to the disease as a matter of expediency and convenience. Indifference to particularity and personhood in attending to the sick was a practice of slavery in the eighteenth-century's system of racial capitalism.

Capitalism is nothing, however, without labor. Labor underlay the conduct of plantation medicine and was also its purpose. In order to capture what medical practice looked like on estates, we must look at how many different hands shaped and tempered its inner operations. By using labor as its main analytical lens, *Slavery's Medicine* brings all the players involved in medicine into a common frame of analysis and reconstructs in greater detail the social relationships that undergirded the recuperation of the sick and the generation of medical knowledge. Care was not the domain of enslaved healers and medical men alone—and their working relations with absentee planters and one another were not static. Medicine was also not the sole domain of people who made it their primary occupation and conducted it on a regular basis. Looking at work, in other words, highlights the entire range of people shaping proprietors' efforts to reform how enslaved people recovered from illness. Patients bargained for rest from their labors and thereby influenced how healers and others executed their tasks and obligations. Proprietors made demands of medical men and overseers, yet these middling men's own interests influenced their commitments to the varied tasks associated with the recuperation of the sick. As both sufferers and healers, enslaved people also shaped the direction of knowledge-making, because trials with drugs and contests over illness were part of these groups' day-to-day negotiations within a brutal labor regime.

The work of medicine set the terms for how and when people could negotiate their circumstances and illuminates the degree to which they could forge common cause with one another. Proprietors' efforts to systemize the management of illness forced people from all corners of the estate and outside of it to interact with one another. As people tried to conduct their work, accumulate resources, survive, and respond to pressures placed on them by their communities, they learned how much their interests aligned and the limits of their reciprocal obligations. As different members of the plantation managerial staff and enslaved people of varied station maneuvered within this new system of intervention, they operated within slippery social logics. In the day-to-day management of illness and health, people often made decisions as individuals and sometimes within smaller groups.

Plantation medicine is thus best understood as a series of working relationships and acts of resistance that developed among the many people within it, each of whom pursued their own objectives. Proprietors intended to make illness management more efficient. What materialized instead was a multifaceted system to recuperate and discipline the sick, one filled with frictions. As hives of activity, hospitals and yaws huts forced the people who used and worked within them to engage in tense negotiations with one another. Medicine's social relations were dictated neither from top down by enslavers nor from the bottom up by sufferers. Instead, they emerged from the interests and lateral maneuvers of the many different players caught in the middle, enslaved and free, who steered this system through the pursuit of their own ambitions and transient alliances with other parties.⁵⁴

We can best understand the people who shaped this program by their bundled sets of interests based on different incentives—most especially the time scales in which they thought, the materials that they favored, the work pressures that they faced, and their obligations to different communities. This book therefore recovers the nature of the work that practitioners, healers, and others performed to care for the sick and generate knowledge about medicine. Their competing expectations, pressures, and interests hammered this system—its compromises and contestations—into its particular shape.

Slavery's Medicine begins by examining the working lives of different figures in this new system. The first three chapters examine patients, plantation medical men, healers, and managers. These chapters argue that pressures external and internal to their working lives shaped their ability to carry out their duties. Their struggles also determined how medicine was practiced. Chapter 4 then focuses on experiments and how managers, enslaved people, and practitioners made knowledge through their exchange of ideas about disease. The same frictions, oppositional social relations, and interruptions that prevailed in the recuperation of the sick also helped to create a highly fractured and imperfect knowledge culture that hindered as much as helped to advance the science of body management.

The changes that took place in medicine and care during the era of improvement were not separate from but rather part of a larger movement to render work, on all corners of the estate, more efficient. Proprietors' and managers' decisions about health care on their Caribbean plantations were local, opportunistic, and efficiency-minded—shaped by the exigencies of the next season's crop rather than the health of the enslaved. Managers aimed to circumvent enslaved healers, the sick, and the people who cared for them. They tried to prevent enslaved people from mounting challenges to managers' interventions and from participating in the decision-making process about the management of illness. Yet enslaved people, in concert with and in opposition to plantation managerial staff, transformed proprietors' interventions. Above all, medicine was used for labor, and it also was itself labor. *Slavery's Medicine* therefore reveals a wider world of contestation, compromise, and survival as people struggled with one another over the terms of their work.

1

Catastrophe's Threshold

ENSLAVED SUFFERERS, SPEECH, AND THE NEGOTIATION OF INCAPACITY

AT SUNRISE in Jamaica in 1790, Golden Spring's enslaved driver sounded the conch, signaling the start of the workday. The previous evening, a fever had seized Prancer, an enslaved girl of around twelve or thirteen years who lived on the estate with her mother, Fanny. It was the end of the harvest. Prancer, Fanny, and the other men and women on Golden Spring had been pushed to their physical limits, cutting, hauling, and thrashing cane for as many as eighteen hours a day while they survived on sugar, molasses, and dietary essentials from their provision grounds. As she rose for work, Prancer realized that she could not endure. She joined with four other enslaved people who were also sick and in need of rest. In solidarity, they staggered from their quarters to the hot-house (hospital), where they encountered John Cumming, Golden Spring's doctor. They begged him for admission into the hot-house, Prancer on the grounds that she had a fever. Cumming made what he would later characterize as "the strictest examination." He concluded that they were "by no means eligible objects of admission."[1] Then he summarily sent them to the field. Cumming later explained that he made it a policy to turn away people complaining of feverishness, "unless there is at the time some evident symptoms of illness." "No inconvenience arises from not being admitted in the earlier part of the day," he argued.[2] Cumming was demanding, essentially, that the people suffering from fever reapply to him several times over. The sick and their families refused to abide by that policy. All too aware that cultivation took its toll, they knew how quickly infirmity of any sort transmogrified into crisis. Negotiating absence from work was often a matter of life and death.

Prancer was still a young girl, and her mother was at work. That morning, she had little choice but to follow Cumming's decision. She stumbled to her station. When Prancer returned to her house after sundown, Fanny was alarmed. Fanny already had her eye on Cumming. Fearing for her daughter's life, the following day she stormed back to the hospital and directed her fury straight at the doctor. In refusing to give Prancer the rest that she needed, Cumming was adding insult to a previous injury. The reasons for Fanny's long-standing anger soon became clear. Prancer, still a girl in early adolescence, had rejected Cumming's predatory advances a few months before. In an angry bid to get her daughter the resources she needed, Fanny took Cumming to task. Using "most insolent and unbecoming gestures and language," Fanny "accuse[d] me of dismissing her daughter from the hot house, (knowing her to be sick) from revenge and disappointment," wrote Cumming when he described the incident. Fanny upbraided the doctor, and not in private. She made her claims "publickly," likely in front of other enslaved men and women in the hot-house.[3] The public nature of her reproach was as damning as its substance. In the ensuing days, the overseer, Dominic Kelly, waved away the doctor's demand to see Fanny punished for openly challenging Cumming. The men and women on Golden Spring now had reason to question whether the doctor was worthy of deference. In the future, they too might challenge his decision to deny them admission to the hospital.[4]

In the era when this conflict occurred, plantation sick-houses, variously referred to as hospitals or hot-houses, had become a standard element of plantation management. They represented a novel component of enslaved sufferers' experience of illness. As anyone requiring a reprieve from work due to illness needed to gain admission to the hospital and was expected to recuperate inside of it, hospital buildings formed an unwelcome but necessary dimension of enslaved people's strategies of survival. This chapter focuses on how managers thought about plantation hospitals, what plantation hospitals meant for enslaved people; and how they responded to the conditions they imposed. Amid the vexed and contested process of rendering illness management on West Indian estates more predictable and efficient, enslaved people were not passive victims but integral shapers of this new system of body management.

Plantation hospitals brought enslaved people's and managers' understandings about illness and remedies into proximity and conflict with one another as never before. These tensions sprung from their rival views about the purpose of hospitals and their struggles over work, rest, and remedies. We can see these conflicts in the protest that Prancer and Fanny mounted in response to Cumming's gatekeeping. Managers did not have a sophisticated grasp of enslaved people's medical cosmologies, which often saw care and medicines in social terms. But they understood enough to recognize that removing the sick from larger webs of care socially isolated them. Managers saw illness as the loss of labor, and one of the reasons for building hospitals was to keep enslaved people working by making the experience of illness deeply unpleasant so as to deter people from seeking admission.[5] In constructing hospitals, managers also had another goal in mind: to make medical care itself more efficient. Hospitals warehoused the sick in a single location and enabled one to streamline the identification and treatment of illness. They also gave managers more control over the substances that sufferers consumed. By separating the sick from family members and other enslaved herbalists or ritualists who might interfere, hospitals thus became a way that managers tried to achieve uniformity and replicability in therapeutics. To that end, they used hospitals to impose their own remedies—usually a mixture of materials appropriated from enslaved healers and imported manufactured medicines.[6]

The medicine practiced in plantation hospitals ran directly against African medical orthodoxy and put enslaved people in a dilemma. Prancer and others like her lived along thin energetic margins and in a perpetual state of exhaustion. They were often one day's work away from serious crisis. When crisis hit, managers forced enslaved sufferers to bargain with them to gain admission in order to acquire the rest they needed to survive. However, hospitals threatened enslaved people with disconnect—admission took the sick out of communities where both illness and remedies were embedded in complex systems of belief related to enslaved people's connections to others.[7] Enslaved people strove to reclaim their personhood in the face of a system of medicine that involved confinement and that threatened to alienate them from others. They worked through plantation hospitals (or around them) to extend the social relations of healing of their quarters into these new buildings. Fanny's assistance of Prancer, which brought the risk of violent punishment, illustrates one of the many strategies that enslaved people deployed, both to survive and to make sure that the experience of illness was less alienating. In confronting Cumming, Fanny reassured her daughter that she would not have to face the plantation's doctor on her own. By working together, enslaved people helped the sick and exhausted acquire vital resources. Simultaneously, they reminded sufferers that they were not alone.

In tracing the emergence of modern medicine, sociologists and historians of medicine have focused not only on the adoption of specifics and a disease-based understanding of illness. They also examine the disappearance of illness narratives in patients' and practitioners' dealings with one another, which is understood to coincide with the erosion of the sick's authority to determine how their illness was addressed. In contrast to the interactions that occurred between patients and practitioners in hospitals or clinical settings, medicine that took place at patients' bedsides and in their homes was person-oriented. Therein orality had a prime role in sufferers' explanations of their illnesses. In clinical medicine, in contrast, doctors' claims to knowledge were not rooted in their interpretations of their patients' stories but rather in what doctors could see and feel. Hospital practitioners focused on the body itself rather than anything the patient might say.[8] Historians of medicine in early modern Europe have probed the neatness of the division between bedside and clinical medicine.[9] But generally, as many hospital patients in Britain, Europe, and colonies were living in various states of unfreedom, patient and practitioner were not on equal social footing, and the person's biography and history diminished in importance. The hospitals in the plantation Caribbean came nowhere near in size to the charity and municipal hospitals discussed by historians of modern medicine. But as the scholar Miles Ogborn has recently demonstrated, speech is a useful way to examine the shifting relations of medical authority between doctors and enslaved people. For Ogborn, enslaved people's talk about the medicinal qualities of plants and colonists' acknowledgment of their botanical know-how created an inversion of the typical relations of medical and scientific power on estates. It is on this basis that Ogborn situates the British West Indian plantation complex as a middle ground between the bedside and clinical paradigms.[10]

Contests over medical authority involving different types of medical speech were not limited to discussions of plants and their medicinal attributes. Building on Ogborn's insights, this chapter uses speech to examine enslaved people's engagement with plantation sick-houses. In looking at enslaved people's speech, this chapter adds precision to our understanding of the moments and places during an enslaved person's illness when they spoke and were heard. It does so in order to challenge the silencing of enslaved people's voices in plantations' records that abstracted men and women into diseases and numbers, such as hospital books, increase and decrease accounts of enslaved births and deaths, and lists of the sick.[11] I treat enslaved speech here as the literal act of communicating and translating across ways of understanding illness that were often incommensurate. Speech is also a metaphor for the variety of ways that enslaved people challenged or accommodated managers' dictates about when, how, and where they would recover from illness.

The encounters between Prancer and Cumming and then Fanny and Cumming reveal that enslaved people talked back in hospitals. In their insistence on speaking to those who did not wish to listen to them, enslaved people refused to abide the primacy of managers' and medical men's interpretations that they were not sick or did not require resources. Enslaved sufferers (and their families) were far more loquacious in their interactions with practitioners and plantation managers in matters of illness and injury than managers and doctors wanted. They went to extraordinary lengths to make themselves heard. For enslaved people, illness was often a matter of life and death; receiving the rest necessary to survive was also a matter of labor and labor bargaining. Their use of talk in their negotiations with managers and doctors required them to render affliction in different terms than the speech-acts associated with divination, rituals, and communal medicine that occurred outside of plantation hospitals.[12]

Because illness was construed as the inability to work, admission was based on the status of incapacity. Managers and the sick assessed incapacity from different vantages. Sometimes persuading listeners entailed making the case that one suffered from a particular disease that was incapacitating—Prancer's insistence that she was suffering from a fever is one notable example. But as Cumming's refutation reveals, rival ways of knowing also came into play. Managers like Cumming often tried to root their assessments about readiness to work on the basis of what they could see or what others told them. As Cumming explained, he (and other doctors and managers) disregarded enslaved people's own testimony. Instead, they relied on "some evident symptoms of illness."[13]

Yet again and again, enslaved people tried to counter managers' reliance on visual evidence with additional speech. Men and women used the speech, and sometimes gesture, to describe sensations and symptoms that were below the surface of the skin and that could not be apprehended by the human eye. Obligated to interface with managers' interventions as a matter of survival, enslaved people learned to speak in a new idiom at the hospital's threshold and outside of it. And plantation practitioners, charged with upholding absentees' interests (which included both detecting feigned illness and keeping enslaved people alive), had to listen in particular ways. Speech did not put the two groups on equal footing. But as Fanny's public scolding of Cumming reveals, enslaved people forced a conversation.

Cacophony shaped sufferers' encounters with managers, but so did silence, as both an intentional tactic and a secondary effect. Some silencing of enslaved people was a secondary effect of managing bodies in the aggregate with the bare minimum of resources. In chapter 2, I will explore indifference to enslaved people's interpretations and individuality in the medical encounter as an effect of practitioners' workloads and practitioners' treatment of individual sick men and women as interchangeable as a means to contend with the large volume of people they saw throughout the year. Yet enslaved people also wielded silence strategically, withholding information as circumstances warranted. If noisiness helped men and women get into the hospital, silence, wielded purposefully, also helped them to evade managers' efforts to impose medicines on them that they did not want. Enslaved people deployed collective loquaciousness at the hospital's threshold and strategic silences outside of it. To get the rest that they needed, enslaved people shrewdly developed a praxis for navigating an onerous and punishing system designed to compel them back to work.

Siting the Hospital

Managers' hopes to make medicine more efficient and better control enslaved people in their recovery from illness began with decisions about the location of plantation sick-houses in relation to other clusters of buildings on the estate. The geographer B. W. Higman has found that slaveholders settled their estates and created three distinctive zones on their plantations according to an ethos of "movement minimization."[14] This principle was built out from the particular demands of sugar production, whose profitability hinged on the capacity of an estate to integrate the production of canes with their manufacture into sugar, molasses, and rum. Creating these commodities required a sugar mill (for grinding canes, often powered by water, cattle, or, less commonly, wind); boiling and curing houses; a still house; and a trash house. Slaveholders typically clustered these buildings together and referred to this grouping of buildings as "the works," a band of buildings that formed what Higman describes as the "productive engine" of estates.[15] Slaveholders placed the works at the center of the estate and built out around them. This arrangement minimized the distance that enslaved people (or cattle) traveled transporting canes from fields to this processing area.

It also allowed overseers and bookkeepers to actively supervise enslaved people's activities in the works. Thus, on a typical sugar estate, the overseer's house and bookkeepers' barracks (as well as the stables, artisans' shops, pigeon and poultry houses, stores, and kitchen houses) sat adjacent to the works. Works and managers' buildings formed the core of estates, a zone of processing activity distinctive from the fields and subject to intense oversight.

Enslaved people's dwellings, sometimes referred to by scholars as "the village," formed a second distinctive space of a plantation's arrangement. Slaveholders sought to minimize movement between the village and the works, and they typically located the two areas in close proximity to one another. Higman found that in the period between 1760 and 1860, the average village was located no more than 384 yards (approximately one-fifth of a mile) from the works.[16] Although they kept the village in close proximity to the works, proprietors and managers recognized that they would not have as much control over enslaved people's activities in the village.

Finally, the great house, or plantation owner's house, tended to sit at a distance from the works. Higman describes them as "satellites orbiting at relatively variable distances."[17] Together the works, village, and great house formed the whole of an estate's built environment. They were "typically located at points of a triangle, very nearly equilateral in shape and fell within a circle with a radius of only 250 yards."[18]

Many estates situated their hospitals in the core, usually in closer proximity to the overseer's house or the bookkeepers' barracks than to the works.[19] The hospital sat between three buildings: the dungeon; a larger complex that contained lying-in rooms, the curing house, managers' rooms, and stables; and the boiling house. In 1824, the attorney John Johnson visited Lavington's plantation in Antigua. His estate report showed that the hospital, works, and managers' buildings were located on the same elevated plane (figure 2).[20]

Efforts to make body management more efficient entailed conserving how enslaved people as well as managers used their time and energy. Although it is not entirely clear where illness was managed officially prior to the improvement movement, we do know that there are instances when enslaved people cared for one another in the village. When an estate's overseer or doctor had to walk to the village to assess readiness for work,

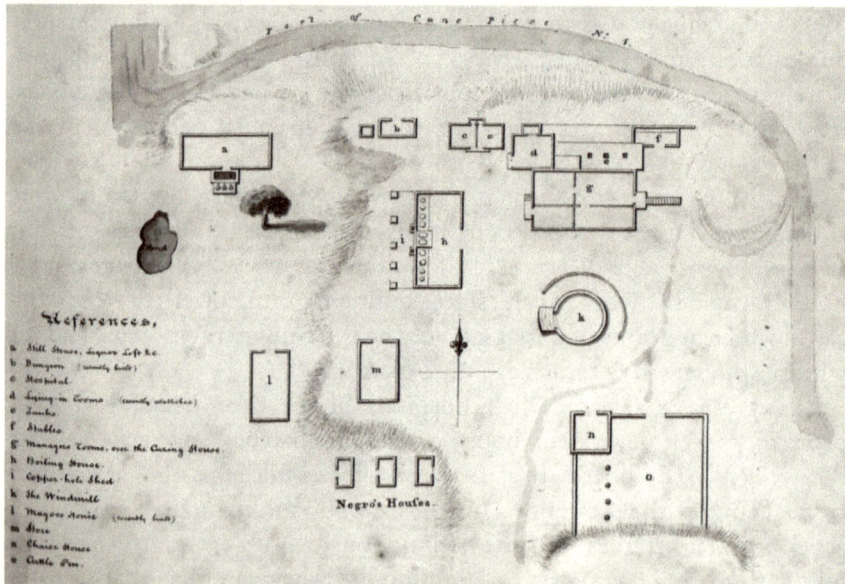

Fig. 2. Lavington's illustration of buildings (*top*) and estate map (*bottom*). The hospital (figure c in the estate map) was flanked by the dungeon to the west and, to the east, by a larger complex of buildings that included lying-in rooms, managers' rooms, tanks, and stables. The estate's boiling house sat to the south of the hospital. (John Johnson, "Reports Relating to Mr. Gordon's Estates in the West Indies, pt 2," M526a, Beinecke Lesser Antilles Collection, Hamilton College)

they lost time. They also lost, potentially, some of their authority. Other people in the vicinity, family members especially, who cared for the sick would insist on being heard. Hospitals like the one at Lavington's relieved overseers and plantation medical men of the obligation to walk to the village to inspect the sick. But as Fanny's brave castigation of Cumming reveals, this arrangement never entirely removed family from the picture.

Managers did, however, compel the enslaved sick to come to the core of the estate. That location allowed overseers to control the movements of enslaved people who were not at work. For one, detention in a hospital kept the enslaved sick within managers' channels of oversight. It also discouraged enslaved people's bids for greater mobility more generally. Proprietors and attorneys claimed that feigned illness facilitated enslaved people's movement outside of their purview. Men and women might "affect illness with a view of getting an uncontrouled [sic] range for a few days."[21] Proprietors viewed hospitals as a tool to combat what they saw as attempts to dress up petit marronage in the guise of illness. Hospitals and the records kept about the people inside of them were interlocking parts in a larger system of surveillance. Sick-houses became standard in treating sickness in significant numbers just as managers adopted record-keeping methods, such as worklogs and lists of the sick that enabled them to identify the location of each man, woman, and child on a given day.[22] At the start of each day, according to plantation advice writer David Collins, a prudent overseer was supposed to read a list compiled by the estate's bookkeeper of those incapacitated and those capable of work. Next, he visited the sick-house and checked the people therein against those on his list.[23] This circuit and its attendant records created a synoptic view of the estate. Overseers and attorneys believed this combination of records and buildings confined the sick (or those not at work) and would direct men and women through a series of defined zones—between field/works, village, and hospital—depending on their level of capacity. Within larger routines of work, recuperation, and crisis, the hospital ensured that the incapacitated remained in place and under supervision.

The location of the hospital in the core area of the plantation was by no means foreordained. There were many reasons to dissuade managers from keeping the sick in one building and in a centralized location. Proprietors and attorneys mulled over the many drawbacks of such an arrangement. Most obviously, the people locked inside did not enter with the same afflictions, and this arrangement potentially spread different diseases among them. Moreover, according to eighteenth-century medical orthodoxy, concentrating the sick, the lame, and the punished in a single space had the potential to make the building into its own biohazard that was a threat to others outside of it. Eighteenth-century medical belief held that some bodies, such as those of sailors, soldiers, the poor, or the enslaved people on plantations, were more prone to putrefaction than others. "Putrefaction" described the internal process of a body rotting from the inside out through the production and stagnation of bile. There were many things that might instigate the process of putrefaction. It nearly always began with the creation of putrid matter, referred to colloquially as "poisons."[24] Many poisons developed internally—from impediments to the expulsion of the fluids in the digestive system or a corruption of the juices caused by a faulty diet or an intemperate manner of living.[25] Those intemperate in their diets, subject to filth, and who tended to live in damp spaces, such as the enlisted and the enslaved, or the urban poor, were reputed to become easily "putrid."[26]

As these groups of people exhaled and respired through their lungs and pores, they released and consumed what was referred to as "effluvia."[27] When a person's body became putrid, poisons escaped the body through putrid effluvia. In instances when the poor, the laboring, the punished, or the sick were concentrated together in a single space with little ventilation, their collective sweat, breath, and evacuations created what Kevin Siena has described as an imagined "pestilential layer of filth."[28] Eighteenth-century people referred to this as "foul air." This corrupted air was destructive—it could render the sick even sicker. Most importantly, it could infect those many yards away.[29] The authors of plantation management guides warned that crowding enslaved people in a single building posed a similar threat to managerial staff. They cautioned proprietors against building the hospital too close to the overseer's house.[30] Still, proprietors prioritized surveillance of the incapacitated ahead of concerns about putrefaction.

Proprietors and attorneys did not ignore the threat of putrid disease and infection completely. Many plantations had separate huts or buildings for people afflicted with yaws, a disease that originates in the bacterium *Treponema pertenue*, which is a relative of the bacterium that produces syphilis. Yaws is most recognizable in debilitating concentrations of ulcerous and raised yellow sores, whose ichor is contagious, that manifest suddenly across the surface of the skin. If left untreated, yaws produces symptoms similar to late-stage syphilis. Attacking human bones, cartilage, and skin, advanced yaws makes the long bones of human limbs swell, causes facial disfigurement, and damages joints and connective tissues.[31] Of all the diseases that afflicted enslaved people, yaws became a major object of managerial oversight—mainly on account of its erosion of enslaved people's long-term capacity for work and the seeming similarity of yaws lesions to the ulcers associated with late-stage venereal disease. Yaws houses were typically situated far distant from the main works. Yet with the exception of yaws, most people who fell sick on a sugar estate would have found themselves confined in a sick-house located in close proximity to the overseer's house or bookkeepers' barracks.

Prescriptive advice writers suggested many workarounds to the problem of putrefaction. Most suggested ventilation.[32] James Grainger recommended "a chamber-ventilator to windward," as well as construction that would allow "some light from the roof."[33] Other authors endorsed features that would enable attendants to periodically rid the building of the corruption produced by patients. To absorb sweat and other evacuations, Thomas Roughley mandated swapping out linens for "clean plantain mats." Roughley probably appropriated a practice already in place among enslaved people. Collins drew inspiration from the British Army. He described a raised platform that enslaved patients would sleep upon, "like the platform of a military guard room." The boards that formed the base could be removed and cleaned by the hot-house healer.[34] These were ideals. There is not enough material in the archival record to determine the extent to which, systematically, they were put into practice.

Surviving evidence suggests that plantation hospitals constructed earlier in the century were cramped and fetid places but that their size and features improved over time. The enslaved patients entering the 576-square-foot sick-house of the Seawell sugar plantation in Barbados would have had between thirty-six and eighty square feet of space each day, depending on the number of people admitted therein.[35] For many sufferers, a common experience of a plantation hospital was crowding into a small building whose walls and floors were rife with stench and decay.

Improvements in ventilation and crowding seem to have occurred over time, but much depended on the whims of the attorney or slaveholder. The Jamaican attorney and slaveholder Simon Taylor had his own plantation, Holland, and managed the Golden Grove plantation on behalf of the absentee slaveholder Chaloner Arcedeckne. Both were located in the Plantain River Garden district in St. Thomas in the east. In 1790, Taylor had a new hospital built at Golden Grove—it had separate rooms for men and women, a bathing facility, a room for people afflicted with venereal disease, and a separate room for the enslaved hospital doctor.[36] The hospital on the Sanderson sugar plantation in Antigua, visited by the attorney John Johnson, was a wooden structure with windows and separate beds. The St. Vincent hospital that he inspected on another estate had two compartments, twelve square feet each, for men and women.[37]

One of the largest and better-documented hospitals was the one at John Tharp's Good Hope estate in Trelawny Parish, Jamaica (figure 3). Built at the end of the eighteenth century, the Tharp hospital was a carefully planned building, designed in accordance with ideas that the careful coordination of medicine, discipline, and adequate ventilation restored the enslaved sick to health. Tharp drafted plans for the hospital in 1798. His design shows a two-story building with fifteen rooms on each floor, approximately 8,600 square feet total. Men and women who entered were assessed in separate lobbies, convalesced in sex-segregated wards, and ate meals prepared in two separate kitchens, one for men and one for women. Medicines were locked away in a medicine room, and a doctor might remain at night in his own apartment to supervise the management of extreme cases.

The timing of Good Hope's hospital suggests that slaveholders like Tharp initially took concerns about overcrowding seriously. Concerns for enslaved people's health often gave way, however, to the desire to maximize profits. Tharp drafted plans for the hospital in 1798, just four years after he married Ann Gallimore.[38] Prior to his marriage to Gallimore, Tharp owned three other sugar plantations. The marriage brought Lansquinet and Cheshire plantations into his estate and put an additional 357 enslaved men, women, and children under Tharp's control, bringing the total number of enslaved people on his sugar plantations to approximately 857.[39] If he was like other sugar barons, Tharp probably expected Good Hope's hospital to serve the five sugar plantations in his roster. The timing of his plans suggests he was responding to the abrupt increase in the number of people brought under his control as a consequence of his marriage to Gallimore.

It was also constructed at the height of slave-trade abolitionism. Thus, the hospital fulfilled several of Tharp's goals. For one, it allowed him to extend the fantasy that he was a rational absentee proprietor, one whose engagement with ideas of the Enlightenment, contemporary medical belief, and metropolitan medicines allowed him to extend enslaved people's capacity for work. That ambition overlapped with another goal. As Sarah Pearsall has observed, in his return to Britain, Tharp wanted to escape

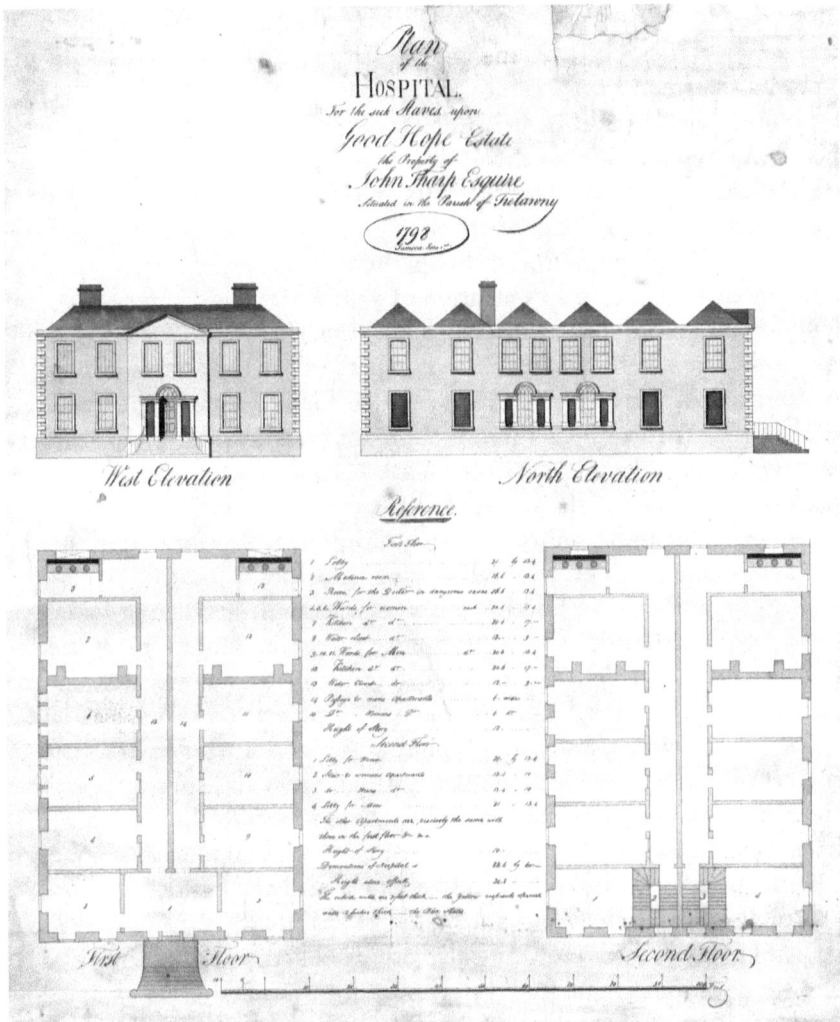

FIG. 3. Plan of the hospital for sick enslaved people upon the Good Hope estate, the property of John Tharp, Esquire, situated in Trelawny Parish, Jamaica, 1798. (Cambridgeshire Archives, KAR55/7/121/16)

not only the day-to-day burdens of managing his estates but the reputation of West Indian men as ruthless despots.[40] It is unlikely that Tharp publicized the construction of Good Hope's hospital widely. Still, it may have been one way for Tharp to imagine himself as a benevolent paternalist; perhaps his hospital allowed him to present this figure to West Indian absentees who were part of his social circle. For the enslaved people held captive on Tharp's plantations, paternalism meant that Tharp used his hospital to extend his hand into the intimate dimensions of enslaved life.

Proprietors' commitments to bettering enslaved people's health were nearly always at odds with their drive for profits. The changing state of hospitals reflects the fact that this group of men and their attorneys nearly always placed the production of sugar above all else. Tharp's hospital at Good Hope followed this pattern. The hospital began as a facility intended to serve a population of 857. Yet it would come to sustain a population more than twice that size as the Tharp family increased the number of people they held in captivity and of acres that they put under cultivation. A pair of Quakers who visited Good Hope in the third decade of the nineteenth century observed that the hospital was provisioning medical care for all nine of the Tharp properties, comprised of more than two thousand enslaved people.[41] As the Tharp family's slaveholding increased, their ambitions to create a healthy and well-ventilated space for enslaved people to convalesce fell in their priorities.

Amid rising costs of building materials, some hospitals that had been constructed earlier in the century under the grand ambitions of the estate's owner had fallen into ruin by the turn of the nineteenth century. At one point, the hospital at the Flamstead plantation in Jamaica had a raised floor, bricked walls, and a piazza. But those who entered late in the century would see a monument to managers' decision to prioritize sugar manufacture over the health of enslaved people. The chimney "had been pulled down for bricks for the works."[42] All buildings in Caribbean colonies weathered faster than those in more arid and temperate climates. Hospitals generally fell low on the list of maintenance priorities.[43] On some plantations, overcrowding also occurred because managers tried to wrench additional value from hospitals as fixed capital. Plantation managers sometimes engaged in informal make-good bargains that allowed for the exchange of resources with other plantations in the vicinity.[44] Thus some estates with large hospital facilities took in the sick from adjacent estates. Taylor intended the hospital at Golden Grove, the estate he managed on behalf of Arcedeckne, to serve the 371 enslaved people who lived on that plantation, as well as the 400 enslaved people who lived at Holland, the sugar plantation that Taylor owned.[45] At one point the two plantations also shared the same medical man.[46]

The fact that some grandees used their hospitals to serve several estates in their portfolio or allowed neighboring estates to use their facilities meant something very different to the enslaved people who were sent to these buildings to recover with people from other plantations. From some illnesses, such as venereal disease, enslaved people required months to recover. When he was the overseer for the Kendall plantation in Jamaica, Thomas Thistlewood sent an enslaved woman, Hannah, to Salt River, an adjacent estate, "to be salivated for the pox," that is, treated for venereal disease. She remained there for over two months.[47] When attorneys allowed the hospitals on the estates they managed to take in the sick from plantations in the vicinity, it meant that an illness event might take the enslaved sick distant from their homes, to hospitals where they would recover in close proximity to people whom they did not know, for months on end.

The discomforts of hospitals were not just in the isolation and dislocation that one might encounter there. They sprung as well from the many ways that managers wrested additional value from these buildings. As Richard Sheridan found in his study of medicine and slavery, managers used hospitals as places to punish men and women and then repair their wounded flesh. On the Hutchinson plantation, in St. Christopher's, "the stocks are adjoining the sick house." The building also had a dungeon.[48] The inventories for the Phillipsfield and Pleasant Hill hot-houses in Jamaica both included a set of stocks alongside pots, chairs, syringes, and brass mortars and pestles.[49]

Here old words associated with domesticity took on new meanings. "Bedstocks" is an antiquated term to refer to a bed's frame. In plantation hospitals, it appears to describe the placement of stocks on beds, to immobilize the sick and the punished (figure 4).[50] The plantation surgeon William Chamberlaine observed that those sent to the hospital for the "slightest scratch or ... the least sore on the leg or foot" were "confined to the stocks, that the sore may not be enlarged by walking about."[51] As they cycled through sickness and punishment, enslaved people confronted similar sets of instruments that curbed their mobility. Anyone entering the building would have found it hard to separate the two purposes.

Sick-houses' design hindered communications between the sick and the people who cared about them and reveal the carceral dimensions to illness management. The windows that let in the light and fresh air were to be "fortified with bars, or jealousies [sic], to prevent the escape of negroes."[52] In the nineteenth century, advice writers advocated expanding single-room buildings into multichambered structures, some with separate quarters for men and women. In some cases, the hospitals had individual rooms for each patient. While patients would have had more

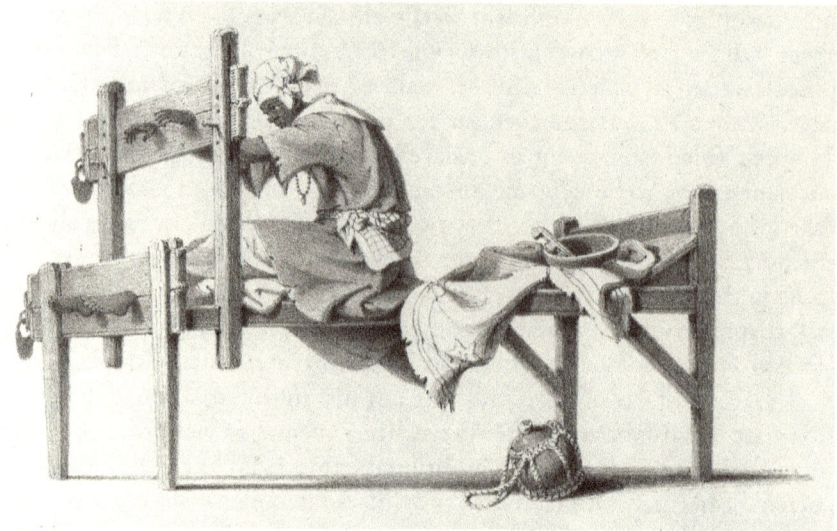

FIG. 4. Stocks were attached to beds in many plantation hospitals. Their presence reveals that these buildings were used for both convalescence and punishment. (Richard Bridgens, *West Indian Scenery with Illustration of Negro Character, the Process of Making Sugar &c.*, London, 1836; Beinecke Rare Book and Manuscript Library, Yale University)

space under this program, their mobility was constricted. Each of these sections might be "well secured with bolts and locks."[53] Confinement, as Rana Hogarth has shown, informed some hospitals' layouts. Separate wards for men and women would empty, Collins advised, into a "common passage, for which, there should only be one outlet, which ought to be the nurse's room, who is to keep the keys."[54] Illness meant imprisonment.

Using hospitals as places to imprison the recently punished or to crowd in as many people as possible inflamed old antagonisms and created new ones. When people were forced to recuperate in such close proximity to friends, foes, and people they did not know, tumults inevitably ensued. In January 1831, a Berbice estate's overseer named H. E. Hockin sent the enslaved woman Mary Gordon to the hospital for her illness. Shortly thereafter, Charlotte entered and, as Mary explained, was "placed in bedstocks in an upper room of the hospital where I was lying sick." Another woman, Queen, convalesced in a bed on the lower level, directly beneath Charlotte's bed on the upper floor. Apparently, there was enough space between the floorboards that served as the lower level's ceiling that sounds and liquids fell from the upper floor to the lower one. Within a few hours,

Charlotte called out to Elias, the hospital's enslaved healer, to "release her for a moment from the stocks to perform an act of nature." She needed to urinate. But only the overseer had the key. A few beats later, Charlotte relieved herself. Queen, meanwhile, "got wet by water [Charlotte's urine]," which trickled down on her from above. What happened next was a matter of perspective. Mary claimed that she chastised Charlotte. "Oh Charlotte, you ought to be ashamed, there are sick people below," Mary clucked. Queen heard something else: Mary was mocking her. Queen ran upstairs to exact retribution from Mary. As Queen confronted her, Mary allegedly cursed Queen's mother, adding insult to injury. Elias tried to stop the fighting, but it spiraled out of his control, and eventually Hockin arrived with other men to restrain Mary.[55]

As Hockin's quick arrival suggests, the decision to locate hospitals in the vicinity of overseers' houses was born not only from a desire to augment overseers' surveillance power but also to enable their greater control over what went on inside the building itself.[56] That priority overshadowed concerns over foul air and ventilation. Thomas Plummer, the attorney for Island sugar plantation in Jamaica, insisted on moving the hospital from its original site. While an expensive proposal, the arrangement would place the building in a more salubrious location on the plantation. It would also allow the overseer, residing in the great house, to keep the hospital "under his eye and inspection."[57] When the absentee proprietor Samuel Vaughan set about updating the buildings on the Flamstead plantation in St. James, Jamaica, he ordered the construction of a paved, three-foot-wide path "from the house to the range of out house and up to the hot house."[58] Vaughan wanted easy communication between the two buildings. The slaveholder Gilbert Francklyn explained that in order to maintain the health of the enslaved people on his estate, he had "built a hospital close to my house, that I might have an opportunity of inspecting the conduct of it; and appropriated two rooms in it for the use of lying-in women."[59] Once managers foreclosed other possibilities for enslaved people's recovery, incapacity became as much a spatial condition as a medical one. The reorganization of medicine and care forced enslaved people to accept hospitals, and the control that overseers exerted within them, in exchange for the rest and food that kept them alive. And, as Francklyn's insistence on inspecting the "conduct" of those inside of the building suggests, for proprietors, overseers, and attorneys, conduct did not just mean how people interacted with one another. It covered what the enslaved sick consumed as well.

"Two Thirds of the Cure"

In addition to using hospitals to gain control over enslaved people's mobility, managers started to use hospitals as an extended and informal place to experiment with different medicines and diets for the sick. Eighteenth-century Britons and colonists looked at diet as a therapeutic, and provisioning the sick was standard practice in hospitals across the Anglophone world. "Good nourishment and care provide two thirds of the cure," the absentee Samuel Cary proclaimed in a private set of instructions that directed his attorneys in the management of his estate.[60] "Under all diseases," the plantation practitioner John Williamson declared, "diet should be regulated and modified according to the circumstances of complaint."[61] Managers wanted to discover the quantum and type of food given to the sick and the type of substances that would restore the sick to a laboring capacity.[62] Thus, in addition to functioning as places to recuperate the sick, hospitals also became sites for what we might call managerial knowledge-making. Managers seemed to have operated on the expectation that uniformity would achieve efficiency in body management. Uniformity would be the basis, moreover, for the creation of replicable knowledge.

In these spaces, managers tried to exploit the confinement of the sick to experiment with different dietaries to determine the most efficacious manner of provisioning. In the early eighteenth century, there were few hospitals, and sufferers' families may well have been expected to provision them. By the late eighteenth century, managers typically fed the people kept inside hospitals, and this arrangement allowed them to control what the sick ate.[63] However, although they publicly proclaimed the provisioning of the sick as an example of their benevolence and charity, privately attorneys and slaveholders were also concerned about the costs. During one particularly bad episode of illness on Island, John Van Heilen, the estate's attorney, wrote that he had "been obliged to give many a good extraordinary nourishing food, such as soups and beef, to keep them alive and recover their strength."[64] Van Heilen's explanation signals that provisioning the sick was an expense that required some explanation to the absentee proprietor. Attorneys and overseers were ultimately beholden to absentees' bottom lines. What enslaved people were forced to consume was determined as much by the expense of different articles of provision as managers' understanding of their therapeutic qualities. Thus, experiments with the enslaved sick's dietaries were carried out to discover not only what was efficacious but what substances could restore the sick at the bare minimum of cost.

Managers did not develop insights about sustaining the sick entirely on their own but often looked to other labor regimes, where laboring bodies were sustained in large numbers, for information on the types of food to feed the sick. Taylor ordered 100 pounds of a portable beef soup for Arcedeckne's hospital. The soup was, he explained, "the same sort as is made in the Navy & costs about 7/6 lb."[65] Different types of afflictions required specific types of diets. Andrew Duncan Sr., the chief physician for the Royal Infirmary of Edinburgh, prescribed three different types of diets for admitted patients: a low (antiphlogistic) diet, comprised of oatmeal or other starchy substances and milk; a full diet, which contained the same ingredients as the low diet but included boiled meats; and a stimulant diet, which contained more nutritious substances.[66] Collins advised that, in cases of dysentery, "the patient must be supported with milk and water, sago, salep, tapioca, Indian arrow root, and pap made of starch and milk."[67] Attorneys followed convention and imposed dietary regimens onto the enslaved sick similar to those used in military and charity hospitals.

Yet forces outside of attorneys' control also determined what the sick consumed inside hospitals and disrupted their efforts to impose uniformity. Sugar estates supplemented enslaved people's diets with imported provisions from North America and Britain, but often just barely enough. They operated on a "just-in-time rationing system" that exposed them to problems in Atlantic supply networks.[68] Managers could plan for annual spells of sickness and thus anticipate increases in the estate's consumption of rations. The sickliest time of the year occurred during the caning and holing season in the fall. But epidemics acted as exogenous shocks to the system, because they increased the amount of food an estate needed, with little advance warning. In these instances, Mother Nature blew attorneys' and commission agents' purchasing schedules off course.

Attorneys found themselves buying from local provisions merchants, which meant taking what they could get. When he acted as the attorney for the Simon plantation in St. Kitts, Samuel Cary wrote to the estate's absentees that he had purchased a nourishing soup for the sick-house. He enthused that the soup would make the hospital "a very desirable place." He explained his decision on the grounds that the beans and peas that the estate's commission agents had purchased had not yet arrived and the estate had been forced to purchase "rice and flour" from local merchants.[69] Purchases from local merchants carried with them convenience costs.[70] So descriptions like the ones that Cary made to the absentees were often attended with promises of rationing. Cary reassured the absentees that "the sick is examined every morning and its [the soup] only given to those who are very low there can be no trouble of turning those into field who are not sick but lazy."[71] What Cary's letter reveals is that although they complained about it, neither attorneys nor absentees experienced the consequences of purchasing from local merchants. Under the cover of suspicions of exaggerated illness, attorneys forced sufferers to bear the costs instead.

Hospital inmates across the Atlantic World expected to submit to the dietary dictates of the institution that housed them. However, most enslaved people sustained and fed themselves largely from produce grown in their kitchen gardens and provision grounds, small plots of land allotted to individual families. They were therefore accustomed to a great deal of dietary autonomy. Because admission to the sick-house transferred the burdens of sustaining sufferers from their families to the estate, managers assumed the prerogative to direct the dietaries of the sick.

The expansion of networks of information exchange among attorneys, absentees, and commercial purchasing agents in London also encouraged managers to vet different remedies that they created and manufactured medicines that they imported.[72] Doctors' and prescriptive advice writers' complaints about the difficulties of administering medicines to the sick reveal the assumption that they should have control. Many managers talked about force as a component of body management. Shortly after he arrived in Dominica, the parvenu surgeon Jonathan Troup observed his employer, the druggist Andrew Fillian, forcing medicines on an enslaved patient with the assistance of the slaveholder Mr. Morson. The slaveholder "was obliged to stand over him [the patient], an hour to make him take bark."[73] The St. Vincent botanist Alexander Anderson wrote to the Philadelphian Benjamin Rush to praise the efficacy of Rush's cure for tetanus. Anderson explained that he had "forced down their throat great quantities of Madeira wine and bark."[74] The attorney John Johnson warned that patients who fled the hospital exacerbated their afflictions "by taking cold or deviating from their regimen prescribed."[75] Managers presumed it was their prerogative to impose remedies on the sick. The isolation of the sick from others who might interfere enabled doctors and overseers to exert such force.

Doctors and overseers complained about the necessity of force because enslaved people were pushing back. Sometimes the enslaved won concessions that resulted in the modification of the substances fed to them. On the Island plantation, managers set aside a hogshead of sugar for the hospital; John Van Heilen explained that the hospital "requires a good deal of sugar when negroes take physic."[76] On the low diet prescribed to patients suffering from diarrhea, Collins warned that "if too long continued, the negro will shew a dislike to it."[77] It is possible that, in moments when there were many inside plantation sick-houses, enslaved sufferers used collective action to convince managers to modify diets. It is also possible that managers made these modifications in response to the cumulative refusals of enslaved individuals or because they aligned with managers' own beliefs about the necessity of certain dietary items for certain medicines.

The dietary and therapeutic restrictions as well as the isolation that enslaved people experienced in hospitals were a novelty and, obviously, unwelcome. Many enslaved people therefore refused to make that concession until they were desperately sick. And yet, hospitals became an important resource in the survival of enslaved people. Overwhelmed by the dual demands of backbreaking field work and scanty dietaries, many men and women endured the building's confines in order to ready themselves against the imminence of total abjection.

That they did so highlights their dire condition. Sugar cultivation was lethal. But before it killed, it broke people's spirits and bodies. Managers regularly pushed enslaved people until they collapsed. In addition to their subjection to ruthless toil, enslaved people lived along thin margins. The nature of provisioning and rationing regimes meant that the vast number of enslaved people who lived on sugar estates consumed only slightly more calories than they expended in work. A combination of exhaustion and dietary privation enfeebled enslaved people and made them far more vulnerable to illness than were their colonial counterparts.[78] Enslaved people thus operated with very little energy.[79] Some of their illnesses were acute, but most were chronic. Sufferers could get medicine and care from other enslaved people in the village. But to survive an illness, most enslaved people needed, at the bare minimum, rest. If they fled temporarily from the estate to the forest or into the arms of a loved one on a neighboring plantation, they would be punished. Admission to the hospital, by contrast, secured absence from work.

Once enslaved people were inside hospitals, managers used their captivity to conduct informal experiments to determine what diets and medicines were best used to address particular diseases. But managers' overarching goal was to keep enslaved people out of hospitals, because illness was lost labor value. The hospital's resources were restricted to those whom managers judged to be incapable of work. That set up a situation in which managers and enslaved people would bargain with one another over the signs of incapacity.

At the hospital's threshold, incapacity was relative because its boundaries depended on the eye of the beholder. Managers tried to keep the definition of incapacity and sickness narrow enough that only the seriously ill would be admitted, and they claimed that many who sought assistance were pretending to be sick. Feigned illness assumes, however, that the person in question was starting from a place of perfect health, which was an unlikely condition for the enslaved. Moreover, managers did need to attend to enslaved people's health as their employment partially depended on it. They also recognized difference in the status of the sick. As enslaved people endured brutality, privation, overwork, and skepticism, they continually pushed to get the care they needed. To secure admission to the hospital enslaved people needed to counter managers' suspicions of feigned illness. That entailed speaking in certain ways at the right place and time.

Managing Crisis and Making Incapacity

Slaveholders established hospitals to shut down conversation—rendering stays in these buildings unpleasant in order to keep enslaved people working rather than convalescing. They also made it difficult to gain admission. Their inclination to turn people away was partially born from emergent assumptions about enslaved people's bodies that metropolitan slaveholders advanced: that Black bodies were all alike and interchangeable. Their defining feature was that they were not as sensitive to pain as white people and thus required less care.[80] But managerial policy to ignore enslaved people's petitions for relief also stemmed from the conviction that enslaved people's interpretations of illness were not credible because enslaved people were inclined to exaggerate their pain. The editors of a British medical and literary journal, likely summarizing the plantation surgeon James Adair, complained about how difficult it was to understand the "true nature" of enslaved people's ailments compared to white people's, "partly from their ignorance, but more from their inclination to imposture."[81] The editors of the literary journal explained that practitioners were instead "obliged to draw their information, and form their indications, from temperamental distinctions, aspect, pulse, and the moral character of the person."[82] Practitioners (and other hospital gatekeepers), in other words, wanted to base their assumptions on what they could feel and what they knew about the person in question—likely from other people such as overseers. To sidestep feigned illness, managers and doctors wanted to eliminate intercession by the enslaved.

Enslaved people, in contrast, pushed managers, including doctors, to render incapacity as a dialogue rather than a reading of signs or presumption of character. Making incapacity required giving the right answers to probing questions and transforming more generalized malaise and exhaustion into signs legible to managers as the symptoms of illness. Establishing incapacity sometimes arose from one-on-one dialogues. Other times it emerged from solidarity among enslaved people. The consequences of talk, moreover, depended on who was doing the speaking and listening as well as when it occurred in the course of contending with illness.

When enslaved people demanded that managers listen, they often risked violent punishment. Managers and absentee slaveholders both situated illness as the loss of labor, but slaveholders had invested in maintaining enslaved people's capacity to work over the long term. Overseers and attorneys, in contrast, were motivated by increases in salary and commissions to place the production of large crop outputs ahead of enslaved people's health. They ruthlessly impelled enslaved people to produce and drove them into destruction.[83] All managers kept their definition of incapacity narrow, but overseers were especially inclined to see feigned illness nearly everywhere they looked. The possibility of punishment loomed over anyone who challenged overseers or drivers directly in claims of sickness or the need for rest. Congo Jack on the Hutchinson's estate in St. Christopher's was murdered by William Rawlins, the estate's overseer. Jack sought rest and resources for his addled body in the middle of the workday and in the field. Jack proclaimed that he "was sick and hungry," and he lay down. Rawlins ordered him to be flogged. Then Rawlins beat him privately. Jack died two days later.[84] Violent spectacles reinforced for onlookers that claims of illness and incapacity brought with them the possibility of physical punishment. They also fortified enslaved people's political awareness—that the time of day, season of the year, audience, and relationship might shape the outcome of their petition. Claims of incapacity may well have been more successful and safer at particular places and times of the day. The official place to negotiate the necessity of rest was just outside of the hospital's threshold.

The first step to gaining the hospital's resources began with a petition for admission. The gatekeepers of the hospital (and others who assessed incapacity) varied from estate to estate. Some of the largest plantations had a medical man living on the estate full-time who "examined into their [slaves'] respective cases."[85] Enslaved hospital healers likely also assessed who was unfit to work, as they often reported on enslaved people's prognosis and progress. While he was in the employ of several estates, Troup attended the two military hospitals at the Cabrits garrison in Dominica: one for enslaved people owned by the Crown and the other for the white rank and file. An enslaved healer named George was stationed in the hospital for enslaved people and seems to have had a large role in running the operation while Troup attended the soldiers' hospital and the plantations in his roster. In one instance, George watched Troup administer several medicines over the course of two days to an enslaved man. George concluded that the case was hopeless and advised Troup to that effect, who wrote down George's interpretation in his diary.[86] Given their responsibilities for assessing patients' progress, enslaved healers like George may well have also had a say in determining who was too sick to work.[87]

Decisions about incapacity were not confined to those with a defined medical role, however. Overseers and bookkeepers also assessed. In fact, when they trained to become an overseer, many bookkeepers "attended the surgeon in his visits to the sick" as part of their apprenticeships.[88] In deciding who was fit for work, overseers weighed competing factors, but they always put their own interests first—which was to make the largest crop possible. To effect that end, they needed to keep as many people at work as possible. Their interpretations of incapacity were shaped by the quantum of people demanded by the phase in the agricultural cycle and the relative strength or weakness of the estate's gangs. Such decisions also hinged, however, on the relationships they had with the men and women whom they routinely worked to exhaustion and punished for evading the physical effects of the field through work stoppages, slowdowns, and marronage.[89] The motivations and asymmetrical positions of power of these different gatekeepers no doubt influenced whom they adjudged as incapable of work, and when. Yet they shared a belief that they could differentiate legitimate incapacity from feigned illness.

Illness could not be read on the basis of physical signs alone. "Some negroes may also be really indisposed," David Collins acknowledged, "though they are without any of the symptoms which would indicate indisposition."[90] By the same token, even with symptoms, it was frequently difficult to identify the affliction in question and its severity. In an era prior to bacteriology and virology, Europeans and colonists acknowledged that some diseases were distinctive, such as smallpox and yaws. They also regularly contended with the ontological instability of diseases and their categories. A fever could be the sign of temporary unease, its own distinct illness (such as bilious fever), or the sign of another illness—such as putrid sore throat (a multipurpose term that described diphtheria) or dysentery, a deadly disease characterized by violent diarrhea and bloody stools. Such ailments required immediate attention and interventions. "If the patient comes to the hospital in the morning . . . no time to be lost, you should begin with a purge," Collins warned. "You must inquire," Collins wrote in his section on dietary complaints, how many bowel movements the person had.[91] When time was of the essence, it was dangerous to rely on physical inspection alone—gatekeepers needed to accept that speech was on the table and to ask probing questions about the onset of affliction, its temporality, and its sensations.

Sufferers gave descriptive accounts of their unease. Enslaved people did not adopt their captors' bland and alienating language of anatomical parts and physiological processes. They probably anticipated that they would be mocked or the integrity of their claims questioned. Instead, enslaved people developed a vocabulary of affliction that was rich in metaphor and description. They drew on everyday objects and sensations to paint a picture of physical states that could not be apprehended by the human eye. In Dominica, for instance, an enslaved woman fell from a precipice and hit several rocks and trees as she plummeted to the ground. The slaveholder "Mr. Trotter" and Troup described the effects as blows to the "temporal bone and breast."[92] Reporting on the effects of a blister that Troup applied to her forehead, the woman stated that "she feels her head like a broken calabash."[93] This language not only challenged the dry and unfeeling vocabulary of elite medicine; it also created vivid images in an effort for sympathy and more precise care.

Collins and other advice writers encouraged overseers and practitioners to speak with petitioners, but it was probably enslaved people themselves who risked a conversation. Their phrases reinforced the need to act in haste. The symptoms of sharp gastrointestinal pain and an urgent need to defecate, sometimes signs of dysentery, were coolly described by colonists as "gripes" and "tenesmus." But enslaved people's terms were more urgent. An overseer searching for the signs of dysentery would need to ask a petitioner "whether his belly cuts him much" or whether there was the presence of "a needy."[94] One enslaved person replied, "I have been in bush twice, holding up his two fore-fingers," which Troup translated as the number of bowel movements.[95] When they looked retrospectively at their encounters with enslaved sufferers, medical writers assumed a haughty posture, at times deriding their patients' phrasing. It was a means by which practitioners-turned-authors positioned themselves as heroic translators of enslaved people's vernacular and amused their readers. On the ground, however, this translation work was not a matter of amusement but of survival for the petitioner and continued employment for the practitioner. Diseases in hot climates turned deadly quickly. Any plantation practitioner who wished to keep his position learned enslaved people's language of illness and learned when to act with haste.

Troup had to master many skills to ingratiate himself within Dominica's medical economy. He had to navigate Dominica's treacherous landscape. He also had to amass a local medical vocabulary. To make his work go easier, Troup kept a diary of his interactions with his enslaved patients (as well as other colonists) during his first two years on the island. It functioned, in parts, as a glossary for the many descriptive phrases that Africans and Afro-Creoles used in their communications with him. Sometimes men and women spoke in their own terms, and much meaning was lost in the process of translation. A boy whom Troup attended who had developed a large ulcer on the side of his head complained of a "yamming pain."[96] Troup speculated that this meant pain while eating. But yams had a much larger social significance to enslaved people and a place of pride in African understandings of protection, belonging, and people's ties to the spiritual world. His invocations of yams suggests that the boy might have understood his illness in these terms. Even mundane matters like how the enslaved people marked passage of time became relevant in deciphering the severity of an affliction. Conferring with an enslaved man who suffered from an irritated bladder, Troup used an enslaved intermediary to translate the man's account of how much time passed between each episode. A woman informed him that the man's affliction reared its head "every new moon."[97] In many circumstances, breaching the linguistic chasm was urgent.

It is entirely possible that enslaved people also assimilated and then redeployed colonists' terms as well—mainly those that communicated severity. Recall the interaction between Prancer and Cumming that opened this chapter. Prancer and the other people petitioning Cumming described themselves as afflicted with fever. Colonists did not usually see fevers as symptoms of other illnesses but as very dangerous afflictions in their own right—indicated by sensations of raised temperature and confusion.[98] Fevers behaved unpredictably in hot climates. Under the right circumstances, a fever could become lethal within a matter of hours. Cumming's interest lay with his slaveholder-employer, and he turned a blind eye to Prancer's plight.

Nevertheless, it is telling that she used this term to describe her condition. Across the West Indies, colonists spoke constantly of tropical fevers—as they imperiled their prosperity and security. Fevers felled soldiers in the British Army and Royal Naval sailors in the thousands, and their deaths made the islands vulnerable to attack, sapped morale, and undercut metropolitan Britons' support for war-making.[99] There was, moreover, an extensive corpus of texts on tropical fevers with authors from across the empire debating and citing one another.[100] Colonists maintained that Black people were less vulnerable to fevers than people of European descent but still maintained that fevers that took hold in the weak, overworked, and poorly fed were more severe.[101] Thus, Prancer was probably aware of the valence of the mention of fever. Other instances suggest enslaved people's awareness of what managers wanted to hear. Colonists maintained that afflictions that immobilized and seized the entirety of the body were the most dangerous. Collins warned readers that men and women who described pains in "their belly, their backs, and their skins ... of the whole together" might be exaggerating their condition.[102] Collins identified this as a stratagem and a design. But his acknowledgment of such ploys shows that enslaved people had learned to speak in a medical idiom that made their dire straits legible to colonists.

Partial translations abounded. Africans saw health and sickness on the skin. A glowing and glossy epidermis was a mark of health, and the maintenance of the surface of the skin kept the interior of the body in good condition.[103] Charlotte, the "sick-nurse" on the Hutchinson plantation in St. Christopher's, revealed this assumption in her testimony about Congo Jack. Her account depicted Jack as healthy (and thus that Rawlins, rather than a prior illness, had killed him). His skin spoke to his condition.

Charlotte testified that she had seen Jack the day of his murder: "he did not complain of any thing; when the deceased came home, his skin shone, by which is meant he was in good health."[104] By the same token, the skin's dullness marked malaise. Yet the deeper significance of this sign was lost on overseers, attorneys, and slaveholders. In his efforts to portray the abundance of medical care given to the sick, the slaveholder Alexander Campbell testified, for example, that enslaved petitioners were readily admitted to the hospital. He allowed inside even those "who have no apparent complaint but that of dry skin."[105] Campbell's understanding was partial, perhaps willfully so. He had taken notice that this complaint was meaningful to enslaved people. Yet in his testimony before members of the House of Commons, Campbell created a different narrative: that West Indian colonists were receptive to enslaved petitioners, even in seemingly trivial matters of dry skin.

Campbell's beliefs and those of the enslaved people he derided were not quite so far apart, but both groups focused on different elements of the skin. For early moderns, the interior of the body was difficult to apprehend. But Europeans maintained that ulcers and sores were windows that revealed the state of the body's juices. Elite and lay medical thought maintained that sores were a sign that a person's blood was putrid and that the body was attempting to purge itself of tainted internal matter. That was a problem to be taken seriously, as many people believed that putridity created illness, sometimes severe. "There is an intimate connection between the surface and the vital parts," a duo of surgeons who weighed in on Congo Jack's death explained.[106] Sores also indicated that a person was, in effect, in a state of decay and that time was of the essence. People afflicted with sores were often treated with aggressive chemical remedies that caused the body to excrete poisonous matter through sweat, urine, and vomit. British medical theory, which was based on examining the bodies of the laboring poor, held that the poor never exerted themselves sufficiently enough to push out the foul substances that their bodies produced. This matter then remained inside the body and caused more corruption. Sores were, therefore, one of the many visible signs of laziness.[107] For officers and slaveholders, it was but a small step to imagine that these groups had often caused their own sores in order to exempt themselves from work.

Many plantation practitioners had come to the Caribbean by way of the British armed forces, where sores and ulcers were a major source of conflict between doctors and the military rank and file. At the garrison hospital, Troup and a soldier, John Rule, argued about an open wound on Rule's leg. Rule tried to persuade Troup that the sore on his leg was an old one and hence a sign of deep-seated corruption. For Rule, the reemergence of this old sore warranted exemption from duty. "This was evident proof besides the symptom said he would not go out his leg was so bad," Troup summarized Rule's reasoning. Troup had a different interpretation. He maintained that Rule was suffering from a minor wound and that Rule's intemperance had created it. "He got Drunk & his leg a little ruffle from the Rum Cask," Troup noted in his diary. "His leg was no hinderence [sic] to his operating on duty." Troup sent him off. The next day, Rule returned to the hospital. To Troup's horror and surprise, the sore was "double the size, a large blister on it." Troup doubted his initial interpretation. Perhaps the sore was a mark of something more serious. But shortly thereafter, Rule's fellow men-in-arms flooded the hospital with sores on their legs. Troup and the corps' sergeant grew suspicious. Troup identified a man, "one Devil Binby," as "the ringleader & his trade is Tinker." Binby had apparently gathered metal alloys from a kettle and offered the scrapings (presumably for a price) to the other soldiers in the corps. Rule had acquired some and applied it to his sore. Troup charged him formally "with having applied poisonous substances to his leg, that he might be up in the Hospital to prevent him from doing his duty as a soldier."[108] Caricatures about idle soldiers and sailors created paranoia about sores that suddenly changed in their size and appearance.

Managers treated enslaved people's sores with a similar level of suspicion because they embedded sores within a larger culture of concerns about illness and idleness and because the West Indies saw the cross-institutional pollination in ideas about managing soldiers, sailors, and slaves. In their advice texts, some medical men, such as yellow-fever writer David Grant, warned that enslaved people "uncover and apply such things [to their sores] that exasperate, extend, and continue the malady."[109] The slaveholder advice writer Clement Caines assumed that some patients "palpably cherished a sore." In reference to the imagined prevalence of this action in military regiments and naval squadrons, Caines recommended a "few stripes . . . to be inflicted, as they are on sailors and soldiers in hospitals, when they voluntarily exacerbate their complaints by indulging in drunkness."[110] For many managers, sores and ulcers that suddenly changed in their appearance signaled feigned illness.

Like the soldier who scraped resin from the kettle, an enslaved person who wanted to irritate a wound would not have had to search very far to find the means. The oxidized substrate that formed on the instruments of oppression, such as iron manacles, chains, and hoes, could be easily harvested. Since enslaved people had been driven to the precipice of crisis and were in desperate need of respite from the rigors of the field, they may have engaged in measures that to us seem unfathomable. What these stories show, in part, is that managers struggled to ascertain what occurred beneath the surface of the skin. They wanted to believe that incapacity could be ascertained through sight, but in practice that was far from certain. They also reveal enslaved people's desperation: enslaved people knew that they would need to appease managers' expectations about what a legitimate illness looked like.

For as much as proprietors and managers grumbled about it, enslaved people's canny manipulation of speech and other signs of incapacity ensured their survival. The necessity of these strategies was particularly acute in the late eighteenth century. During this period, managers worked enslaved people harder than ever before, and enslaved people saw far more medical crises per year.[111] After one particularly grueling and productive harvest, the absentee slaveholder Chaloner Arcedeckne received a letter from Simon Taylor urging him to look outside of Golden Grove for additional manpower during the holing and planting season. The current crop output could not be maintained, Taylor warned, "without murdering the Negroes."[112] Enslaved individuals engaged in a number of activities to survive, from struggling to get admission into plantation hospitals to temporary marronage. Managers sometimes accommodated enslaved people to ensure the viability of the functioning of the estate. But they made such concessions on an ad hoc basis and only as a result of enslaved people's cumulative challenges and requests, many of which were met with punishment.

Enslaved people's petitioning was not an organized and collective activity against their conditions. Yet it allowed individuals or small groups to endure. Moreover, few overseers were willing to slow down production schedules entirely, which meant that one person's relief became another person's burden. When illness was rampant or the estate did not have enough people capable of taking out the crop, managers externalized cultivation's burdens onto hired hands—jobbing gangs.[113] As jobbing became a more standard component of managers' pursuit of efficiency, total strangers were often made to carry the weight of others' afflictions (and overseers' pursuit of profits).

Sometimes the people who carried the burden lived close to home. Attorneys and overseers admitted people on the brink of catastrophe into the hospital and then reapportioned the cost of cultivation onto other members of the estate. The bare life minimal subsistence to which managers subjected enslaved people incentivized them to police one another. According to the proprietor Matthew Lewis, the men and women on his Cornwall plantation in Jamaica regularly castigated Nato for his extended stints in the hospital. They attacked him "for his laziness and leaving them to do his work for him he told them plainly that he did not mean to work and nobody should make him."[114] Enslaved people generally did not resent the sick but generously took up additional labor to support them. But in certain instances, they also criticized feigned illness not out of a conservative impulse to uphold the integrity of the plantation system but to ensure their survival by regulating incapacity among themselves.

At the threshold of plantation hospitals, both managers and sufferers understood that they were engaged in a type of bargaining—they were negotiating the capacity to work and the necessity of rest. Managers and the enslaved approached incapacity from oppositional interests—overseers especially wanted to extract more labor from the enslaved, and enslaved people wanted the rest that would enable them to survive.

Enslaved people spoke about their unease in an era when political and medical thought demarcated hierarchy and race on the basis of who could feel and emote. Colonial gentlemen and men of letters argued that what marked them as distinct from Indigenous and enslaved people, as well as the lower sorts, was their own exquisite capacity for sentiment.[115] These beliefs were of consequence when they met with enslaved people's own traditions of verbal expression. Enslaved women, for instance, customarily remained silent during childbirth—it reaffirmed motherhood and childbirth as sacred. Colonists had long racialized gender and maintained that women of African descent were more fecund than European women. Yet in the late eighteenth century, slaveholders and plantation managers now pointed to enslaved women's silence during childbirth as evidence that they did not feel pain and thus did not require extensive medical care and could be made to bear children in significant numbers with little respite from agricultural toil.[116] Against this backdrop of beliefs, enslaved people described many symptoms and states. They constructed a rich metaphorical language and a series of colloquialisms to communicate to managers and vocalize the imperceptible. They used speech to contest managers' contentions that they were not sensate and thus did not deserve to be heard.

Given the bleak conditions of the hospital, it should come as little surprise that many enslaved men and women contended with their afflictions and those of their kin outside of sick-houses and on their own terms. Such actions took several forms, from using remedies from the Afro-Caribbean therapeutic arsenal to simply keeping their afflictions hidden from view for as long as possible. We catch a glimpse of this world, of course, in managers' complaints about it. The visible signs of illness—venereal disease especially—did not manifest in forms that could be read on the surface of the body until the advanced stages of the disease. Managers acknowledged the "impossibility of examining minutely and regularly into the state of every individual amidst such a variety of important concerns."[117] "The women," Simon Taylor complained, "treat the symptoms [of venereal disease] with some sort of bushes and plumtree bark, and never come to the hospital till they are as rotten [sick] as can be." Colonists could not control the willingness of sufferers to speak about symptoms that were perceivable only to the person experiencing them. One of the ways that enslaved people ensured that they could manage sickness on their own terms, then, was not through negotiating but through prolonged silence. "The men don't complain until they pass blood," Taylor grumbled about enslaved people afflicted with venereal disease.[118]

Because managers maintained that enslaved people's bodies belonged to them, they believed that they should be in possession of all of the information about enslaved people's condition, including their health. They therefore situated enslaved people's efforts to heal with their own medicines not as silence but as concealment. Troup noted that a woman he treated named Lydia had definitely been "clap'd" (afflicted with venereal disease) and that she had made an effort "to prevent discovery."[119] Sufferers did not turn to the hospital, at least not immediately. There were many good reasons why an enslaved person would choose to be silent instead. To gain rest and sustenance that they needed to survive, sometimes men and women made the body speak in a language intelligible to managers. But just as often, they managed sickness out of earshot.

Social Remedies

Isolation and temporary displacement were probably the hardest elements of a hospital stay for both the sick and their families and a major point of contestation in the social relations of illness. In a sense, sickhouses represented managers' efforts to muzzle the sick, to break off their communications with others on the estate. Apart from their dim view of the salubriousness of the foods and medicines given to the sick, one reason that the enslaved sufferers hesitated to go into plantation hospitals stemmed from foundational differences in the ways that Europeans and Africans understood medicine and illness. Enslaved people did not always situate medicine and care in narrow therapeutic terms but maintained a relational view of health and sickness—illness concerned a person's connections to others. In her study of the British slave trade, Carolyn Roberts explains how Biafrans linked their illness in the Middle Passage to their unmooring from families, homelands, traditional modes of care, and the protective web of community and spirits. The social and spiritual dislocation that captives endured during the Middle Passage was not equivalent to what hospital sufferers and those who cared about them experienced. Still, connection during moments of illness was important, and enslaved people worked to recast hospital medicine in relational terms to countermand sufferers' potential disconnection.[120]

Enslaved people probably viewed hospitals as extracting the sick from important webs of social connection that brought about restoration from illness. Hospital sufferers, one attorney observed, "have a great aversion to being kept in the sick house during their illness, and if they can escape to their huts they will do so."[121]

They sought familiar surroundings of course. But their reasons for doing so were probably also related to enslaved people's beliefs about landscapes. Enslaved people moved through a sacralized natural world comprised of the spirits of ancestors, personal spirits, and what Ras Michael Brown refers to as nature spirits.[122] Place held a welter of meanings—it could animate spiritual forces that conveyed either material prosperity or peril upon the living. Spirits converged in particular places, such as silk and cotton trees, forests, grasslands, waterways, and enslaved people's burial grounds.[123] Variously malevolent and assistive, nature spirits, the dead, and malevolent spiritual entities inserted themselves into human affairs. They issued illnesses, brought natural disasters, and thereby apportioned resources.[124] These entities could be summoned by human agents. In response to interpersonal strife, enslaved people often consulted shamans and ritualists, known as Obeah, or Obi, men and women, who could cause afflictions and remedy infirmity through their interactions with this larger, invisible, and mysterious world. In exchange for payment,

Obeah ritualists intervened in disputes between parties and offered protection for the sick or cast curses by directing malevolent forces. A sudden and abrupt illness that followed on the heels of conflict between the sick and other members of the community was often seen as evidence of social and spiritual rupture—a person's movement out of the protective web of human and spiritual entities.

Enslaved people worked collectively to redress illness. When they suspected Obeah as the source of harm, they looked for signs that other members of the community had consorted with a ritualist to cause harm. Search parties dug up the earth in the huts and gardens of people whom had been cursed by ritualists—hoping to discover the ritual objects, such as rags and pieces of glass bottles, that the ritualist had buried therein. Just as often, the family members of aggrieved parties raided the huts of ritualists to find the tools of their trade—knotted cords, human hair, as well as animal parts consisting of blood, bird feathers and beaks, the teeth of cats and dogs, and claws.[125] Silk and cotton trees, burial grounds, woods, the floors of enslaved people's huts and their kitchen gardens collectively formed an Afro-diasporic topography of health, sickness, and social relations. Restoring the sick might entail material redress to the injured party, locating an Obeah ritualist to intercede, or appeasing a nature spirit by building an altar with sacred objects and plants. But on a more prosaic level, it entailed provisioning with sacred plants, foods, and care to bring the sick back into the fold. That was difficult to achieve when people were forced to convalesce in hospitals and kept under lock and guard.

In a variety of gestures, enslaved people worked to combat the social isolation of sufferers. Many enslaved people's responses to sufferers' isolation were surreptitious out of necessity. Managers took enslaved people's efforts to assist as interference in managers' large and informal experiment to identify the consumables that sustained enslaved life. So families engaged with the sick and affirmed their connections within one another in fugitive acts that have largely evaded archival capture but can be perceived in managers' frequent warnings about enslaved people's persistence in visiting and bringing food and other articles of comfort. The plantation surgeon Robert Thomas decried plantations that did not have hospitals, as this allowed the sick to receive "improper things brought to them by their friends."[126] Thomas's criticism reveals managers' fixation on imposing their dietary and pharmaceutical remedies and achieving uniformity. But one might also read managers' warnings as observations about how enslaved people responded to their dilemma. Speculating on what activities and beliefs lay behind managers' grievances draws into view the more specific ways that enslaved people mitigated the terror of displacement and isolation to remind the sick that they were not alone.

Substances and provisions held the power to heal, especially those tied to homelands. Troup reported on a recently arrived African captive at the Woodbridge plantation who expressed his illness in terms of his dislocation from his native country. The man had fallen into fits and requested warm water, which he drank, and candle tallow, which he rubbed on his stomach.[127] Woodbridge's manager demanded that the man eat hard biscuit. The man refused. He ascribed the persistence of his condition to his displacement from his place of origin. "He complains greatly to get back to his country to get strong food, for that the hard biscuit hurts his stomach," Troup recorded.[128]

The ways that enslaved people produced sustenance created commonalities and affective ties that mapped onto African beliefs about the relationship between food, homeland, and health. The bedrock of enslaved people's maintenance as well as their communal life lay in their provision grounds.[129] These were parcels of land, usually located at the margins of estates, that slaveholders gave to individual men and women, who used them to sustain their family's subsistence. Working with fixed amounts of energy, it was advantageous for men and women to work their grounds collectively. Ground foods, such as yams, cassava, eddoes, plantains, and tannia were especially common articles of cultivation. In addition to provision grounds, enslaved people maintained kitchen gardens close to their cabins, where they raised petty livestock and cultivated additional vegetables, such as squashes and callalou (a type of green).[130] Some enslaved people sold the excess from their provision grounds at market and thereby enhanced their family's personal wealth. Enslaved people held their particular provision grounds dear because they depended on them to live and because they represented their families' attachment to place. When the Jamaican absentee planter Joseph Foster Barham proposed to displace some of the carpenters on his Mesopotamia plantation to another one named Island, the carpenters protested. "They would consider themselves," Barham's attorneys warned, "without a home and their provision grounds, houses, and families would be neglected."[131] Enslaved people defined their communal life, homeland, and family around provision grounds that were vital to their survival.

Yet enslaved people's subsistence was precarious. Overseers' seasonal claims on enslaved people's time took them away from their provision grounds. Domesticated and feral pigs wandered into grounds, destroyed fragile root systems, and consumed the fruits of enslaved people's labor. Natural disasters such as hurricanes or droughts blunted the energy that people expended bringing roots and crops into maturity. Incapacity meant that the sick could not work their provision grounds. Other family members picked up the slack. The healthy sometimes assisted and carried another's wares to market. Others might slash plantain suckers and "green-meat" to feed the sick's hogs and other livestock.[132] Enslaved people distributed their energetic resources across the kin-group and between kin-groups, which probably bestowed emotional meanings on the crops and livestock they raised and stored as well as the precious and scarce food rations that managers provided.

Still, managers ignored such affective meanings because they wanted to control and standardize sufferers' dietaries. Collins advised against allowing enslaved people to consume pepper-pot and salted herrings during their convalescence.[133] The advice writer Clement Caines locked up enslaved people afflicted with yaws so that "they did not eat one ounce of salt provision (herrings or salted beef) during their confinement and cure."[134] Many authors anticipated that others would comfort the sick by bringing them food. Collins recommended deputizing the hospital's healer (or sick-nurse) to act as a guard and "not to let the negroe eat any thing that may be brought to him by the other negroes."[135] Probably the most direct and common expression of care, then, was through foodstuffs smuggled in to the sick. Some of the articles may have contained not just affective but also spiritual resonances that offered hope of recovery, including boiled or roasted yams. As Roberts explains, Biafrans attribute yams' growth to the yam deity in the region, and thus the yam today has powers associated with "life force."[136] Roasted yams were probably among the forms of sustenance brought into plantation hospitals. Men and women who cared about the sick had to move these materials into the hospital surreptitiously, which likely enhanced their potency.

Enslaved people fought against sufferers' sense of disempowerment in simpler ways, too. When possible, they kept company with the sick and put collective pressure on the people who attended them. The most effective way to do so was to mobilize their own awareness of the internal struggles and frictions among white managerial staff, especially practitioners' concerns about their own employment. They often spoke about practitioners to the people who hired them. "The negroes in general are remarkably sensible and if you are successful they will sound your praise give them little pain," Troup recorded in his diary only a few months after his arrival.[137] Fanny, Prancer's mother, was one of many enslaved people who made practitioners aware of their watchful presence. There must have been many others. In one instance, Troup was palpating the muscles of a man whom "locked jaw" (tetanus) had stricken. "And some negroes," Troup reported, "being inclined to be funny with him made him laugh and use the muscles of his face."[138] As helpful as the man's friends were, they were also, as Troup seems to have been aware, watching the doctor and taking note of what he was doing.

For enslaved people, visiting and accompanying the sick alleviated sufferers' isolation. Even after the construction of hospitals, such visits—when possible—became fugitive gestures of care. The scope of enslaved medical subversion can be glimpsed in the development of a cottage industry of hospitals operated by independent practitioners, who promised better control over the sick than what plantation hospitals could achieve.[139] The surgeon William Mann, for instance, hung out his shingle in Kingston and announced the opening of his hospital. Managers could send men and women suffering from yaws, ulcers, and venereal disease to Mann for their confinement and rehabilitation. Mann's hospital was meant to fill a gap in the medical marketplace—the diseases he proposed to treat often required long-term convalescence and care. Yet Mann also distinguished his hospital from the yaws houses and hospitals on estates by touting, in part, the amount of control he would have over the sick. The patients sent to him had "the proprietor's own attendance and inspection thrice a day, who sees every medicine given to them [the sick] to prevent deception." Mann's constancy would ensure that "they [patients] have no possible means of getting at any thing which may impede their cure, as all communication between them and their outside acquaintances is forbid and prevented by confinement and strict inspection (within the place)."[140] Mann's advertisement was an attempt to differentiate his offerings from what was available on estates. Yet the fact that managers might seek out such proprietary hospitals is a powerful testament to the persistence of enslaved people in taking measures large and small to care for their friends and family who were suffering.

ALTHOUGH PLANTATION sick-houses were not originally intended only to reduce enslaved mortality explicitly but rather to facilitate managers' control over the sick, their meanings changed over time. During the last decades of the eighteenth century, Britons were increasingly concerned about slaveholders' dependence on the murderous Atlantic slave trade; even after its abolition, Britons remained concerned about rampant mortality and morbidity among enslaved people. In Parliamentary hearings, therefore, politicians wanted to know what was being done to curb these outrages. In speeches before the House of Lords and Commons and in reports sent by colonial assemblies, attorneys and proprietors pointed to the construction of plantation sick-houses as evidence that they were taking action. "There is no plantation where a hospital is not provided, and generally on an extensive scale, and under good regulations, in respect to cleanliness and ventilation," read one report that the Jamaican Assembly had sent. That same report claimed that even a person who was not "laboring under any real sickness, but wishes a day of rest and relaxation," would gain admission.[141]

By speaking about these hospitals in public, proprietors fashioned themselves as benevolent paternalists who manifested care and concern to their enslaved dependents, whose care and longevity was their responsibility. Like the benefactors of English voluntary hospitals who touted their charity as a means to grow a productive population and to paper over deep inequalities, defenders of slavery invoked the proliferation of plantation hospitals to obscure that in their extremely coercive labor regime the work itself was the principal cause of illness.[142]

The story that the members of Parliament heard from slaveholders and colonial assemblies was a quite different tale from the ones that absentees hoped to receive from managers on the ground. In their correspondence, overseers and attorneys reassured absentees that they shared the same time-horizons as concerned convalescence from illness. Managers were not bargaining with enslaved sufferers but using coercive measures to drive them out and back to work and controlling what they consumed. Sampson Wood, the manager at Newton plantation in Barbados, assured the absentee that he pushed men and women back to their stations as soon as he saw that "their digestion good & their appetite keen." Proprietors expected colonists to regard enslaved people as bodies that could keep enduring work and who were incapable of interpreting their own illnesses. Managers, in turn, postured and gave the impression in correspondence that they were not listening to the patients' speech. Since colonists believed that white people alone should possess and wield the power of speech, they feared that feigned illness, effected by speech, undermined their authority. Still, there are signs in managers' correspondence that they often stumbled in their efforts to interpret illness and incapacity by reading signs and symptoms. Wood acknowledged that it was "impossible to tell when a person is sick or not."[143] The sick, in turn, strategically deployed talk, unwilling to grant colonists the sole power to interpret illness or to meekly accommodate their managers' denials of rest.

Living along thin margins and vulnerable to illness, hospitals operated for enslaved people as an unwelcome yet necessary component in enslaved people's bids for survival. Managers tried to deter enslaved people from demanding the resources they needed, mounting punishing criteria to determine whether someone was incapacitated enough to warrant rest, medicine, and dietary assistance from the estate's stores. To acquire hospital admission and to survive required enslaved sufferers to negotiate—they had to contend with the figures who were tasked with determining who was too sick to work and who was healthy enough to keep cutting cane. At the hospital's threshold, sufferers and managers were trying to determine their customary obligations to one another over work, sustenance, and rest. Men's and women's demand for admission to the hospital was part of the moral economy of illness that was hammered out in these everyday interactions. That these were negotiations does not mean that enslaved people had the upper hand. Enslaved bids for admission into hospitals were made under dangerous conditions. Men and women faced violent reprisal if they were adjudged as feigning illness. Enslaved people thus learned to speak in particular ways to make themselves heard and secure their safety. In the medical encounter between colonists and enslaved people, therefore, practitioners and managers had a monopoly on speaking in safety and judging the truth of enslaved speech, but they could not wholly dominate the orality of the enslaved.

In exchange for rest and sustenance, men and women had to accommodate managers' new expectation that the enslaved should convalesce in plantation sick-houses rather than in their own quarters. Outside of plantation sick-houses and well before managers had begun to interfere, enslaved people had for many years engaged in collective efforts to support the infirm. In sacred plants, food, and in carework, enslaved people made sure the sick were not disconnected from others. In the era of improvement, men and women worked to resist depersonalization and disconnection by affirming bonds of affinity and reclaiming their personhood under duress. They advocated for themselves and their families through speech or hid from managers with strategies of silence and concealment. They helped sufferers draw strength from the concern of their loved ones. They knew that without one another's assistance, managers' medicine might harm them. So they banded together in small ways to make hospitals into a resource they could use and mitigate that threat.

Into this clash of wills stepped plantation doctors, many of whom struggled to handle large rosters of clients with hundreds of sick people under their care at a time. Those working conditions encouraged practitioners to mimic the managers' indifference to the ways that an enslaved patient's life events and habits had shaped her or his illness and how it ought to be treated. Enslaved people had overcome one obstacle by forcing the hospital's gatekeepers to hear them. Now, as they subjected their illnesses to treatment and prescription, they encountered another set of difficulties: the economics of plantation medicine rendered most practitioners deaf to enslaved sufferers' voices. This type of silent treatment reflected an assembly-line approach that accompanied proprietors' efforts to take control over the ways enslaved people contended with affliction.

2

The New Business of Plantation Medicine

Across the Anglophone world, the quack, or medical charlatan, was a familiar figure of animus. His itinerancy, showmanship, as well as his extravagant boasting in print transgressed the boundaries of tasteful self-promotion. He was not dealing in bad medicine per se. Rather his theatricality and immoderate use of printed instruments of publicity, such as handbills and newspapers, suggested that he prioritized financial gain over his customers' well-being.[1] In the final decades of the eighteenth century, British Caribbean colonists developed their own version of this figure. The tales they spun had a very specific point of inflection, however. They cast the Caribbean quack as a young, male itinerant whose inexperience and neglect of the enslaved people under his responsibility imperiled colonists' prosperity. As storytellers explained, swarms of "young doctors," comprised of "raw inexperienced youths," "apothecaries' boys," "apprentice boy[s]," and "young and transient practitioners in the army and navy" who had only "a smattering of Latin" and "perhaps a voyage or two on board and African trader," had become ubiquitous in the West Indies.[2]

In his *History of Jamaica*, the absentee slaveholder and proslavery lobbyist Edward Long gave this Caribbean quack a name: Mr. Apozem, a reference to charlatans' medical mixtures of questionable quality and safety. Apozem was born in Britain as the son of a carpenter. By the time he reached his early adulthood, Apozem had little to no experience with medicine. He had served as a footman (and not an apprentice) to a British apothecary. After completing his "apprenticeship," Apozem was hired as the surgeon for a Guinea (slave) ship. He did not last beyond the second stage of the itinerary. By the time the ship had crossed the Atlantic from the African coast and docked at Kingston's quay, his medicines had killed most of the crew and African captives. If Apozem remained aboard, the ship would not have the manpower to steer it back to Britain. The captain thus foisted him upon an unsuspecting plantation owner, who, in turn, let him loose in the care of his estates. Thereafter, Apozem spent his days riding his horse between plantations in Jamaica's hinterlands. Colonists could easily spot him, "continually upon high-trot, riding post, and spreading depopulation far and wide."[3]

As Long's satire suggests, the stories that colonists told about charlatanism concerned the young men, later called plantation surgeons by historians, who derived their income entirely or in large proportion from attendance on enslaved people on plantations. One reading would see these stories as yet another example of slaveholders displacing blame for the ghastly morbidity and mortality among enslaved populations onto the middling white men whom slaveholders hired to manage their estates. This chapter proceeds from a different angle. The end of the eighteenth century saw the omnipresence of young and inexperienced practitioners across several genres of writing. Their ubiquity is a sign of several changes taking place on Caribbean estates that had happened several decades earlier: the practitioners' relationship to their slaveholder-employers, the structure of medical care on plantations, and the experience of illness among enslaved people had all been transformed. The plantation surgeon emerged as a differentiated figure of the larger medical economy at the end of the eighteenth century as result of multiple forces internal and external to the plantation complex that were a consequence of war-making and the development of the plantation system much earlier.

Scholars have argued that the activities of colonial legislatures, whose members included slaveholders and attorneys, drove the provision of medicine on plantations. Starting in 1780, these bodies passed laws, known as amelioration laws, mandating that each plantation employ a practitioner.[4] But an even larger and insufficiently studied element that drove the development of plantation medicine took place well before amelioration legislation. During the second half of the eighteenth century, Britain went to war with its European rivals as well as with the region's Maroons. War-making multiplied the number of surgeons and surgeon's mates in the region as well as the number of civilian practitioners. The army's presence was, however, like blacksmith's bellows. It swelled with imperial rivalry and Anglo-Maroon conflict, and it shrunk with the cessation of hostilities. Peacetime brought cuts to the military establishment, including its medical staff.[5] Civilian and military migration created a surplus of young medical men in need of work. Established physicians monopolized the more lucrative positions in seaports. Young medical men, in turn, migrated to the Caribbean's hinterlands in search of work, which created a surplus of young practitioners. Consequently, medical men's time and labor were far cheaper to purchase after 1763 than in previous eras.

Slaveholders might have responded by hiring medical men to live directly on their estates. But that would mean yielding arable land and building housing, which increased rather than reduced the cost of producing cane. Instead, they took advantage of the practitioners' diminished bargaining power and hired them at an annual rate to visit their plantations several times a week. To offset their expenses, plantation practitioners increased the number of estates they took on, which expanded the ambit of their work. Indeed, the number of patients who were a practitioner's responsibility as well as the amount of ground that one needed to cover were, to its practitioners, the definitive features of plantation medicine. This type of medical practice and its attendant economic arrangements was a distinctive arena of medical commerce. It was poorly remunerated and laborious, often chaotic. Its personae were young and peripatetic autodidacts on the make. Plantation medical men were just as colonists described them: young, recently decommissioned regimental surgeons or surgeons' assistants or recently arrived civilian doctors who rode to multiple estates per day.

Their working conditions gave them too little time with any one of the thousands of enslaved people under their responsibility, warping the empirical approach to medicine they had learned in the British Army and on slave ships into a type of medical practice that seemed alien to observers, to their patients, and to themselves. Although they were charged with the provision of care to people in significant numbers, plantation practitioners' workloads meant that practitioners could not even provide minimal attention to the sick. Most enslaved people therefore experienced plantation medicine not as the surveillance and ongoing monitoring of their bodies but as neglect and the cursory treatment of their symptoms with aggressive chemical remedies. Practitioners' working conditions intensified the place of violence within medical men's practice. Coercion facilitated the expedition of their tasks and quickly became central to their business model.

This chapter lays out the economic organization of this type of medical practice in order to identify how the larger forces that structured the relationship between medical men and their slaveholder-employers also shaped medical men's relations with enslaved sufferers and healers.

Medicine on the Move

THE EIGHTEENTH-CENTURY Caribbean was the cockpit of European rivalries. The sugar economy of the British and French Caribbean was lucrative, and mining industries on the Spanish Main sustained this waning empire's power. The region was therefore critical to the success of the British imperial project. From the War of Jenkins' Ear in 1739 until the conclusion of the Haitian Revolution in 1804, the region operated as the main theater where Britain, Spain, France, the Netherlands, and Denmark squared off, subverting one another's economic clout and geopolitical position through the seizing and occupying of different territories. In addition to its status as a major theater of European conflict, the Caribbean was also a major site of internecine warfare between bondspeople, Maroons, and colonists. Consequently, British Caribbean islands had a far larger military presence in the eighteenth century than did the mainland North American colonies. Only New York and Nova Scotia had their own garrisons manned by British regulars before 1776. After the American War of Independence, British imperial power in the Atlantic World had its heart in Jamaica.

Consequently, the British armed forces mobilized practitioners to the Caribbean in large numbers, especially at the ranks of regimental surgeon and surgeon's mate. As early as 1730, the rudiments of what would become the West Indian Garrison were set in place as a sprawling network of batteries, coastal fortresses, fortified refuges, and mountainous hill camps in Jamaica, Barbados, and Antigua.[6] Prior to 1754, independent companies and provincial militias manned these fortifications.[7] After 1763, when Britain gained new islands from the French, the imperial government authorized the permanent establishment of three thousand redcoats in the West Indian Garrison. The number of permanent soldiers thereafter fluctuated with each war, reaching its apogee in 1795, when the establishment consisted of twenty-two thousand regular troops. From 1763 onward, British regulars were a visible presence in the Caribbean.[8] Yet while the size of the West Indian establishment grew steadily over time, the presence of the British Army fluctuated. It expanded with imperial and Anglo-Maroon conflict and withered with the suspension of hostilities.

Movement from the lower ranks of the armed forces to plantation medicine was common. William Wright exemplified this trend. Wright entered the Royal Navy as a surgeon's mate in 1758. By the time Britain had seized and occupied Martinique in 1762, Wright had become a surgeon in the naval hospitals in Fort Royal and Saint Pierre.[9] Wright seems to have acquired his M.D. in a matter of months. In 1764, he returned to Scotland and matriculated at the University of St. Andrews, one of several new diploma mills, which granted Wright an M.D. To earn it, he sat for an oral exam administered by the father of a friend whom Wright had met in the Royal Navy. Later that year, Wright ventured to Jamaica, first to Savanna-la-Mar (a port in Westmoreland Parish). But because of the deluge of practitioners, Wright could not operate independently. He then relocated to Kingston and settled for working as an assistant to a man named Dr. Gray. A few months later he formed a joint medical proprietorship with a man named Dr. Steele. The two serviced and lived on absentee slaveholder James Stirling's Hampden plantations, located in Trelawny Parish on the north side of the island.[10]

The economic expansion that typically accompanied war-making also stimulated transatlantic ethnic, professional, and family networks, which channeled practitioners from North America and Britain to the Caribbean.[11] After the American War of Independence, many civilian networks mobilized to secure employment for doctors in the Caribbean. "The war being at an end," the Jamaican plantation surgeon William Chamberlaine observed in 1784, "the number of medical practitioners, migrating to the West Indies, will be daily increased."[12] These social, educational, and family networks operated alongside those of the British Army and Royal Navy to bring practitioners to the torrid zone.[13]

Meanwhile, changes to the economy of slaveholding generated additional demand for medical attendance. From approximately 1750 to 1790, the real price of Atlantic slaves doubled. Then, during the last decade of the eighteenth century, pressure on British planters to hasten sickly enslaved people's return to work intensified even further. The Haitian Revolution put a halt on sugar production in Saint-Domingue, creating an opening on the European market that drove up the price of sugar by 40 percent. The overthrow of the most profitable sugar colony in the world incentivized planters in Dutch, Danish, Spanish, and British colonies to increase sugar production. The number of Africans dragooned into slavery skyrocketed, as did the number of acres put under cultivation. Between 1791 and 1800, nearly twice as many Africans arrived in the British Caribbean as had arrived between 1751 and 1760. The years immediately following the Seven Years' War and the Haitian Revolution represented two periods of surge in the slave trade to the British Caribbean. A leveling off took place in the 1780s. These patterns suggest that warfare played an important role in increasing both the numbers of doctors in the region as well as the numbers of enslaved people. The two appear to have coincided with one another.[14]

With the capture of Tobago, Trinidad, Demerara, and Suriname, the real price of slaves imported from Africa jumped a further 140 percent in the sixteen years between the Haitian Revolution and the abolition of the British Atlantic slave trade. Since prices of African captives were, on average, 56 percent higher than sugar prices during this period, concerns about the opportunity costs of enfeebled manpower likely drove slaveholders to use practitioners to police and treat enslaved people felled by yaws, venereal disease, and a variety of deficiency diseases so as to hasten their recuperation for work. Concerns about the abolition of the slave trade also encouraged enslavers to hire surgeons to supervise enslaved midwives, nurses, and mothers in the management of childbirth and the illnesses of infancy.[15]

What did young practitioners hope to gain from the Caribbean? What did they think after they arrived? As practitioners and colonists, young men chose to migrate to the Caribbean and then often came to regret it. All colonists who journeyed to the Caribbean confronted a Janus-faced world of potential fortunes and dangers. The region offered natural abundance on the one hand, and the hazards of disease and natural disaster on the other. Tropical climate and rich soils rendered the Caribbean a "biodiversity hotspot," which attracted botanists and fortune-seekers alike.[16] Yet for every reason that favored a person's migration to the Caribbean, there were as many against it. A major disincentive was the abundance of disease, particularly the tropical fevers that notoriously felled newcomers, especially those who hailed from temperate climates.[17] As the Jamaican doctor Benjamin Moseley observed, "there is no climate in which so much care and circumspection are required to secure the body from diseases, and where they are so rapid."[18] West Indian environments held resources from which colonists stood to make great riches. Yet the spectacular natural world that dazzled European newcomers also threatened their survival.

Quotidian violence between colonists and enslaved people presented another threat. British Caribbean colonies' value was predicated on the backbreaking regimes of sugar cultivation that consumed the lives of enslaved Africans and Afro-Creoles. Slaveholders maintained their workforces only by purchasing African captives, usually from West or West Central Africa.[19] As colonists, the young medical men who ventured to the Caribbean were direct participants in this system of violence. As practitioners of medicine who adjudged when the sick were well enough to return to work, they served as handmaidens to a brutal regime.

Yet colonists' grip on power was shaky. Like slave ship crews, colonists maintained their dominion through what Stephanie Smallwood calls the "arithmetic of racial violence."[20] In Jamaica, enslaved people outnumbered colonists by a ratio of ten to one. Colonists convinced themselves of their security and maintained a tenuous hold on authority through routine and violent attacks on the men and women whom they held in bondage.[21] The routinized nature of violence is captured in the diary of Jonathan Troup. The Scottish transplant came with an A.M. (the equivalent of a bachelor's degree) from the University of Aberdeen. He worked initially as an assistant in the medical firm of Andrew Fillian, which was located in Roseau. Shortly after his arrival, Troup witnessed a violent brawl between a person he described as a "mulatto man" and a clerk that ended in the clerk's death. Troup read the conflict as an example of the vulnerability of the colony's managerial class. "Drs and managers of estates die more than any set of people from their greater exposure on all occasions," he opined in relating this anecdote in his diary.[22] In these extractive and brutal plantation economies, enslaved people and colonists were perpetually engaged in a low-grade war with one another.[23] Middling managerial staff imagined themselves as the vanguard in a larger battle between colonists and the Africans they held in bondage.

As semi-skilled laborers, Troup and men like the Jamaican overseer Thomas Thistlewood were part of a particular exodus of young, middling bachelors who went to the Caribbean from the British Isles during the second half of the eighteenth century. They fled Britain because of the limited opportunities for men of middle rank. Collectively they represented what Trevor Burnard has described as the foot soldiers of the British Empire. They filled local militias and comprised the labor force of white bookkeepers, overseers, doctors, coopers, carpenters, petty shopkeepers, and millwrights. Many of them were young men. Bookkeepers were in their teenage years. They expected that if they could survive the

Caribbean, they could amass enough of a fortune to retire to Britain. Within a few months of most young men's arrival, however, the image of the Caribbean as a place of easy abundance was replaced by one of competition, disease, and violent conflict. Yet many remained for the sake of the more certain economic prospects offered by Caribbean slaveholding.[24]

In contrast to the people who became overseers, young medical men professed a trade, and they imagined slightly different itineraries for themselves than someone like Thistlewood. Most hoped to land in London, the world's largest metropolis, or Edinburgh, the capital of British academic medicine and a center of medical knowledge-making. There was a handful of people who followed this route and whose itineraries would have been familiar to venturing practitioners. Some of the most well-known practitioners of military medicine, namely the army physician Sir John Pringle (1707–1782) and the naval surgeon James Lind (1716–1794), rose through the armed forces. Both had launched careers on the basis of campaigns in European theaters. But after the Seven Years' War, the Caribbean produced a roster of practitioners who had become famous for their writing on the diseases of warm climates, fevers in particular.[25] The careers of these fever writers, who were mostly army physicians, offered object lessons on how one could use the Caribbean to advance one's station. At best, a Caribbean venture would yield metropolitan appointments and connections. Second best, they hoped, would be a steady and comfortable existence in a seaport. The worst—and most likely—fate was an early death.

Benjamin Moseley's remarkable rise may well have encouraged some young medical men to follow his example. Although he had studied medicine in hospitals in London, Paris, and Leyden, Moseley came to Jamaica without an M.D. in 1768. There he worked in the island's military hospital, held a position with the Seventy-Ninth Regiment, and published *Observations on the Dysentery of the West Indies* (1781) to great acclaim. Moseley remained in Jamaica until just after the end of the American War of Independence, when he left for Britain. Within the next decade, he acquired an M.D. from St. Andrews University (1784), became a Licentiate of the Royal College of Physicians (1787), published *A Treatise on Tropical Diseases and on the Climate of the West Indies* (1787), and developed a roster of wealthy and well-connected patients in London. In the years before his death, he held a post as the personal physician to the Duke of York.[26] That Moseley had been able to remain in Kingston and carve out a career in the seaport almost immediately following his arrival was exceptional, possibly owing to the strength of the patronage network that he had developed even before he had arrived.[27] Few of the military surgeons and civilian practitioners who ventured to the Caribbean in Moseley's wake would exit as quickly. Most would not even be able to join the medical world of the region's ports.

The medical marketplace of British Caribbean colonies was a variegated arena. Healers and herbalists of every origin and specialty offered cures, remedies, carework, and counsel on either a full-time, as-needed, or seasonal basis. One might seek assistance from an enslaved person or a free healer of color; a midwife; surgeon; apothecary; or physician. This last group had an M.D. attached to their name, which meant that they had graduated from a university with a medical degree. In London, titles, including physician, surgeon, and apothecary, were tied to social and intellectual hierarchies. They held little purchase in the Anglophone Atlantic. As medical practitioners arriving in Britain's Caribbean colonies learned, one needed patronage and experience with the medicine of hot climates in order to develop proficiency.

Among practitioners, however, there was a loose hierarchy. Printed rosters of practitioners, such as *The Medical Register*, where editors listed the name, title, and location of local practitioners, make visible the economic fault lines among white medical men that loosely correspond with hierarchies of prestige in London.[28] The geographic distribution of the white practitioners followed a pattern. Work in seaports was the most desirable and the most difficult arena to penetrate. Among the Jamaican practitioners listed in *The Medical Register* for the years 1780 and 1783, 84 percent did not have an official title or identify as a surgeon. Physicians in Jamaica were a minority, comprising only 16 percent of the people listed in the *Register*. However, nearly 80 percent of the physicians hung out shingles in Jamaica's major ports of call (Kingston, Spanish Town, Montego Bay, and Savanna-la-Mar). In Jamaica, elites clustered in seaports rather than in the island's hinterlands. Thus, those who left Britain as physicians, that is with an M.D. in hand, dominated this highly desirable pool of clients.

This was also the arena where patients demanded personalized attention to their unique constitutions. Claims to a systematic understanding of the "fundamental underlying causes of health and disease" and how illness materialized in the bodies of their individual clients were a potent means by which physicians distinguished their medical counsel from that of the practitioners against whom they competed.[29] Physicians promoted themselves by offering to provide advice tailored to the unique constitutions of their elite patients and the enslaved dependents within their households.

Yet the physicians' claims to deep knowledge of illness did not earn them deference from elite patients. In elite households, patients shared interpretive primacy with the medical men they patronized. Practitioners who waited on elites, according to Troup, were required to "cringe and bow and be continually attending upon triffles, just to keep patients."[30] This norm stood in stark contrast to practitioners' experience attending enslaved people, who were expected to be deferential to attending medical men. Seaport medical work, in other words, required practitioners to spend considerable time listening and deferring to clients. Still, practitioners of all stations saw seaport work as more desirable than that of plantations.

Attendance upon elites was probably as time-consuming as it was for those who attended plantations. But it was far less physically arduous. Medical work in seaports did not require the same amount of travel as that in the islands' hinterlands. A roster of deep-pocketed clients enabled one to take on fewer patient-clients. Physicians spent far less time than plantation practitioners hoofing it between households in the torrid zone's heat and humidity. Moreover, if a physician could not survive on his roster of elites alone, relationships developed with elite patients often generated opportunities for other employment. These usually came in the form of appointments to public offices. These appointments included the head of the island workhouse or jails, or one of the several charity and Royal Naval hospitals.[31] The Jamaican colonist Elizabeth Lichtenstein Johnston observed that "in Kingston whatever merchants the doctors attend they have the attendance of all of the ships consigned to them."[32] These appointments enabled the practitioner to attend to multiple patients who were concentrated in particular seaports. Because the roads in these urban areas were better maintained than those elsewhere, seaport practitioners could travel easily by carriage.

Additionally, a person stationed in port had access to Atlantic cosmopolitan literary and scientific culture—in the form of coffeehouses, taverns, newspapers, lending libraries, and scientific societies. Living in a seaport, one developed transatlantic connections to other medical men situated in other centers of medical knowledge-making such as

Philadelphia, Charleston, or Edinburgh. Through reading, writing, and correspondence, medical men stationed in seaports advanced their reputations and drummed up additional business. Access to ephemeral materials, which included case histories circulated in manuscript as well as short-run printed medical periodicals, helped a medical man anywhere compare what they had seen in the field with what other medical men in other climates had observed. Access to these materials, in other words, helped medical men substantiate the claims they made in print.

Plantation practitioners stumbled into many obstacles to knowledge-making. Compare the efforts of an elite medical man and a plantation practitioner as they tried to access a new edition of a medical periodical. In the same two-year period, Benjamin Turney and Alexander Anderson sought the most recent edition of the Edinburgh-based periodical the *Medical Observations and Enquiries*. Turney was the doctor for the Golden Grove estate, owned by the Jamaican absentee Chaloner Arcedeckne. Anderson was a physician and botanist to the botanical garden in St. Vincent. Anderson had a relationship with Benjamin Rush, the private Philadelphia physician, faculty member of the medical school at the University of Pennsylvania, and physician to the Philadelphia Hospital. Stationed in the printing epicenter of the North American mainland, Rush used his proximity to the vibrant world of medical print to establish reciprocal relationships with elite West Indian practitioners. In exchange for much-sought-after and often ephemeral medical texts, people like Anderson sent Rush botanical specimens, weather observations, and their own case studies on infectious fevers in West Indian microclimates. In 1791, Anderson thanked Rush for sending the newest edition of the *Medical Observations and Enquiries*. Anderson remarked that he "had heard much of it and therefore much wished to see it."[33]

Turney had a much more trying experience securing a copy of the *Medical Observations and Enquiries*. The plantation doctor relied on Arcedeckne, the London absentee for whom he worked, for medical periodicals. And unlike the relationship between Anderson and Rush, Arcedeckne and Turney did not stand on equal footing. Turney served at the absentee's pleasure. Arcedeckne proved somewhat indifferent to Turney's scientific endeavors. In 1789, as a gesture of goodwill, Arcedeckne had promised to send to Turney the *Medical Observations and Enquiries*, the same periodical that Anderson had received from Rush. Turney thanked Arcedeckne for his generosity in requesting that "Messrs Long to send me" the journal. "I hope it will not escape their memory," he closed this letter.[34] But his gratitude proved premature. Five months later, Turney had yet to receive the promised journal. "I have not yet read the *Medical Observations and Enquiries* you was so good as to mention, but hope Messrs Longs have not forgot them," he gently prodded in a subsequent letter sent to Arcedeckne.[35] Texts from Rush in North America moved into the hands of elite West Indian practitioners in a steady flow as a consequence of their networks and geographic proximity, but they reached the West Indies' hinterlands much more slowly. Medical practice in seaports, in other words, better positioned its practitioners to accumulate the financial and social resources that would hasten their return to Britain or help them generate prestige and elite clients locally. And it gave them access to the world of medical print and manuscript that helped practitioners develop new insights into the nature of diseases in hot climates through reading of diseases elsewhere.

Only a limited number of elites lived in seaports, so practitioners faced high barriers to entry. The seaports were impenetrable to the wave of newcomers who materialized during moments of war and peace. "In towns," the Jamaican Charles Leslie explained, "there are generally one or two eminent [medical] men who have the employment and soon get to be rich."[36] One gained a toehold in the medical economy of seaports by invitation to join an existing partnership or by inheriting the client roster of someone who died or who was leaving the island.[37] The surgeon John Williamson, for example, was able to maneuver from plantation medicine into a joint-partnership with Dr. Rennalls in Spanish Town only after Rennalls's partner had died. Williamson was probably offered this position because he had already worked in Jamaica's interior for several years in partnership with the physician Thomas Clarke. By the time he relocated to Spanish Town, Williamson was a known persona. In reference to the difficulty he had experienced moving from Jamaica's hinterlands to Spanish Town's medical arena, Williamson remarked that "it is an arduous task for a professional man to gain general good opinion; and, in entering on a new scene, that line of conduct has again to be renewed."[38]

Most newcomers, surgeons, and surgeon's mates, who were young and had been crowded out of work in ports, were consequently compelled to work in the region's hinterlands. Colin McClarty arrived in the Caribbean from Scotland at the conclusion of the American War of Independence; his grievances spotlight the saturation of the medical labor market that ensued with formal declarations of peace. Demobilization, combined with the arrival of North American Loyalists, had led to the saturation of the plantation medical market. "There are two things which I regret," he wrote to his sister in Scotland. "The first is that I did not come here some years ago, and the last, that I came here when I did." Had McClarty arrived in Jamaica prior to the war's termination, he might have stood a chance at finding work on one of the many estates, but, "owing to the vast number of medical people who are either refugees or deprived of employment by the peace," the colony "is so perfectly overwhelmed with them that almost every small plantation has got its doctor."[39] Most entered plantation medicine as a final recourse when they became demoralized by the paltry options in seaports. More work needs to be done to trace, systematically, what happened to surgeons and surgeon's mates once regiments were decommissioned. However, as we shall see, proprietors and attorneys clearly understood that there was a link between war-making and an excess of medical men. Stiff competition to find work on estates gave proprietors and their attorneys the upper hand in setting rates of compensation. The need for medical services and attendance on estates created a safety valve through which Caribbean seaports expelled its surplus medical men.

The abundance of practitioners was immediately visible to slaveholders and their attorneys, who took advantage of the situation. In 1777, Simon Taylor, a slaveholder and an attorney for the absentee Chaloner Arcedeckne, poached a doctor from a plantation that neighbored Arcedeckne's. He lost little sleep over it. "Was there not another doctor to be got ... it would be something," Taylor remarked, "but there are very great plenty."[40] Writing near the end of the Haitian Revolution, one attorney optimistically assessed the possibility of getting a competent practitioner for the estate he managed. "Medical men have been very scarce during the whole of the war, but we hope now from the numbers that will of course be dismissed by the reduction of the army and navy soon to have plenty among us," he explained.[41]

Occasionally, it was not just young men but established practitioners who were drawn into this arena of practice, typically after poor turns of fortune. This was the case for the Jamaican physician Thomas Clarke, who started what he described as a "large negroe practice," after he lost his appointment as island botanist.[42] The previous appointment as island botanist had provided Clarke with an annual income of £420. By comparison, the salary of the Jamaican overseer Thomas Thistlewood ranged, in the 1760s, between £200 and £300 per year.[43] When the Jamaican colonial assembly terminated the botanist position, Clarke experienced a significant loss of income.⁴⁴ It was then that he, in the words of one acquaintance, "turned plantation doctor by which he gets £1000 per an. and dared not look at a plant."⁴⁵ Plantation medicine could provide a landing spot for individuals like Clarke with established connections in the island. But it also required investment. When they set up shop, people like Clarke incurred costs associated with transportation and the purchase of goods and supplies. And because it was labor-intensive, it was no practitioner's first choice. Clarke, for example, lasted only five years before he reorganized and relocated to Kingston.⁴⁶

The British Army and Royal Navy trained legions of surgeons and surgeon's mates to set bones, amputate limbs, repair hernias, and identify and treat illnesses among the enlisted. Its undulations in size then produced a surfeit of practitioners. In combination with the flood of practitioners coming to the region through civilian networks, the armed forces helped to produce a surplus of medical men. These young men were compelled to reduce the price of their services to the point that it was within the grasp of many plantations to purchase them. Britain's imperial war machine provided an indirect subsidy to the plantation complex.

Circuit Surgeons

The surplus of medical men undercut their bargaining power with slaveholder-employers, leaving practitioners with poorer compensation and more estates under their care. Plantation practitioners had far less capacity to negotiate their pay in their relationships with attorneys and proprietors in the second half of the eighteenth century than in earlier eras. In fact, the well-known system by which plantation practitioners were paid an annual salary to visit but not live on a sugar estate seems to be a product of the second half of the eighteenth century. But to perceive that, a brief excursus into earlier arrangements between slaveholders and doctors is necessary. From the start of the sugar revolution in the Anglophone Caribbean until roughly 1770, medical care on sugar estates had been organized along two configurations. Most practitioners did not service estates exclusively. And they did not often live in their immediate proximity. Instead, they tended to be stationed in towns or seaports, where they provided medical goods, services, and counsel to a variety of clients. Estates paid these practitioners on a fee-per-service basis for difficult childbirths, smallpox inoculations, surgical accidents, and mysterious and immobilizing illnesses. Practitioners came out when summoned.

This arrangement left enslaved people to convalesce from illness without oversight from a practitioner. The administration of expensive medicines was, in turn, delegated to the estate's overseer.

As Richard Sheridan has described, other practitioners worked under a residential contract. Because of its cost, only sugar barons (the wealthiest slaveholders with massive estates) were able to enter into such arrangements. In those cases, the slaveholder contracted with a practitioner to live on the slaveholder's primary estate and attend to all of their properties exclusively. The practitioner was situated as salaried, and, if all went according to plan, he would become a permanent member of an estate's managerial hierarchy. His annual salary was computed as a "fee-per-head": the price per person under the doctor's care, multiplied by the number of enslaved people on the particular estate. But his actual compensation was far larger. It included housing, and sometimes it included additional stores of sugar and molasses that he could market. Most importantly, it included pasturage for his transport animals, which meant he could afford to see other estates for individual services as needed. John Williamson noted that when he was the residential practitioner on the Williamsfield estate, he had few expenses. "Every comfort [was] afforded for my horse and servants etc," he wrote.[47] Many of the practitioners entering into these agreements were recruited from the British Isles.[48] The absentee William Vassall asked his attorney to "inform me whether he can procure a proper person to go out as a surgeon & reside on my estate and take care of my negroes—if he can, on what terms he will."[49] Because they were recruited, they had greater power to negotiate their salaries in advance than surgeons who had come to the islands by way of the army or without a contract in hand.

A third paradigm emerged after about 1763 in response to the changed status and position of practitioners in relationship to their slaveholder-clients. Because of the glut of doctors that surfaced at the conclusion of the Seven Years' War, which increased at the terminus of the War of American Independence, doctors worked under conditions that somewhat resemble the twenty-first-century gig economy.[50] Most slaveholders did not hire them to live on their estates. Instead, practitioners were now forced to make individual visits to each estate in their roster of clients. They did have an annual contract, whose amount was determined on "fee-per-head" terms. On the surface, the compensation structure was similar to those for plantation doctors who enjoyed the residential arrangement. However, significantly, the circuit arrangement did not include the compensation of food, housing, and, most importantly, pasturage (and fuel) for practitioners' transport animals. The emergence of this circuit-based arrangement marked the devaluation in practitioners' goods and services. Contemporaries recognized immediately that plantation medicine was a cutthroat arena; practitioners had to meet slaveholders' terms or risk losing them as clients.

Veteran practitioners responded to these circumstances by hiring young, recent arrivals as assistants. Normally, expansion suggests greater profitability. These veteran practitioners, like slaveholders and their managers, may also have been taking advantage of the possibilities afforded by the sudden influx of young, healthy, able-bodied medical men seeking work. The hiring of young assistants may have enabled them to expand the reach of their firms by relying on this inexpensive labor. But perhaps veteran practitioners' activities should be seen as a bid for survival in a changing labor market that required a great deal of physical strength—to remain viable they took on more plantations and then hired young, able-bodied men to absorb the burdens of this work.

Colonists liked to complain about greedy practitioners, but plantation medical practice was rarely profitable. Moreover, as most medical counsel and services were provided on credit, payments were difficult to collect. Williamson called this arrangement the "procrastinating system of payments."[51] On the books, the Jamaican doctor Alexander Johnston earned approximately £490 in 1774 from his attendance to 1,959 enslaved people on nineteen different plantations.[52] Yet Johnston once remarked that he had only a guinea on hand.[53] Troup quickly arrived at a dismal appraisal of his prospects, even if he were to succeed as an independent plantation surgeon. "One in many only makes a fortune in West Indies out of 500. It is long before he goes into business and when he is in business, he risques so much by bad pay and loss of negroes, that in the space of 20 years he will not be able with great frugality to make more than £3,400. In Britain when one gets into business he will make a vast deal more," he noted with regret.[54] According to Troup's calculations, a practitioner would have made £170 per year, which meant that in the 1790s, it would have taken him approximately 172 years to purchase a medium-sized sugar plantation in Jamaica on his salary as a plantation practitioner alone.[55] Ascendance to the class of sugar proprietors was not an option for plantation medical men.

Practitioners, like other creditors, rarely collected the entirety of what slaveholders owed them, even when the law stepped in. Medical services had marginal significance compared to an estate's other annual expenses that kept enslaved people alive, such as provisions. Within proprietors' list of debts and credits, slaveholders prioritized repayment to metropolitan merchants. Local creditors were paid last. In the late eighteenth century, colonial lawmakers enacted debt-priority legislation that mandated the repayment of local creditors first. Significantly, however, these laws prioritized debt payments to local provisions merchants (who sold the foodstuffs that sustained enslaved people) over services provided by doctors.[56] This legislation shows that lawmakers viewed practitioners' counsel as a secondary priority for the maintenance of the lives of enslaved people.

The terms of compensation were sensitive to the saturation of the local medical labor market. We can see this dynamic in variations in the price per head and compensation for other services. Practitioners' rates varied, the advice writer David Collins wrote, "according as the faculty are more or less abundant."[57] Those who landed in the Ceded Islands and new frontiers of the sugar complex were in a more favorable position than those in older and more settled plantation economies. In Dominica, they could set the rate at six to ten shillings per person.[58] In older British islands, competition among practitioners was fierce. Jamaica's hinterlands arguably experienced the greatest influx of practitioners as a result of the movement of Loyalists to the island in the wake of the American War of Independence. In Jamaica, the fee-per-head price remained, from 1773 until at least 1801, five shillings per person.[59] For most practitioners, these annual fees represented, in the words of one Nevis slaveholder, "the least part of a surgeon's profit."[60] Surgeons rarely drew income from annual contracts alone. They made up the difference by charging for additional services such as night visits, inoculations, surgeries, and childbirths.[61] Amputations and childbirths were the most expensive services, and the rate varied between islands.[62] The price of a smallpox inoculation also varied depending on the number of practitioners offering the service. In Jamaica inoculations were cheapest. The rate was consistently five shillings per person.[63] But in St. Vincent, practitioners could charge four times that amount.[64] Wherever they resided, practitioners typically performed inoculations in the aggregate, which yielded a substantial portion of a practitioner's annual income.[65] These additional sources of income were important.

The real value of practitioners' compensation plummeted at the end of the eighteenth century, however. It was then that practitioners had to hustle to stay afloat. In Jamaica (and possibly other islands) both the fee-per-head rates and the earnings from other services stayed flat amid skyrocketing inflation, especially between 1795 and 1804.[66] "The allowance made for negroes does not, by any means, compensate for the trouble they [practitioners] generally have," Williamson observed.[67] The Antiguan plantation doctor and smallpox inoculator Thomas Fraser noted that "the scanty allowance we have for the care of these [enslaved people] will not afford any great expense of medicines, and is but a pitiful consideration for the fatigue we undergo in their service."[68] The downward movement in the real value of practitioners' income meant that practitioners needed to take on more estates in their roster in order to turn a profit, especially anyone trying to profess physic as a solo practitioner. John Williamson summarized this scope of practice as "the extensive charge which practitioners are obliged to take on themselves to earn a complete maintenance."[69] In response, practitioners began to operate as what one might call circuit surgeons—each year they added or lost plantations as clients and created a circuit of estates in their roster that they visited in succession.

Comparatively, Caribbean doctors who worked a circuit had more people under their care than did their contemporaries in Britain. In Jamaica, a practitioner could have between ten to fifteen estates under his care, with 1,500 to 4,500 enslaved people under his responsibility annually.[70] In the Ceded Islands, where sugar estates were generally smaller and salaries higher, the ratios were less extreme.[71] John Castles, a surgeon in Grenada, testified that he had between six and ten plantations under attendance annually, with 1,200 to 1,500 enslaved people as his responsibility.[72] Much depended on the composition of a surgeon's clientage—the size of each estate and the number of estates in the surgeon's roster. In London, by contrast, during roughly the same period of time, the ratio of doctors to the general population was 1 to 850.[73]

Any calculation of the enslaved-to-practitioner ratio must also account for the total number of patients in a practitioner's circuit (that is, how many sick they might have under their care at a time). Estimates for the number of patients at a time are rough and based on limited data of hospital numbers from two estates. Taking the total number of estates and patients together, the data suggests that a practitioner in Jamaica could be responsible for from 150 to 450 patients at a time. That is more than the number of sick people whom medical men attended in Caribbean seaports, but it is only slightly more than the number of patients for whom practitioners in Britain's voluntary hospitals were responsible.[74] In 1783, the smallest charity hospital in London, Westminster, held 110 beds; the largest, Guy's, held 430.⁷⁵ From 1744 onward at Guy's, there were three full physicians on staff, one assistant physician, and three full surgeons.⁷⁶ Most plantation hospitals had an enslaved hospital healer, so plantation practitioners were not going it alone. Still, even when the amount of time that plantation practitioners spent moving between estates is taken into account, the differences between metropolitan and plantation hospitals appear even starker.

Circuit surgeons had less time and attention to give to an individual patient than did their contemporaries in Britain and the armed forces because of the distribution of hospitals in their respective landscapes. Practitioners at Guy's might have patients elsewhere, but they were moving between hospitals located within a city so their time was not consumed moving extensively across many miles in a single day. Sugar plantations occupied vast amounts of space.

The largest plantations extended across slightly less than two thousand acres.⁷⁷ According to Edward Long, a plantation of medium size in Jamaica could occupy six hundred acres. His own Longville estate was among the larger estates in the island. It held 304 bondspeople in captivity and totaled 1,800 acres.⁷⁸ The estates that practitioners visited, moreover, were not always contiguous with one another. One Jamaican practitioner, Robert Jackson, estimated that "the exercise of my profession led me daily to the distance of eight, ten, or more miles."⁷⁹ Troup characterized one plantation he visited as "almost inaccessible."⁸⁰ A single plantation practitioner could have the same number of patients as the six practitioners at Guy's, distributed in sick-houses that sat miles apart from one another. Thus, because each individual practitioner took on many estates and had to travel among them, the amount of time given to any individual enslaved person was probably far less than that given to patients in one of London's institutions of care. The scale and ambit of plantation medicine distinguished it, for practitioners and consumers, from the larger medical marketplace of goods and services. Plantation medicine was especially laborious because of long days on horseback traveling among a circuit of clients.

Because of the distance between estates as well as the number of them necessary to visit each week, transport animals increasingly functioned as animate capital for plantation surgeons. Williamson cited "the great expense in horse, stock, and carriages" as necessary to engage in the industry with "any comfort."⁸¹ When Troup left Andrew Fillian's household in Roseau and courted his own slaveholder-clients, one overseer advised him that he would need to secure a horse before he moved to the northwestern part of the island. Another suggested that Troup would need two horses to work three estates. Troup had to borrow the 13½ Johannes to purchase his first horse and saddle.[82] Since the cost of a horse ranged from £20–35 to £100–200, Troup's was a bargain.[83] For reference, Williamson estimated that in the 1790s he brought in £1,100 per year and carried considerable debts; his horse's feed was a major part of his expenses.[84]

Plantation doctors were differentiated from others on the basis of the length of their travels, which made them visible figures in the arena of mounted movement. Mobility and movement were markers of rank in the early modern Atlantic. Horse-keeping was widespread among elites as well as white middling sorts who used their mounts to police the movement of enslaved people and to maintain racial hierarchy.[85] Britain and many colonies in North America had, by midcentury, a burgeoning network of paths and roadways in the countryside and cobblestoned streets in seaports. But in the West Indies there were only so many routes connecting seaports within islands and connecting plantations. Although enslaved people moved between estates through many different means, rivers and poorly hewn pathways were the most common routes between plantations among whites. Elites and nonelites were using the same roads, encountering and sizing up one another's transport animals with greater frequency in the Caribbean than in Britain and North America.

There was considerable variation in the capacity and height of different mounts. The Caribbean's elite—its officers, slaveholders, and merchants—appear to have monopolized the stock of horses imported from England. These horses tended to be larger and swifter than the mules and horses imported from North America and the Spanish mainland. Lewis Gordon, who came to Jamaica to act as an attorney, complained that he had difficulty finding a horse befitting his status: "There's not a horse in Kingston above fourteen hands high [4.69 feet] and such creatures, most of them are that a man may be ashamed to lay a leg over if there is one of a tolerably handsome make he sells at a very great price £50, £60, £70."[86] The planters, merchants, and attorneys like Gordon who settled in seaports with defined channels of movement prioritized their own mounts' power and speed.

Plantation doctors had to cover more ground per day, and difficult ground at that. The eighteenth-century historian of Jamaica James Knight described one road in the island as so dangerous that "very few horses can travel that road, and only those as have been bred or used to rocky and mountainous places."[87] Practitioners chose transport animals that generations of colonists had decided were best suited for this type of terrain. They preferred mules bred in Jamaica, horses imported from Cuba and the Spanish Main, or Narragansett pacers bred in Rhode Island. Knight described "the Spanish breed" as "small, very few exceeding fourteen hands; but they are full of spirit, well shaped, and make very good pads."[88] Pacers were a smaller saddle horse (up to fourteen hands tall—4.69 feet) whose ambling gate was more comfortable than a pacing gate, enabling horse and rider to traverse over many miles with minimal discomfort.[89] Mules were an uncomfortable mount. But to their credit, as Knight observed, they were "strong, hardy and sure footed ... undoubtedly better for long journeys ... because they are cautious of danger and very careful in chusing their way."[90] "After trying all kinds of horses if I could get a good riding mule I would prefer it," Troup concluded.[91] Mules had an added benefit. They were "maintained easier and at much less expense, for they will browse on trees and shrubs, and eat many things that cattle and horses will not touch."[92] Mules were hardy and fuel-efficient—perfectly suited for the needs of the circuit surgeon. Compared to other occupational and economic groups in the West Indies who used mounted passage, plantation doctors' equestrianism was decidedly pragmatic.

Plantation medicine demanded that its practitioners travel far and wide and in rough conditions. Newcomers registered this phenomenon as distinctive. Troup used his diary to record the many natural wonders, social curiosities, and novel customs he observed in Dominica. He included in this group his horse (figure 5).[93] The botanist and plantation doctor James Grainger became famous for "The Sugar Cane," a Georgic poem on plantation slavery and the natural world of Saint Kitts. He composed it, as he relayed, "mostly in my rides to different parts of the island to visit my patients."[94] In the stories they told about themselves, practitioners linked their ridership and mobility to the particulars of their trade.

Plantation doctors' transport animals cemented their reputation as ambitious and perhaps reckless men who failed to live up to the ideal of the gentleman practitioner. Pacers ambled. Mules did not bend easily to their riders' demands. Mules moved, Knight explained, at "a shambling pace between a trot and gallop."[95] Satirists of plantation medicine mocked practitioners' efforts to mimic the men whom David Bell has described as the era's charismatic men on horseback—George Washington and Napoleon Bonaparte. Edward Long's Mr. Apozem, for example, was "continually upon high-trot, riding post."[96] The absentee Stephen Fuller

FIG. 5. Troup's sketch *My Spanish Brown Horse, with Black Mane and Tail*. Plantation medicine was workable only so long as practitioners could scale up their work and take on many plantations. Transport animals were essential to practitioners' work. (Journal of Jonathan Troup, catalogue number MS 2070/14, University of Aberdeen Museums and Special Collections, licensed under CC by 4.0)

decried the negligent practitioners who "gallop to a plantation" to compensate for the many estates they had to visit each day.[97]

Yet practitioners' horses and mules were at the forefront of their occupational identity because travel constituted the most dangerous part of their work. Jamaica's physical geography is characterized by high, rugged limestone plateaus that "run through the middle of it, almost from one end to the other," and enshroud narrow valleys of alluvial plains.[98] In the early eighteenth century, many of its roads were not of wide enough berth to allow a carriage. Most could only hold, Knight observed, "two horsemen passing one another."[99] Knight described one major road in Jamaica as extremely dangerous in rainy weather. Riders "often plunge into great holes where the waters reach as high as the belly of a mule."[100] Dominica had volcanic rainforests, forested ravines, cliffs, and river valleys. Maroons took advantage of this topography, and it limited white settlement to Dominica's coastal plains.[101] As one officer described Dominica's settlement patterns: "distances are not here estimated by miles, but by time; the neighbour you can hail with your voice, you cannot shake by the hand, but by a weary traverse."[102] Troup noted the necessity of remaining vigilant about the "crab holes, a dangerous trap to horses feet."[103] Threats from the natural environment imperiled horse and rider, as did the colonies' rough roads and fragile bridges. Moving between agricultural behemoths entailed navigating, on mounted passage, uneven and poorly cleared roads. Often it required crossing rivers. As they rode between clients, circuit surgeons straddled a knife's edge between the exigencies of haste and compulsory attendance on the one hand and their personal safety on the other. The need to hasten among plantations often compelled circuit surgeons to take extensive risks.

Troup's ambitions as a rider exceeded his ability. Over one four-month span, he was unseated five times.[104] Returning from dinner after visiting one of the estates in his roster, his horse stumbled over a tree stump in the dark, which made him "fall down from a gentle trot and I fell for the first time over his head."[105] Another time, as he tried to pass over a landslide that had spilled onto one of Dominica's paths, a freshet engulfed his horse's hocks, which trapped it in the muck. Troup eventually unearthed the animal by "lifting and loosening them pulled him to one side." But as he worked, the waters overpowered the animal and sent it tumbling "down into the sea amongst the rocks on his side and his head lowest the waves of sea getting into his mouth." Troup "got him up with great difficulty" and continued on his way.[106] Troup seems to have been new to horsemanship, which may have been the case for many young practitioners.

Jamaica's topography imperiled veterans as well. Alexander Johnston took a serious fall returning from a visit to a plantation sick-house. "Passing the timber bridge my horse fell thro' the broken and rotten planks," he recalled in his daybook. Johnston was ejected onto "a ridge of rough sharp edged stones." The accident left him incapacitated for over two months. Johnston owed his recovery to a woman, likely enslaved, whom he described as "Sabina at Blenheim," one of the plantations in his roster of clients. Johnston did not pay her with currency, but with chintz and two hams.[107] This practice of plantation medicine was more physically demanding than other medical trades, and more dangerous to boot.

Transport animals also loomed large because their upkeep occupied a significant proportion of annual expenses. It cost a lot to maintain hooves that transported riders across hundreds of kilometers per month and perhaps thousands each year. Generally, healthy horses can cover between twenty-five to thirty miles in a day. This modern-day estimate assumes adequate sustenance and clear passage.[108] While the value of practitioners' income decreased, the price for the fuel that powered their transport animals did not; if anything, the late eighteenth century was an era when keeping transport animals fed became more expensive.

Feed was the largest expense of transport animals, and its cost was a major source of concern. Securing it for horses was especially difficult in the British Caribbean, where monoculture and trade embargos created shortages of hay and oats. Although Jamaica's uplands and swampy lowlands contained an abundance of guinea-grass and livestock pens, much of the island's pasturage and hay fueled the transport and draft animals on sugar estates, with little surplus for market.[109] The problem of feed became particularly acute after the American War of Independence, when Parliament prohibited British merchants from trading with the United States. In the wake of that conflict, many colonists dispensed with their transport animals, as the slaveholder Joshua Steele observed, because "the price of corn, since the interruption of free trade with North-America, has rendered horse-keeping too dear to support them."[110] Even troops of horse had trouble locating sufficient stores of bat and fodder to maintain their animals. But by many accounts, plantation practitioners also struggled. As one colonist observed, the small premiums given them for their services made it "impossible for them [plantation doctors] to get the keep of one of their horses."[111]

Practitioners tried to price the cost of travel into their negotiations with attorneys and proprietors. To newcomers, it seemed self-evident that slaveholders would compensate practitioners for the cost of transportation. When Troup struck out on his own, he negotiated with one attorney and demanded twenty shillings per head, nearly double the going rate in Dominica at that time. He explained that he had "some knowledge of this quarter, of the roads and distances to the above the estates." This rate, he explained, covered his: "visit [to] the estates once a week, but when sickness and accidents occur, to be ready day and night."[112] The attorney rejected Troup's terms. A friend advised Troup that the newcomer would need to build up his reputation before he could make such demands. Troup retorted, privately in his diary, that "I will not kill myself for nothing."[113] Once he became a solo practitioner, Troup linked his mount's periodic hungriness to his own position. "But my horse I wish to accustom to hardship as well as myself till I find a safe harbor," he wrote in his diary after he forced the animal to go without grass one evening.[114]

The maintenance costs of transport animals and the perils of visiting made it difficult to practice plantation medicine as a single-man venture. When the Jamaican practitioners Alexander Johnston and Alexander Fullerton set up a joint medical firm, their horses were one of the two annual costs singled out in their articles of copartnership whose expense they agreed to split between them (the other was "medicines in the shop").[115] All of the copartnerships listed in *The Medical Register* for the years 1780 and 1783 were located in Jamaica's hinterlands, likely because these individuals were engaged in plantation medicine and had a great deal of ground to cover.[116]

The joint use of transport animals sometimes created tensions between copartners. The Dominican doctor William Bremner complained that in retaliation against him for a disagreement, his copartner had sent the firm's horse "to graze during his [copartner's] absence at a neighboring plantation."[117] The centrality of these animals to practitioners' livelihoods meant that in disputes, transport animals were sometimes weaponized in petty, yet potent, ways.

New requirements of extensive travel affected veteran plantation doctors immediately, who quickly registered the demands that attendance made upon their bodies. "The labor of plantation practice," Williamson elaborated, "is very great. It requires bodily health, vigor, and spirit, to get through with it."[118] Robert Thomas, a Nevis surgeon, explained that his plantation medical business was initially undertaken with a copartner. But when forced to work independently, Thomas quickly "found my health injured from too great fatigue."[119] The Jamaican physician-botanist Thomas Clarke explained to a friend that as soon as he had been able, he had shifted from plantation medicine to urban drug retailing and hospital proprietorship in Kingston because the "gout or rheumatism with a string of complaints" made it difficult to keep up with the physical demands of "a large country business."[120] Although the toll of this type of plantation medicine was negligible compared to that borne by the enslaved people they attended, practitioners still complained that it exacted a physical price.

To reduce the physical burdens of travel, firms employed assistants—the recently arrived "young bachelors" who flooded the region.[121] The copartners John Williamson and Thomas Clarke of Jamaica, for example, mentioned "our assistant Mr. F.P.," who attended on the Peartree Grove plantation.[122] Robert Thomas also hired an assistant to bear the physical weight of attendance.[123] Troup joined Andrew Fillian and Thomas Clark's medical firm in Roseau, Dominica, in 1789.[124] In exchange for room, board, and a minuscule share of the firm's profits, Troup and his contemporaries worked as assistants in established medical firms. Some put up bonds of security that bound them to the firm for a period of time. For Troup and other assistants, these medical firms offered opportunities to build up a local reputation and thereby move upward in the medical marketplace. Fillian's firm serviced both householders in Dominica and estates in the hinterlands. Troup was hired to attend, primarily, to the firm's roster of plantations under contract. The tension between slaveholders and doctors over the expectation of frequent attendance remained. But veteran practitioners changed how the aggravations of plantation medicine were distributed. Copartners absorbed the expense of transport animals' maintenance but externalized the dangers of the circuit onto their young assistants.

Assistants were expected to bear the physical burdens of plantation medicine, which was a major point of conflict between Troup and Fillian. During the fourteen months when Troup was Fillian's assistant, he visited twenty-four different plantations.[125] Yet when Troup first arrived to work in Fillian's firm, the recent arrival was not yet acclimated to the tropical environment. In accordance with the widespread belief that newcomers from temperate climates needed to "season" their bodies to the Caribbean before undertaking physical exertion, Fillian waited approximately one month before he dispatched Troup on visits outside Roseau.[126] Not surprisingly, on Troup's first extended visit, to a plantation six miles out of town, he observed the sensation of a "Prickly heat in my throat . . . or . . . pushed in to the skin—very sharp."[127] Heat rash was a small price of initiation. But once Troup was acclimated, tensions increased over the frequency of his attendance on the estates in Fillian's roster. "Feel desperate with Dr. Fillian respecting the Bath negroes," Troup wrote early into his assistantship.[128] He was referring to the responsibility of the daily visits to the Bath estate. It is possible that the clients in Fillian's portfolio were new contracts—that Fillian had taken on Troup in order to extend the firm's reach beyond Roseau and into Dominica's coffee neighborhood.

Circuit surgeons such as Troup found it difficult to square the demands of hoofed transportation with the claims of white homosociability. At dinners, overseers, plantation practitioners, and residential plantation owners propped up white racial solidarity by forming relationships that crossed the lines of rank and status. Yet alcohol magnified the perils of the circuit. After one evening where he consumed many cups of wine, Troup "tumbled off my horse 3 different times."[129] Troup's accidents imperiled his reputation. The wife of a slaveholder, "Mrs. Bell," snubbed him, "owing to my falling drunk from my horse."[130] Circuit surgeons' blunders and falls amplified plantation medicine's reputation as an industry for the young and disorderly.

In Britain, institutions such as universities or colleges of medical faculty regulated members and formalized the transmission of knowledge across generations. In the absence of these institutions in Caribbean colonies, colonists used age as a proxy for the competence of white practitioners.[131] But the physical constraints of age, combined with poor infrastructure, limited the mobility of seasoned practitioners such as Thomas, Fillian, and Clarke by hobbling their capacity to ford rivers and navigate washed-out roads. For the rugged and overgrown trails that led to the Caribbean's coffee estates as well as the frequent flooding of the pathways that wended through its sugar landscapes, the islands needed a steady supply of younger men to practice plantation medicine. For all that their youth and second-rate horsemanship tarnished their image, the plantation doctors' reputation suffered most from the second-rate way they were forced to practice medicine.

Calculated Indifference

The expanded ambit of practitioners' operations undercut the amount of attention they could provide to each estate. The slaveholder John Stewart understood that the distance between estates made it difficult to visit the sick-house twice per week. Jamaica was an island, he wrote, where "estates etc. lie scattered over any great extent of country." "Indeed," he continued, "at a sickly period, strict medical attention to all the patients under their care must become utterly impracticable."[132] It "often happens," the Jamaican surgeon William Fitzmaurice testified, "where the proprietor does not live upon the estate, and the attorney at the distance of thirty, fifty and one hundred miles from the plantation, that the negroes suffer very severely indeed from the want of medical attention."[133] With a large roster of clients and the necessity of visiting several plantations per day, plantation practitioners likely came to place an even greater priority on expedition than did their counterparts attending the sick in other unfree labor regimes. Managers warehoused the sick in plantation hospitals in order to keep everyone in a centralized location. Such an arrangement allowed for easier inspection and therefore engendered greater efficiencies in the management of affliction. Slaveholders and their attorneys may have imagined that this arrangement might allow as much attention to enslaved people as was given to the enlisted. Practitioners' caseloads, however, worked against that assumption. Close physical inspection and diagnosis of enslaved patients after their admission to the hot-house were not prioritized in the same ways as they were in those military and metropolitan settings. Such neglect had detrimental, sometimes lethal effects on enslaved patients.

Given that they were responsible for the provision of medicine and counsel to unfree populations, it is tempting to imagine that circuit surgeons replicated exactly the practices of doctors in naval, army, and voluntary hospitals. The surgeons in these settings practiced "empirical, practical, and 'clinical'" medicine that evolved out of the exigencies of provisioning medicine and care to unfree populations rather than individual clients.[134] The ways that they understood and treated illness among these unfree populations cut against medical orthodoxy. Both experts and laypeople still adhered to orthodox "constitutional conceptions of disease."[135] They conceived of their bodies as "idiosyncratic," that is, as individualized "sacs of fluids whose consistency, balance and free movement were the basis of health."[136] A person's idiosyncratic constitution had been molded by their distinctive diet, work, rest, and emotions. The individual constitution also determined the way that a disease manifested: its duration, severity, and movement between different systems of the body. A person's physiology therefore pointed to how they ought to be recovered from illness. In this orthodox tradition, a good physician engaged in an ongoing dialogue with their clients and provided dietary and medical advice bespoke to their client's constitution.

Practitioners in the armed forces, as well as those in voluntary hospitals, did not have the wherewithal to give this type of individualized attention to their patients. Although attention to the patient's individual body was known to be crucial in the recovery of a person from illness, the doctors who attended large, unfree populations could not easily scale up to this level of attention. In hospitals, therefore, practitioners adopted and endorsed a "take-this-for-that" approach. Instead of focusing on the distinction between different bodies, they tended to see bodies as universal. They argued that diseases were distinctive and manifested the same way from person to person. This made it easier to treat hospital patients with standardized dietaries and medicines suited for individual diseases.[137] Yet there were limitations to this approach, and old habits of thought persisted even amid ideas of universal bodies. Hospital practitioners in Britain tracked their patients' improvement or decline. Most importantly, they contended that a person's age, sex, and strength influenced the expression of a disease, especially its virulence and lethality.

The provision of health care en masse was one thing. But the treatment of enslaved populations took health care in bulk to a perverse extreme.[138] Plantation hospital books exemplify the gap between treating patients thoroughly and treating illness efficiently that was particular to plantation medicine. Based on descriptions of their contents, it appears that each entry had far less information than those for patients of other hospitals in the British Atlantic World. In the hospital notebooks of charity and military hospitals, for instance, surgeons recorded case and prescription notes for each patient. Most entries contained additional observations and remarks that tracked the patient's changing condition.[139] These records tracked what ailed each patient and the nature of their illness, as well as changes in symptoms over time.

Plantation hospital books, however, had many fewer of these meaningful details that directed practitioners' actions. Instead, they functioned as recordkeeping devices that enabled managers and doctors to coordinate the care of the sick across different parties. None has survived for the eighteenth century, but it is possible to reconstruct the information they contained and prioritized by tracking their interaction with other records on the estate that overseers created. On plantations without a medical man in residence, it was often the overseer or bookkeeper who acted as the hospital's gatekeeper and wrote down, as one absentee slaveholder enjoined, "ye nature of their [a petitioner's] distemper" in the hospital book.[140] He might also compose his own "list of the sick," which identified the people confined for sickliness. These records usually accompanied an overseer's worklogs (a running record listing the different enslaved people on the estate and the station they were assigned for the day).[141] I have located only one "list of the sick." It was produced by the overseer of the Phillipsfield plantation in Jamaica (figure 6). Its contents suggest what types of details a nonresidential plantation practitioner might have received during his visit: one-word symptom descriptions. With the exception of distinctive diseases, diagnosis was not a priority, nor was the minute tracking of symptoms for the purposes of eliciting the attributes of the illness in question. "Sore leg," "venereal," "bloated," "itch," and "worms" all appeared as explanations for why the named people were not at work.[142] The slaveholder John Baillie later described how doctors and overseers used these books together. The overseers' one-word descriptions of illness were entered into hot-house books. When the surgeon called upon the plantation, "the book," Baillie explained, "is open to him, and he

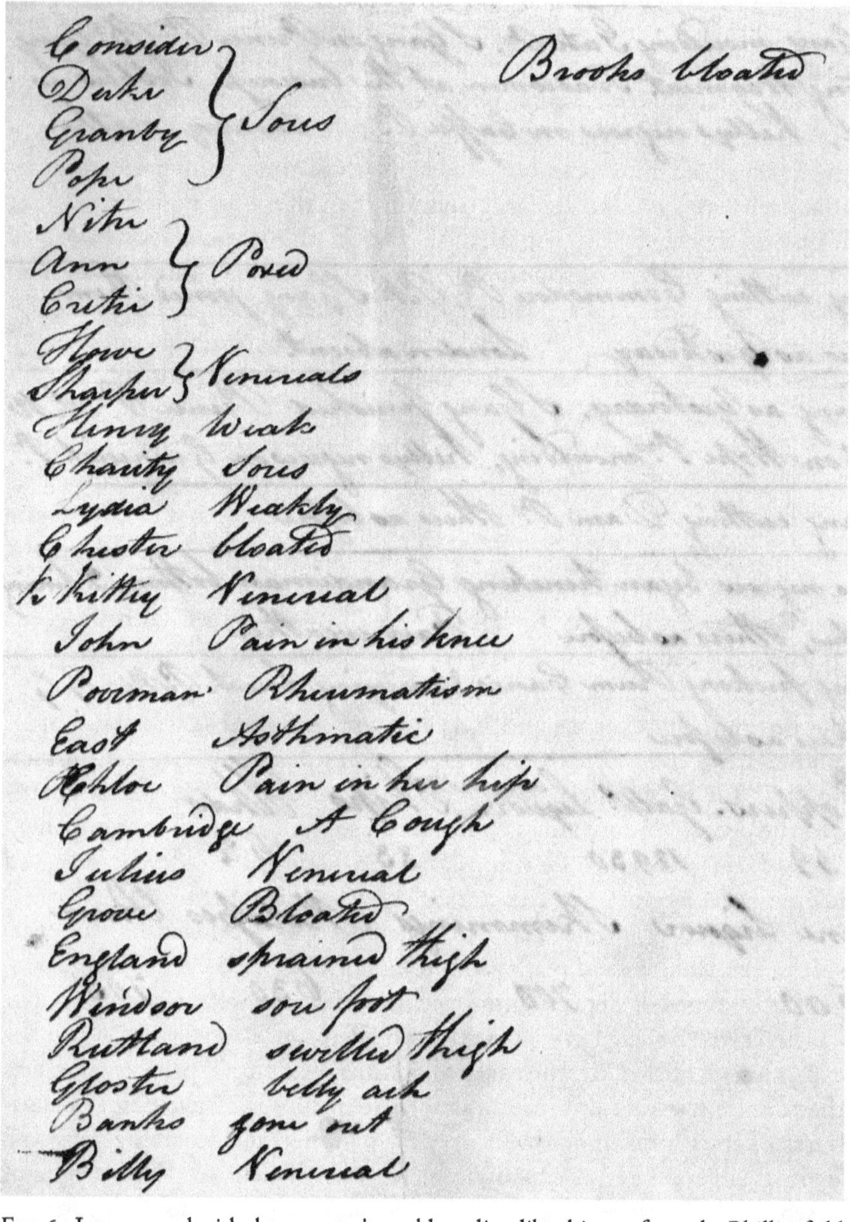

Consider }
Duke   } Sores
Granby }
Pope   }
Nitu   }
Ann   } Poxed
Cuthi   }
Howe   } Venereals
Sharper }
Henry   Weak
Charity Sores
Lydia   Weakly
Chester bloated
Kitty   Venereal
John   Pain in his knee
Poorman Rheumatism
East   Asthmatic
Chloe   Pain in her hip
Cambridge A Cough
Julius   Venereal
Grove   Bloated
England sprained thigh
Windsor sore foot
Rutland swelled thigh
Gloster belly ach
Banks   gone out
Billy   Venereal

Brooks bloated

FIG. 6. Interspersed with the overseer's worklogs, lists like this one from the Phillipsfield plantation in Jamaica probably mirrored the bare-bones descriptions of enslaved people's illnesses that appeared in plantation hospital books. (Slebech Estate Records, MS 8489; Llyfrgell Genedlaethol Cymru/The National Library of Wales)

prescribes for the sick accordingly in that book."[143] For practitioners with heavy caseloads, these entries provided just enough information for the surgeon to prescribe his remedies before riding off to the next client.

Rather than a means to chart a patient's progress in response to medicines or delve deeply into the particularities of what had made them sick, hospital books facilitated the dispersal of medicines in great numbers.[144] They encouraged practitioners who had learned about their patients' symptoms secondhand to barrage the sick with drugs. Unwanted surveillance and control over what the sick consumed characterized the relationship between overseers, attorneys, and the sick. However, neglect or indifference was also built into the relationship between plantation doctors and their patients. Absentee slaveholders would often depict themselves as the victims of practitioners' heavy workloads and dispersed attention. It was in fact enslaved sufferers who bore the consequences of the expanded ambit and scope of plantation practitioners' work.

Practitioners' workloads incentivized the development of a turnstile approach to the treatment of illness that had serious consequences for enslaved patients. Eventually, elite medical writers in Caribbean seaports and abroad would come to theorize that the constitutions of Africans and people of African heredity were distinctive from those of white people. They would argue that race should be a guide to diagnosis and prescription.[145] But in the day-to-day management of illness, medical racism did not necessarily take shape in habits of thought that purported to explain racial difference while stipulating the ways that practitioners should prescribe medicines. Medical racism instead manifested as practitioners acknowledging that sex, age, and strength *should* direct their diagnoses and prescriptions but nonetheless forging ahead to treat enslaved people's bodies as interchangeable with one another. With their attention dispersed across plantations situated miles apart from one another, a plantation practitioner's medical violence took the form of a calculated indifference to the conditions of the people they presumed to heal.

Indifference to particularity had real consequences. Such neglect informed how practitioners engaged in preventative technologies, particularly smallpox inoculations. Eighteenth-century Britons considered smallpox a distinctive disease caused by external poisons rather than an ailment that manifested as a consequence of humoral imbalance. But the way that smallpox materialized, especially its severity, depended on the constitution of the afflicted person. Consensus held that smallpox inoculations required attentiveness to the particularities of the body of the inoculation's recipient. Expediency led many plantation practitioners to ignore this convention in inoculating enslaved people.

The Antiguan surgeon James McKittrick-Adair noted that he often inoculated "without regarding the circumstance of pregnancy or chronic complaints."[146] "In negro practice," the Jamaican surgeon John Quier callously explained, "the nature of things will hardly permit a choice of patients to be inoculated, it must necessarily be supposed that many of them are very ineligible subjects." In determining *who* would receive an inoculation, practitioners ignored conventional ideas about the importance of particularity. They tended to perform inoculations serially, without regard to the people's age, rank, gender, health, or kin relations. By forcibly and indiscriminately subjecting enslaved populations to the disease, they showed their indifference to whether everyone would survive the ensuing smallpox infection. Practitioners did not inoculate in this manner on the premise that enslaved people's bodies were necessarily interchangeable in their nature. They recognized caution was warranted but still blew past it, prioritizing property rights over enslaved people's health.[147] Over and over again, they recognized difference in the types of people they attended, but they did not incorporate this into their actual practice.

Expediency meant that practitioners typically did not speak to the people they treated. Consequently, the sick were forced to consume medicines in doses that far exceeded what circumstance warranted. In 1809, the doctor for the Trout Hall sugar plantation gave Ivey, a cooper, far too much tartar emetic, the formal name for the chemical compound antimony potassium tartrate. The dose killed him.[148] Unless it was a case that required multiple visits, Troup never recorded his enslaved patients' names. Sometimes Troup did not speak to staff on the estate who might have filled him in. Troup appears to have prescribed by consulting the hospital book. "I inadvertently gave a vomit of T. Emit [tartar emetic] to a Boy for a man without asking his complications," Troup recorded. "He vomited blood from it—so make it a rule never to give without seeing or knowing except it be simple things," Troup concluded the entry.[149] The early nineteenth century saw the racialization of the nervous system and the corresponding belief that Black people were indifferent to pain. That set of beliefs no doubt also encouraged surgeons to use medicines, mercury especially, that outstripped normal rates of use.[150] But the disasters that Troup and Trout Hall's doctor created in the eighteenth century arose from plantation medicine, which was set up to manage sickness in large numbers and to get people back to work.

Although the work of plantation doctors superficially resembled that of other hospital practitioners, it produced cognitive dissonance among observers. Plantation medicine departed from norms that governed expectations about the doctor-patient relationship between elites; it was even distinct from the type of medicine and care given to unfree populations in the British Army and Royal Navy.

The physician Thomas Dancer had once held an appointment as the physician to the Sixty-Ninth and Seventieth Regiments during their invasion of Fort San Juan (in present-day Nicaragua). He had also held a position as the physician to the Bath Hospital in Saint Thomas in the East, where Jamaica's authorities sent white invalids to recuperate in the bathing waters. By the time he was writing about the plantation system, he was settled in Kingston and tending to its elite. Dancer had never worked as a plantation practitioner; nevertheless, he weighed in on how medical assistance was organized on Jamaica estates because he had contacts with many plantation practitioners and an abundance of experience tending to laboring populations as well as individual clients.[151]

For Dancer, the ways medicine was practiced on estates represented a perversion of good medical care. He seized upon the duration of ulcers among enslaved people on sugar estates to show how the short-time horizons and limited resources with which plantation practitioners worked had undermined their efforts to heal. They were ineffective, according to Dancer, because they did not have the wherewithal to tailor their remedies to the individual. "Ulcers," he wrote, "are of several kinds, and require a very various management, according to the state of discharge, the constitution and habit of the patient etc."[152] Among many enslaved people, ulcers were said to arise from the salt-heavy rations forcefully fed to them during their confinement onboard slave ships. But their severity, appearance, and type also varied based on the circumstances of the patient once on an estate.[153] Ulcers therefore required a regimen that was specific to the individual. This plan of action also needed to be flexible, modified according to the different states of the person's sores as they changed over time. "It is seldom in the power of plantation surgeons to pay" the sustained attention necessary to recover a person from sores, Dancer lamented. It was for that reason, he explained, that "ulcers are of such long duration, and frequently become incurable."[154] Ulcers' persistence among enslaved people was a microcosm of the tensions of early modern body management—that is, between an approach that treated the disease *tout court* and one that took into account the way the individuated body of each patient shaped a disease's appearance as well as how it ought to be remedied.

Slaveholders maintained unrealistic expectations of plantation practitioners in terms of the amount of time that practitioners could spend on their estates, creating tensions between slaveholders' expectations and doctors' workloads. Attention became a major point of conflict and contestation among practitioners, attorneys, and absentee slaveholders. Absentees conceded that the practitioners who managed hundreds of people at a time operated with fixed capacity. They did not have the wherewithal to practice medicine on enslaved people with the same attention to individuation and constitution as they did with colonists or even the enlisted. Yet absentees still had high expectations for their underpaid practitioners. Even when treating distinct diseases with manufactured medicines made to target the specific disease, medical men were supposed to know the people whom they treated—because a sufferer's life history or basic autobiographical facts informed the expression of the disease. Slaveholders did not expect practitioners to theorize the entire race of enslaved Africans and people of African descent, but they still expected practitioners to understand the men and women who lived on each particular whether or not they lived there themselves. More specifically, they expected practitioners to amass an extensive knowledge of each plantation's enslaved men and women, as though they had undertaken something like a longitudinal study of its people. In absentees' view, long-term residence ought to enable the practitioner to understand the origins of varying afflictions and to prescribe accordingly.

This was not just a matter of understanding a plantation's microclimate. It was instead taking stock of a population holistically, on the grounds that its members' bodies had been molded by the estate's particular labor regime. That included factoring in the age of the people; the proportion who had been born in the Caribbean or Africa; and how they were fed, clothed, and worked. The absentee slaveholder William Vassall, for instance, wrote to his attorney John Wedderburn beseeching him to incorporate the insights of his previous attorney, James Wedderburn (John's cousin).[155] James had managed Vassall's Green River plantation in Jamaica. In that capacity, he had compiled a book "containing all that he had observed particular in managing negroes and their diseases." James attributed the numerous sores among the enslaved people on Green River to the particular microclimate, the enslaved people's diets, and the fact that the majority of them were adults who had come from Africa. In addition, there was the problem of Green River itself—it was old (and presumably its soil was exhausted), and so it was "more laborious."[156] Collectively, James Wedderburn concluded, these factors accounted for the preponderance of sores on Vassall's plantation.

Absentees and attorneys expected plantation practitioners to amass the cumulative knowledge that James Wedderburn had offered. The absentee slaveholder James Chisholme stipulated that his attorneys should employ a doctor with "the most knowledge and [who] pays the most attention."[157] Europeans and colonists expected a dialogue between patient and client, but when doctors treated enslaved people, colonists expected attention and attentiveness through ongoing scrutiny and observation of their larger life circumstances. Managers judged a practitioner's knowledge not on the basis of his education but his experience—which came from the time he spent tending to the sick and watching the healthy on their particular estate.

Based on this set of assumptions, slaveholders and attorneys like Simon Taylor hired plantation practitioners who had lived in the vicinity of the plantations they managed. In 1794, Taylor poached a doctor, Bolton, from Duckenfield plantation for Golden Grove. Duckenfield and Golden Grove sat adjacent to one another on the south side of the Plantain Garden River, in the Plantain River district in Jamaica's easternmost parish, St. Thomas in the East. In fact, the two "shared a common trench and weir."[158] Taylor rationalized his decision on the grounds that Bolton was familiar with the neighborhood and the people on Golden Grove: "as he has lived several years at Duckenfield, & knows the nature of the Complaints of the Negroes."[159] Bolton, Taylor believed, understood "the complaints of the negroes" in both local and historical terms. He understood how the two estates' soils, provision grounds, microclimates, as well as the origins, dietaries, and work routines of the enslaved people who lived on Duckenfield and Golden Grove, had molded their bodies, enough so that Bolton could apply the insights he had amassed tending to Duckenfield's enslaved people to those who lived on Golden Grove. Taylor expected that this arrangement would engender greater specificity in diagnosis and prescription, not to the individuals on Golden Grove but to its enslaved population.

Sugar barons like Taylor and Vassall were also willing to pay for a certain degree of attentiveness and to hire medical men to live on the estates they managed and owned. Eventually Vassall abandoned the use of local practitioners. Instead, he requested that his agent in Britain find someone who would agree to come to Jamaica and live on his plantation. He directed his agent in London to find "for my estate at a stipulated yearly sum & for him to reside on my plantation & take care of my negroes so that my estate may have nothing to do with the doctors in the parish, nor give them any longer 5/p head yearly for doing nothing."[160] Taylor also pursued this strategy. This arrangement, slaveholders maintained, would keep their enslaved captives healthier, as doctors' attention would be devoted to their properties alone.

Sugar barons could command this level of service. Taylor's strategies were exceptional. He was the wealthiest man in Jamaica, an island that was the crown jewel in the British Empire. Extremely brutal and violent in his approach, he nevertheless managed with the long term in mind, intending to prolong not life expectancy but the number of years in which the enslaved people on Golden Grove and the other estates he managed could toil in the fields.[161] Taylor hired medical men to live on-site because he believed that this arrangement allowed the practitioner to amass a more specific understanding of the people that Taylor held in bondage. But most slaveholders were short-term thinkers who wanted doctors' attention but were unwilling to pay for it.

Instead, slaveholders tried to claim as much of practitioners' time as possible, sometimes by bullying them from across the sea. Some wrote letters that probed into other claims on the doctor's time. In 1794, Arcedeckne was content to see Taylor poach a doctor [Bolton] from Duckenfield plantation to live on his own. Yet twenty years earlier in his absenteeship, Arcedeckne presumed that absentee and attorney could monopolize the time of the practitioners hired for their estates. In 1774, Arcedeckne had permitted Golden Grove's overseer, John Kelly, to find a doctor for Golden Grove. Kelly appointed Dr. Hayward. Shortly thereafter, Kelly became the managing attorney for Duckenfield, and he hired Hayward to work that plantation as well. Arcedeckne was incensed when he learned that Hayward was attending both plantations. Hayward "should not act as doctor there and at Golden Grove," Arcedeckne wrote in anger to Taylor.[162] Eventually Arcedeckne relented and allowed Hayward to attend to the sick on both plantations.[163] After the doctor Robert Pinkney and the attorneys for the Jamaica absentee slaveholder Joseph Foster Barham completed articles of agreement, Pinckney received a letter directly from Barham. The absentee demanded to know "the number of estates I practice upon with their distances." Pinkney reassured Barham that the further plantations were "only two miles with Mr. Dunns, Mr. Vassals estate and Mr. Woolery's."[164] Fully aware of the large pool of practitioners in search of work, slaveholders leveraged a tight labor market to compel attendance upon their estates. At the same time, they also kept compensation so low that practitioners were forced to attend to many at a time. Slaveholders put practitioners in an impossible bind: they drove practitioners to spread themselves thin and then complained about their inattentiveness.

Even resident practitioners may have suffered under the new economic circumstances and tried to expand the ambit of their work. They seemed to have anticipated slaveholders' objections to taking on more plantations. They tread carefully. Around 1782, the practitioner Benjamin Turney was hired by Simon Taylor to attend Taylor's plantation, Holland, and Arcedeckne's Golden Grove. But Arcedeckne refused to lease or grant Turney any acres of land, which Turney wanted presumably to put under cultivation. He wrote that he "wish[ed] to be doing something before I grow old which I cannot do without your generous assistance." He also proposed an alternative: extending his practice within a limited geographic circuit (figure 7). The attorney at Amity Hall had extended an offer to Turney, and he petitioned Arcedeckne to allow him to take it

FIG. 7. Benjamin Turney's proposed circuit, which would see him starting at Holland, stopping at Amity Hall, and then ending at Golden Grove. *Map of the County of Surrey, in the Island of Jamaica*, James Robertson, 1804. (National Library of Scotland, https://maps.nls.uk/view/74428067)

on. Turney justified the request on the grounds that Amity Hall's proximity to Golden Grove and Holland would mean that no attention was diverted from the enslaved people on the two plantations: "I hope you will consent to my taking, you know its situation and that I ride thro it [Amity Hall] every morning in my way to and from Holland, its vicinity to G Grove and the convenience with wh [ich] I can attend it is the reason why I venture on this request."[165] There is no record of how Arcedeckne responded. But given his concerns about Bolton's engagements, he may have refused to honor this request.

Most practitioners had too many estates to attend. Slaveholders' parsimony had widened the scale of practitioners' work, which made for a type of medicine that was utterly different from that given to soldiers and sailors in the British armed forces or to the poor in Britain's voluntary hospitals. On plantations, there was not much in the way of diagnosis or the tracking of symptoms in response to medicines. Nor did practitioners take into account the basic biological facts and medical histories of the people they treated. The paucity of detail in hot-house books was related to the fact that admission to the hospital was not intended to achieve full restoration through a deep understanding of the disease in question. Instead, surgeons, overseers, and attorneys, working sometimes in alliance and often at cross-purposes, created a system that treated symptoms so as to engender patients' return to work. This was an even more coercive form of "bulk medicine" than that of armies, navies, and voluntary hospitals.[166] But unlike regimental colonels or hospital governors, estate owners had a proprietary interest in their enslaved populations and the land they lived upon. Managers wanted to treat their patients as interchangeable for the sake of efficiency but also demanded (beyond their willingness to pay) a level of localized attention and experience from the practitioners they hired.

As THE prosecution of imperial and Anglo-Maroon warfare facilitated the expansion of slavery and accelerated the African diaspora, it produced a surplus of practitioners comprised of Loyalist refugees and decommissioned surgeons and surgeon's mates. In spite of the demands for medical men within the plantation complex, the surge of practitioners generated competition between them and lowered the cost of their services. Consequently, the owners and managers of sugar estates were able to purchase medical labor at a lower cost than before midcentury.[167]

Mass migration created a surplus of medical men. Yet it was slaveholders' drive to make their estates more productive and efficient that casualized the trade of those who professed physic. This, in turn, transmogrified the ways that medical men plied their craft and incentivized the treatment of enslaved people's bodies as fungible. With an expanded roster of clients and the necessity of putting in adequate face time on many different estates, plantation practitioners prioritized expediency over care and attention. Although practitioners complained about the paltry pay, it was the enslaved sick who bore the cost of this arrangement, to the point of being force-fed an excess of medicine.

Slaveholders' and plantation practitioners' labor conflicts with one another produced a paradox that sat at the heart of medicine in the age of improvement. This was an era when slaveholders were building hospitals and hiring medical men in order to engender greater efficiencies in body management. Yet slaveholders also forced practitioners to divide their time across many different estates and to absorb the physical and financial costs of transport. This arrangement created inefficiencies in the delivery of medicine as well as in the supervision of hospital healers and the enslaved sick. As we shall see in the next chapter, enslaved hospital healers fell victim to a second paradox created by the first. The healers' work was also transformed. They were put in the contradictory position of imposing harsh remedies in the absence of these doctors while also supplying the care and attention that doctors had no time to provide.

3

"All Lesser Matters Related to the Sick"

Enslaved Healers and the Greater Work of Improvement Medicine

---

By the fifth decade of her life, Parthenia, an enslaved woman, had worked as a healer in the hospital on the Mesopotamia sugar plantation for several years. But as she approached advanced old age, she could no longer endure the physical demands of attending and caring for large numbers of the sick. The plantation's attorneys assigned her to attend a man named Old Primus, a blind octogenarian who had been Mesopotamia's boiler.[1] Located in Jamaica's Westmoreland Parish, Mesopotamia was one of the island's largest sugar plantations. Between 1762 and 1811, its absentee owners kept an average of 302 enslaved men, women, and children in captivity. Every season, a significant number of them fell sick. Parthenia's departure now left the hospital without a head. Mesopotamia's attorneys decided that they needed someone who would administer medicine to sufferers in an official capacity and work under the estate's bookkeeper as well as John Horsley, Mesopotamia's medical man.[2] So Mesopotamia's overseer, the hard-driving John Graham, appointed Kickery, a midwife, to temporarily act as both midwife and hospital doctress, expanding her workload.[3] As enslaved hospital healers, Parthenia, Kickery, and their counterparts would play a key role at Mesopotamia. They carried out managers' and proprietors' efforts to make healing more efficient by imposing order in plantation hospitals and administering their own remedies as well as imported pharmaceuticals.

Kickery, Parthenia, and other women healers functioned as Jills-of-all-trades within their communities. They facilitated childbirths, tended to wounds, and prepared and administered medicines more or less on their own terms, and they had done so for decades. They were esteemed and sometimes intimidating. Yet enslavers' efforts to bring healing under their control put healers' relationships with other enslaved people under stress. To extend their power into areas of enslaved life that were previously beyond their reach, managers and proprietors rendered healing into an official station and gave the people who held it a great deal of control over others. Healers of the early eighteenth century had probably worked in the houses of family, friends, and foes; some others worked in the great house. Kickery, Parthenia, and others now spent their days (and sometimes slept) in specific sites on the estate where, in addition to administering medicines and care, they were expected to constrain the mobility of enslaved people who were not at work and keep the punished confined under lock and key. Doctresses worked in hospitals, midwives attended in lying-in houses or in enslaved people's own quarters, and yaws healers were stationed in the yaws house.[4] Proprietors' system of body management put healers in positions that asked them to undermine the bodily autonomy of others. The reorganization of medical care could occasion the creation of solidarities with other enslaved people on the estate and from nearby. But it also brought healers into conflictual relations and intensified old enmities.[5]

As much as the improvement movement placed healers in a position of power, it also saw managers drawing boundaries around healers' work. To achieve efficiency and replicability in body management meant controlling the substances that the sick consumed, standardizing what remedies would be used for which afflictions, and attempting to predict the quantity of medicinal substances an estate would consume over a particular period of time. In the era of improvement and on most plantations, overseers and doctors now prescribed medicines. Yet proprietors attempted to achieve this control and track medicines' use by placing bookkeepers on their estates to act as apprentices to overseers. Bookkeepers were men in early to middle adolescence who lived on the estate and kept records of sugar output, the increase and decrease of stock and enslaved people, and accounts of expenses.[6] They were also supposed to make the remedies that practitioners and overseers prescribed and keep track of who went into and left the hospital.[7] Healers' role was now to administer medicines prescribed by other white people on the estate. One doctor explained to a Parliamentary committee that healers worked in coordination with medical men and described what they did: they performed "all lesser matters that related to the sick."[8] Efforts to systematize body management and render medicine more predictable presented a significant challenge to healers' therapeutic autonomy.

At any given moment, therefore, healers were caught in a tug-of-war between the expectations of sufferers and their families, on the one hand, and managers' demands, on the other. To maintain their station, healers needed to show managers that they could maintain hospitals as places of order and that they dutifully administered medicines prescribed by doctors and managers to the sick. Yet in order to make their own working lives easier, healers needed to secure sufferers' trust and deference by showing that they were knowledgeable people who understood managers' medicines and figures of authority who could intervene on sufferers' behalf.

The novelty and complexity of healers' position went unrecognized by managers and proprietors. Popular images of healers that arose from plantation management guides, chatty doctors, and boastful proprietors variously depicted hospital nurses as unfeeling drones, schemers, and dupes. Their inability to feel meant that they could not summon the concern necessary to attend to their patients. "The nurse," the plantation management author David Collins wrote, "is frequently ignorant, and generally inattentive to her charge; indeed what nurse is otherwise, longer than while the eyes of the master or mistress is upon her?"[9] Allegedly concerned only with their self-interest, healers connived to shirk their work responsibilities. Or their simplemindedness meant they were easily manipulated by others. Either way, the consequence was that the sick did not receive the medicines that doctors had ordered for them.

Scholars have emphasized Africans and Afro-Caribbean healers' ingenuity and creativity—showing how they located medicinal flora and fauna in the Caribbean basin equivalent to those used in Africa.[10] A related literature has revealed that the colonial Caribbean functioned as an emporium for divergent Amerindian, European, and African healing traditions.[11] Within this arena of hybrid knowledges, free and enslaved people of African descent ingeniously and successfully competed for clients against European rivals by incorporating various medical practices from Europeans and Amerindians into their therapeutic repertoire.[12]

Still, we know very little about the creative ways that healers responded as their work was transformed when plantations grew into massive agricultural behemoths, with dozens of sufferers to care for at a time.

To make this system of body management work for them, healers acted as go-betweens and negotiated among the expectations of managers and sufferers.[13] Foremost, they drew on the advantages of old age. Healers were expected to function as the subordinates and auxiliaries of doctors, overseers, and bookkeepers. They worked closely with men, in other words, who were much younger and who often had less experience than they did. Yet the transactions and negotiations intrinsic to the hospital's operation favored people with extensive experience. It required information that healers wielded about the people pleading for admission, the doctor who would attend them, the nature and severity of their ailments, and the medicines that would be applied. Healers integrated and responded to the therapeutic and temporal expectations of doctors, overseers, slaveholders, and the sick. Healers drew on their institutional memory, their diplomatic sensibilities, their social connections to others, as well as their extensive botanical know-how. Proprietors and attorneys situated Kickery, Parthenia, and their counterparts at the bottom interpretive rung of a hierarchy of people making decisions about the sick, with overseers, bookkeepers, and doctors on the upper most rungs. By operating as intermediaries, healers retained some of their power amid organizational and spatial changes that threatened to erode it.

Metropolitan Medicines and Meddling Managers

Understanding why changes in the organization of body management on estates forced healers to operate as intermediaries requires first examining managers' attempts to encroach on healers' long-standing role in selecting and making medicines. One of the most visible expressions of healing power lay in the autonomy to select and make remedies. It took ingenuity to identify particular plants as efficacious and manufacture them into a medicine. Colonists had long credited enslaved and Indigenous people with possessing this type of know-how. The colonists who arrived in the Caribbean in the seventeenth century, for example, well understood that they could not survive without Africans' and Amerindians' botanical knowledge.[14] But over the course of the eighteenth century, British colonists increasingly disdained the truth-claims that enslaved and Amerindian people made about the natural world. Colonists across the British Atlantic World began to characterize enslaved informants as "cunning," called their beliefs about plants "superstitious," and feared their dexterity with poisonous materials.[15] Proprietors and managers sought to gain better control over what the sick consumed in part because of concerns about poisoning and superstitious medicine; yet their efforts also arose in response to the increase in the size of individual slaveholdings and shifts in estates' consumption patterns. The integration of estates into larger Atlantic circuits of manufactured goods, capital, debt, and credit opened up new channels for the flow of consumer medical goods and information that would come to abet proprietors' and managers' encroachment on healers' territory.

Sugar plantations could not function without English manufactured goods and dietary provisions from North America, Scotland, and Ireland. With the exception of food that enslaved people grew in their own provision grounds, nearly every article that facilitated the production of sugar and sustained enslaved labor forces—from textiles for enslaved people's clothing, to barrels, hoes, nails, axels, manacles, and chains—arrived from abroad, their purchase made available on credit extended by metropolitan commission houses to absentees in exchange for a percentage of sugar sales.[16]

Medical consumer items available in Britain were part of this world of manufactured goods. Merchant-apothecaries in Britain responded to overseas demands for pharmaceuticals that were capable of treating sick populations. Manufactured medicines were especially appealing to the managers of unfree laboring populations. They "offered a convenient solution to the omnipresent challenge of manpower by the logic that certain treatments could work on anybody irrespective of external characteristics or internal complexion," explains Zachary Dorner.[17] Eighteenth-century proprietors and their agents purchased substances and manufactured (pharmaceutical) medicines from British merchant-apothecaries more and more.[18]

The invasion of healers' domain can be attributed not only to the availability of medical consumer goods but to long-term changes in the ways that laypeople understood themselves in relationship to medical authorities. The growth of what historians call the medical marketplace in the early modern period saw the decline in the authority of medical regulatory bodies and the growth of a new, complex arena of commercial medical provision. Practitioners and healers of all stripes now competed against one another for clients. "In any year a sick person might visit a wart-charmer, get a remedy from a neighbor or bookseller, pay a surgeon and hire a horse leech," scholars explain.[19] Across the British Atlantic World, a veritable cornucopia of practitioners, merchants, healers, and writers offered advice and goods, remaking sick people into customers and "every man his own doctor," as the title of an extremely popular medical advice guide boldly proclaimed.[20] As they engaged in a commercial economy abuzz with getting and spending, proprietors, attorneys, and managers stylized themselves as savvy consumers of medical goods and advice who often operated independent of practitioners' counsel.[21]

Popular medical advice texts and locally circulated recipes joined manufactured medicines as items that helped proprietors and managers determine which medicines to employ. Such texts explained to readers "how to do something, whether that is to gather herbs, choose a diet, make a remedy or figure out what ails a person."[22] Domestic medical advice texts published in the eighteenth century often promoted the consumption of manufactured medicines and locally made remedies that targeted particular afflictions. These texts helped to entrench the idea that people suffered from distinctive diseases for which there existed a remedy particular to their cure.[23] The most popular medical reference book in the eighteenth-century Caribbean was James Grainger's *An Essay on the More Common West-India Diseases* (1764). Grainger's book provided practical advice on the cure of illnesses on plantations—it listed thirty-one afflictions and diseases that commonly afflicted enslaved people and showed readers how to make remedies for them. Historically, the plantation management guide belonged to an agricultural genre that for nearly a century was mute on the subject of medicine. In the late eighteenth century, these guides underwent a metamorphosis.[24] The titles of these texts, such as Clement Caines's *Letters on the Cultivation of the Otaheite Cane* (1801), continued to advertise these books as agricultural guides on the cultivation of cane, its manufacture into sugar, and the organization of labor. Yet some of these guides now also operated as popular medical advice manuals. Several portions of Caines's text discussed sores, yaws, and leprosy. It contained information similar to what readers would have found in Grainger's *Essay*, where he discussed these afflictions. Indeed, many West Indian plantation management authors lifted their material directly from Grainger and other popular medical authors.[25] Competent managers and proprietors, these texts argued, did not defer to enslaved healers and practitioners; instead, they should select medicines, prepare remedies, and apportion doses on their own.

Such texts were, as Katherine Paugh has observed, ideological.[26] They painted the world as authors wished it to be. Yet by the time plantation management advice guides doubled as medical texts, managers had already taken measures to develop remedies for specific diseases that they would force onto the afflicted. In addition to copying from other popular medical advice writers, plantation management texts likely also codified material that overseers and attorneys had developed in local networks for trying and circulating medical recipes. Printed advice texts repackaged locally produced remedies (which creators had appropriated from enslaved people) for larger audiences and made them ready for transport.

Together local remedies, plantation management guides, and imported pharmaceuticals emboldened proprietors and managers to try to push healers aside from their selection and making of medicines. Yet efforts to dislodge healers from these activities did not go uncontested. At various points in the recovery of the sick from illness, hospital healers and yaws-house nurses resisted managers' efforts to arrogate healers' historical decision-making as their own. To reconstruct the contentious process by which healers defended their ground, we should examine yaws, a disease that healers had historically managed. Estates now acquired information and materials to contend with this affliction (and others) through four channels: healers, proprietors, managers, and practitioners.

For centuries, healers had operated with a great deal of autonomy in sourcing ingredients and manufacturing them into medicines. They sometimes supplied ingredients grown in their kitchen gardens adjacent to their houses. Just as often, they foraged for materials in forests and savannas. In the early eighteenth century, the enslaver and naturalist Henry Barham remembered that an enslaved man had restored his strength. As Barham recovered from a fever and soaked his limbs in a warm bath, an enslaved man "going through the house" proclaimed, "master I can cure you." He brought bark and leaves harvested from a hog plum tree, which he instructed Barham to mix in a basin filled with water. He then directed Barham to immerse his swollen legs in it. Barham recovered. In recounting the event, he made clear that, although he thought the enslaved man's knowledge was credible, it was not a sign of enslaved people's sagacity. Barham attributed his recovery to God, whom he credited for placing such powerful substances in "mean and common plants," and the "knowledge of them should be made known to so vile and mean objects as negro slaves and Indians."[27] Whatever else Barham thought about enslaved people, he was desperate enough to rely on the enslaved man for help.

The emphasis on the enslaved man's movement in Barham's story is suggestive of what independence in selecting medicines might have meant to healers. Their historical role in selecting remedies was tied to their autonomy to forage for individual ingredients. Healers' mobility was more circumscribed than that of plantation medical men or enslaved tradespeople. But because estates depended on healers' knowledge of the local environment, they might have allowed healers to move about the estate and its environs to gather ingredients.

Historically, healers held a great deal of interpretive and therapeutic autonomy in the treatment of yaws especially. Colonists had long observed that enslaved people had many means for contending with this disease. The eighteenth-century historian of Jamaica James Knight observed that enslaved people "very seldom prescribe any thing to be taken inwardly."[28] Knight was speaking generally about enslaved people's remedies. But his observations seem especially pertinent when one examines men's and women's beliefs about yaws. Many of the treatments they applied suggest that enslaved people thought that remedies for yaws needed to work on the disease from the outside in rather than the inside out. One popular remedy encouraged sufferers to soak the parts of their body afflicted with yaws sores in herbal baths or to stand in them to produce sweat. The overseer A. J. Alexander wrote about an enslaved man "who understood the method of treatment in their own country." The man's method "is making them stand in a pot and sweating them powerfully in it twice a day giving them decoction of 2 woods in this country called Bois Royale and Bois fer and applying an ointment of lime juice and rust of iron to their sores."[29] Other enslaved people, especially people from the Gold Coast, inoculated children from yaws. As Katherine Paugh explains, this practice reflected the necessity of "opening up the skin and inviting illness inside." At other times, they "encouraged the disease to flow freely back out across the boundaries of the body by scrubbing open the skin's lesions."[30] Knight probably exaggerated enslaved people's aversion to internal medicines. He was not off the mark, however, in noting that many therapeutic traditions from West Africa involved managing the body from the outside: exfoliating sores and immersing sufferers in therapeutic baths that promoted sweating.

Colonists also liked to see sweating, but they came at it from a different angle—they wanted to encourage the body's juices to move. The enslaver and practitioner David Collins recommended that "the prisoners [patients at the yaws house] may, occasionally, be indulged with a walk out of their bounds, under the escort of their nurses, who should never lose sight of them." When the excursion was finished, the yaws nurse was enjoined to "conduct them back again to the yaws-house and lock them in it at night."[31] Yaws-house attendants kept patients in place or forcibly moved them around and between estates as necessary. Thomas Thistlewood was a Jamaican overseer for sugar plantations in the 1750s and 1760s. By the 1770s, he owned his own animal and guinea grass pen. He had extensive experience with yaws. Thistlewood believed that a successful yaws cure required keeping the sufferer "warm by night and worked by day." Thistlewood sent a man named Simon to live with a woman named Old Bella, who "will make him stir about" during the day.[32]

But it seems unlikely that Thistlewood could have compelled Old Bella to enact his demands from a distance. Colonists argued that yaws originated in Africa; on this premise many argued that enslaved people's remedies for yaws were safer and far more efficacious than those promulgated by plantation medical men.[33] Thus, for many years yaws remained almost entirely under the control of enslaved healers, some of whom worked in yaws houses. In many instances, yaws healers might take on afflicted people from adjacent plantations. Egypt, the sugar plantation that Thistlewood supervised in the 1750s, does not appear to have had its own yaws house. Some of Egypt's enslaved people were subjected to Thistlewood's remedies; he sent the more severe cases to Old Sharper, a watchman, barber, and yaws healer on Salt River, a plantation near Egypt.[34]

Enslaved people also maintained control over yaws management because many practitioners were terrified of becoming infected with yaws. "Physicians or surgeons who are employed on estates are not understood to have the immediate charge of Negroes in the yaws," the plantation practitioner William Wright explained to readers. "Should a medical man contract this filthy disease," he continued, "his fortune and future prospects are ruined."[35] Because Africans had familiarity with yaws and medical men had such aversion to it, managers readily delegated yaws management to enslaved people.

The interactions between Thistlewood and Old Sharper illustrate yaws healers' autonomy. After Hector, Cloe, Morris, and Clara arrived at Salt River, Old Sharper kept most of them for nearly half a year. Hector was with Old Sharper and apart from his family for nearly nine months.[36] At the six-month mark, Old Sharper marched Cloe, Morris, and Clara back to Egypt. Thistlewood decided that this was premature: "as none of them are well yet, made him take them back, and Morris with them."[37] Old Sharper then escorted them back to the yaws house. Yet, tellingly, Thistlewood's disagreements with Old Sharper centered not on what he used to recover people from yaws but whether the sufferers were cured. Because Old Sharper carried out his work at a distance, the overseer could ignore the fact that he was not fully in charge. Managers told hospital healers what remedies to use, but their authority was especially thin in yaws houses, where healing took place far from the core of the estate or on another estate entirely. At midcentury, healers operated with considerable leeway and autonomy.

Autonomy had its burdens. Work in the yaws house could be isolating. Yaws healers spent their days far distant from the main areas of activity on the estate. On Mesopotamia, the yaws house sat on a distant hill.[38] Thistlewood referred to Old Sharper's location on Salt River as "Hill." The name suggests that the building sat on a place that was elevated and possibly topographically separate from the razed areas of the plantation.

Enslaved people believed that yaws remedies needed to address the affliction from the outside in. Colonists, by contrast, believed that remedies needed to target the disease on the inside. Their understanding of yaws was informed by their understanding of venereal disease. Many believed that they were the same affliction, wherein the symptoms represented different stages of the disease's progress.[39] The conviction that the two had a relationship to one another informed colonists' understanding of yaws and how yaws remedies ought to work. Both afflictions were caused by the internal process of putrefaction, which "rotted" the body from the inside out. The internal processes of an illness indicated what was required to recuperate someone from it.[40] Understanding how colonists thought about remedies for yaws and venereal disease thus requires learning about how Britons imagined the internal workings of afflictions that they believed were caused by putrefaction.

In the eighteenth century, for instance, practitioners arrived at a consensus that the fevers of hot climates were bilious in nature—their symptoms were the product of internal putrefaction. Putrefaction originated in putrid matter, often referred to as poisons, which caused the bilious fever.[41] Since practitioners and laypeople believed that bilious fevers were caused by poisons that instigated the processes of putrefaction, they also maintained that bilious fevers needed a particular therapeutic: antiseptic medicines, such as cinchona, which would halt putrefaction; antimonial medicines, which purged the poisons that had initiated the process; and mercury in the form of calomel, which would cleanse the digestive organs of putrid matter.[42]

Colonists used the same conceptual toolkit for yaws and venereal disease as they did for bilious fevers. Yaws symptoms were, for colonists, the visible effects of internal poisons that had instigated an internal process of decay. If poisons remained, colonists imagined, they would corrupt the afflicted in phases until the person's body became irreversibly putrid. One or two primary sores, which one colonist described as the size of a coat button, marked the first phase of yaws. As the disease progressed, the sores transformed into either several large ulcers or many tiny ones that covered most of the body. If left untreated or treated with tepid medicines, the disease advanced to a more dangerous stage, moving into the deep anatomical structures of the body, where it damaged the integrity of bones, producing what enslaved people and colonists described as "bone ache."[43] The ulcers and lesions characteristic of yaws' first phases signaled that the body was trying to rid itself of the poisonous matter.[44] Medicines assisted and sped up that process.

This way of conceptualizing yaws as poisons comes through in the notations that Thistlewood made about Dick, an enslaved man suffering from yaws. "As Dick has the yaws coming out sent him in the field," Thistlewood wrote in his diary. Thistlewood reasoned that since Dick's body was in the process of expelling the yaws poisons, he was well enough to work. A month later, Thistlewood revised his conclusion and mused that the yaws poisons still lingered. "Dick is too full of the yaws," he wrote. The overseer determined that Dick was now too ill to hire him out to work on a neighboring estate.[45] Whether they thought yaws and venereal disease were distinctive or the same, all conceptualized the diseases as engendered by poisons and wanted to prescribe remedies for both afflictions that worked violently to hurry yaws and venereal poisons out of the body through the force of expulsion. The remedies that colonists made aimed to expel the morbid matter by "throwing the disease to the skin," whereupon sweat vented yaws poisons, preventing the blood from becoming irreversibly putrid.[46]

When Thistlewood was an overseer at Egypt, he received a recipe for yaws from John Cope, the resident owner. The ingredients in the recipe that Cope recommended reveal colonists' thinking about how to manage yaws—that it should start from the inside. The first component of Cope's remedy was a drink. Like drinks for venereal disease, Cope probably assumed that it operated as an internal astringent that rid the body of putrefaction. Cope's drink started with two pounds off lignum vitae wood chips (a powerful diaphoretic, diuretic, and cathartic evacuative made from the trunk and branches of the gum guaiacum plant).[47] It also included one ounce of sarsaparilla, "to be beat or bruised to powder in a mortar." "Then an Ounce & a half off [sic] Senna Mixed with them: to be divided into 14 papers: One paper off which powders to be put in an Iron Pott, to 3 pints off water, and build to a Quart." Senna achieves its effects by irritating the colon and forcing the discharge of feces. Taken in significant amounts, it causes gripping stomach pain.[48] The recipe directed sufferers to drink the mixture four times each day.[49] The remedy also included a dose of flower brimstone. This ingredient was sublimated sulfur, a pale, yellow powder that is diaphoretic and cathartic, and was, in Britain, used primarily to blunt the side effects of mercury.[50] Colonists believed that it worked as an evacuant. The sulfur powder, Thistlewood noted, would "drive the yaws out well."[51] Yaws healers working under managers' directives would have carried out remedies that contained many different phases. Charged with imposing enfeebling remedies that achieved their effects through expulsion, healers were supposed to help overseers and practitioners accelerate the body's healing process according to European ideas about the temporality of yaws poisons.

Managers' proclamations about their ability to manage yaws became especially strident in the late eighteenth century. Yet as Thistlewood's exchange of remedies with Cope suggests, managers and practitioners had been pushing healers out of the conversation about remedies and botanical medicine for some time. In the early eighteenth century, colonial botanists corresponding with metropolitan patrons openly touted their contact with enslaved informers so as to situate themselves as important "translators of the vernacular."[52] Yet by the middle of the century, colonists' face-to-face engagement with enslaved people about the properties of different plants was becoming more infrequent. Part of the reason for this stemmed from changes in remedies themselves. Colonists' remedies increasingly combined local botanical substances with chemical substances imported from abroad. Thus, the discussion of cures among colonists no longer focused on the attributes of individual plants (and the enslaved person who made those attributes known) but on whether different combinations of botanical and chemical substances were effective cures.

Another development was the increased interactions among overseers and practitioners, who learned from one another and from what was written down in an estate's hospital book and from local networks of recipe exchange. Enslaved people like Old Sharper and Bella would continue to inform colonists' ideas about yaws and influence which remedies were applied for that affliction until the abolition of slavery in the nineteenth century. But they saw their claims challenged as managers and proprietors took a greater interest in the management of illness and insisted on their prerogative to impose their own remedies.

In colonists' recipe exchange networks, enslaved people's role became that of silent experimental objects rather than speaking, authoritative subjects. This dynamic appears in the ways that Thistlewood used and cited information passed to him from another enslaver, Mrs. Wheatley. After Wheatley gifted her remedy for yaws to the overseer, Thistlewood transcribed the ingredients and instructions in his diary in full. It is almost certainly the case that Wheatley had vetted the recipe on the enslaved people she held in captivity before passing the recipe to Thistlewood. Since the recipe had already been tried, Thistlewood was more willing to apply it.[53] In his diary, he listed hog plum tree root as one of its ingredients.[54] The roots of the plum tree were a staple of enslaved people's therapeutic warehouse. They used and sought out this material in recipes for venereal disease. The plant was abundant in Jamaica's lowland woods and savannas.[55] It is a strong possibility that Wheatley, or someone in her own network, had learned about this ingredient from an enslaved informant. Yet it was in trialing the remedy on enslaved people and observing its effects that Wheatley came to think of the recipe as hers. That is likely how she presented it to others. In his diary, Thistlewood cited Wheatley alone. This was a pattern he repeated many times over as he received recipes from people across the parish of Westmoreland, Jamaica.[56]

In the mid-eighteenth century, when Thistlewood was exchanging recipes with his neighbors, healers still retained input, though they were not officially credited as the authors of information. Before he received Wheatley's recipe, Thistlewood tried to cure an enslaved woman named Abigail of yaws. Before he began, he dispatched the enslaved man Coffee to gather "maiden plum tree root to assist curing the negroes crab yaws."[57] Coffee or someone else had probably suggested this ingredient to Thistlewood. Just as importantly, Thistlewood understood that Coffee knew where to locate it. But he never credited Coffee as possessing any knowledge about plum tree root in his diary. At the same time, Thistlewood's dependence on Coffee's environmental know-how allowed Coffee the mobility to forage for the materials that Thistlewood would mix together to make a bath for Abigail's sores.

Still, as local networks of recipe exchange matured and managers tried recipes many times over, colonists like Wheatley and Thistlewood repackaged and claimed knowledge appropriated from enslaved people as their own. In so doing, they formed a closed circuit of collective knowledge-making. Colonists cited one another; meanwhile, enslaved people disappeared from the historical record through colonists' secondary and tertiary appropriation of their knowledge. Even though enslaved people sometimes remained involved in gathering ingredients, their disappearance in discussions about remedies probably reinforced managers' sense of their proprietary ownership of the information they exchanged with one another. Just as significantly, enslaved people's exclusion from this discussion bolstered managers' assumptions about their right to select and manufacture the substances that they would impose on men and women suffering from yaws and venereal disease.

Local networks of recipe exchange formed just one channel for the exchange of information and substances among colonists that would underwrite managers' invasion into healers' domain. Another incursion arrived from abroad. Increasingly, proprietors and attorneys acquired medicines directly for the estates under their charge, using metropolitan commission agents who purchased materia medica (substances) and patent medicines (pharmaceuticals) from merchant-apothecaries. Merchant-druggists supplying pharmaceuticals packaged their materials in bottles and packets and provided instructions on doses.[58] Agents then sent these materials overseas to the Caribbean. Many of these materials were stored in the estate's medical chest.

Pharmaceutical medicines attracted proprietors and attorneys engaged in managing illness en masse, especially with the growth in the size of their estates. As Zachary Dorner has explained, merchant-druggists promoted the idea that it was more efficient to treat diseases with "bulk medicines rather than by individualized constitutional ones." Manufactured medicines were promoted as treating specific diseases. Instead of tailoring remedies to the particular body of the sufferer, manufactured medicines "offered the possibility of treating anybody, whether free or unfree, old or young, poor or rich, suffering from a certain ailment with a similar pill or tincture from a laboratory in London."[59] The purchase of pharmaceuticals and substances as part of an estate's annual supplies was also less expensive than allowing surgeons to provide medicine from their own coffers.[60] Many estates acquired medicines and substances in shipments from Britain and then purchased individually from plantation practitioners on an as-needed basis—sometimes as a stopgap measure until the next supply ship arrived.[61]

Proprietors and attorneys prided themselves not only on knowing what substances to use in different remedies but from whom to purchase them in an arena filled with merchant-druggists whose honesty varied. The knowledge they developed, in other words, was that of customers as much as it was as makers. Shortly after the Seven Years' War, for instance, the Jamaican attorney Malcolm Laing wrote to the British absentee Philip Perrin about a cure that he had developed for yaws. Laing needed ingredients, and he asked Perrin to send them out from Britain. Laing's supply list included corrosive sublimate (mercuric chloride) and "Edinburgh Treacle," a mixture that contains a proportion of opium. Laing planned to mix these materials with a "decoction of sarsaparilla," a perennial climbing plant native to the Caribbean. The entire mixture would then be dissolved in ten gallons of rum.[62] Laing warned Perrin against purchasing from urban druggists, as "the apothocarys, [sic] are apt to send arsenic in place of corrosive sublimate." Laing directed Perrin to an alternative source. Perrin should seek these ingredients from another resident of England (Benjamin Cowell), who was also the brother-in-law of another Jamaican absentee (Chaloner Arcedeckne). Laing gained information about the properties of the diverse ingredients in his remedy from his interactions with other managers and enslaved people. Laing's warning to Perrin about conniving druggists reveals that his involvement in larger Atlantic circuits of provisioning, which included working for other absentees, was just as significant for the composition of the remedy as was information about the attributes of the remedy's individual ingredients. In his letter, Laing needed to assure Perrin of his medical authority. Yet he did not situate himself as a colonial collector of enslaved people's knowledge. Instead, he painted a picture of himself as a canny consumer of Atlantic goods.

Over time, absentees grew more strident in their opinions on the expeditiousness of certain substances. In many cases, they attempted to dictate from across the ocean what managers would impose. In one of his receipt books, James Chisholme reminded himself that he had written to his attorney forbidding the use of corrosive sublimate for enslaved people afflicted with venereal disease. Instead, he ordered his managers to apply mercurial ointments and "plenty of sarsaparilla in powder."[63] A few years later, Chisholme revised his opinion and complained that his attorney relied too much on sarsaparilla, which he described as "money thrown away; as a decoction of sarsaparilla is of no more use in medicine than ditch water, this I have proved myself beyond contradiction."[64]

Once proprietors began purchasing imported medicines as part of the annual supplies, they became accustomed to tracking their rates of consumption. After agents shipped medicines overseas, absentees received receipts, enumerating the amounts of the substances and medicines they had purchased by weight and volume (pounds, ounces, and quarts). In 1810, for example, agents for the Jamaican absentee William Chisholme (James's brother) sent his estate approximately 128 pounds of different medicinal powders, oils, and salts.[65] Looking over such receipts, absentees became better-informed consumers about the costs of particular substances in designated amounts. Comparing them with previous years' requests, they developed a measure of how long such materials could be expected to last. At the same time, they could not control entirely how those substances were used once they left their agents' hands. Substances and pharmaceuticals functioned in labor regimes in ways similar to food and textile provisions: they were vulnerable to theft, misuse, and overcharge. Still, as absentees scoured their receipts and compared them to requests for annual supplies sent from resident attorneys, they told themselves that they could spot the signs of excessive use and theft. When James Chisholme explained to his manager that "the medicines now sent, if properly used, and none suffered to be carried way, would serve the whole of the properties for seven years," he expressed an expectation about the rate of use and warned the manager that Chisholme would be keeping an eye on their consumption.[66]

Managers assured absentees that they limited who could access the medicine chest. "I declare," William Anderson wrote to Chisholme, "the medicines are the only supplies of which I keep the key." "They are kept," he continued, "in the closet of my room with the remnants of cloth and the gunpowder; and none is under the hand of white or black doctors, but what is used for the day."[67] Proprietors' concern with theft suggests healers' and other enslaved people's awareness of the location and value of pharmaceuticals and the appeal of some of these materials. The very need to calm proprietors' concerns shows that healers probably had greater access to imported medicines than proprietors would have liked.

Estates also acquired substances from medical men who supplied medicines from their own coffers, an arrangement that also threatened to cut healers out of the process of deciding what the sick would consume as well as the process of transforming substances into medicines.[68] The Jamaican practitioner Alexander Johnston, for instance, regularly sent medicinal substances in bulk to the plantations of his clients. In one instance, he charged the estate for one pound of antimony powder for the plantation's horses. It was also common for practitioners to send medicines that they had prescribed and compounded as remedies tailored to particular individuals, though, as discussed in chapter 1, such a privilege was primarily granted to managerial staff and a handful of individual enslaved people. Thus, Johnston charged Pinnock for medicines that he compounded for the estate's managers and one enslaved man named George.[69]

When practitioners prescribed remedies and made medicines off-site, enslaved people often retrieved them. Collins described the custom of dispatching enslaved people to practitioners' shops and homes to obtain medicines for sick individuals on the estate. Collins frowned upon this arrangement, arguing that it delayed the administration of medicines. The "negro who is dispatched to bring them [the medicines] . . . is possibly detained half the day on the errand before he can get served."[70] Nevertheless, this arrangement appears to have been a common one. Over a ten-month period in 1770, the enslaved woman Bess walked from Breadnut Island Pen to Dr. John Drummond's shop six times, carrying a letter from Breadnut's owner, Thistlewood, describing her illness. Later Bess returned to Breadnut with medicines and instructions from Drummond. Perhaps on her walk home she inspected the materials. She might have sniffed the packets and shifted them between her fingers to ascertain the qualities of the materials inside. Maybe she held up bottles to the sunlight and shook them to watch the way their liquids moved. Perhaps these signs signaled to Bess the medicines' potential threat or value. She also may have scanned Drummond's instructions.[71] Though overseers and plantation doctors assumed that their exchanges were private, enslaved people often functioned as conduits for communications between these two groups. Still, there was a difference between making medicines oneself and fetching those made by another.

Indeed, we can see how estates' reliance on outside sources for substances and medicines curtailed enslaved healers' autonomy and mobility, especially when estates purchased prefabricated medicines in large volumes. One of the best examples of prefabricated materials comes from Johnston's entrepreneurial activities. Throughout the 1760s and 1770s, Johnston prescribed and made individual remedies for individual afflictions on an as-needed basis. During this time, he started putting together ready-made prefabricated units of "yawey ingredients," which contained multiple substances and which he sold and sent to at least three different sugar estates in northwestern Jamaica.[72] The amount of this remedy that he sent ranged. When Johnston sent units of "yawey ingredients," he measured them out in amounts appropriate for different quantities of liquid. His instructions directed recipients to either mix the packets with "1 quart" or for "two bottles" of liquid, either rum, wine, or water. The premade packets of yaws ingredients appear to have included substances from local and transatlantic sources. On one occasion Johnston sent a packet "with the gum [gum guaiacum]," and on another, "without the gum."[73] The papers also included ingredients, such as corrosive sublimate, that Johnson either purchased from local druggists or agents abroad.

The addition of gum guaiacum in Johnston's remedy is suggestive of how, when practitioners gathered together different substances and packaged them into individual units, they may have constrained healers' mobility. Gum guaiacum is a resin made from the trunks and branches of the guaiacum tree, which grows in Jamaica. The wood from this tree is called lignum vitae. Europeans had known about Indigenous people's (and possibly enslaved people's) use of gum guaiacum and lignum vitae wood chips in place of mercury to treat venereal disease since the fifteenth century. Gum guaiacum had been adopted in Europe as a substitute for mercury. It was also a staple ingredient for yaws remedies. Cope's recipe contained lignum vitae wood chips. Some colonists used the lignum vitae to fence in their estates.[74] It would have been easy for estates to send enslaved healers to collect this resin themselves. It is possible that the enslaved man Galen who lived in Johnston's household and worked as his assistant collected some of the materials for the gum guaiacum resin: perhaps he also made it. But the enslaved healers living on the plantations who purchased Johnston's packets might have had a different experience of Johnston's entrepreneurship. Managers may have purchased Johnston's packets to increase efficiency and control over the process of making medicines and to exclude healers from making yaws drinks. If that was the case, Johnston's ready-made packets may have indirectly curtailed healers' mobility, as the need to source materials, gum guaiacum especially, disappeared.

Premade medicines and mixtures using colonists' tools of measurement threatened to alienate healers from their work. But to understand how, one must reconstruct what making medicines looked like when enslaved people like Old Sharper were in control. At midcentury and in healers' hands, the transformation of ingredients into a medicine drew from the material culture of West African and Afro-Caribbean medicine. Specifically, enslaved people used a variety of clay and ceramic bowls as well as gourds, often calabashes, of various shapes and sizes to transport solid and liquid matter and to mix ingredients for poultices and liquid medicines.

One can glimpse enslaved people's vessels in action in Thistlewood's interactions with Old Sharper. In middle of the eighteenth century, Thistlewood suffered from venereal disease, and he sought Old Sharper's counsel and purchased medicines from him. In several instances, Thistlewood noted that Old Sharper sent a "diet drink in a gourd" to him.[75] Gourds were not a novelty to Thistlewood. He had witnessed enslaved people transform gourds into drums.[76] Still, Thistlewood may have associated Old Sharper's gourd with a world of religious healing that for him seemed both dangerous and superstitious. Such resonances may have enhanced his perception of the potency of the gourd's contents.

Thistlewood would not have been far off the mark. Gourds were part of a larger culture of healing that some scholars refer to as social medicine. Africans maintained that "the presence of sickness and strife must prove the influence of some evil intent."[77] Sometimes diagnosis and healing required a ritualist or diviner to connect with this world of spirits and receive instructions on how appease or protect others from them.[78] Analogues of this system of belief existed throughout the colonial Caribbean. Enslaved people believed in a numinous sphere peopled by the dead, where ancestors offered important sources of protection and a means of redress. Enslaved people also lived amid a variety of nature spirits. Both entities could intrude upon and shape the realm of human affairs.[79] Gourds occupied a place of prominence in the rituals that medical diviners conducted to beckon spirits into the temporal realm of the living. Handled correctly, gourds acted as power objects. They grounded the healer's power to identify the spiritual origins and cure for illness in a tangible thing, one that belonged and was specific to the individual healer.[80] The many gourds of different shapes, colors, and sizes that Old Sharper and other healers used operated as part of the world of ritual medicine and the more prosaic acts of care and healing that took place in the everyday. These vessels formed the fundaments of a maker-centric culture of medicine that tied efficacious medicines to particular healers and their instruments.

A healer derived their instruments from many sources. Gourds were but one type of measuring and making instrument. Just as often, healers used their own bodies—their knowledge of making medicines was tacit and haptic. Healers determined the amount of a particular ingredient in a cure on the basis of what they could grab, pinch, smell, touch, or taste. In an article published in a British medical periodical, a writer from Jamaica described the use of cabbage-bark in a remedy for treating intestinal worms. His observations on the ways enslaved people prepared this remedy offer a glimpse of this sensory epistemology in action: "The negroes or nurses, to whom the general exhibition of this bark is intrusted [sic], commonly prepare it, by taking a handful of it bruised and boiling it in water, till the decoction, well sweetened, they give for three successive mornings, a small table-spoonful to a child of two years of age."[81] Hands, fingers, tongues, and gourds were the building blocks of a healer's individual and highly particularized skill. To be sure, they intermingled with colonists' tools of measurement—note the tablespoon in the remedy. Healers' knowledge of how to make medicines was built up over time and through repetition. Their knowledge was bodily—they measured on the basis of how a certain quantity of leaves felt in their hands or the particular sounds that a liquid made as it sloshed inside a calabash, depending on its viscosity. As was the case for artisans in early modern Europe and sugar boilers on plantations, healers' know-how was haptic, and the mysteriousness of their processes likely contributed to the perception of healers as powerful.[82] That type of haptic, bodily knowledge was difficult to replicate, let alone standardize.

Old Sharper's name places him within this world of maker-directed medicine. The term "old sharper" was one that enslaved people assigned to men and women who possessed intercessory powers. The term "sharper" was both a metaphor for the ways that healers cured illness and a description of tools they used. These men and women wielded the power to sever the ties between the sick and the malevolent entities that caused illness, thereby releasing the sick from their suffering.[83] Knives and other tools used for cutting featured in their ceremonies. But ritualists could also connect with these entities and direct them to harm others. Some of the enslaved women in Dominica whom the plantation doctor Jonathan Troup attended encircled their children's wrists with red string to protect them from the "old sharpers who principally reside about grand bay."[84] Just as important as the gourds themselves were the things that healers put into them. It is likely that some of the substances that Old Sharper placed in his gourd were ones that his enslaved clients associated with a larger and sacralized natural world where spirits resided in trees, stones, and plants.[85]

Thistlewood needed Old Sharper's assistance but struggled to fit the gourd that Old Sharper put his medicine in into units of measurement that were familiar points of reference. When Thistlewood recorded in his diary, repeatedly, that he consumed "a bottle off old Sharper's diet drink" or "drank a quart bottle of old Sharper's diet drink," the overseer was trying to translate the gourd into a unit of consumption that was meaningful to him. Perhaps he also wanted to measure the gourd's contents so that he could know the exchange value of the drams in which he paid Old Sharper.[86] At midcentury, Thistlewood could do little but adapt and accommodate. He did eventually seek assistance from the estate's doctor. But he also repeatedly returned to Sharper and would have to integrate and translate Sharper's vessel into his routine by pouring the gourd's contents into the bottles he had at hand.

Yet, by the era of the American Revolution, bottles of imported substances, boxes of pills, and prefabricated envelopes of "yawey ingredients" threatened to eclipse the vessels that enslaved healers had used to mix, apportion, and transport materials. As estates became ever more integrated into the Atlantic consumer economy, a new system of measuring and knowing took shape that was divorced from the individual maker of medicine. British manufactures related to cookery and manners were more widely within reach to colonists of all ranks, and standardized systems of weights and measurements took on great importance in everyday exchanges where it was necessary to stabilize the relationship between quantities and costs. Proprietors and attorneys prided themselves on knowing the macro-measurements of bulk purchases, which overlapped with the development of a local culture preoccupied with micro-measurements in the making of remedies. The haptic knowledge and ritual vessels that were part of a healer-centric model of medicine competed with a system of weighing, measuring, and valuing derived from colonists' units of measurement, which largely relied on tools external to the body. These measuring tools helped to push aside remedies whose potencies were tied to their particular maker and replace them with manufactured medicines. The units colonists employed trafficked in the expectations that good medicine was not tied to an individual maker but was replicable on a broader scale. The remedies that colonists consumed and made, in turn, operated on the precept that anyone could compose a medicine if they had common tools of measurement or received a prefabricated packet of ingredients to be mixed with liquids on hand.

Vernacular remedies in popular medical and plantation management guides provide a window into this transformation. In instructions for how to make different remedies, authors used official units of measurement and those that were not formalized but that were nevertheless common points of reference for colonists engaged in a larger Atlantic consumer culture. In his recipe for fevers, Collins counseled readers to "mix thirty-two grains [of tartar emetic] in a quart of water, give a wine glass-ful to an adult, about the half, or a third of the quantity, to children according to their ages and constitutions."[87] In the appendix to his book, he supplied a conversion table that helped readers translate apothecaries' measurements, such as drachms, scruples, and grains, into more familiar quantities, such as pounds and ounces. Some of these measuring tools, such as bottles, derived from merchant-apothecaries who organized the sale of their pharmaceuticals into "divisible units" like the bottles in which they sent their medicines in.[88] Wine glasses and teaspoons, by contrast, were consumer objects that colonists associated with manners, cosmopolitanism, and the discipline of the body. Authors assumed that estates would have these on hand as well as other measuring tools that gauged the amount of a given substance in ounces and quarts.

Authors were not wrong. The measuring materials enumerated in estate inventories and annual supply lists indicate some of the instruments that overseers and bookkeepers used to make medicines using particular amounts. The hot-house of the Phillipsfield sugar plantation contained a brass mortar and pestle and a syringe.[89] James Chisholme purchased one quart pewter syringe for Trout Hall in 1804.[90] Both consumer and official measuring tools created expectations that remedies were predictable and replicable. Among colonists, a wine glass, a quart, or a drop were common enough ways to measure the size or amount of something, and anyone could replicate another's recipe numerous times over, with neither expertise nor lengthy experience required.

Colonists used their tools to determine quantities and sizes to disparage healers' involvement in making of medicines. The Jamaican surgeon Peter Dugid wrote about healers' creation of a cabbage-bark remedy. Yet he characterized these healers as unmethodical. The cabbage bark, he explained, "is commonly given in decoction, but not in any regular quantity; the negroes being generally the preparers of this medicine, and therefore no wonder that it sometimes has very violent effects."[91] Claims about enslaved healers' imprecision in apportioning ingredients or doses provided a rationale for challenging healers' involvement in the making of remedies. Colonists operated on the premise that a good remedy or cure used colonists' points of reference.

A good plantation owner should "prescribe for his own negroes," Collins proclaimed.[92] Still, as much as proprietors and managers tried to impinge on healers' historical role, their efforts were never fully realized. In 1823, the enslaver and plantation management author Thomas Roughley stated the expectation that managers would mix and administer medicines. "An experienced ... overseer or book-keeper ... will perform cures in ordinary, simple cases, compound and administer the medicine to the afflicted and the sick," he wrote. In the same section, Roughley exhorted readers to exclude healers from these activities. "Of deleterious drugs they [healers] should never have the mixing up; and the utmost caution should be observed when they are allowed to administer any such." Written several decades after proprietors and managers had first begun to creep in on healers' territory, Roughley's descriptions reveal that proprietors and managers had been unsuccessful in displacing healers. Instead, they had to compete with them. "The hothouse or hospital doctoress ... midwives &c. ... in the course of the year ... [have] the whole proportion of the estate—white people, mixed, coloured, and black—under their care," Roughley complained.[93]

Although a gap remained between proprietors' fantasies and the reality on the ground, healers' working lives had changed. Proprietors had made sustained efforts to better systematize body management so as to streamline healing and anticipate the costs of medicine—its manufacture and administration. What types of work were healers supposed to perform amid this new world of standardized ingredients and mass medicines? Instead of acting as speaking agents who collaborated with managers to diagnose, select, and create, healers were now expected to act as mute extensions of managers' and doctors' own bodies—more specifically their ears and hands. They were supposed to exist on the receiving end of managers' and practitioners' instructions, to listen but not speak, administer managers' medicines to the sick, and hurry them back to work. This is probably how the surgeon testifying before Parliament imagined hospital healers' role when he described them as performing "all lesser matters related to the sick."

Putting Hands on the Sick

Managers and proprietors construed healers' work as unthinking physical drudgery. Yet healers put their hands and ears to many uses and would continue to employ a haptic and sensory epistemology to carry out their obligations. Although managers and proprietors focused on the administration of medicines, healers' responsibilities were far greater. The physical dimensions of healers' work included everything from myriad acts of carework to different forms of manhandling, restraining, and guarding. It also entailed observing and listening—not only in regard to the sick. They observed the conflicts, animosities, and affinities among different groups and individuals on the estate so that healers might know when they could intervene and push back. As discussed in chapter 1, plantation hospitals sat at the juncture between enslaved people's need for succor, rest, and sustenance, and managers' determination to use these buildings to control the movements of enslaved people and to enact exemplary punishment on men and women. Managers expected that healers would act as their proxies in exchange for additional resources and privileges. That belief created one possibility for how healers would use their hands—as individuals they would lift themselves up by holding others down. Simultaneously, healers used touch to articulate a different set of values—they expressed affinities in the provision of succor and care. Hospital and yaws-house nurses were in a wrenching position of trying to find a middle ground between the competing demands of managers and the sick. This physical and psychological pressure motivated healers to draw upon their ingenuity and their awareness of the estate's inner workings to try to preserve their own position while meeting the expectations of the people around them.

Healers felt the expansion in the size of sugar estates and changes in the larger Atlantic consumer economy most acutely in the administration of medicines. Healers were envisioned as mere ears and hands because proprietors were trying to provide medicine en masse, on some estates that held as many as five hundred men, women, and children in captivity. Hospital healers worked with many different ailments and administered many different remedies on any given day. To retain their positions and their power to intervene, healers learned to manage a great deal of information and the many commands directed at them. Some of these commands came from medical men who did not live on-site, and therefore were unavailable, but who would return to gauge the sick's progress or decline.

The number of prescriptions to administer, already quite extensive, became even more so as estates grew in size. Archival sources demonstrate how many patients a hospital healer had under their care on large-sized sugar plantations (those with more than 250 enslaved people). The amount of sickness varied according to the time of the year. Late summer and early fall were the unhealthiest periods of the year. There are two lists of the sick that survive from the Phillipsfield plantation in Jamaica. With 394 people held in captivity, it was one of the largest plantations on the island. There, two women ran the hot-house: Rachel, the hot-house doctress, age forty, and Princess, her assistant, age seventeen.[94] In June 1789, these two women juggled nearly thirty patients between them.[95] Their experience approximated that of another hospital healer, Hampton, who lived on Island, a medium-sized sugar plantation in Westmoreland, Jamaica. Owned by Joseph Foster Barham II, Island's enslaved population was half that of Phillipsfield's. Hampton would have contended with between twenty and thirty people in early June.[96] Out of the 402 enslaved men, women, and children on the Braco plantation in Jamaica, on average sixty-eight were in the yaws house or the hospital during June.[97] These were relatively healthy months. The sickly season of fall was far more difficult. Mesopotamia's hospital doctress sometimes had enslaved assistants, usually girls younger than fourteen or older women. But the work was always burdensome: in October 1793, the hospital healer Quasheba contended with between sixty and eighty enslaved people in the hospital with assistance from Horsley and Graham.[98] There were far more patients to attend now that estates were larger. Hospital healing represented a considerable increase in healers' work.

Healers administered medicines in several stages. To recover someone from illness, one had to continually attend to them and adapt to their changing condition. Colonists maintained that illnesses contained different phases—each with its own distinct set of symptoms. Diseases were "constantly shifting ... requiring the trained physician to constantly adjust his diagnosis and treatment," as Randall Packard writes.[99] It is true that estates began to consume manufactured pharmaceuticals that promised to relieve sufferers of particular diseases. Yet these medicines were sometimes also used with other therapeutic remedies. There were pills, boluses, ointments, oils, and dietary soups to administer at different phases of an illness.[100] Additionally, managers placed the patients with many different types of illness in hospitals. Hospital healers therefore had to apply different remedies to different individuals.

Medical men and managers often delivered their instructions out loud. J. B. Moreton, a visitor to Jamaica who sought to reform the practice of slavery in the island, took note of medical care on estates. The overseer "*reads* back to some old black man or woman" from the hot-house book, Moreton wrote disapprovingly.[101] The "apprentice boy," the absentee slaveholder William Vassall complained, did not record his prescriptions but only "*tells* the hot-house woman" what to administer.[102] These critics scoffed at the verbal transmission of information—they believed that these verbal exchanges accounted for the many errors and inefficiencies of plantation hospitals. Nonetheless, healers learned to absorb the instructions they received. To assist their memory, healers probably drew from a range of verbal traditions that prioritized sound over the written word. Speech was an important component of ritual work among Africans and Afro-Caribbean people, especially in communal settings.[103]

Healers also applied old haptic techniques to new challenges—they used their bodies to encode information about who would receive what remedy and to make these directives easily retrievable. The attorney John Johnson observed one such technique at work. As the overseer transferred the medicines and explained who was to receive what, Johnson reported that the healer "places each packet between several of her fingers, each of which it is to be presumed represents in her mind the patients to whom they are to be administered."[104] As Pablo Gómez has shown, enslaved people in the seventeenth-century Spanish Caribbean maintained a sensory epistemology that saw the natural world as populated by "numinous entities" that were perceivable by taste, smell, sight, and sound. Johnson distrusted the tactile nature of this mnemonic device. But for the enslaved women themselves, it was probably an adaptation of a way of knowing the natural world that they had developed outside of the hospital. Johnson proposed a method that prioritized spatial relationships instead; the overseer would place the medicines "in such order on the spot as to preclude the possibility of an error."[105] These mnemonic devices were important, and yet managers and doctors did not see that this memorization and deciphering were evidence of healers' ingenuity. These groups valued obedience and loyalty over intellect. They expected healers to act as their hands, while transforming the sick into unwilling consumers of the compound remedies that managers and proprietors selected.

Some of managers' medicines, especially those for venereal disease, could be dangerous and disfiguring. At the very least, they were deeply unpleasant. Through their discussions with proprietors and in recipe exchange networks, managers claimed an in-depth understanding of the materials inside these remedies. Healers were probably more aware than managers of the effects of these compound remedies, because they had long-standing experience with them, sometimes as both sufferers and hospital attendants. Many healers may have been especially reluctant to enforce managers' remedies for venereal disease and yaws on their patients. Colonists' remedies for venereal disease were particularly gruesome. Early modern people maintained what Kevin Siena has described as a unicist view of venereal disease; they did not draw sharp distinctions between gonorrhea (clap) and syphilis (pox). Instead, they maintained that these two terms described distinctive stages of venereal disease, which began with clap, and if not treated properly, matured into pox.[106] Because one had to expel the poisons that caused gonorrhea before the sufferer became syphilitic, the medicines and therapies that colonists applied to venereal disease were far more violent than those for other ailments.

Patients and practitioners treating venereal disease sought combinations of treatments; through the body's discharges and excretions (such as salivation), these treatments would "flux" the morbid matter out of the body.[107] Although they disputed what drugs would best promote evacuations, most eighteenth-century British people discussing venereal disease agreed that some quantity of mercury, or mercurial salivations, was necessary. Regimes of salivation typically lasted from a month to a month and a half.[108] People undergoing a mercurial salivation for venereal disease "spit several pints per day."[109] While the application of mercury took many forms, it nearly always involved mercurial pills. In more advanced stages of the disease, sufferers applied ointments and rubs to their genitals and elsewhere. Usually patients were counseled to take additional medicines—these were intended to dampen mercury's side effects or prime the sick for their entry into the mercury regimen. Other medicines eased their transition out of it.[110]

Anyone taking mercury medicines would need to ready themselves for a wrenching ordeal. In 1770, Thistlewood gave mercury pills to Phibba, his enslaved consort. They "made her sick & purged her much in the night."[111] Her unease did not end there. Mercury taken in significant amounts often caused internal poisoning, nausea, swollen gums, and loose teeth.[112] A week later, Phibba reported that the pills had made her mouth sore.[113]

Some healers at Mesopotamia had themselves been subjected to remedies for yaws and venereal disease earlier in their lives. Managers may have operated under the assumption that such experiences would make healers more familiar with the administration and effects of mercurial and botanical remedies. Kickery had survived venereal disease and had probably been subjected to repeated rounds of mercurial medicines that Mesopotamia's managers imposed on her.[114] She may well have been reluctant, therefore, to force mercury pills on other members of the estate who were in her immediate social circles, especially those she had known since her childhood.

But how far would she extend her compassion if it meant jeopardizing her own position? Under what circumstances did she refuse to carry out orders or impose a medicine? In 1786, when Kickery assisted Quasheba, the head doctress, in the hospital, Mesopotamia's attorneys purchased and brought to the estate some sixty-five newcomers from Three Mile River, a nearby sugar plantation. An enslaved woman, Marina, was part of this group. Marina was also afflicted with venereal disease. Managers noted in the inventory that Marina "was said to be diseased," a euphemism for a venereal affliction.[115] The passive voice cloaked a bricolage of people and things that had mediated Marina's experience of illness outside of managers' purview. The men and women who were displaced from Three Mile River along with her may have known about her condition beforehand. Marina and others may have sought out local remedies such as hog plum tree root that Marina or others sought out on her behalf, possibly in secrecy. The new men and women of Mesopotamia may have learned of her condition from her or another newcomer. But when Marina's condition became known to managers, what happened then? There are not any extent hospital records for Mesopotamia. Yet it may have been Kickery's or Quasheba's responsibility to administer remedies to Marina that had once robbed Kickery of her own strength.

Marina was a newcomer, so Kickery's dilemma might have been easier to bear. But when did a stranger become a foe, friend, or family member? And were those ties likely to be built inside the hospital or outside of it? Eight years after Marina came to Mesopotamia, she gave birth to a girl, Sarah.[116] Kickery, then Mesopotamia's oldest midwife, most likely attended Marina in childbirth, possibly with assistance from Cretia.[117] That same year, Marina was thirty-one years old and also "learning to be a midwife," probably under Kickery.[118] Sometimes identification might be forged along the lines of gender, motherhood, and skill. But ethnicity, color, rank, as well as enslaved healers' own struggles to survive along thin margins could cut against any affinities that healers might form with the people under their supervision. As was the case with the relationship between Marina and Kickery, identification and enmity probably evolved as time passed and status changed. An enslaved healer might find herself administering unpleasant and unwelcome medicines in one season, deliberately forgetting to administer them at another time, and then working alongside that same person at another.

The expectation that healers would undermine the bodily autonomy of others undergirded the entire system of medicine that managers and proprietors were forging in the name of productivity. If the sick's resistance to alien medicines formed a choke point in practitioners' visiting circuits, then assigning healers to struggle with the sick allowed practitioners to move along to their next client that much sooner. As they galloped off to the next estate, practitioners left hospital nurses in their dust to absorb the sick's sour resentments.

Jonathan Troup recognized that his own comfort depended on this configuration of the physical, emotional, and interpretive labor on the plantations in his roster. One enslaved woman resisted his attempt to "bring off a stool." That same day, Troup declared (privately, in the pages of his diary) that administering medicines was beneath him. "It detracts from a man's character. The patient says give me this & this damned stuff," he seethed.[119] Troup also understood that distancing himself from coercing the sick might help him to retain his position. "The negroes in general are remarkably sensible and if you are successful they will sound your praise give them little pain," Troup recorded in his diary.[120] "Hence forth to give no medicine by myself but always make the nurses do it," he declared.[121] He wriggled out of direct responsibility by compelling healers to coerce his patients. Practitioners cast a skeptical eye on healers' independence in the *preparation* of medicines. But they welcomed an arrangement that saw healers *administering* medicines to patients, since this allowed practitioners to position themselves as figures of benevolence.

Healers often impeded the administration of dangerous and enfeebling medicines that managers or practitioners ordered, even though this carried the threat of punishment. Healers' obstructions, particularly in the administration of yaws and venereal disease remedies, arose from deeper conflicts between managers and healers over enslaved people's safety and long-term health. Such disputes arose from oppositional time-horizons. Managers thought in the short term: they wanted to get people back to work. In pursuit of that end, many espoused medicines for yaws that seemed to rid sufferers of the disease but that had secondary effects that were dangerous and enfeebling. Healers worked with managers to recuperate the sick from illness. But as enslaved people, healers understood that health was a precious resource necessary to combat the alienation that sat at the heart of slavery. Health secured futurity. The health of the individual ensured one's long-term survival and was also crucial to ensure the survival of one's family. A healthy woman bore children who stood a chance of surviving infancy and childhood. Healthy adults possessed the strength to amass dietary resources and material wealth (from their provision grounds) that they could share with other family members. Healers had firsthand experience with managers' medicines for yaws and venereal disease. They undoubtedly knew that many remedies celebrated for their capacity to engender quick recovery potentially sapped the health of the afflicted over the long term. The therapies that the two groups espoused reflected their different priorities—and the risks they were willing to achieve them.

Overseers, proprietors, and attorneys recognized that healers commonly obstructed them or refused to carry out their demands. Collins recommended mixing mercury with corrosive sublimate and rum and giving it by the tablespoon each night as a cure for yaws. He warned, however, that managers would need be involved. "When you attempt the disorder in that way," he wrote in his advice text, "it is necessary that you should devote a good deal of attention to it yourself, as you cannot safely trust the conduct of the process to your negroe nurse." William Beckford, the historian of Jamaica, lamented that practitioners did not have a "more controlling power over the hospital nurses." When John Johnson visited the Sanderson sugar plantation in Antigua, he noted the "want of attention in administering medicine." Since healers were sometimes cut out of determining what went into remedies, they tried to assist in other ways. By interrupting the administration of medicines, they tried to protect the sick from further harm.[122]

Without a doubt, hot-house and yaws-house attendants forgot steps, reversed their order, or did not act with the haste expected of them. Hospital healing made demands that everyone struggled to meet. However, colonists were probably not far off the mark in suspecting that healers' failure to follow directions to the letter were an expression of deeper opposition to managers' and practitioners' claims on the sick's time and health. The slaveholder Samuel Cary, for instance, stressed that his overseers needed to "oblige the nurses to do their duty and see that the doctor's orders are punctually observed."[123] Cary's stipulation suggests that nurses, managers, and doctors fought over the timely administration of medicine. As an attorney and a plantation owner, Cary probably had his own expectations about the amount of time it took his or others' remedies to achieve their intended effects for particular afflictions. Yet healers might have deliberately delayed giving enfeebling remedies or skipped them altogether in order to give the sick more time to recover and to create the circumstances for the sick to retain their health by regaining their strength from diet and rest alone. Proprietors and attorneys erected plantation hospitals to engender greater efficiencies in the management of illness. But by refusing to administer medicines as demanded, healers created frictions in the system of producing bodies capable for work.

Healers understood that managers characterized them as inept and imprecise. They knew that they would shoulder the blame for this system's malfunctions, regardless of how well or earnestly they executed others' demands. By absorbing liability for the larger failures of this system, they maintained the appearance of trying their best; at the same time, they worked covertly to combat the ways that the production needs of the cultivation schedule subordinated enslaved people's health. Their refusal to carry out managers' directions probably also reflected more immediate concerns. Healers took pride in their knowledge—technical, physical, social, and affective—that drew from their connections to others, their knowledge of the local environment, and their assessments of managers' medicines, which they refused to sell short. They hoped to reclaim a sphere of power that managers had taken from them and earn the trust of sufferers. Healers understood that their ability to elicit deference from other enslaved people hinged on their ability to intervene on sufferers' behalf. Sometimes that took shape in challenging overseers' orders directly. At other times, healers quietly forgot or delayed administering remedies on sufferers who did not want them.

Occasions for the expression of solidarity occurred in other types of physical carework that colonists characterized as unskilled. Much of healers' daily labor took the form of what historians of medicine refer to as bodywork—feeding, watching, cleaning, and attending the sick.[124] Historians of medicine have shown that bodywork was the heart of early modern medicine. Recent studies reveal the politics of bodywork. Sasha Turner's examination of the "reproductive bodywork" carried out by midwives reveals how activities that readied parturient women for labor were a means to combat the threat of isolation and alienation that accompanied the treatment of enslaved women and their children as commodities and chattels.[125] We might examine what bodywork meant in a context when managers sometimes humiliated the sick as a strategy to discourage the sick from seeking relief. In this context, healers' drudgery could also operate as an act of affinity and concern. Through carework, healers affirmed that sufferers were not just their work responsibilities but rather people worthy of attention.

Healers cleaned the sick and sometimes collected and cleaned their undergarments.[126] In his discussion of what a hospital should contain,

Collins directed blankets "large enough to lie upon, and to wrap round the body," that could be "freed from their dirt by washing," as well as bed pans "for such negroes are too weak to rise from the board to ease themselves, and also for the use of dysenteric patients, who, when perspiring, ought not to go to the privy."[127] The medicines that estates forced upon the sick were often a mixture of emetics, expectorants, and purgatives that encouraged the body to expel various fluids—vomit, stools, urine, sweat, or menses.[128] "Good medicine," as Mary Fissell writes, "was expectorant: it involved provoking the body to heal itself often by expulsive means that required a great deal of intimate bodily care."[129] The enslaver Henry Barham endorsed the elder-shrub plant in the treatment of venereal disease because it "brought away such a quantity of slime and urine it was incredible."[130] As Sharla Fett has pointed out, healers' proximity to the body's various excretions designated such work as manual and menial labor.[131]

For healers and the sick, cleaning could also be an act of opposition. Healers cleaned, wiped up, and restored the sick's dignity even as overseers routinely laid assault to it. There was, already, much to wipe up and absorb, but the amount was made even greater by managers' use of the hospital as places of punishment and humiliation. Charlotte, the enslaved woman in Berbice introduced in chapter 1, urinated in her hospital bed because the overseer, Hockin, had shackled her to the bed. Elias, the healer, could not release Charlotte from the bedstocks because Hockin kept the key. When she soiled her bed and clothes out of desperation, what Elias could do was to clean her, as best he could, so as to combat Hockin's dehumanization of Charlotte and restore her dignity. Although such tasks seem mundane and self-explanatory, wiping, drying, and cleaning were profound gestures. Enslaved people reclaimed their bodies against overseers' assaults on their physical person by bathing and pursuing other pleasures. They affirmed that their bodies were not just for work and ultimately belonged only to themselves.[132] Under the circumstances like the ones Hockin imposed, anything enslaved people could do to clean one another reasserted their humanity.

Outside of hospitals, bodywork's burdens were often distributed across different members of the community. In an era when homes were heated by firewood and most water had to be fetched from a stream or well, cutting wood, hauling water, and emptying privy pans were significant components of carework. Family and neighbors almost certainly helped in the recovery of the sick—sometimes watching and attending. They may have also prepared hearty soups composed of foodstuffs grown on their provision grounds and in small gardens adjacent to their individual cabins. Enslaved people were just one hurricane or drought away from serious privation, and this type of provision was a potent gesture of affinity. The collective nature of healing outside of plantation hospitals—its social as well as therapeutic dimensions—gave people engaged in bodywork a means to repudiate managers' contention that illness primarily meant the inability to work. Working to keep the sick clean, comfortable, and fed, enslaved people tried to ameliorate unease and relieve suffering rather than treat bodily deterioration as the depreciation of capital held in human flesh. The displacement of the sick and infirm from webs of assistance and their placement in hospitals magnified, however, the burdens of carework and made it more impersonal. In 1785, when Kickery was Mesopotamia's doctress, the enslaver Barham held 305 enslaved people in bondage. That same year, sixty-five of the enslaved people on Mesopotamia were recent arrivals from other estates in the vicinity, total strangers to Kickery.[133]

The impersonal nature of this office may have made it easier for healers to use their hands to hold people down. Hospitals could quickly become sites of unruliness and unrest. In hospitals and yaws houses, enslaved people could not choose with whom they convalesced or who cared for them. Consequently, new disputes erupted and old conflicts came back to life among sufferers inside these buildings. At the outbreak of these fights, the control of combatants devolved, initially, onto the healer. Chapter 1 reconstructed a verbal conflict that became physical between two women patients in a hospital in Demerara. As the fracas escalated, Elias, the hospital healer, tried to physically subdue one of the women and pin her to the ground. Elias could not control her. Eventually, the overseer arrived with three other enslaved men. The four of them dragged the woman to the dungeon, shackling her so as to keep her in solitary confinement.[134] Managers hoped healers would command deference, but sometimes healers relied instead on their physical strength.

Healers sometimes used their hands to push the sick away. Just as they had to make difficult decisions about when to impose managers' medicines on the sick, healers working under the thumb of managers also might determine when the sufferers would be admitted into the hospital. At the hospital's threshold, life, death, and affinity were at stake. On the Canefield plantation in Dominica, an enslaved man tried to convince "the sick nurse[,] a mullattoe [sic] woman," that he was too weak to work. The plantation surgeon Jonathan Troup recounted that the woman "told this negro he was shamming... against his assertions to the contrary [she] would have him sent to the field & that too [sic] do the hardest work of digging and holing the earth." Canefield's overseer "saw [that] he was unequal to the task," but he decided to lighten his load rather than offer him vital rest. He "sent him up to a cane piece to weed which was much easier employment." Within a few hours, the man collapsed and expired. A group of men and women saw that "he was carried home dead to the mullattoe nurse."[135] The overseer was just as culpable in the man's death as the sick-nurse. But the men and women did not feel that they could or perhaps should hold the overseer accountable. Instead, they tried to prick the sick-nurse's conscience and make clear that she had betrayed their expectations of solidarity. The Canefield nurse's actions, and her status as a mixed-race person, are suggestive of the range of political actions that hospital nurses could pursue. As much as they could use touch to create solidarities across social divisions, healers sometimes used their position to reinforce status differences based on rank, race, and lineage.

The status of the woman in Troup's account as mixed-race suggests the type of people who held the office of hospital healer as well as the meaning of the office itself. On many estates, people of mixed-race heritage held positions of privilege. We need to ask whether the woman's mixed-race identity meant that hospital healing was a station of privilege, one typically occupied exclusively by members of the enslaved elite.

The adjective "privileged" is a capacious designation that scholars use to denote the people who performed various types of work and, in turn, the stations that allowed the people who held them to amass material wealth, gain greater access to resources, social standing, and superior health. Since field work hastened people into infirmity or the grave faster than other positions, enslaved people who did not labor in the fields enjoyed greater health relative to others on the estate, and scholars have considered them privileged. Typically, privileged groups engaged in non–field work in the prime of their adulthoods. Some enslaved people in roles of privilege, such as drivers, had worked in the field but then ascended into a supervisory role that gave them decision-making power over others.[136] A position of privilege created reserves of energy that people used to engage in petty economic activities. They might, for instance, cultivate excess provisions for market. Such advantages helped these individuals to acquire wealth and power over others. Positions of privilege also allowed the people who held them, and often their descendants, to live longer, healthier lives: they had reduced workloads and access to more material goods that enabled survival. People who held positions of privilege therefore constituted the enslaved elite. Managers believed that privileged enslaved people placed their own interests above collective action and were therefore less inclined to join rebellions.[137]

Who tended to hold these positions? On many plantations, women who formed romantic partnerships with white managerial staff and the children produced from these unions acquired positions of privilege. Others were Creoles, people born on the plantation or who had grown up on the estate. Still others, such as drivers, came into these positions as a consequence of their reputations and leadership abilities.[138] The status of the hospital nurse at Canefield as mixed-race suggests the possibility that the office of hospital nurse was considered a privileged station. Possibly the woman who held it was part of the estate's elite.

Was healing work privileged work? Hospital and yaws healing falls under the category of work that many would describe as "socially reproductive labor," such as cooking, sewing, laundering, nursing children, gardening, and the tending to small livestock, such as chickens. This type of work helped plantations "meet their basic biological needs."[139] Some historians have described this as "marginal" work in the sense that this type of work was not as important to slaveholders as cane cultivation.[140] It also tended to be performed by elderly enslaved women who could no longer endure field work. Hospital and yaws healing held much in common with other forms of socially reproductive or marginal labor. The people who held these roles typically aged into them, weakened by field work.

Yet it was also distinct. Healers' position required them to communicate across the lines of rank and race, to amass information about the medicinal attributes of local flora and fauna, and to develop a working familiarity with the estate's people and their afflictions. All the while, they acted in a position of power over others. In some ways, hospital nurses' position as people working to meet the competing expectations of other enslaved men and women and enslavers bore similarities to the dilemma of enslaved drivers. Drivers were men (and a few women) who supervised enslaved workers in the field and used violence to extract greater work from them on behalf of managers and proprietors. Healers did not use violence to extract greater work from men and women. But they sometimes used their strength to keep sick-houses as places of order. Moreover, healing was distinctive from driving in that healers had seen their historical roles transform over time. Driving had been at the heart of the integrated sugar plantation since its inception in the seventeenth century.[141] Although managers had always envisioned healers as restoring the sick for work, historically managers had exercised little control over the administration of medicines and care before the mid-eighteenth century. Then, as managers and proprietors tried to appropriate healers' knowledge and authority for their own ends, they positioned healers as overseers' and doctors' proxies.

Thus, healing was distinct from other types of marginal work that women performed in that healers wielded power over others in the service of producing wealth for proprietors. In judging who was too sick for work, healers controlled access to precious resources, not managers' medicines, but rest and dietary provisions for the sick. They were expected to impose violent medicines onto the sick in accordance with managers' demands. They monitored who went in and out of the building and kept patients admitted confined. The position required a great deal of physical strength, not only in caring for but in disciplining the sick—as healers sometimes broke up fights or assisted in keeping the punished locked up and confined. Much of healers' work served managers' broader goals: to cut down on the costs of production and to recover sufferers from illness within managers' time-horizons. Healers continued to understand their role as affirming men's and women's humanity and provisioning comfort. Yet in the era of improvement, they were also charged with working alongside doctors and managers.

The nature of the office meant that the people who were appointed to it needed to be those whom others held in high esteem. Plantation management authors, such as Collins, explained that a healer could only execute her responsibilities insofar as she could gain sufferers' assent. He cautioned managers from using people who were "superannuated" and "infirm." A person who was very old and very enfeebled "has no authority over the negroes, will often have her orders disputed, and, being rather afraid of them, than they of her, she will wink at their irregularities, rather than provoke their resentment." Healers, as Collins summarized, had to "command the respect of the sick and to insure their obedience."[142] For Collins, a healer whose authority was weak would undermine managers' efforts to impose new, efficacious remedies. But for healers, the absence of respect posed a different problem. They could only keep their office and maintain their credibility with managers insofar as they could elicit deference from others. That required gaining sufferers' confidence that healers would do their best to keep the sick safe and that they could rely on managers and other enslaved people to back them up in moments of conflict. Managers did not treat hospital healing as skilled, thinking work. Nevertheless, they recognized that the people they appointed as healers would need to be people with considerable authority that they would co-opt and redirect.

Knowledge, Respect, and Senescence

WHAT TYPES of people did managers appoint as healers? Some authors counseled managers to choose men for this position. James Grainger recommended replacing women who were "so old that they cannot take proper care of the sick" with men who were "strong, sensible, and sober."[143] Roughley proclaimed that he would "prefer a male to a female attending the hospital."[144] These writers advised slaveholders on the basis of gendered assumptions about the type of power necessary to mediate social conflict. They may also have been thinking about the physical demands of healing on large sugar plantations, where the number of the sick exceeded what an elderly person could manage. Managers and proprietors also struggled to accept women operating in a role that involved power over others, whether as drivers or healers.[145]

But not all colonists believed physical force was necessary to secure deference. Collins acknowledged that the selection of people who had the "experience of age" was useful, since this group tended to be less reactionary and emotional. Managers and proprietors did not select enslaved people for healing offices on the basis of certain skills or medicinal knowledges alone, though this was clearly important. They also identified people with certain characteristics as suitable for this position. "There must be sobriety, somewhat of feeling, principle, strength, and respectability of character," in the person selected for hospital healing.[146]

The most important characteristic for healers was prior familiarity among managers and other enslaved people on the estate, which meant that most healers were people of advanced age. Indeed, age and experience on the estate often went hand in hand. The relationship between the two is evident in biographies of the people who became hospital or yaws-house healers on the Mesopotamia. Between 1762 and 1811, Mesopotamia's hospital had four different hospital healers in succession—Warwick, Parthenia, Kickery, and Quasheba. Kickery worked primarily as a midwife, though she also operated as the hospital healer for two years. During these same years, there were three yaws-house healers: Suckey, Augustine, and Lydia. None of the healers began their working lives in the hospital or yaws house. Most of them were in their late thirties to early forties when they were placed in their stations.[147]

The limitations of Mesopotamia's records make it impossible to identify all of the healers' places of birth. Yet the people who staffed Mesopotamia's hospital had grown up on the estate. There is a strong possibility that Warwick was born on Mesopotamia. In 1751, the estate's attorney listed him as a boy. When Warwick died at approximately fifty years old, he had passed all of his adult life on Mesopotamia. Roughly the same age as Warwick, Parthenia had gone through the transition from adolescence to adulthood with him on Mesopotamia. Kickery had been born on the estate, and Quasheba almost certainly did as well.[148] The place of origin of the three yaws-house women varied. Because Mesopotamia's inventories did not begin to record births until 1774, we cannot identify Suckey's place of birth or parentage. Augustine was part of a group of people whom Mesopotamia's proprietor-enslaver, Joseph Barham, had purchased and displaced from Three Mile River. Lydia had been born in Africa.[149] All of these individuals were clearly known to many on the plantation, since all of them had passed through either their adolescence or early adulthoods on the estate.

Long-standing ties to a particular estate was a common trait among healers. One colonist described an enslaved man (originally from Africa) under his care who was also a yaws healer and had learned of a treatment for yaws "in their own country." The colonist observed that the healer had "lived many years upon the estate."[150] The Kingston physician Thomas Dancer described Thomas Fuller, his patient and an enslaved man, as "between fifty and sixty years of age ... a creole (that is[,] one born in the West Indies)." Fuller had worked, Dancer remarked, "many years a hot-house doctor, that is, an attendant on the sick in the plantation hospital."[151] Some absentees were involved in determining who would be a hospital healer, which suggests the importance of a personal relationship formed over many years. The absentee James Chisholme decided who would become Trout Hall's hospital doctor. He prioritized familiarity and experience over strength. When his attorneys informed Chisholme that the "constitution" of a man named Chamba Tom's "won't do for a cooper [a barrel maker]," the absentee directed his attorney to station Tom in the hot-house. "He used to be," Chisholme relayed, "a very steady fellow and I dare say he will make a good doctor."[152]

In their formal assessments of most enslaved people's value, health and youth held great importance for managers and proprietors. These features typically indicated a person's capacity to produce sugar and wealth for others. According to this system of valuation, healers' advanced age rendered them of little worth because they were too weak to work in the field. Yet a person both gained and lost value as they aged. Colonists and enslaved people considered enslaved men and women who reached their forties and fifties to be old.[153] Old age was, therefore, rare enough that the people who survived to that point had experience on the estate that was extremely valuable in its own right.

Such value could not be measured by the number of cane stalks cut. Healers had instead amassed specific knowledges and skills necessary for success in this station over the span of their lives. A person engaged in healing needed a deep understanding of the social relationships, animosities, and hierarchies within the enslaved community and among its managers. Healers had to keep the sick in line and negotiate with managers about their admission, therapies, and length of stay. Their value to managers and other men and women lay in the advantages and wisdom that inhered in old age.

Healers also drew on their botanical knowledge, having engaged with the local environment over the long term. Hospital doctresses and yaws-house attendants did not immediately learn how to heal upon their appointment. Instead, over the course of their lifetimes, they gathered information about the preparation of poultices, herbal baths, and dietary drinks; mastered the cultivation of healing herbs in provision grounds and kitchen gardens; learned where in the savannas and wetlands to locate ingredients for different remedies. On Breadnut Island Pen, a provisions and livestock estate in Westmoreland, Jamaica, for example, Nanny frequently dressed the feet of people afflicted with what was called crab yaws.[154] She probably inspected the feet of family and neighbors for "chigoes" (chiggers), a burrowing insect; removed them with the point of a knife; and applied a greasy substance where the skin had been punctured in order to protect the wound.[155] For many enslaved, healing entailed identifying plants in the local environment that had properties equivalent to the materials in Africa or one's place of origin.[156] As most enslaved populations struggled to reproduce themselves, this type of know-how came to healers through their social networks. Nanny came by much of her knowledge from firsthand experience and her connections to others. Women like her learned how to heal as either mothers themselves or in their role as someone's daughter, niece, or friend.

As both managers and enslaved people well understood, healing knowledge and authority was not just medical and environmental but also social. Aisha Finch has recently argued that awareness of the social sphere, its ruptures and frictions, formed important components of enslaved women's political life.[157] Enslaved healers on Mesopotamia and elsewhere amassed knowledge of the social, institutional, and natural world over the course of their lifetimes. The decisions that Mesopotamia's healers made were informed by their awareness of different personalities and personae they would need to adopt to establish credibility with managers, and their assessment of the relationships between other enslaved men and women on the estate.

Yet given that hospital and yaws-house healing often entailed acting in concert with managers as much as opposing them, what reasons did healers have for occupying these stations? There is no question that healers sympathized with the sick. And yet managers had many levers to pull in order to ensure that healers carried out orders as given. Quite often the conditions of slavery—the sheer difficulty of surviving and creating families—incentivized healers to act on the estate's behalf in order to keep an office with privileges attached to it.

The threat of being moved back into field work discouraged healers from openly subverting managers' demands, aligning with others, or using the office in ways that went against its purpose. In one instance from the second decade of the nineteenth century, the overseer of another estate named Canefield accused Philip, the hospital healer, of drunkenness. The overseer punished Philip by putting him in the stocks for four days. Then the overseer demoted Philip. "I am taken out," Philip explained, "of the hospital as sick-nurse, and put to work with the carpenters." When the overseer accused Philip of lingering on an errand, he punished him by sending him into the field. Both changes of station saddled Philip with drudgery and physical demands that he insisted were not his to bear. It was a circumstance that Philip "objected to, being the sick-nurse."[158] He sought assistance from the colony's protectorate to ensure that his demotion was not permanent.

Many, if not most, hospital healers and yaws attendants had spent the prime of their adulthoods in the field, and their poor health and the sheer difficulty of surviving incentivized them to remain out of the field once placed elsewhere. The working lives of the hospital and yaws-house healers at Mesopotamia, for example, reveal that the people who occupied these stations were like the majority of enslaved people on sugar estates—they did not start out in stations of privilege. Instead, they had followed the typical cycle of most enslaved people, which put them in poor health. Enslaved people on sugar estates passed through a work cycle that consisted of at least three phases, the first of which began in childhood, as early as age six.[159] By their early adolescence, men and women began the second phase of the work cycle and moved into their primary working positions. For most enslaved people, their primary occupation was in the field, which robbed them of their strength and health.[160] When they could no longer endure their primary jobs, men and women (if they survived) passed into a tertiary position that was less physically demanding. The trajectories for men and women after the field were different. For most of the enslaved women, managers sought to wrench additional value from them by placing them in marginal work where they helped keep an estate's people cleaned, nursed, and fed.[161]

That was certainly the case on Mesopotamia. All of the women who worked in the hospital and yaws house came to it by way of the field, many of them weakened by it. Quasheba and Kickery had been in the field since adolescence. We can learn from Mesopotamia's inventories that Parthenia had been in field work since her twenties; almost certainly she began in her early adolescence.[162] Quasheba and Parthenia were appointed hospital healers (and left the field) in their early forties.[163] Kickery became a midwife in her late thirties. Most of the midwives left the field in their thirties, suggesting that midwifery was treated as skilled work on Mesopotamia.[164] The picture of Warwick's working life is murky—because Mesopotamia's inventories did not begin recording station until 1762, it is impossible to say whether Warwick was in the field prior to the hospital or was a healer from his adolescence onward. Many hospital workers began in poor health—both Warwick and Parthenia were listed as infirm, and the attorneys described Kickery as suffering from venereal disease.[165] Quasheba, however, remained healthy for much of her time in the field and the hospital.

Mesopotamia's yaws-house attendants had similar stories. They had spent their adolescence and early adulthood in the field.[166] For the yaws-house healers, this position was often their third station in their adulthood. It usually followed a less isolated position, most often in domestic work. Prior to Lydia's time in the yaws house, for example, she had been stationed at the estate's chapel, presumably attending its missionaries. Suckey had been at the fowl house and the slave quarters, where she recuperated from a lingering illness. Managers had moved Augustine between the stations of field cook and children's driver.[167] The people conscripted into this office were in an even poorer state of health than were the hospital healers. Everyone who served in the yaws house had been sick or an invalid for many years prior to their appointment. On average, a yaws-house attendant remained in that station for a mere four years. The yaws-house station was their last working station—they died or became too infirm to work thereafter.[168]

The enslaved women healers on Mesopotamia were like other women across the plantation Caribbean. They were subjected to a double burden—compelled to bear children while engaging in physically demanding and enfeebling work. Then, in the second half of the eighteenth century, women on sugar estates shouldered the burdens of field work so that enslaved men could progress. During this period, proprietors sought to reduce the costs of production and increase the wealth they held in enslaved people by diversifying the types of work that men performed.[169] Managers took enslaved men out of the field and put them into apprenticeships where they learned specific trades. Enslaved men became carpenters, masons, boilers, and coopers.[170] Men entered apprenticeships (and left the field) when they reached their thirties, whereas women toiled in fields well into their forties.[171] Men in skilled work obtained the material advantages of nonfield work in their prime adult years. Labor diversification, in sum, created sizeable numbers of enslaved women who had spent a decade longer in the field than men. Healers' health was significantly compromised by the age of forty—a result of their extended time planting, slashing, and hauling cane.[172]

Mesopotamia's women belonged to the cohort that saw gendered divisions in health magnified by labor diversification. Their creaking joints, strained tendons, angry scars, and aching backs were painful reminders that women bore the brunt of labor diversification and that herbal and surgical know-how offered no security from the hardship and exhaustion associated with the field. Instead, they spent their adolescence and young adulthoods in the field alongside men. Yet some men left early to learn trades. By the time both groups reached the fourth decade of their lives, wearied women healers tended to these men of privilege (and everyone else on the estate) during their illnesses.

By the time she reached the hospital at nearly forty, Quasheba had experienced multiple illnesses and had borne witness to sickness and death among legions of friends, antagonists, and kin. During her adolescence and early adulthood, she had seen epidemic diseases such as smallpox, tuberculosis, and measles as well as endemic afflictions such as yaws cut down friends and foes. If she was not stricken by dysentery or another gastrointestinal disease during the sickly and wet seasons of the year, she must have watched in horror as other members of her gang fled to the bushes and then limped to the hospital as these ailments liquefied their insides.[173] She understood that as a field worker, backbreaking work, inadequate sustenance, and violent physical attacks as punishment increased her chances of becoming sick and could make ordinary illnesses fatal. Life for sugar workers was fragile. Quasheba watched Mesopotamia's managers purchase scores of African captives to replace friends, loved ones, and rivals lost to death. Over the course of her long life, Quasheba experienced illnesses in common with other enslaved people.

She also formed family bonds and her own circles of affinity. She understood how fragile those bonds were and how slavery could easily threaten her family's survival. Among the 1,103 slaves who resided on Mesopotamia between 1762 and 1833, 20 percent died before the age of sixteen.[174] As she watched drivers, skilled tradesmen, and women of mixed-race form families, acquire wealth, and sustain health, Quasheba learned an important lesson: material resources were necessary to ward off an early death and to protect the integrity of family units. Slavery subjected men and women to premature death, threatening survivors with social isolation and alienation that accompanied such a brutal existence. Survival motivated healers to oblige managers' demands.

The additional rations that managers gave to hospital healers made this office distinctive from other positions that women occupied after they left the field. Quasheba, for instance, enjoyed some advantages equivalent to those of privileged men. An 1802 inventory created by one of Mesopotamia's attorneys lists Quasheba as the recipient of a significant rum ration, just like other people of very high status and power. Quasheba was one of eleven enslaved people out of the 214 adults on Mesopotamia who received a weekly rum ration. She was one of seven (including tradesmen) who received a quart of rations, the second-largest portion. Only Hector, Mesopotamia's head driver, received more than the other members of Quasheba's group. There was only one other woman on Mesopotamia who received a rum ration: Camilla, the driver of the children's (grass) gang. Camilla was, however, one of three people who received the smallest quantity of rum.[175] When Quasheba received her ration amid these privileged men, her status became visible to onlookers. Mesopotamia's managers and others elsewhere may have made it a policy to give healers rum rations alongside other people of high station, so as to secure healers' loyalty in exchange for these additional resources.[176]

Rations may have also incentivized healers in other ways too—to secure their children's survival. In 1802, Mesopotamia's attorneys distributed additional food rations to women with large numbers of children as well as elderly people who were not healthy and strong enough to tend to their own provision grounds. Quasheba also received them, and the amount that managers allocated for her was the second-highest amount of all the people given rations—forty plantains, one quart of oatmeal, and one quart of sugar each week.[177] If Quasheba sold her rum rations in exchange for provisions, she could have acquired additional dietary resources to offset the physical price that field work had extracted from her. The additional rations also probably helped Quasheba keep her children alive. Quasheba had four children: Sally, Bob, Bernard, and Claret. I have been able to determine that three of her children—Bob, Bernard, and Sally—survived into adulthood. (I have not been able to determine Claret's fate, as he was a child in 1811, the year this survey ends.) The rewards accorded to hospital healers were not as large as those that enslaved drivers received. But they still helped to secure futures, which was not otherwise possible for most mothers. Rum helped healers and their families numb their senses to the rigors of plantation life, while food helped them recover from the effects of the field and minimized dietary precariousness.

While it is difficult to draw a direct link between this incentive structure and healers' health, rations may have enabled healers to outlive other people on the estate and to remain in their secondary adult station for more extended periods of time than other women. Using what is known about the working lives of Kickery, Parthenia, and Quasheba, a healer had forty-seven working years on average. Twenty-two of these years they spent in a healing role.[178] For some it was not their final station in adulthood. When she was approximately fifty, Parthenia left the hospital to attend Old Primus.[179] When Primus died almost fifteen years later, Parthenia minded the poultry on Mesopotamia.[180] She remained in that station until 1801, when she could no longer work. She died in 1810, at around the age of seventy-five. Though she started at approximately the same age as the others, Quasheba endured longer than her predecessors, at least twenty-five years. Her tenure may have extended beyond 1811, the year when this survey of Mesopotamia's healers ends.[181] Quasheba lived until she was at least sixty. Kickery died at age sixty-three.[182] Warwick died in his station in his late forties.[183]

These were long lifespans for enslaved people generally. In his study of Mesopotamia, the historian Richard Dunn found striking distinctions between the life expectancies of drivers, field workers, domestics, and marginal workers. On average, female domestics (45.1) and field workers (44.9) died almost a decade sooner than male field workers (53.4). Male drivers, who died at age sixty-eight on average, outlived female domestics and field workers by over two decades. Female marginal workers (60.6) lived almost as long as drivers.[184] Hospital healers fell under the category of marginal worker. They did not experience any of the material advantages of privilege during the prime of their adulthoods. Yet once they occupied the office, healers received the vital rum and dietary rations that augmented their health, extended their longevity, and kept their families alive.

But appointing people to this position who were in advanced years would prove, for managers, a double-edged sword. The women and few men who became healers were often several decades older than the white men—whether bookkeepers, overseers, or doctors—who gave them marching orders. Healers' advanced years meant that they had developed an awareness of who was weak, who was powerful on the estate, and who could be manipulated.

Mesopotamia's healers had witnessed considerable managerial turnover. Plantation overseers came and went: some died, some broke with their employers, and some left in search of better salaries. Kickery, for example, had survived the arrival and departure of at least one overseer, Daniel Barnjum, as well as one doctor, Robert Pinkney.[185] Whether the new practitioner, John Horsley, would keep his post for many seasons was by no means assured. People like Kickery, consequentially, understood the animosities and affinities among the estate's white middling staff—its overseers, attorneys, and doctors—and the relations between managerial staff and other enslaved people on the estate. They could identify points of vulnerability and use that knowledge to map the social spheres where they lived. As figures of constancy on Mesopotamia, these healers had spent years assessing and deliberating the estate's multiple social relationships. On Mesopotamia, Kickery, Quasheba, Warwick, and Parthenia became faces of institutional continuity. They probably manipulated expectations about their age and experience to manage their relationships with the plantation's white staff as well as the sick. They would push to be met on their own terms.

Institutional memory was almost certainly relevant for helping healers negotiate the terms of their work. Kickery remembered that midwife and hospital doctress were separate offices and had been for several decades. It is possible that she was displeased about being asked to fulfill the demands of both. When Quasheba became hospital doctress in 1786 and thereby relieved Kickery of this double burden, perhaps Kickery had pressured Graham using her knowledge of the historical division of labor on the estate. But Graham seems to have pushed back. Kickery was "distempered and sickly," but Graham would not allow her to rest.[186] The first year that Quasheba was the hospital doctress, Kickery was assisting her there. Perhaps Quasheba had requested the additional assistance, or maybe Kickery insisted on supervising or helping Quasheba. Because they had grown up on Mesopotamia, hospital healers had deep and complicated relationships with its managers, which they used to negotiate the terms of their work.

Healers had helped to define the contours of the estate's social sphere over several generations. They had learned much of what they needed in the hospital outside of it. Like enslaved women healers in the nineteenth-century U.S. South, the hospital healers on Mesopotamia had learned how to engage in carework and medicine as they tended to siblings, raised their own families, and tended to the needs of other adults and children on the estate.[187] They also saw up close that carework mitigated the vulnerability of enslaved life and affirmed ties of affinity. They had spent years contesting power from a place of disempowerment: they had survived slavery and the strictures and demands of patriarchy. In their old age, they could readily identify who was in control, who could be pushed, and who would push back.

For healers as well as the sick, hospitals and yaws houses were sometimes sites of struggle. Both the people who put healers in hospitals and the people who worked in them sought to transform the balance of power. Healers did so carefully and as circumstances permitted. They may have been engaged in so-called marginal tasks. But they made the office one of the few places on the estate where such "marginal" people amassed the material privileges and social power associated with rank. At the same time, they also used this power to resist and repudiate slaveholders' treatment of the sick as insensate units of manpower.

THE WAYS that proprietors and managers responded to the challenges that arose from managing illness en masse fundamentally transformed the nature of healers' labor and threatened to alienate them from their work—to render them mere hands. Managers increasingly used remedies that were part of an expansive world of commercial pharmaceuticals and substances, operating on the premise that medicines could target specific diseases. Their remedies brought together ingredients from the farthest reaches of the British Empire and beyond. Laing's remedy contained old chemical and mineral standbys as well as ingredients, such as sarsaparilla and gum guaiacum, that were drawn from the storehouse of native and Afro-Caribbean medicine. Cope's contained sulfur mined in Saxony and senna pulled out of Egypt, among other local substances. Other slaveholders and colonists managing yaws and venereal disease would mix sublimated sulfur from Saxony with Barbados tar, a pitch from Barbados that was used as a balm.[188] Managers and proprietors stylized themselves as savvy consumers of a dazzling world of medical goods and information. They never granted to healers the authority to interpret and analyze so many local and Atlantic substances.

At first glance, it might appear that managers and proprietors were alone in acting on a global scale. But the integration of the plantation Caribbean into larger circuits of global capitalism also modernized enslaved people by placing men and women, as objects, as well as consumers and producers, at the center of global circuits of commodity consumption. Whether they collected a remedy off-site, put different ingredients together on the orders of someone else, or administered manufactured substances to the sick in significant numbers, healers remained at the center of managers' projects to make medicine more efficient. Their work now involved gaining sufferers' confidence that healers could decipher what was safe and what was dangerous in the substances they would force others to consume. In familiarizing themselves with the materials they would impose onto others, healers also became more worldly. They gained a savviness about the attributes of imported medicines and the points of vulnerability of the people prescribing them.

As they grew old, they also grew attuned to the ways that colonists made and sustained medical truth-claims about the efficaciousness and safety of different remedies and substances. That entailed becoming more aware of the figures of authority and substances that were meaningful to managers, doctors, and the sick. A healer who had reached their elder years could influence what the sick would consume. Not only by forgetting or refusing to administer remedies that others ordered but also by influencing what remedy a doctor or manager might reach for in moments of crisis. Through age and experience, healers assimilated what different audiences wanted to hear and which points of reference to invoke—their own experience, lore within the enslaved community, or managers' own traditions—in order to reassure sufferers and managers of their credibility.

For instance, enslaved people called the tall, verdant plant with white flowers that we know as sesame by many names. They termed it vanglo, wangla, whangla, wongola, wangle, oil-plant, and whangra.[189] They cultivated it in their gardens. They ground the seeds into a paste that resembled cornmeal.[190] The botanist Sir Hans Sloane noted that women took it as an emmenagogue, but they perhaps were using it as an abortifacient.[191] Some used it to cure intestinal distress. One tale saw an enslaved man named Edward venture into the woods at midnight to uproot an entire stalk. When he returned, he picked off its leaves, boiled them in an iron pot, and whispered mysterious words. He was not done. Next, he cut the root into three parts, gave each a Christian name, buried two outside the plantation's gates and burned the other. As soon as he did, Pickle, his brother-in-law, was seized with pain in his side and stumbled to the hospital—he later complained that Edward had used the plant's root to put a curse on him.[192] For Black Jamaicans, this plant could be many things in the course of a lifelong campaign to stay alive—sustenance, a means of controlling fertility, a medicine, and a weapon. Vernon, the enslaved healer on Dovehall plantation, was familiar with wangla. He almost certainly knew that the enslaved men and women on Dovehall used it for both ritual and therapeutic purposes. He may have also suspected that if the estate's new doctor, John Williamson, knew about its use in ritual contexts, that might discourage him from using it. Vernon understood that to convince Williamson to use it, he would need to restage the plant's meaning and emphasize its historical use by colonists.

Vernon, "the hospital negro doctor," had worked for many years amid the expectations of enslavers and the enslaved. He had cemented his utility to the estate's enslaved people and its managers by translating between the two groups, whose access to information was unequal. Both sides probably had questions about his trustworthiness, especially managers, who often suspected enslaved people of subterfuge as they tried to take greater control over what the enslaved sick would consume. By 1800, Vernon probably knew that different audiences wanted to hear different things, and he knew what to say to achieve his intended outcome. Thus, when Williamson became Dovehall's doctor and the two worked together to manage an outbreak of dysentery, Vernon exercised discretion. To bolster his credibility, Vernon used the right point of reference—not his own experience or that of other bondspeople. Instead, he cited Williamson's predecessor. "Vernon informed me . . . that he knew our predecessor, Dr. Thomson, use the wangla leaf in dysentery twenty years before," Williamson reported.[193] The mention of the time that had elapsed gestured to the duration of Vernon's experience—he had worked as a healer at Dovehall for two decades prior to Williamson's arrival. Vernon had seen enough to understand that young, male bookkeepers, overseers, and doctors were insecure about their status and that direct challenges to their authority could elicit violence. So perhaps Vernon's reference to Williamson's predecessor was an act of diplomacy. But this information might also have functioned as a subtle assertion. The healer was now the bearer of therapeutic memory on Dovehall. He knew what was safe, efficacious, readily available, and amenable to the sick. Williamson would have to work alongside not above him.

Colonists like Williamson would dismiss what healers like Vernon did as "lesser matters," but these people were engaged in greater matters than their managers were willing to admit. They acted as a consistent presence, gave care, weighed competing expectations, and found avenues to work around them. It can be easy to narrate healers' responses to historical changes in the organization of medicine as a story of complicity and opportunism—whereby men and women seized the opportunities that managers extended to them in exchange for their willingness to implement various forms of pharmacological and psychological violence. Another interpretation would see healers as victims, thrust into positions whose social stresses and strife outweighed the rewards.

Healers recognized that they could not determine entirely how hospitals and yaws houses would operate. Nor could they hold off the arrival and integration of imported chemical substances and pharmaceuticals. But they understood that their work and presence was crucial to the extension of dignity and care in these spaces. They knew as well that success in this position required a deep understanding of the social relationships, animosities, and hierarchies within the enslaved community and among its managers. Healers had to keep the sick in line and negotiate their admission, therapies, and duration of stay with managers. To do so, they worked with the advantages that inhered in old age. They drew on their institutional memory, their diplomatic sensibilities, their social connections to others, as well as their extensive botanical know-how. Healers maintained plantation medicine as a system of top-down body management that operated as a series of time-sensitive delegated tasks. In so doing, they retained some decision-making power over how those tasks would be executed. They helped preserve the dignity, health, and humanity of the sick in a space that was hostile to it.

4

Uncontrolled Experiments

AT THE height of antislavery sentiment and abolitionist pressure in the late eighteenth century, a chorus of West Indian writers called attention to the paltry intellectual output of plantation practitioners. More specifically, they noticed that they had yet to produce a corpus documenting the infectious diseases of the plantation complex that was equivalent, in scope and volume, to the texts on infectious fevers that had emerged in the previous fifty years from the hospitals of the armed forces. "We are," John Hunter, the expert on infectious fevers and surgeon-general of the army in Jamaica, wrote, "hitherto much in the dark respecting several disorders, that are in a great measure confined to the negroes."[1] Likewise, Alexander Anderson, the director of the Royal Botanical Garden in St. Vincent, bristled, "There are several common diseases in these islands, which the Drs know nothing of, moreover attempt to the care."[2]

Slaveholders piled on. In his advice intended to ameliorate the conditions of slavery, St. Vincent slaveholder and physician David Collins placed a slew of fever writers—"Town, Warren, Hillary, Bisset, Blane, Hunter, Mosely, Chisholme"—in the pantheon of West Indian scientific grandees.[3] But, he noted, their theories of contagion as well as their proposed modes of treatment and prevention about the "diseases of the climate are much more applicable to the condition of whites." For Collins, this asymmetry potentially qualified the gains made in the previous fifty years on the nature of infectious diseases in tropical climates. That was because white people, he explained, "have all the advantages of good nursing, lodging, and medical attendance, than do that [sic] of our slaves, who possess none of them, at least in equal degree."[4] More was needed, these writers explained, to understand how similarly infectious diseases prevailed among overworked and inadequately sustained bondspeople.[5]

It is not difficult to see how these writers arrived at this conclusion. The number of printed, book-length texts on, for example, yaws or other infectious ailments that debilitated and killed enslaved people because of overexposure, overwork, and inadequate sustenance could not compare to those produced on fevers and other infectious diseases associated with the sequestered spaces where infantry and sailors were housed and confined. By approximately 1770, Britain's war machine had produced a veritable cornucopia of texts that examined the origins and progress of infectious fevers.[6] These texts not only described the nature of the disease, but they also were brimming with empirical examples of its effects on different laboring populations, their symptoms, and the appearance of their remains upon dissection. Colonial medical writers operated in a world where medicine distinguished diseases similar in their symptoms to one another according to their causes. In accordance with this expectation, colonial fever writers analyzed the circumstances that had preceded outbreaks among different regiments and squadrons—what these groups ate, how much they worked, the environments they entered, and how disorderly they had behaved. They did so on the grounds that this comparative work would settle debates about the identity of each disease in question. They sought, for instance, to establish whether yellow fever, which many maintained was an entirely new disease entity, was actually a variant of a nervous fever. The authors of these texts also maintained that the vulnerability of different groups to different infectious fevers as well as the infectiousness of the diseases depended on the unique circumstances of the group. Hence, writers' close attention to the circumstances of the group that preceded the outbreak of particular diseases: these circumstances could explain why the same disease could become more virulent and contagious in one group than in another. Such comparative work aimed to determine the best modes of prevention and treatment of these fevers. This was not an intellectual exercise. In the Caribbean, significant numbers of British soldiers and Royal Naval soldiers were felled by infectious fevers.[7] The discovery of the causal origins of various fevers and the ability to distinguish between them would go far to secure Britain's triumph over France in Caribbean theaters of warfare.

Plantation practitioners, these critics observed, had forsaken an opportunity to understand how infectious ailments manifested and moved among enslaved plantation populations. In these writers' view, enslaved populations represented a differently enfeebled but similarly sequestered laboring population as the military rank and file. Moreover, the failure of plantation practitioners to investigate infectious ailments with equal rigor meant that plantation practitioners had abdicated their responsibility to mobilize science in the service of an equally pressing economic and political problem: the morbidity and mortality of the enslaved that drove slaveholders' reliance on the Atlantic slave trade. Solutions to this problem, these critics maintained, would come in publications that described the precise etiology, prevention, and remedies of ailments that menaced the enslaved. They would also point the way forward to particular remedies for particular diseases. Such discoveries would potentially eliminate slaveholders' reliance upon the Atlantic slave trade. Yet, with the exception of Collins, these critics were armchair outsiders. They were deeply unfamiliar with the considerable differences of medical knowledge-making in the hospitals of the armed forces and those on West Indian plantations. What these writers did not comprehend was that enslaved people's medical care, as given by plantation practitioners, typically took place along a plane of neglect rather than of sustained attention and control.

Historians of medicine have demonstrated how, in clinical settings such as urban and military hospitals where patients were treated in the aggregate, confinement facilitated knowledge-making.[8] Many circumstances, unique to the setting of the eighteenth-century hospital, contributed to this dynamic. For instance, hospital patients were drawn from either the urban poor or the military rank and file. Their status as dependents—as either the beneficiary of a hospital benefactor or the charge of an officer—positioned them as the institution's wards and removed family members from aiding in their recuperation and determining the disposition of their bodies upon death. The history of premodern European medicine has underscored this last component, as the social isolation of hospital inmates engendered the new scale of postmortem pathologies. Practitioners in these institutions produced a torrent of writing on the manifestation of disease in different tissues and organs.[9] More prosaic forms of knowledge-making also developed in these spaces. In fact, a well-demarcated structure of authority enabled practitioners to conduct exhaustive physical examinations on a large and sequestered patient population, to take extensive notes, and to experiment with different remedies and dietary regimens. The centralization of information on patients' symptoms and postmortem findings in hospital books enabled the creation of consecutive medical records.[10] Such records, in turn, created the datasets that practitioners used to publish texts describing the origins, behavior, and lethality of the different ailments they treated.

There are many similarities between the hospitals examined in this literature and those of the plantation complex. As discussed in chapter 1, the development of hot-houses were part and parcel of the project to increase efficiencies in the delivery of medical care and to compel the sick to return to work. They also represented a new geography of containment that rendered enslaved suffers into patients through their social entombment.[11] As sites for the confinement and social isolation of the sick, hospitals also enabled the development of a new culture of experiment. Yet, although the paradigm of plantation medicine was one of control, its implementation was experienced, for better or worse, as neglect. Enslaved patients received little direct attention from practitioners once confined in the hospital or other spaces designated for their care. Practitioners' large workloads exceeded their capacity to remain very long on individual estates. Enslaved healers' intellectual and manual labor was, as a consequence, central to the hospital's operation—especially as an institution that enabled colonists' interventions into the ways enslaved people recuperated from illness.

This chapter argues that a secondary effect of the delegation of the labor onto enslaved people was that they often foiled practitioners' efforts to exploit them as a captive population to produce knowledge. They leveraged abandonment and neglect to thwart and shape the execution of practitioners' experiments far more extensively than scholars have appreciated. In the face of practitioners' and managers' efforts to render the enslaved sick into socially dead experimental subjects, the relatives of enslaved doctors, nurses, and sufferers seized on gaps in practitioners' attendance to reposition the enslaved sick as part of a larger community and to affirm their social connection to one another.[12] In so doing, enslaved people constrained plantation surgeons' intellectual output, which came nowhere near that of practitioners working in the other clinical settings of the Atlantic World. By looking closely at the on-the-ground interactions between slaves and practitioners, this chapter reveals how enslaved people ensured that the hospital would not become a space of unfettered knowledge-making. At the same time, enslaved people also contributed to medical case histories.

Ambition and Observation

In the corner of the British West Indies, plantation doctors' processes were utterly unlike those enjoyed by physicians to regiments in the British

Army or those stationed in seaports. The latter monopolized seaports' shallow pool of aristocratic and well-to-do clients as well as appointments in the islands' civilian hospitals. Practitioners stationed in seaports thus dominated a knowledge economy primarily concerned with infectious diseases that prevailed among Europeans, particularly the military rank and file. By the last quarter of the eighteenth century, however, colonists' concern with the impending abolition of the Atlantic slave trade increased seaport practitioners' interest in the medical world of plantations. Medical men, such as the Kingston-based physician Thomas Dancer, had the training and access to books, medical journals, and manuscripts necessary to grapple with and differentiate among different infectious diseases. They quickly pivoted to expand their coverage—publishing texts that described the remote, proximate, and pathological origins of ailments that commonly befell enslaved people.

Such interest altered the ways that plantation practitioners formed relationships with their better-heeled peers. For most of the eighteenth century, plantation practitioners found it difficult to breach this arena of intellectual development and publication that developed in centers of calculation in the seaports of Britain, North America, and the Caribbean. Therein, elite physicians were largely concerned with epidemic disease, and they sat atop a patronage system that provided important appointments in military and civilian hospitals. Yet, increasingly, plantation medical men attempted to mobilize their attendance upon overworked and inadequately sustained enslaved patients to enter the knowledge economy of Caribbean seaports. They positioned themselves as intermediaries, forcing scientific men of eminence to rely upon them for information.

But unlike the fever-writers of seaports and the army, who tended to publish books, plantation surgeons disseminated their observations in short case histories that were either circulated in manuscript or published in medical periodicals of short run. Although they garnered little acclaim from the larger British medical world, case histories fit with the circumstances of most plantation surgeons. They hoarded the data necessary to make them and gifted the finished product selectively to grandees in Caribbean seaports and centers of medical education in Britain. From enslaved confinement, surgeons incrementally generated intellectual movables, and they hoped that these products would broker their entrance into the patronage relations that might facilitate their escape from the backwaters of the British Empire. The growth of hot-houses thus remade the plantation Caribbean from a site of botanical bioprospecting into a nursery for the proliferation of medical case histories.[13]

Put into circulation, case histories had similar attributes to the botanical specimens that West Indian and North American colonists gathered from Afro-Caribbean healers and gifted to scientific grandees in Britain. Diverse plants had rich meanings in Afro-Caribbean healing cultures and were associated with a sacralized natural world. These local meanings were lost as scientific elites received different plant and animal objects from colonial brokers, placed them in Linnaean classification systems, and thereby transformed them into pieces of universal knowledge.[14] Case histories derived from enslaved people similarly represented a means by which writers hoped to abstract from myriad particulars to produce something universal. The study of sickness and its treatment among enslaved people represented an opportunity for elite medical writers to observe how disease unfolded in an overworked population reduced to a bare life subsistence. "A better history of them [the diseases that prevailed among the enslaved] would enlarge our knowledge of pathology, and teach us ... many new and interesting facts in the animal œconomy," the military physician John Hunter remarked.[15] In the late eighteenth century, elite medical writers claimed to have discovered a new universal biological principle: racialized imperviousness or vulnerability to disease.[16] And yet, as we shall see, the case histories that provided the fodder for elite medical men's racial abstractions were suffused with the particularity of the patient's circumstances, based on enslaved patients' own testimony.

Case histories found their final resting place in larger printed texts or medical periodicals of short run. But this textual journey masked the labor involved in producing them over the course of hundreds of encounters and negotiations among enslaved patients, practitioners, and observers. At the core of any case history was a curiosity or an unusual event—something that did not often occur in nature. Practitioners then explained the circumstances that surrounded this curiosity and produced a story of a strange ailment or recovery that was awash with what Steven Shapin and Simon Schaffer have described as the "circumstantial details" of what had happened.[17] To do so they gathered minutiae from patients' bedsides and onlookers and juxtaposed them against known facts. The labor involved in transforming a natural curiosity into a medical case history added to its value. Their credibility and worth were then enhanced by the elite status of people who received and published them.

Indeed, as they moved through patronage networks, case histories took on the qualities of currency. They enhanced the reputation of the colonial writer and augmented the intellectual capital of recipients situated in centers of calculation.[18] The transmission of a case history—between giver and recipient, or between middling practitioner and scientific patron—often initiated a relationship.[19] Numerous case histories gifted to patrons could bind men of uneven status in relationship to one another and transform an unknown practitioner into a permanent correspondent of a scientific grandee. Such a relationship could lead to employment or an appointment elsewhere. Men of middling status in the Caribbean's hinterlands often sent case histories to scientific grandees stationed in Caribbean seaports as well as in the British Isles and North America, hoping for their acceptance. Norms of genteel sociability and the patron-client model structured interactions between plantation practitioners and practitioners in seaports and abroad. Not surprisingly, intense rivalry for patrons structured middling practitioners' relations with one another.[20] Anecdotes about diseases and their remedies were requisite to produce a case history, but the cutthroat economy of information hoarding in the Caribbean's hinterlands also impeded the exchange of these vital details between practitioners on the make.

The efforts of the surgeon Jonathan Troup to compose a case history in 1789 illustrate the potential difficulties of amassing information in the Caribbean. That year Troup was still a newcomer to Dominica. Of middling economic status, he occupied the lowest rung of a far-reaching transatlantic Scottish community of medical men. He was an assistant in the household of Andrew Fillian, the Roseau physician-apothecary who controlled two-thirds of all the seaport's medical business. He had also been recruited to Dominica by Fillian's copartner, James Clark, a fellow of the Royal College of Physicians of Edinburgh.[21] Even before Troup arrived in Dominica, he likely saw the island and his new employers as a springboard into this larger knowledge economy, so long as he played his cards right. Similarly, to local people who might want to breach James Clark's transatlantic network, Troup provided a potential point of entrance. But other medical men and amateur naturalists might have hesitated to rely too heavily on a mere assistant.

In fits and starts during the month of July, Troup attempted to compose an account of the birth of quadruplets by an enslaved woman. Slaveholders' and managers' displacement of enslaved midwives from the birthing room brought many plantation doctors closer to childbirth. At the same time, late eighteenth-century efforts to coercively extract additional value from the reproductive bodies of enslaved women helped the European medical world to learn more about the processes of reproduction.[22] In this era, therefore, medical periodicals contained many case histories from across Britain, recounting birthing complications, unusual presentations, and multiple births. While the womb was becoming less mysterious, the processes of reproduction were still imperfectly understood.[23] Instances of twins, triplets, and quadruplets were particularly valuable to medical men because they believed that multiple births illuminated the processes of fetal development.

The woman at the center of Troup's account was never under his attendance. He gathered the details of her case from eyewitnesses. On approximately July 14, she gave birth to one boy, George. His birth was facilitated "by a negro woman on the estate." But the mother was carrying additional babies, and so Gemmet, the plantation's overseer, sent to Roseau for a mixed-race man named Joseph, "reckoned an excellent accoucheur" (male midwife).[24] Joseph arrived the next day and assisted in the delivery of the other three infants: Faith, Hope, and Charity. They were born within a half hour of Joseph's interventions. Incredibly, the mother and her quadruplets survived. It was a preternatural event that captured the attention of people within miles of the estate. Without skipping a beat, Troup set out for the estate to gather details.

From information provided by Gemmet, the enslaved mother, her attendants, the enslaved midwife, and the rest of the plantation's enslaved community, Troup composed the delivery's general plotlines. He learned from the mother that she had believed she was only carrying one child. But "the people" declared, "from the size of her abdomen," that she was bearing twins.[25] Still, many questions remained. Did the fetuses share the same amniotic sac and placenta? Did each have a separate umbilical cord, and did they ever join together? How did Joseph know whose limbs he had pulled as he maneuvered the head of the first of the remaining three to the mouth of the birth canal? Were the arms or legs attached to the body whose head he had directed? These points were important for transforming an anecdote about a preternatural event into a case history that might bring Troup a patron.

Troup's labors were in utter contrast to those experienced by the enslaved woman whose delivery he attempted to leverage for personal gain. Throughout her labor, delivery, and lying-in, the Coromantee woman was subjected to numerous violations of her bodily integrity that her enslaved attendants, in all likelihood, attempted to mitigate. At the onset of contractions and after delivery she may have been bathed by attendants in a nearby river. These rituals provided assurance to enslaved mothers that they would safely deliver and recover from their ordeal.[26] But in the days following her delivery, the estate's attending practitioner, Dr. Spencer, arrived. He took measurements of her newborn infants as well as of the length and diameter of her pelvis.[27] In the ensuing days, it is unlikely she had as much time to recuperate and nurse as a recently delivered indentured servant or a free woman. For instance, the historian Sasha Turner found that on the Potosi estate in Jamaica, an enslaved woman named Sarah was sent back to work in the cane fields two weeks after her delivery. Two other Potosi women, Nelly and Molly, were forced to return to work within a few days of their delivery. Because of the exceptional nature of this delivery, the woman may have been given a longer time than usual to nurse and convalesce. But it is just as likely that Gemmet forced her to return to work, giving her only brief periods of respite to nurse. It would not have been unusual for Gemmet to compel the woman to leave her infants in a weaning house while she toiled in the field. And if she refused, she was likely flogged or confined in the lying-in house rather than her hut. Such a confinement would hinder her capacity to renew and succor affective ties that she and her attendants had forged in the course of her pregnancy and delivery.[28]

Having gathered some preliminary details about the childbirth, Troup returned to Roseau, where he hazarded answers to his questions, drafting "A Particular History of the Case."[29] But as soon as he set down the details, he scratched them out, likely because his queries had been answered by people—Gemmet, the mother, the enslaved midwife, and onlookers—who had not manually guided the other three infants to and through the birth canal. The only person who had those details was Joseph. The next day, Troup beat a path to his house.

Joseph probably held similar ambitions as Troup—he also wanted to use the preternatural childbirth to move up in the knowledge economy. And he was, without a doubt, an adept navigator of the competitive world of information exchange. He understood that he had to keep the details of the quintuplet birth close to his chest in order for the information to retain its value. Troup's interrogation was likely one of many that Joseph endured following the birth. At each, Joseph probably sized up the situation—what he might gain from giving his account of the childbirth and what its release might cost him. Troup had few levers to pull. But he may have believed, erroneously, that he had an edge on Joseph, a mixed-race man. Perhaps Troup imagined that Joseph would not be able to enter local and transatlantic networks. At their first meeting, Joseph checked that assumption. He relayed that he had studied at Paris and Montpellier "and other capital places where he had learned anatomy and surgery with midwifery," Troup noted in his diary. Joseph then sent Troup into the night with a promise "to give me a history of the negro woman's delivery at Mr. Gemmet's at Tuesday."[30]

As Troup persisted, Joseph protected his information. Its value lay in its novelty, and Joseph was not going to release it to Troup. But Troup was slow to apprehend Joseph's motivations. Or perhaps Troup thought he could badger Joseph into getting what he wanted from him. Following his initial visit, Troup "called on Joseph French midwife [the accoucher] but not receive his history of Negro woman."[31] A week passed. Then Joseph had the misfortune of encountering Troup at another's household. There Joseph promised "to give me a history of case of a woman's 4 children."[32] After three pestering visits from Troup during the next fortnight, Joseph decided that Troup might be a useful associate in the island. Like others, he might testify to the safety of different remedies or pass along a cure. Joseph promised "to call me [Troup] upon extraordinary occasions—in midwifery," but he "declines giving me a History of case of Mr. Gemmets Negro." Therefore, Troup concluded, "I must write it as well as I can."[33]

The next day, Troup cast his net far and wide. He sent his case history, titled "Mr. Gemmets Negro woman who brought forth 4 children of a birth," to Sir Joseph Banks, president of the Royal Society of London. He also sent a copy to Alexander Monro (Secundus), the famous anatomist and professor of medicine at the University of Edinburgh. Troup padded his letters with other scientific observations that he hoped would capture the interest of Banks and Monro. The miscellanies included: "my tour of Scotland, my storm in Bay of Brescay, Gemmet's account, my own measurements, Joseph's account and remarks, the negligence of physicians here—what only related to the case."[34] His bids went unanswered. In the months following, Troup modified his ambitions—turning from the Royal Society and the University of Edinburgh to Dominica's garrison. Successfully entertaining several officers with his large collection of natural specimens, he gained admission into the scientific circles of the eastern Caribbean.[35] His association with this group, in turn, facilitated his appointment as the garrison's surgeon, an office that enabled him to leave the household of Fillian—the practitioner-apothecary who had employed him as his assistant.

Experiments on the Fly

By hook or by crook, practitioners generated medical knowledge. But as Troup's failed efforts to create his case history suggest, plantation practitioners did not typically generate knowledge as systematically and successfully as their counterparts working in the British Army and municipal hospitals. The administrative structures in the British Army and municipal hospitals that organized the collection of information on diseases and remedies for doctors working in these institutions did not exist for plantation practitioners in the Caribbean.[36] In the Caribbean's hinterlands, individual practitioners interacted with managers, rather than bureaucracies, to collect and circulate medical knowledge that concerned the diseases of laboring populations. They did so on their own initiative and in chaotic conditions. Overseers, bookkeepers, and attorneys collected information on the total increase and decrease of an estate's population, the days enslaved people were not at work due to illness, and kept hospital books to track the disbursement of medicines. But that was not the same as systematically amassing this into a working knowledge about the nature of particular diseases and their remedies. Practitioners did try. Many "experienced gentlemen of the faculty," the enslaver and politician Edward Long wrote, had amassed a "treasure of experimental knowledge" for their personal use. Yet as colonists' lives were brief, knowledge-making in the plantation Caribbean was shaped as much by rupture as permanence; death and departures for elsewhere undermined possibilities for generational and institutional continuity. What little knowledge had been developed, Long mused, might never see the light of day. Long maintained that unearthing these jewels and readying them for publication was a race against time before such records were "buried with him [the practitioner] or passed away to another country."[37]

The notes of the Jamaican plantation doctor John Williamson, which he initially kept in his memoranda books and later published, exemplified what Long imagined was in practitioners' records. Williamson composed "monthly memorandums" and recorded "minute details of cases." Williamson attributed his diligent recordkeeping to the fact that he "was fortunate enough to enjoy a less interrupted state of good health," which provided the constancy necessary to produce them.[38] Williamson was able to transform his notes into natural histories of disease similar to those that emanated from practitioners in the armed forces, but for many other practitioners, the physical demands of plantation medicine left them little opportunity. Indeed, they were more likely to perish than publish: rampant mortality among newcomers and the absence of consistent running records meant that there was little institutional continuity in the arena of plantation medicine—even within individual firms.[39] Williamson's two-volume *Medical and Miscellaneous Observations, Relative to the West India Islands* (1817) makes clear that he intended to harness his experience to join the ranks of medical writers who theorized and racialized the pathological and remote origins of distinctive diseases. Yet while he was still in Jamaica, Williamson had neither the time nor the resources to achieve this end. It was some thirty years after his relocation to the British Isles that he polished the notes for publication. The scope of his writing, moreover, makes Williamson the exception rather than the rule.[40]

In terms of what practitioners actually committed to paper, the notes of Troup are probably more representative. Troup's memoranda book functioned as a repository for nearly everything he saw and did. He wrote most often about the weather, griped frequently about his employer Fillian, and commented the least about his medical practice. The passages in his diary that related to his visits to estates typically relayed the date of his visit, the ailments he had treated, and what he prescribed.[41] It is difficult to differentiate between his own thoughts and those of someone who had already seen the sick—but his diagnostic notes were unlikely entirely his own. They were probably copies of what the overseer had written in the estate's hot-house book, supplemented by Troup's own impressions.

There were considerable differences in the types of information that a plantation practitioner would receive about his respective patients, compared to urban and military hospital doctors. Urban and military hospitals conducted exhaustive physical examinations, and their surgeons offered detailed descriptions of symptoms and observable signs—these were hallmarks of clinical medicine, but they were almost entirely absent in hot-houses. In urban hospitals, Susan Lawrence writes, "medical men of science discovered a numerous and sequestered population of the sick poor whose illnesses they watched, whose treatments they controlled, whose bodies they autopsied, and whose cases they counted."[42] In contrast to accounts of the rise of hospital medicine in Britain, which emphasize doctors' surveillance over and intrusion into patients' bodies, doctors simply neglected sufferers in the hot-house. They treated symptoms but did not investigate their deep physiological origins.

In charity and military hospitals, on the other hand, the new emphasis on physical examinations was accompanied by the rise of "hospital books." In these small notebooks, hospital surgeons recorded case and prescription notes for each patient, and many entries contained additional observations.[43] Charity hospitals, moreover, had students, and the hospital books thereby had a pedagogical purpose.[44] The notation of symptoms and clinical signs in hospital books collated data from patient-practitioner interactions and made it available for consultation. The intensification of recordkeeping in hospitals, in turn, facilitated a steady stream of book-length publications on the various diseases and pathologies that practitioners in these institutions encountered and treated. Notably, metropolitan institutions of care instantiated analytical practices that facilitated the production of texts even as they eroded patients' agency to reckon with illness on their own terms.

In plantation sick-houses, in contrast, there was no incentive to take extensive notes on patients. Those books were far less detailed than hospital books, since overseers and not practitioners did the work of assessing and recording illness in its first stages. Since overseers and bookkeepers, as well as enslaved healers, generally decided who would be admitted, these groups determined what information the doctor received when he visited patients.[45] Because Jonathan Troup and other plantation doctors relied on the contents of these hot-house books, their notes were not very extensive. Plantation practitioners saw far more patients per year than did doctors working in London's charity hospitals. Yet the expansion of surgeons' workloads, discussed in chapter 2, reduced the number of hours that they could give to each individual estate and increased the number of days between each visit. Consequentially, plantation practitioners did not prioritize close physical inspection and diagnosis, since they had little time to do so. The brevity of practitioners' visits meant that they were rarely around long or frequently enough to sustain the communication and control necessary to generate knowledge about diseases and conduct experiments with remedies.

Certain procedures and circumstances, however, extended the number of visits and amount of time that practitioners spent on estates, providing opportunities to conduct experiments with remedies in large numbers. Smallpox inoculations, childbirths, surgical operations, and complicated illnesses tended to affix surgeons upon estates for a more sustained period of time than usual and encouraged their return in the ensuing day. That was because, for these procedures, surgeons received additional compensation outside of their annual salary. These circumstances made it more difficult for enslaved people to control the terms of the sick's recovery and, in turn, augmented opportunities of practitioners to trial new drugs. Enslaved people's own maneuvering—as both healers and patients—did, however, merge with the structural features of the surgeon's working conditions to limit what type of medical knowledge came out of the plantation complex. Consequently, enslaved people's interventions impeded the steady production of case histories more extensively than one might imagine.

One must distinguish between two different ways of generating new knowledge about remedies. Elaine Leong and Alisha Rankin define and differentiate between two "ways of making and doing" in early modern medicine, while also showing that they often overlapped.[46] On the one hand, there was testing drugs. Leong and Rankin define this as the countless ways that early modern people uncovered the medicinal properties of different substances. And on the other, there was the trying of cures—which entailed subjecting humans and animals to experiments that were intended to reveal the safety, efficacy, and application of substances or recipes composed of myriad substances for different afflictions. Plantation practitioners engaged in both of these processes: interacting with enslaved people to learn about new drugs and testing cures on enslaved subjects.

Smallpox inoculations represented a particularly charged moment for testing different cures. Practitioners in Jamaica charged five shillings per smallpox inoculation, a fee that covered the procedure itself as well as their time and expertise readying the bodies of inoculation patients.[47] Significantly, this compensation increased the amount of time that surgeons spent upon the estates. It also increased the amount of surveillance and supervision over enslaved doctors and nurses in the administration of the medicines that they prescribed. For these reasons, smallpox inoculations often became episodes where surgeons vetted alternatives to especially harsh chemical substances that were usually standard in the preparation for inoculation.[48]

A smallpox inoculation entailed deliberately embedding a piece of pocky material, collected from a person infected with the disease, within an incision made on the recipient. The purpose of this procedure was to convey a case of smallpox. Colonists were initially hesitant to adopt this new technology, since it mirrored no known medical intervention. Moreover, it went against conventional medical ideas, which situated bodies as individualized. Sickness, even that caused by distinctive diseases, was held to manifest differently from person to person, depending on their constitution.[49] Finally, the idea that one might survive smallpox by deliberately infecting oneself with the material was utterly at odds with prevailing ideas about the prevention of illness—which tended to focus on the management of diet and the environment for the individual and quarantine for populations.[50] But from the mid-eighteenth century onward, advocates of inoculation convinced skeptics of its safety and utility.

These advocates argued that inoculated pox allowed recipients to better plan for and thus survive smallpox than if they had contracted the disease naturally. Because they could time and plan their infections, the recipients of inoculation stood a better chance of survival. Crucial to convincing the public was the idea that the people who performed the procedure could prepare recipients for the ensuing smallpox according to the needs of their individual bodies. "Different bodies will necessarily require different degrees and modes of evacuation," the South Carolinian smallpox inoculator James Kirkpatrick explained.[51] Readying the patient's body according to its specific needs was an important component in securing practitioners' authority to perform inoculations. Thus, the cost of an inoculation covered the transmission of the pocky material to the recipient as well as the reduction of the patient's body with medicines and other therapeutics prior to the engraftment. Typically, colonists guarded their authority to interpret their own as well as enslaved people's bodies. Smallpox inoculation was, however, one of the handful of experimental medical practices supported by overseers and slaveholders.[52]

As smallpox inoculation originated in Africa, it was a practice familiar to many of the enslaved people subjected to it. Yet the ways that surgeons carried out inoculations were potentially disruptive to enslaved people's kin relations. As Elise A. Mitchell has shown, West African healing cosmologies situated health and sickness in collective rather than individual terms. Inoculations in particular were a means to make and reaffirm the bonds of kin and secure futurity. "Rather than focusing on healing individual bodies," inoculation as practiced by Africans, "centered and addressed whole communities." It was a "collectivist practice that enabled West African, North African, Arab, and East Asian groups to preserve themselves against a scourge of a disease . . . to have intergenerational connections and opportunities beyond their homelands."[53] Having survived the ensuing infection, the recipient was indifferent to the disease of smallpox.

But slaveholders did not take the same approach to the inoculation of enslaved people as they did with their own family members. More specifically, proprietors and attorneys calculated that in a smallpox epidemic a number of enslaved people would die from either natural or inoculated pox. Eager to preserve their capital in enslaved flesh, attorneys planned to inoculate enslaved people en masse, without concern for the readiness of each person to survive the inoculated pox. Neither did they bother to have practitioners prepare the recipients of inoculated pox according to the needs of their individual bodies. In so doing, they treated enslaved people as disposable—in a cruel and calculated anticipation of wastage in the process of inoculating an entire estate. Consequentially, practitioners inoculated an estate's enslaved people serially.

With upward of one hundred enslaved people inoculated in sequence, these industrial-scale smallpox inoculations created the conditions for doctors to test other remedies that, they argued, would work universally across many different types of bodies. Often, for instance, surgeons used their inoculations as occasions to identify and experiment with substitutes for mercury. Mercury was a principal ingredient in inoculators' preparatory regimens. Since physicians widely believed that smallpox was an inflammatory disease, medical orthodoxy counseled that preparation for smallpox inoculation required an antiphlogistic routine. This was a regimen that involved bloodletting, a "low" diet of broth and vegetables, and, often, medicines that had antimony or mercury as key ingredients. Collectively, these things cooled the body and ensured that it did not overheat in response to the inoculated pox.[54] There were many other reasons to trial alternatives to mercurial medicines. For example, mercurous chloride, often listed in plantation inventories and lists of medicines as calomel, was a standard remedy for venereal disease. Colonists also used it as a treatment for yaws. They maintained that, once rooted in the body, yaws required remedies that coaxed the poisonous matter to exit through the fluids or the surface of the skin.[55] Mercury was a principal ingredient in medicines for the treatment of venereal disease. Thus, slaveholders and practitioners externalized the risks of trying a remedy that was to have many applications, for colonists and the enslaved, onto the enslaved people who were the recipients of inoculated pox.

Mercurial remedies were excruciating for everyone. Prompting intense salivating and sweating, mercurial medicines wore down those subjected to them. Plantation managers and doctors recognized the deleterious effects of mercury upon people subjected to it repeatedly. In fact, John Quier maintained that the constant use of mercury for both yaws and venereal disease rendered the ingredient potentially lethal when used in smallpox inoculations. "When a spitting is attempted to be raised," he warned, "if much caution is not used there is a danger of instantaneous suffocation."[56] Colonists were perpetually engaged in a project to identify an alternative to mercury because they were concerned that the overuse of mercury eroded enslaved people's capacity for labor.

The confinement of enslaved sufferers during their smallpox inoculations and their isolation gave practitioners the opportunity to experiment with botanical alternatives. The plantation surgeon William Chamberlaine, for example, used his smallpox inoculations to identify a new antiphlogistic (a medicine intended to curb inflammation). Although he failed to discover a viable substitute for mercury, in the process of trying different African-originated remedies, he learned from the enslaved healers on the plantation that cabbage-bark and cowhage functioned as a universal treatment for worms.[57] What Chamberlaine learned about these two plants was incidental to smallpox itself. But his so-called discovery of their attributes and applications nonetheless derived from experiments with medicines that he used to ready enslaved people's bodies for smallpox inoculation.

The volume of tests that Chamberlaine conducted with cowhage and cabbage-bark was made possible by three circumstances: a long history of the exchange of botanical know-how between enslaved healers and plantation managers; the fact that Chamberlaine executed his trials while preparing enslaved people to receive smallpox inoculations; and the assistance of enslaved healers in carrying out his trials. In the span of a few months, he tested his decoctions on colonists and enslaved people (primarily) of different strengths, ages, sexes, and health. Chamberlaine prepared 254 enslaved patients situated on different estates in his roster of clients for smallpox inoculation.[58] The first mercury substitute that he attempted to test was a decoction of cabbage-bark and jalap. Chamberlaine forced it upon an "adult, of a robust constitution." Following "a few more trials with equal success," he prepared a large quantity "as a common purging powder for negroes of all denominations."[59] The surgeon envisioned that the seriality afforded by the circumstances of his smallpox inoculations would yield information about the effects of his new remedy across many different types of bodies.

Chamberlaine's experiments relied upon the existence of a rich Afro-Caribbean therapeutic arsenal that colonists respected and exploited. Alexander Anderson, the aggrieved superintendent of the Royal Botanical Garden in St. Vincent, proclaimed that several illnesses in the island were better treated "by old intelligent negroes" than by its medical men.[60] Indeed, cowhage, the principal ingredient in Chamberlaine's trial, was a plant remedy that enslaved healers had made known to colonists many decades ago. At midcentury, the Jamaican botanist Patrick Browne described cowhage as a plant well-known throughout Jamaica "on account of its sharp itching hairs." "The root," he continued, "is looked upon as an aperient and diuretic and both the decoction and juice are frequently used among the negroes for those purposes."[61] Healers taught colonists as well how to render these plants into medicines. "The negroes or nurses, to whom the general exhibition of this bark is intrusted," one colonist relayed, "commonly prepare it, by taking a handful of it bruised and boiling it in water, till the decoction, well sweetened, they give for three successive mornings, a small table-spoonful to a child two years of age, fasting; and they increase the dose according to the age and strength of the patient."[62] It was enslaved nurses, then, who had originally informed colonists about the identity and attributes of cowhage and cabbage-bark, the two plants at the center of Chamberlaine's experiments.

As was typical of many botanical encounters in West Indian slave societies in the late eighteenth century, Chamberlaine's knowledge about cowhage as a worm medicine sat at several degrees' remove from its original source. Information about the safety and efficacy of cowhage came to the experimenter thirdhand. He received intelligence from other overseers and slaveholders who themselves had appropriated this know-how from enslaved informants. These managers, in turn, then tested its effects in different proportions and weights upon the enslaved sick.[63] For many colonists and readers in the metropolis, cowhage was one of a plethora of African and Afro-Caribbean healing remedies that had long been assimilated into European pharmacopeias.

Although the attributes of cowhage were well known, there was no consensus on the number of pods to use in transforming the plant into a worm medicine. Chamberlaine thus did not position his experiments to test a substance to discover its properties—he had already learned from others that cowhage was effective. Instead, he situated his trials as a means to expand upon what was already known—how cowhage achieved its effects. With his particular concoction of cowhage and other substances, he might also discover the safest proportions of each ingredient in his drink. His experiments therefore entailed a refinement of both colonists' and enslaved people's understandings of the mechanism by which the plant killed intestinal worms. To show that the effects of the medicine arose not from an attribute intrinsic to the pods but from the sharpness and elasticity of the bristles that encased them, he shaved some of the pod's bristles into a "calabash full of very large ones [worms] of the *teres* kind, in full vigor." When he applied the bristles, the worms began to "writhe and twist themselves in a usual manner." Notably, the worm he subjected to the cowhage "had been voided by a poor emaciated patient, [which] was brought to me."[64] Chamberlaine, in other words, learned of cowhage's safety from other plantation managers, but he relied upon the enslaved to collect the material—the worms—that was essential for his experiment. In using the passive voice to discuss how he had acquired the worms, however, Chamberlaine erased the role of the healer in this process.

But the mechanical skill of enslaved healers, a know-how rooted in the African diaspora, was in fact central in substantiating the novelty of Chamberlaine's claims: his witnessing of the effects of the bristles upon the worms. Africans and Afro-Caribbean people were familiar with many different types of worms. Guinea worm, a parasite that resides in the subcutaneous layer of the skin and causes the infection known today as *Dracunculiasis*, afflicted natives of and visitors to the West African littoral and was pervasive among enslaved people in the West Indies, as a consequence of the living conditions to which colonists subjected them. These worms were notoriously difficult to extract—requiring the dexterity of someone long familiar with their appearance in different types of flesh. In his visit to São Jorge da Mina (Elmina Castle in present-day Ghana) in the seventeenth century, the Dutch goldsmith Michael Hemmersam witnessed the ways that Guinea barbers removed them. He reported that experienced barbers could recognize the presence of a worm even when it was just underneath the top of the skin. Barbers identified its location and made a small incision at that location. Thereafter, Hemmersam explained, "there then appear two little white hairs, which grow on the head and are called the worm's beard." The barber then returned daily to tug on the hairs until they had excised the worm.[65] The extraction of worms remained enslaved people's remit well into the late eighteenth century. It was a technique, John Williamson advised, that "must be performed with great caution, by rolling it around a small piece of wood as it is removed.... [I]f the Guinea worm breaks in the operation of extracting it, the labour hitherto has been in vain." That involved great technical proficiency, and it was "so well performed by the negro doctor in charge of the sick, that any further description is unnecessary," Williamson explained.[66] Plantation practitioners were quick to rush past enslaved people's medical competency in order to direct the readers' focus back on themselves. At the same time, this move upheld a division of knowledge especially important to aspiring medical men. Those lower in the hierarchy, such as enslaved healers performed manual labor involving the surface of the skin, whereas practitioners interpreted what was deep within the body and developed theories that explained how certain substances achieved their effects.

Slavery's Knowledge-Making

For all of his claims about the success of his trial, Chamberlaine's knowledge-making appears much more troubled upon closer inspection. Indeed, as he was forced to acknowledge, the extent of his experiment was cut short by many factors. First, slaveholders' stipulations about costs interrupted his trials. Slaveholders kept the expense of medicines down by purchasing them in bulk from metropolitan merchants and shipping them annually, alongside provisions. And they quarreled with plantation practitioners who tried to use medicines from their own supply. These conflicts constrained the scope of Chamberlaine's experiments. He had 254 enslaved patients upon whom he had intended to trial the cabbage-bark and jalap remedy but he was only able to execute his experiments on 216 of them. That was because some of them, as he explained, lived on estates that "supplied their own medicines."[67] Although slaveholders complained endlessly about charges for mercury, some of Chamberlaine's slaveholder-clients also refused to pay for the remedy that Chamberlaine proposed. Instead, they insisted that Chamberlaine use ingredients already on hand in their estates' medical chests. Medicines— their cost, disbursement, and origins—represented major sources of friction between slaveholders and plantation doctors and an impediment to practitioners' trials.

Enslaved sufferers-turned-patients also disrupted Chamberlaine's experiment, playing a far more substantial role in limiting what he learned. The patients whom Chamberlaine compelled to drink his preparatory cabbage-bark and jalap purgative were not passive recipients. Of the 216 inoculation patients given his original formula, 23 cases remained inconclusive. Several of the enslaved subjects or the enslaved healers attending them did not relay to him any information about its effects. There were also "others," he explained, from whom "I could expect no account."[68] On the one hand, this may have been a communication barrier. In fact, Chamberlaine noted that recently arrived African captives were among the people he subjected to his experiment. On the other, it was an example of patients remaining strategically silent—perhaps anticipating that if they did not report on the effects of cabbage-bark they might avoid being subjected to an additional round of Chamberlaine's remedy. While their reasons for not reporting to Chamberlaine remain unknown, it is clear that the people who received his concoction were uninterested in facilitating his scientific inquiries.

In response, Chamberlaine attempted to make his remedy (and his presence) more palatable. He ground the bark into a powder, mixed it with rum, and offered the liquid by the wine glassful for free to anyone willing to drink it, thus engineering a delivery mechanism he hoped would encourage interaction between himself and enslaved people upon whom he forced his drink.[69] Chamberlaine's potential patients forced him to dilute his harsh remedies as a condition of his experiment. Similarly, William Wright's enslaved patient, a young boy named Frank who was suffering from tetanus, also sought to determine the conditions under which he would take his doctor's cure. In the same years as Chamberlaine was testing different dosages of cabbage-bark, Wright, a plantation doctor in Jamaica, attempted to vet the effects of cold bathing in the cure of tetanus. Frank was receptive to cold bathing (likely because it was a known practice among West Africans for the cure of sores). He refused, however, to take Wright's remedy of cinchona bark, aqua fortis, and gum arabic until Wright supplemented it with "a few glasses of claret."[70]

The recipients of Chamberlaine's mixture, furthermore, used it in ways contradictory to his original intentions. He was only able to interact with this group during the medicine's uptake. "Two or three" enslaved men whom Chamberlaine maintained were afflicted with worms "came regularly for it." But that was the extent of his interactions. Although he wanted to know if the rum had blunted the effects of the cabbage-bark, he "never could find whether it [his new mixture] had the desired effects."[71] Other enslaved patients, however, vocally registered their displeasure. Chamberlaine noted that he was forced to experiment with new proportions of the mixture in one instance when the "largeness of the dose rendered it disgusting."[72] He attempted to speak to the enslaved people to whom he administered this powerful purgative, but the medicine's recipients communicated with him on their own terms.

Moreover, power cut both ways when practitioners relied upon enslaved healers to administer surgeons' prescriptions, undertake carework, and relay patients' status. Enslaved hospital and yaws-house attendants frequently leveraged their positions as an opportunity to disrupt practitioners' experiments. Hospital and yaws-house attendants did not differentiate between when practitioners had prescribed substances and compounds as a cure or as part of an informal experiment. Yet surgeons' infrequent attendance provided openings for attendants to disrupt practitioners' trials. In one instance a plantation doctor, William Bowie, attempted to determine whether liquid laudanum (a mixture of opium and alcoholic spirits) and warm baths were an appropriate means to curb the spasms characteristic of tetanus. In his letter to the Edinburgh professor William Cullen, Bowie observed that the laudanum he had administered to an enslaved boy had given him "the smallest relief." He then left the estate (presumably to attend upon another). But before his departure, he instructed the enslaved nurses to continue to administer the drug in his absence. When Bowie returned to the hot-house a few days later, however, the nurses had not disbursed the medicine. In so doing, they had foiled his experiment.[73] Bowie's frustration mirrored that of many other plantation surgeons who complained of being thwarted by enslaved healers who did not follow practitioners' directions for the disbursement of medicines.[74] Bowie referred to this as the "carelessness" of the women he presumed to direct.[75] The term "careless" was a charged one, as it held multiple meanings accreted in the elaboration of plantation medicine.

In this context stood the inverse, and thus ideal, "careful." It concerned attention to the niceties of a person's body, their constitution, and how their particular body shaped the expression of illness and its treatment. Practitioners were expected to reckon their patient's constitution, watch attentively, and adjust their treatments accordingly.[76] In this setting, "careful" indicated attention to minute particulars in illness management. Slaveholders and advice writers stipulated that carefulness and attentiveness were qualities requisite in a good sick-nurse. The plantation practitioner William Wright advised readers that each hot-house required a "good careful nurse to attend them and keep them clean."[77] The botanist James Grainger likewise maintained that yaws required the assistance of a "careful and discrete matron."[78] Attention to the patient's individual body, so necessary to recover a person from illness, was not, however, easily disbursed when attending many patients at a time. Given the number of people whom healers were expected to treat, carefulness was difficult to manifest.

"Careful" also shared semantic space with emergent concepts of domesticity that naturalized the deference to male authority as part of a woman's affect. The slaveholder and reformer Clement Caines, for instance, fantasized about placing wives in the position of the hospital attendant because a wife would act as his surrogate and subordinate. A wife, he wrote, "carefully notes the periodical returns of administering medicine, scrupulously conforms to its directions, and increases the efficacy of whatever is prescribed, by combining it with the care of a nurse and the watchfulness of an attendant."[79] Unwilling to dispatch their own wives to the West Indies, enslavers dragooned enslaved women to perform this role instead. When the enslaved midwives at the lying-in house on the Golden Grove plantation refused to follow the attorney Simon Taylor's orders, he removed them from their stations. In their stead, he posted other enslaved midwives, whom he described as "more careful and well disposed."[80] With traditional relations of medical hierarchy inverted in West Indian estates, including expectations that hot-house attendants would be subordinate to medical men, the charge of being "careless" was a freighted one that the nurses in Bowie's experiment deftly navigated.

In all likelihood, the nurses were, rather than careless, merely unwilling to submit to Bowie's instructions. They were, in fact, deliberate in their actions. They were fully aware of their centrality in healing on the estate; they knew that colonists resented the degree to which they relied upon them to recuperate the sick; and they also justifiably feared what might happen were they to confront Bowie directly about his prescription. To intervene, therefore, they leveraged the fact Bowie would not remain on-site to superintend their work. Like other enslaved nurses and hot-house doctors described by plantation doctors as "careless," the nurses Bowie ordered around identified an opening. And by cloaking interpretive independence in the veil of ineptitude, enslaved healers encouraged white practitioners to believe that they were careless, which gave them room to maneuver.[81] They made this decision from their vantage as the primary administers of medicines. It was a strategy predicated on practitioners' and plantation managers' simultaneous underestimation of and dependence upon them. As Chamberlaine summarized the difficulties he encountered as a practitioner, it was "out of the power of any practitioner to get justice done to his prescription."⁸² In Chamberlaine's experiment with cowhage, the plant's place in the enslaved healers' therapeutic arsenal had enabled him to proceed with his experiments without interruption from the healers. Without healers' sanction, however, he might have found himself in a position similar to Bowie, his demands indifferently administered.

Because practitioners sometimes relied on the family members of the sick to carry out the activities associated with practitioners' experiments, kin could also constrain what practitioners could learn. In his trials with cold bathing for the treatment of tetanus, Wright described the "difficulties [that] happened in getting people to throw cold water upon him [his patient, a boy named Frank]." Returning Frank to his mother's supervision, Wright "directed the cold water to be thrown on him every three hours; in the daytime; that his food and drink should be cold; & when in bed, to be lightly covered." For the most part, Frank's mother complied with Wright's prescriptions. At daybreak, however, "his mother thought it cold . . . and covered him with bed cloaths, she also gave him his water-gruel warm," directly contravening Wright's orders. Possibly, Frank's reaction confirmed Wright's hypothesis on the necessity of cold bathing. "By these means," Wright explained, "he [Frank] had several smart attacks of the spasms before eight o'clock in the morning when I visited him." Frank's mother may have trusted and even valued Wright's interventions. But instead of following them blindly, she adjusted them according to her ideas about what Frank needed as his condition and circumstances changed.⁸³

In many ways, Wright's directives to throw cold water on the shivering Frank and expose him to the night air followed medical orthodoxy. European medicine was oriented around expectorant dietary and medical regimes and copious bloodletting—what historians have called heroic medicine.⁸⁴ Jessica Marie Johnson has recently described the flesh as a site of freedom amid slaveholders' efforts to police enslaved women's bodies. Frank's mother's actions in response were another expression of freedom. In pursuing pleasure, according to Johnson, enslaved women repudiated slaveholders' claim that their bodies should only be used for work.⁸⁵ In a similar vein, Frank's mother rejected Wright's claim that her son's body should endure discomfort for the sake of Wright's experiment. Instead, she imposed her own paradigm—one of comfort.

Kin also limited what practitioners could learn about the internal progress of the diseases they treated, specifically, by prohibiting practitioners from opening up the dead for postmortem anatomies. As Mark Harrison has shown, practitioners who were stationed in Caribbean port cities had far more opportunities to conduct postmortem anatomies than their contemporaries in North America and the British Isles, because they lived near the garrison hospitals of the British Army and the civilian charity hospitals in town. Enslaved people's kin-sustaining, however, kept the plantation complex from replicating the constant assaults on sufferers' afterlives that was pervasive in other institutions of clinical medicine in the Atlantic World. Plantation practitioners may have wanted to purchase or expected to have access to the remains of the dead; yet few managers would have complied with this request. Enslaved people reminded overseers, again and again, that the fragile peace the two groups had etched out depended on the enslaved people's ability to bury and mourn the dead without interference from managers. "Surgeons sometimes have been obliged to desist," the Jamaican historian James Knight wrote of dissections, "in order to pacify them [enslaved people], altho[ugh] they were acquainted to the motives and reasons, and many arguments made use of to convince them of their absurd and ridiculous notions, tho[ugh] to very little purpose."[86] Of a dissection that an overseer and plantation surgeon requested to perform on an enslaved boy, Jonathan Troup noted succinctly that "the people would not allow it."[87] On one occasion John Williamson wanted to dissect the body of a young enslaved man whose death he attributed to worms. "Dissection," he wrote, "could only have determined it [the cause of death]; but no opportunities were permitted of this kind by negroes; at least, it was very rarely they could be persuaded of its propriety."[88] Surgeons' knowledge-making could not keep pace with their brethren in the armed forces because of enslaved people's determination to assert bonds of kinship through the memorialization and preparation of the dead. Military practitioners thus experienced near unfettered access to the remains of the rank and file, but enslaved people collectively formed a defensive flank against their family members' desecration.

Of course, in an era saturated with discourses about bodily difference, one would expect that practitioners used these encounters to advance and investigate the medical dimensions of race. In this era, elite writers were using epidemics to prove the medical dimensions of race—that vulnerability or imperviousness to particular diseases originated in racial difference.[89] While plantation practitioners had no doubt assimilated many of the ideas of racial distinctiveness promulgated by the elite writers of their day, two different dimensions of experiments on plantations challenged claims about the hard-and-fast distinctions between Black and white bodies.

One element was the genre in which they wrote—case histories demanded that their authors deal with particulars. Case histories might be examined in the aggregate to suggest universals. Case histories often positioned an ailment's behavior as the product of specific circumstances or sought to showcase the benefits and efficacy of the medicines under study. Second, the actions of enslaved family members, sufferers, and healers directed practitioners' attention to bodily difference. More specifically, these groups drew attention to the bodily effects of plantation slavery—inadequate sustenance, exposure, and overwork—and successfully made the case that, as a result of their enfeeblement, they required different methods of treatment than the expectorant and purgative therapeutics commonly imposed upon them.

Slavery itself, in other words, had devastating effects on the human body. Both laypeople and practitioners claimed that the blood of enslaved people was thinner than that of colonists. Yet they gave different reasons why they thought this was the case. Slaveholders maintained that it was generated in the abuse of mercury—beginning with slave ship surgeons and continuing with plantation practitioners.[90] Chamberlaine and other surgeons pointed to quotidian conditions of overwork and the abjection characteristic of enslaved life on sugar plantations. "The blood of such negroes," he wrote, "as work hard in hot climates, take but little rest, and live mostly upon a vegetable diet, will, even in a healthy state, be found much thinner and less disposed to coagulate, than that of white people." "Mercurial medicines," he concluded, "therefore, are hurtful, by breaking down and destroying the texture of the blood, already too much dissolved, by heat, and the nature of their provisions."[91] Whether they attributed the physiological difference to the living conditions of slavery or the overuse of mercury in the treatment of yaws, both groups concluded that enslaved people's blood was not the same as that of colonists.

Although few practitioners would say so outright, it is clear that enslaved sufferers contributed to these lay and expert claims about bodily difference. As a means to reduce their exposure to dietary and harsh medical regimens as a component of their restoration, enslaved sufferers testified to the effects of mercury or other environmental factors that had caused their illnesses or condition. Sometimes this occurred through enslaved intermediaries. In one instance, from Grenada, a trio of yaws patients were put under the care of an enslaved healer, renowned for successfully recovering those afflicted with yaws. While in his custody, his yaws patients communicated the dire effects of previous mercurial medicines upon them. And in the process of explaining to the estate's overseer why his remedy had failed, the enslaved healer relayed what his patients had told him. They were "affected with pains in their bones, which the negro alleged were owing to the mercury they had taken before they were put under his care."[92] The statement of the Grenadian yaws patients is characteristic of numerous enslaved patients' actions and testimony that, in the aggregate, directed colonists' attention to the cumulative effects of harsh medicines.

Enslaved people assimilated the grammar of colonists' medical narratives, particularly when they accounted for the effects of climate in either producing illness or rendering an existing affliction more severe. This was the case especially during experiments. It is possible to see these processes at work in practitioners' case histories, in spite of the fact that a silencing mechanism is also at play, a feature inherent in the archives of slavery.[93] In 1778, an enslaved watchman in Westmoreland, Jamaica, was suffering from an illness that had been made worse by his inadequate shelter. The watchman may have contributed to colonists' medical narratives as a way to agitate for much-needed resources. Having hobbled down from his station in the plantain-walk to the main works to ask for aid, he suddenly experienced a "stiffness of his jaws, neck and spine, with acute pain." The overseer waited a few days but eventually summoned the estate's doctor, a man named John Drummond. When Drummond arrived, the overseer informed him that the watchman's abrupt stiffness and spasms were probably linked to cocobay, or "cocbia" (what colonists maintained was a variant of leprosy), a chronic complaint that had seized the watchman three years earlier.[94] And yet there were, as Drummond soon learned, possibly from the watchman, other precipitating factors that had thrown the watchman into spasms. In his case history, Drummond relayed that the watchman's hut was in poor shape. It was, moreover, "situated in valley, in the midst of woods and plantain walks." Drummond concluded that the sudden appearance of "moist and foggy weather" had transmogrified the watchman's chronic disease to an acute crisis that immobilized his entire body.[95] He prescribed a cold-bathing remedy. But this prescription was experimental—he therefore visited the estate over a period of two weeks to watch its effects unfold.

It seems likely that the information that Drummond received and transformed into a case history was coproduced. But by whom and how?

From the overseer and possibly the watchman, Drummond received information on the remote origins of the man's crisis—the long-standing cocobay. He may have even learned about its proximate causes—the abrupt turn to damp and cold weather. But who told Drummond that the man's house had increased the watchman's exposure to Jamaica's fog and damp? Drummond almost certainly did not visit the watchman's station. It is also unlikely that the watchman could have told Drummond in the midst of his crisis—he could barely move his jaws. Perhaps the overseer filled in these details. Perhaps the watchman did during his numerous encounters with Drummond. The doctor's cold-bathing remedy was experimental. That brought him into more frequent contact with the watchman than was usually the case. Drummond was invested in seeing the effects of his remedy. Cold bathing brought the watchman great relief and opened up additional opportunities to speak. "He speaks distinctly and swallows better," Drummond relayed in his case history.[96] As the watchman recovered and conversed with Drummond, perhaps he elaborated on the overseer's account. In any case, the information about the watchman's deteriorating hut and the flash of cold weather was front and center in Drummond's case history. It was right there alongside the overseer's description of the cocobay. Yet it is unclear whether the watchman's hut was repaired or removed to a more salubrious place. In encounters with overseers, practitioners, and enslaved healers, enslaved people developed an understanding of how to narrate their own illnesses to colonists in order to make a compelling case. Moreover, they deployed this know-how strategically on particular audiences in order to encourage managers to oblige their demands. Certain precipitating causes, they came to understand, needed to be stressed, but which ones depended on the listener.

As an assemblage comprised of "careless" healers, talkative sufferers, and determined kin, slaveholders' system of intervention in the plantation Caribbean created a bricolage of people and things that were a far cry from the "tightly controlled authoritarian communities" of the hospitals of the British Army, the Royal Navy, as well as the social relations of care and discipline in the charity hospitals of metropolitan Britain.[97] In their own day, the intellectual output of practitioners working in British hospitals and the armed forces set the bar for what types of knowledge ought to be produced. Their orderly archives, in turn, have shaped our own understandings of medical education and medical knowledge-making in institutions of care. There were, however, dynamics specific to West Indian hospitals and other spaces and relations of managerial oversight that complicate the larger historiographic narrative about the relationship between surveillance, confinement, and the trying of cures and dietary regimens.

To be sure, plantation practitioners produced knowledge. But not in the volume or scope that might be anticipated from medical men whose work abetted the manpower needs of racialized labor regimes. Despite their claims to the contrary, slaveholders and managers depended almost entirely upon enslaved healers as well as sufferers' kin for the recuperation of the sick. Yet, although plantation practitioners helped to consolidate a medical regime whose power was derived from the separation of sufferers from kin, enslaved people's interventions rendered practitioners' power unsteady and precarious. In competition with one another and embattled with the personnel of estates, practitioners built rickety information infrastructures that were ultimately unable to support the types of knowledge-making expected by outsiders.

Enslaved people, in turn, became as attuned to the routines of plantation medicine as they were to those of labor—alert to the possibilities for when and how they might contend with illness on their own terms. Enslaved healers noticed what afflictions colonists did not understand and what remedies might be used; how much oversight they would receive from managers and plantation practitioners; and when they could expect these interlopers to visit the hospital. And slaves also observed what concepts colonists used to explain and describe illness. Colonists spoke often of the cumulative weight of work, diet, emotions, and exposure in producing bodily differences—that is, in predisposing a person to particular types of illness or in rendering a person's body unfit for the use of certain remedies. Actions such as the omission or misplacement of medicines, silence about their effects, and demands for alternatives slowed managerial knowledge-making and ultimately undermined practitioners' efforts to exploit patients' suffering for professional gain.

Efforts to manage enslaved affliction from above and opportunities to experiment with new remedies sometimes brought overseers, plantation practitioners, hot-house attendants, and enslaved sufferers into more regular contact with one another. Amid this top-down effort to delimit the geography of sickness and restoration in particular spaces, enslaved people, in whatever stations they occupied, adapted. In so doing, they came to shape the printed, manuscript, and oral archive of case histories—that is, the snippets of data and stories that informed local practice, remedies, and concerns. As plantation practitioners circulated these details to patrons, case histories came to inform the elite world of medical print; however, much of these case histories' particularity, including their accounts of the testimony and medical labor of enslaved people, was lost and compromised in the process.[98]

Conclusion

IN 1786, a distemper that colonists called "putrid sore throat" engulfed the island of St. Vincent. It killed many enslaved children and probably adults as well.[1] Colonists typically treated throat distempers with Jesuit's bark, antimony wine, and blisters. But these seemed to have no effect. As the illness spread unchecked, the enslaver John Collins conducted a massive trial with material culled from a red pepper plant.[2] Confident that it would reverse the distemper, he mixed it with vinegar. He then summoned mothers and their sick children to the hospital on his plantation, kept their children in the building, and had the remedy administered to them every two hours.[3] Collins claimed that his remedy recovered the sick. Shortly after his experiment, Collins returned to Britain, where he composed an essay based on his interventions. "On the Species of Angina Maligna and the use of Capsicum in that and several other diseases" (1790) outlined the course of the epidemic in St. Vincent and his experiments. Benjamin Vaughan, a fellow absentee enslaver and scientist living in London, facilitated the essay's publication in the Edinburgh-based periodical *Medical Communications*.

Privately, proprietors and attorneys had built sick-houses to minimize economic risk and unpredictability in the cost of healing and to extract more work from the men and women they held in bondage. Hiring medical men, appointing healers, and importing medicines enabled proprietors' control over sufferers and healers. Collins's trial shows how these buildings also facilitated larger experiments with different remedies that proprietors hoped would yield new protocols in matters of illness.

At the end of the eighteenth century, however, proprietors publicly recast their management strategies in a different light. These were not efforts to gain control and usurp enslaved people's customary activities. In essays like the ones that Collins published and in testimony before

Parliament, proprietors presented their activities in medicine as valiant, benevolent efforts to reduce the loss of enslaved life (and decrease their reliance on the Atlantic slave trade).

To do so, they recast their economically calculated decisions in health care, first begun in the middle of the century, as the actions of benevolent paternalists, whose rationality and empiricism enhanced the viability of their interventions. In his account, Collins used Linnaean nomenclature to identify the disease he battled and the remedy he used (he called the red pepper plant "capsicum" and the putrid sore throat *Angina maligna*). Although he cited enslaved women in nearby Grenada as some of the sources for his knowledge about the red-pepper plant, his larger narrative obscured the role of enslaved healers and the kin of the sick on his plantation in shaping trials with the remedy; there was nothing to suggest that health and healing had emerged from a vernacular Caribbean setting or that his interference might have elicited enslaved people's opposition and resistance. Significantly, he also drew a division between white and Black capacities for sentiment and concern. As he narrated how the illness spread across the island, Collins drew a distinction between Black and white responses to it: white parents and Collins were attentive and concerned, whereas enslaved mothers were indifferent to the dangers it posed and careless with the administration of the medicines he ordered.[4] Yet his actual experiment made knowledge by separating children from parents. This method was the practice of an enslaver-businessman who sought to minimize parents' involvement in order to maximize his own control. In his account of the trial, Collins echoed what would come to be the position of many proprietors in the nineteenth century in managing health care—their superlative capacity to both feel and reason underwrote their authority to decide what the sick would consume and where they would recover. Many elements of Collins's experiment had deep roots in proprietors' long-standing project to make plantation operations more efficient by reorganizing the work of health and healing by undermining enslaved people's control over medicine and illness management.

The sick-houses that proprietors built and the loose and informal research infrastructures that grew around them were originally intended to manage illness among adults. Yet as Collins's experiment reveals, by the last decades of the eighteenth century, proprietors had a new concern: children. The assemblage of people and things that proprietors had brought together to enact their control over adult illness earlier in the century provided a platform that facilitated proprietors' and attorneys' encroachment into childbirth and childrearing, a domain that enslaved women had previously controlled. Indeed, many of the lying-in houses that proprietors erected in order to supervise childbirth were not located in enslaved people's quarters but were additions made to existing sick-houses.[5]

The reorganization of medicine to make plantations more productive by making care more efficient transformed how enslaved people experienced illness as both sufferers and healers. In previous eras, the sick were less isolated. Sufferers may have recuperated in their own quarters or, possibly, in the Great House. Family members, friends, neighbors, and healers expressed affinity and concern in gestures of care—fetching water, drawing fires, cleaning, watching, preparing food, and making and administering medicines. Plantation medicine challenged enslaved people's pharmaceutical autonomy, imposed time-sensitivity to tasks, and erected a tiered hierarchy that allowed for the work of care to be delegated across different parties. The drive for efficiency threatened to reduce enslaved people's input. Removing the sick from their homes and placing them in sick-houses transformed illness into a medical event. Of course, not all illness was addressed in hospitals—people living with chronic conditions or those who were too infirm to work for long periods of time remained in their homes. Enslaved people would continue, moreover, to practice and avail themselves of what scholars have described as social medicine, including its ritual and spiritual elements.[6] Still, through managerial and enslaved intermediaries, proprietors came to exercise more authority and control over where the sick recovered, whom they consulted, and what they consumed. But enslaved people made sure that they were never entirely shut out of the process.

In sickness and as healers, enslaved people strove for autonomy, advocated for themselves, formed ties in carework, and struggled to survive, all while contending with a punishing system that wore down their bodies in the creation of sugarcane. Parthenia tended to Old Primus. Kickery took on more tasks than a healer could normally handle out of concern for the parturient women she helped in childbirth and the sick she fed, watched, and cleaned. Fanny risked a painful punishment to stand up to a lecherous doctor on behalf of her twelve-year-old daughter. A mother in Jamaica wrapped her son suffering from tetanus in a blanket rather than leave him exposed as the doctor William Wright ordered. The enslaved men who demanded Chamberlaine's rum and the people in the hot-house who insisted on sugar with medicine wrenched small comforts from managers' interventions. Enslaved hot-house healers subverted and thwarted practitioners' dangerous experiments. In these acts of love and yearnings for pleasure, we get a sense of enslaved people doing their best to survive, make the most of uncertainty, and create affective ties in a labor regime that cared only about their ability to work.

Their expressions of concern and care foiled managers' efforts to standardize medicine and to treat the sick as fungible. Enslaved people's opposition to tests and investigations conducted by plantation doctors and overseers compromised the integrity and scope of impromptu trials. The inconstancy in plantation doctors' presence and the rampant churn of managerial staff due to death and turnover, meanwhile, magnified the effects of enslaved people's opposition and made it difficult for managers to fully realize their objectives. Proprietors' program of body management required the labor of people whom slaveholders wanted to be involved—overseers, attorneys, doctors, and healers. Yet it also forced the sick to bargain with managers over absence from work. So the sick and the people who cared about them came to play a role as well.

The work of enslaved healers was transformed in this new system. Many of the activities they undertook looked the same—they watched and fed the sick, administered medicines, and cleaned. But these activities took on new political dimensions as care for the sick became about restoring their dignity and allowing them small measures of comfort. For healers, the plants that they used in plantation hospitals and that they saw incorporated into managers' remedies were drawn from a sacralized natural world and therefore had a different resonance than the meanings managers gave to them. They were part of a therapeutic practice that saw people, plants, and animals as interconnected through nature and ancestral spirits. Healers' work entailed mending illness by manipulating this larger sacralized world. The relocation of healers' work into hospitals or yaws houses did not entirely change the meanings of the plants that healers used. But these changes coincided with efforts to standardize the making of medicines according to colonists' system of measurement, which meant that healers' decision-making in the selection and making of remedies was subject to greater scrutiny. The number of people whom they attended also increased, and healing itself became more impersonal. Hospital doctors and doctresses now worked as both healers and guards and in exchange acquired resources for their own families. Further, they were situated as managers' proxies, whose purpose was to administer unpleasant imported medicines to the sick who might not want them.

Healers continued to wield important botanical know-how that colonists respected. They drew on their knowledge of the landscape to acquire substances and transform them into medicines. Yet their power and authority now derived as well from their capacity to broker between the competing demands of expectations of the young male managers they worked under and the sick they served.

Making body management more efficient required keeping better records about the sick and incorporating medical specifics into strategies of plantation management, which shaped the ways that plantation practitioners and managers saw bodies and disease. The hospital book that Collins and others used transformed the boys and girls afflicted with putrid sore throat into a series of entries in the record, whose responses to the remedy Collins tracked from above. Accounts such as lists of the sick, worklogs, and hot-house books gave managers a synoptic view of the estate at any moment in time. Lists of the sick abstracted individuals into felled units of manpower. Hospital books reduced illness to a cluster of symptoms or a disease and tracked which remedies worked on them. Orthodox medical practice and bedside medicine offered by family members prioritized extensive communication between sufferer and practitioner, or sufferer and healer, attention to the person, and remedies bespoke to both their affliction and their constitution. Treating the disease rather than the person encouraged the use of manufactured medicines and homemade remedies that could target the individual disease or symptom rather than a therapeutic paradigm that treated the individual's body with its particular idiosyncrasies guiding the analysis.[7] Aggregating people and symptoms onto paper kept conversations with the sick short. Plantation practitioners did not need to consult extensively with the people they treated, if at all. Instead, they could read about them in the hot-house book. Hospital books and the industrial scale of body management encouraged among practitioners and overseers a drift from older models of illness that were highly personalized and toward a more empirical and disease-oriented approach. Orthodox medicine did not go by the wayside. Rather, race and class were sustained and enacted through access to personalized, person-centered care.

Many of the British Empire's laboring populations, such as sailors and soldiers, experienced this highly impersonal style of medicine that operated according to a "take-this-for-that approach."[8] However, the context in which medicines were administered mattered, and the circumstances of the enslaved and the enlisted were not the same. Because they attended to fewer people at the same time and were supported by hospital staff, British Army and voluntary hospital surgeons had more resources to attend to the sick. Plantation practitioners rarely had the wherewithal or the inclination to speak to the enslaved sick. Without the will or capacity to attend to sufferers' strength or their improvement and decline, practitioners' chemical medicines were often deadly. Overseers and attorneys, moreover, were incentivized to extract as much labor as possible from enslaved people because their salaries were dependent on crops produced, not lives saved. There was more incentive to standardize remedies and adopt a one-size-fits-all approach than to augment the amount of medical attention to the enslaved sick. They could also treat enslaved people's bodies as disposable to a degree that was not possible in the British Army and the Royal Navy, where the loss of armed manpower sapped morale and diminished Britons' support for war-making.[9] It was increasingly common across the British Empire to use specific medicines to treat specific diseases. Yet the circumstances mattered as much as the theory behind them, and enslaved people experienced a considerable degree of neglect and indifference compared to other laboring and unfree groups.

The terms that practitioners developed to describe their work provides a glimpse into the ways that practitioners' strategies to administer medicine on a nearly industrial scale paved the way for reading racial difference onto enslaved populations. Toward the end of the eighteenth century, plantation practitioners developed a number of compound phrases particular to this arena of medicine. Plantation medical men were described as "country practitioners" who engaged in "country practice," "plantation practice," and "negroe practice."[10] These terms partially described the geography of this particular arena of medicine—that it concerned large estates in the Caribbean's hinterlands rather than the households of its seaports. Across the Anglophone world, "negroe" denoted Africans and people of African descent. But when plantation practitioners used this term, they were often discussing (and generalizing about) enslaved people who lived on plantations whom they treated. The term "negroe practice" is an artifact of a set of working conditions that motivated practitioners to generalize about the large numbers of people whom they saw too quickly to treat adequately. Practitioners simultaneously neglected enslaved people's bodies and treated them as fungible. The treatment of Black bodies as interchangeable helped practitioners expedite their work.

The creation and naturalization of racial difference in the late eighteenth and early nineteenth centuries was thus abetted by the reorganization of body management in midcentury, which saw practitioners shuffling through hundreds of enslaved sick at the same time. Ideas of predisposition—that bodies were malleable and that a person's habits had a cumulative and determinative effect in shaping their constitution and the expression of illness—continued to hold sway. And practitioners used this as part of their analytical toolkit. They did not have the wherewithal, time, or resources to attend to the idiosyncrasies of the bodies of the individual people under their care. Instead, they generalized using ideas of predisposition. When they looked comparatively and retrospectively at Black and white bodies' responses to illness, they saw differences and tried to account for them by generalizing about enslaved people, attributing those differences to race rather than slavery. A handful of plantation practitioners, such as John Williamson or David Collins, wrote books that they published in the nineteenth century that calcified a variety of firsthand observations into notions of racial difference, visible in the differences in Black people's nervous systems and their vulnerability to illness. Whether they argued that Black people were less sensate than white people or less vulnerable to tropical fevers, race came to have explanatory power in diagnosis and treatment.[11] Practitioners-turned-writers like Collins and Williamson developed the theories of racial difference that retrospectively justified the calculated indifference and therapeutic violence to which ordinary plantation medical men subjected enslaved people. By the middle of the nineteenth century, race science came to have even greater purchase in the United States, particularly in the practices of ordinary medical men attending to plantations. Medical schools and medical museums naturalized and formalized vernacular ideas of racial difference in their collection of objects and in their curricula. Engaging in comparative anatomy, they purported to offer scientific proof of the theory of polygenesis—the idea that mankind descended from different human origins—by showing that differences between Black people and white people were not in the cutaneous layers of the skin but, rather, in the deep anatomical structures of the human body.[12]

Amid this brutal system, men and women engaged in gestures, small and large, to contend with slaveholders' interventions and claw back their bodily autonomy. They pushed managers to see them as people and not as fungible units whose bodies all behaved the same way. They accompanied one another to the hospital and surreptitiously offered food and other items of comfort. Telling their stories brings awareness to the historical origins and resonances of contemporary problems, where a combination of racism and particular financial structures in the U.S. health care system continues to shape the experience of illness and create vastly different health outcomes.

Newer forms of scientific racism persist in the most advanced biomedical research into the human genome.[13] But one does not have to enter the laboratory to find medical racism—it structures encounters with and access to the U.S. health care system. The systemic racism that organizes patterns of segregation in the United States deepens health inequities by limiting access to education and employment prospects for people of color, creating racial disparities in access to health care in the form of pharmacy and hospital deserts in low-income neighborhoods.[14] A system whereby access to medicine and health care is dependent on employment means that the health consequences of job loss fall disproportionately on the poor, among whom people of color are overrepresented. We still live under a system designed to deny the physiological effects of racism and to use medicine to get us back to work.

The experience of medical racism is not limited to low-income people of color. For those who can access health care, racial discrimination has lethal consequences. Medical racism materializes in denials of pain and pain medication; in racist attitudes of providers that result in shorter visits, paternalistic communications, and reduced access to preventative care; ghastly Black maternal mortality rates; and in the longer wait times in emergency rooms that Black patients experience.[15] Although civil rights law dismantled formal segregation decades ago, the financing structures of the contemporary health care system that are the product of neoliberal austerity, and the market orientation of many hospitals have also created systems of health care segregation. In many deindustrialized cities, academic medical centers have replaced factories as the largest urban industries and employers.[16] The result has been the consolidation of the health care market around academic medical centers (AMCs). This has created an urban health care landscape wherein "AMCs disproportionately care for White and affluent patients, whereas underinsured Black patients remain hypersegregated in neighboring, lower-resourced AMCs and community hospitals."[17] Looking at the economics of the U.S. health care system reveals in short order how people of color have been made to bear the lethal inequities of neoliberalism.

Some of the strategies that Black Americans have developed to contend with these lethal challenges in the present echo the ingenuity and creativity of enslaved people in the past. They also reveal the ways that contemporary medical racism burdens Black Americans with sustaining a double consciousness as a matter of survival.[18] A recent large-scale study of Black Californians' experiences with the health care system captured some of the many measures that Black Californians must employ to get the care they need in everyday encounters with a racist health care system. In addition to remaining intentional about their health care, survey respondents mentioned speech as a prominent strategy. They tailored their speech to put providers at ease, to avoid being perceived as difficult, or to ask important questions to ensure they received the information and attention they need. Many asked a companion to accompany them to make sure they were taken seriously and to create expectations of accountability.[19] Individuals have adopted and improvised these strategies to contend with medical racism, but it should not be individuals' problems to manage and solve. Instead, it will take a broader, collective vision to dissolve the intertwinement of racism, finance, and health care that slavery produced.

NOTES

Notes on Sources and Methods

1. Lena Cowen Orlin, "Fictions of the Early Modern English Probate Inventory," in *The Culture of Capital: Properties, Cities and Knowledge in Early Modern Europe*, ed. Henry S. Turner (New York: Routledge, 2004), 51–84; Marisa J. Fuentes, *Dispossessed Lives: Enslaved Women, Violence, and the Archive* (Philadelphia: University of Pennsylvania Press, 2016), 1–6; Stephanie E. Smallwood, "The Politics of the Archive and History's Accountability to the Enslaved," *History of the Present* 6, no. 2 (Fall 2016): 117–32.
2. Stephanie Smallwood, "Commodified Freedom: Interrogating the Limits of Anti-Slavery Ideology in the Early Republic," in *Whither the Early Republic: A Forum on the Future of the Field*, ed. Michael A. Morrison and John Lauritz Larson (Philadelphia: University of Pennsylvania Press, 2012), 139–48.
3. Saidiya Hartman, "Venus in Two Acts," *Small Axe*, 12 (2008), 4.
4. Jennifer L. Morgan, "Accounting for 'The Most Excruciating Torment': Gender, Slavery, and the Trans-Atlantic Passages," *History of the Present* 6 (2016): 186.
5. Jennifer L. Morgan, "Archives and Histories of Racial Capitalism: An Afterword," *Social Text* 33, no. 4 (2015): 156.
6. Vincent Brown, *The Reaper's Garden: Death and Power in the World of Atlantic Slavery* (Cambridge, MA: Harvard University Press, 2008), 10.
7. Brown, *The Reaper's Garden*, 10.
8. Lauren Kassell, "Casebooks in Early Modern England: Medicine, Astrology, and Written Records," *Bulletin of the History of Medicine* 88 (2014): 595–625; Gianna Pomata, "Sharing Cases: The Observationes in Early Modern Medicine," *Early Science and Medicine* 15 (2010): 193–236; Gianna Pomata, "*Praxis Historialis*: The Uses of *Historia* in Early Modern Medicine," in *Historia: Empiricism and Erudition in Early Modern Europe*, ed. Pomata and Nancy G. Siraisi (Cambridge, MA: MIT Press, 2005).
9. Steven Shapin and Simon Schaeffer, *The Leviathan and the Air-Pump: Hobbes, Boyle, and the Experimental Life* (Princeton, NJ: Princeton University Press, 1975).

Introduction

1. West Indian proprietors recruited young male adolescents as bookkeepers (Richard Pares, "A London West-India Merchant House," in *Essays Presented to Sir Lewis Namier*, ed. Pares and A. J. P. Taylor [London: Macmillan, 1956], 75–107, esp. 91–92). George Stewart, the young nobleman in disguise who is depicted in *Marly; or, A Planter's Life in Jamaica* ([Glasgow: Richard Griffith, 1828], 15, 30), is sixteen when he is first employed as a bookkeeper on a sugar plantation.
2. Chamberlaine's visit and Edmonds's entries are described in William Chamberlaine, *A Practical Treatise on the Efficacy and Safety of Stizolobium, or Cowhage Internally Administered in Diseases Occasioned by Worms* (1784), 69–70.
3. Bookkeepers' activities in medicine have been reconstructed from *Marly; or, A Planter's Life in Jamaica*, 49–50.
4. When describing the enslaved people ensnared in colonists' sites of medical care, I use the terms "sufferers," "the sick," and sometimes "patients." These terms foreground that, for many, illness was not conceived of primarily in medical terms. On the use of the term "sufferer" versus "patient," see Roy Porter, ed., *Patients and Practitioners: Lay Perceptions of Medicine in Pre-Industrial Society* (Cambridge: Cambridge University Press, 1985), 3; and Flurin Condrau, "The Patient's View Meets the Clinical Gaze," *Social History of Medicine* 20, no. 3 (2007): 525–40.
5. On the "paper panopticon," see Elena Serrano, "Bookkeeping for Caring: Notebooks, Parchment Slips, and Enlightened Medical Arithmetic in Madrid's Founding House," in *Working with Paper: Gendered Practices in the History of Knowledge*, ed. Carla Bittel, Elaine Leong, and Christine von Oertzen (Pittsburgh, PA: University of Pittsburgh Press, 2019), 78. On the implementation of sophisticated systems of recordkeeping in the British Caribbean from the mid-eighteenth century onward as a strategy of labor management, see Caitlin Rosenthal, *Accounting for Slavery: Masters and Management* (Cambridge, MA: Harvard University Press, 2018); and Justin Roberts, *Slavery and the Enlightenment in the British Atlantic, 1750–1807* (Cambridge: Cambridge University Press, 2013), 27–79.
6. On the history and concept of medical arithmetic, see the essays by Ulrich Tröhler, Andrea Rusnock, and Harry Marks in *Body Counts: Medical Quantification in Historical and Sociological Perspective*, ed. Gérard Jorland and George Weisz (London: McGill Queen's University Press, 2005); Serrano, "Bookkeeping for Caring," 77–78.
7. I have reconstructed the limited scope of hot-house books' records (and how they were used) from the following sources: Chamberlaine, *A Practical Treatise;* "Mr. Richard Beckford's Instructions," box 11, folder 18, Series 3, Thomas Thistlewood Papers, Beinecke Rare Book and Manuscript Library,

Yale University (hereafter cited as Thistlewood MSS); [John Cumming], *Daily Advertiser* (Kingston), July 15, 1790; Stephen Fuller, *Notes on the Two Reports from the Committee of the Honourable House of Assembly of Jamaica Appointed to Examine into, and to Report to the House, the Allegations and Charges Contained in the several Petitions which have been Presented to the British House of Commons, on the Subject of the Slave Trade, and the Treatment of Negroes* (London, 1789), 59–60; J. B. Moreton, *West India Customs and Manners* (London, 1793), 21–23; William Sells, *Remarks on the Condition of the Slaves in the Island of Jamaica* (London, 1823), 15; Thomas Roughley, *The Jamaica Planter's Guide* (London: Longman, Hurst, Rees, Orme, and Brown, 1823), 93; and John Baillie's description, as quoted in Richard B. Sheridan, *Doctors and Slaves: A Medical and Demographic History* (Cambridge: Cambridge University Press, 1985), 294 (original citation: *Accounts and Papers [Parliamentary Papers]* 305, no. 127, pt. 2 [1832]: 63).

8. Historians lack systematic rates of sickness for the eighteenth century. Our overall picture comes from numbers derived from individual estates. For example, on Mesopotamia, one of the largest sugar plantations in eighteenth-century Jamaica, men "endured" field work, on average, for a mere 17.7 years and women for 19.6 before they were transferred to so-called marginal roles. Mesopotamia's slaves spent 44 percent of their lives weakly and 11 percent incapacitated. Their average age of death was 46.6 years (Richard Dunn, *A Tale of Two Plantations: Slave Life and Labor in Jamaica and Virginia* [Cambridge, MA: Harvard University Press, 2014], 436–37, 142–43). Much of the violence of slavery lay in its destruction of enslaved people's bodies. Holing put acute stress on tendons and ligaments in people's shoulders and hands. Planting and manuring strained backs and hips (Justin Roberts, "The Whip and the Hoe: Violence, Work, and Productivity on Anglo-American Plantations," *Journal of Global History* 6 [2010]: 108–30).

9. Catherine Hall, "Racial Capitalism: What's in a Name?" *History Workshop Journal* 94 (2022): 5–21, quote on 11.

10. Christer Petley describes planters as "risk-taking industrial capitalists" (Petley, *White Fury: A Jamaican Slaveholder in the Age of Revolution* [Oxford: Oxford University Press, 2018], 9). Scholarship that describes the methods and strategies that British sugar plantation owners deployed to commodify enslaved men and women, increase productivity, and maximize profits is extensive. For recent studies, see Rosenthal, *Accounting for Slavery*; Trevor Burnard, "Collecting and Accounting: Representing Slaves as Commodities in Jamaica, 1674–1784," in *Collecting across Cultures: Material Exchanges in the Early Modern Atlantic*, ed. Daniela Bleichmar and Peter C. Mancall (Philadelphia: University of Pennsylvania Press, 2011), 177–91; Roberts, *Slavery and the Enlightenment*; Randy M. Browne, *The*

Driver's Story: Labor and Power in the World of Atlantic Slavery (Philadelphia: University of Pennsylvania Press, 2024); Nicholas Radburn, "'Managed as If They Were Beasts': The Seasoning of Enslaved Africans in Eighteenth-Century Jamaica," *Journal of Global Slavery* 6 (2021): 11–30; and Christer Petley, "Managing 'Property': The Colonial Order of Things within Jamaican Probate Inventories," *Journal of Global Slavery* 6 (2021): 81–107. On women's experiences of profit-maximizing in plantation management, see Sasha Turner, *Contested Bodies: Pregnancy, Childrearing, and Slavery in Jamaica* (Philadelphia: University of Pennsylvania Press, 2017); Katherine Paugh, *The Politics of Reproduction: Race, Medicine, and Fertility in the Age of Abolition* (Oxford: Oxford University Press, 2017); and Barry W. Higman, *Plantation Jamaica, 1750–1850: Capital and Control in a Colonial Economy* (Kingston: University of the West Indies Press, 2005).

11. Scholarship examining medicine's role in enslaved people's resistance to slavery has tended to focus on the use of medicine and medical ritual in collective, coordinated action against the plantation labor system (see Karol K. Weaver, *Medical Revolutionaries: The Enslaved Healers of Eighteenth-Century Saint Domingue* [Urbana: University of Illinois Press, 2006]; Diana Paton, *The Cultural Politics of Obeah: Religion, Colonialism, and Modernity in the Caribbean World* [Cambridge: Cambridge University Press, 2015]; Vincent Brown, *Tacky's Revolt: The Story of an Atlantic Slave War* [Cambridge, MA: Harvard University Press, 2020], 105–11; and John Garrigus, *A Secret among the Blacks: Slave Resistance before the Haitian Revolution* [Cambridge, MA: Harvard University Press, 2023]).

12. Empire and slavery created similar material conditions as metropolitan charity hospitals. In bringing together large patient populations and creating the research infrastructures for the aggregation of data, all three encouraged practitioners to "see" disease as ontologically distinctive and track how they moved (Mark Harrison, *Medicine in an Age of Commerce and Empire: Britain and Its Tropical Colonies, 1660–1830* [Oxford: Oxford University Press, 2010]; and Jim Downs, *Maladies of Empire: How Colonialism, Slavery, and War Transformed Medicine* [Cambridge, MA: Harvard University Press, 2021]). These new studies are in dialogue with scholarship that locates the lineages of modern medicine in Paris's urban clinics, American centers of medical education, and British metropolitan hospitals (see Michel Foucault, *The Birth of the Clinic: An Archaeology of Medical Perception*, trans. A. M. Sheridan Smith [New York: Pantheon, 1975]; Guenter B. Risse, *Mending Bodies, Saving Souls: A History of Hospitals* [Oxford: Oxford University Press, 1999]; and John Harley Warner, *Against the Spirit of the System: The French Impulse in Nineteenth-Century American Medicine* [Princeton, NJ: Princeton University Press, 1998]).

13. On power as the central question guiding the study of politics and culture of slave societies, see Trevor Burnard, *Jamaica in the Age of Revolution* (Philadelphia: University of Pennsylvania Press, 2020), 18–19. On the threat of social death as central to slavery and the driver of enslaved politics, see Stephanie Smallwood, *Saltwater Slavery: A Middle Passage from Africa to American Diaspora* (Cambridge, MA: Harvard University Press, 2007); Vincent Brown, "Social Death and Political Life in the Study of Slavery," *American Historical Review* 114, no. 5 (December 2009): 1231–49; Turner, *Contested Bodies*; and Jennifer Morgan, *Reckoning with Slavery: Gender, Kinship and Capitalism in the Early Black Atlantic* (Durham, NC: Duke University Press, 2021). On survival, see Randy M. Browne, *Surviving Slavery in the British Caribbean* (Philadelphia: University of Pennsylvania Press, 2017), 2–5.
14. Selwyn Carrington, "Management of Sugar Estates in the British West Indies at the End of the Eighteenth Century," *Journal of Caribbean History* 33 (1999): 30–43; Richard B. Sheridan, *Doctors and Slaves*: 293, 301, 325; Betty Wood and T. Clayton, "Slave Birth, Death, and Disease on Golden Grove Plantation, Jamaica, 1765–1810," *Slavery and Abolition* 6 (1985): 99–121.
15. Turner, *Contested Bodies*; Paugh, *The Politics of Reproduction*; B. W. Higman, *Slave Populations of the British Caribbean, 1807–1834* (Kingston: University of the West Indies Press, 1994), 348–54.
16. Justin Roberts, "Surrendering Suriname: The Barbadian Diaspora and the Expansion of the English Sugar Frontier, 1650–75," *William and Mary Quarterly* 73 (2016): 225–56, quote on 230.
17. Trevor Burnard and David Geggus, *The Plantation Machine: Atlantic Capitalism in French Saint-Domingue and British Jamaica* (Philadelphia: University of Pennsylvania Press, 2016), 3–5.
18. On Worthy Park's enslaved population, see Michael Crayton, *Searching for the Invisible Man: Slaves and Plantation Life in Jamaica* (Cambridge, MA: Harvard University Press, 1978), 18. On York's, see Nicholas Radburn and Justin Roberts, "Gold versus Life: Jobbing Gangs and British Caribbean Slavery," *William and Mary Quarterly* 76 (2019): 223–56.
19. Petley, *White Fury*, 7.
20. Philip D. Morgan, "Slavery in the British Caribbean," in *Cambridge History of World Slavery*, vol. 3: *A.D. 1420–A.D. 1804*, ed. David Eltis, Stanley L. Engerman, K. R. Bradley, Paul Cartledge, Craig Perry, David Richardson, and Seymour Drescher (Cambridge: Cambridge University Press, 2011), 386.
21. Sheridan, *Doctors and Slaves*; Kenneth F. Kiple, *The Caribbean Slave: A Biological History* (Cambridge: Cambridge University Press, 1984); Higman, *Slave Populations of the British Caribbean, 1807–1834*, 261–301; J. R. Ward, *British West Indian Slavery, 1750–1834: The Process of Amelioration* (Oxford:

Oxford University Press, 1988), 160–65; Betty Wood and T. Clayton, "Slave Birth, Death, and Disease on Golden Grove Plantation, Jamaica, 1765–1810"; Amanda Thornton, "Coerced to Care: Thomas Thistlewood's Account of Medical Practice on Enslaved Populations in Colonial Jamaica, 1751–1786," *Slavery and Abolition* 32 (2011): 535–59.

22. On the increase in attrition rates in the second half of the eighteenth century, see Morgan, "Slavery in the British Caribbean," 378–406, esp. 385. Efforts to ameliorate slavery did produce improvements in enslaved people's health as early as the 1790s (J. R. Ward, "The Amelioration of British West Indian Slavery: Anthropological Evidence," *Economic History Review* 71 [2018]: 1199–226).

23. Roberts, *Slavery and the Enlightenment*, 167–201; Ward, *British West Indian Slavery*, 119–89.

24. On productivity and plantation management in the second half of the eighteenth century, see Roberts, *Slavery and the Enlightenment*, 27–30; Burnard, *Jamaica in the Age of Revolution*, 70–102; and Petley, *White Fury*, 127, 130–31.

25. Marcus Rediker describes the slave ship as a "war machine, mobile prison, and factory" and also discusses how these vessels made race by transforming Africans into "negroes" as well as Europeans into whites (Rediker, *The Slave Ship: A Human History* [New York: Penguin, 2007], 9–10). "Factory-like" and "industrial-style" are the descriptive terms Burnard and Geggus use in *The Plantation Machine*, 3–8. Sidney Mintz was the first to characterize plantations as industrial. He describes "factories-in-the-field," "land-and-factory combination," and the "agro-industrial enterprises" (Mintz, *Sweetness and Power: The Place of Sugar in Modern History* [New York: Viking Penguin, 1986], xxii, 50–51, 61). I have found Carolyn Roberts's analysis of how the social, biographical, and biological elements of illness were erased in the process of commodifying slave-trade captives similar to what proprietors attempted on their estates (Roberts, "Pharmaceutical Captivity, Epistemological Rupture, and the Business Archive of the British Slave Trade," *Business History Review* 97 [Summer 2023]: 283–305, esp. 295–96).

26. "Cowhage" is the vernacular term. The modern scientific term for cowhage is *Mucuna pruriens*. My omission of the Latin in the body of the text is a deliberate effort to avoid "retro-botanizing," a term that Projit Mukharji uses to describe the retrospective imposition of modern or learned understandings of the natural world onto people who did not endow these objects with the same identities and frameworks as modern readers (Mukharji, "Vishalyakarie as *Eupatorium ayapana*: Retro-botanizing, Embedded Traditions, and Multiple Historicities of Plants in Colonial Bengal, 1890–1940," *Journal of Asian Studies* 73 [2014]: 65–87).

27. My thinking on medicine, capitalism, and slavery, particularly on the emergence of the interchangeable body in medicine, is deeply indebted to Zachary Dorner, *Merchants of Medicines: The Commerce and Coercion of Health in Britain's Long Eighteenth Century* (Chicago: University of Chicago Press, 2020).
28. In the first decades of settlement, colonists heeded the counsel and botanical insights of Indigenous and Afro-Caribbean healers and depended on them for their survival (Pablo F. Gómez, *The Experiential Caribbean: Creating Knowledge and Healing in the Early Modern Atlantic* [Chapel Hill: University of North Carolina Press, 2017]; Londa Schiebinger and Claudia Swan, introduction to *Colonial Botany: Science, Commerce, and Politics in the Early Modern World*, ed. Schiebinger and Swan [Philadelphia: University of Pennsylvania Press, 2005], 8–13).
29. On Africans' and Afro-Creoles' botanical knowledge and Atlantic cultures of natural history, see James Delbourgo, *Collecting the World: The Life and Curiosity of Sir Hans Sloane* (Cambridge, MA: Harvard University Press, 2019); Londa Schiebinger, *Secret Cures of Slaves: People, Plants, and Medicine in the Eighteenth-Century Atlantic World* (Stanford, CA: Stanford University Press, 2017); Natalie Zemon Davis, "Physicians, Healers, and Their Remedies in Colonial Suriname," *Canadian Bulletin of Medical History* 33 (2016): 3–34; Tinde van Andel, "The Reinvention of Household Medicine by Enslaved Africans in Suriname," *Social History of Medicine* 29 (2016): 676–94; Judith Carney and Richard Rosomoff, *In the Shadow of Slavery: Africa's Botanical Legacy in the Atlantic World* (Berkeley: University of California Press, 2009); and Susan Scott Parrish, *American Curiosity: Cultures of Natural History in the Colonial British Atlantic World* (Chapel Hill: University of North Carolina Press, 2006). On the incorporation of African and Native materia medica into European pharmacopeias, see Benjamin Breen, *The Age of Intoxication: Origins of the Global Drug Trade* (Philadelphia: University of Pennsylvania Press, 2021); Matthew James Crawford and Joseph M. Gabriel, eds., *Drugs on the Page: Pharmacopoeias and Healing Knowledge in the Early Modern Atlantic World* (Pittsburgh, PA: University of Pittsburgh Press, 2017); Matthew James Crawford, *The Andean Wonder Drug: Cinchona Bark and Imperial Science in the Spanish Atlantic, 1630–1800* (Pittsburgh, PA: University of Pittsburgh Press, 2016); Susan Scott Parrish, "Diasporic African Voices in Enlightenment Knowledge," in *Science and Empire in the Atlantic World*, ed. James Delbourgo and Nicholas Dew (New York: Routledge, 2008), 281–310; and Timothy D. Walker, "The Medicines Trade in the Portuguese Atlantic World: Acquisition and Dissemination of Healing Knowledge from Brazil (c. 1580–1800)," *Social History of Medicine* 26 (2013): 403–31. Much of the literature on Europeans'

engagement with Afro-Creole pharmacological know-how casts these encounters as Afro-Caribbean people's contributions to European medicine. I follow the insights of Sara E. Johnson, who sees the erasure of enslaved people's intellectual work in Moreau de Saint-Méry's scholarship as exemplary of enslavers' predation (and theft) of Black knowledge (Johnson, *Encyclopédie Noire: The Making of Moreau de Saint-Méry's Intellectual World* [Williamsburg, VA: Omohundro Institute of Early American History and Culture, 2023], 4).

30. Roy Porter, "Lay Medical Knowledge in the Eighteenth Century: The Evidence of the *Gentleman's Magazine*," *Medical History* 29 (1985): 138–68.
31. Dorner, *Merchants of Medicines*, 6.
32. Harold Cook, "Markets and Cultures: Medical Specifics and the Reconfiguration of the Body in Early Modern Europe," *Transactions of the Royal Historical Society* 21 (2011): 123–45.
33. Dorner, *Merchants of Medicines*, 5–6.
34. Quotation from Sara Stidstone Gronim, "Imagining Inoculation: Smallpox, the Body, and Social Relations of Healing in the Eighteenth Century," *Bulletin of the History of Medicine* 80 (2006): 258.
35. Harold Cook, "Practical Medicine and the British Armed Forces after the 'Glorious Revolution,'" *Medical History* 34 (1990): 1–26.
36. In the middle of an epidemic of putrid sore throat, for instance, the surgeon James Stephens in St. Christopher's mixed dried and ground red-pepper plant with other ingredients and administered it to some four hundred patients (James Stephens, "An Account of the Use of the Pepper Medicine of the West Indies in the Cynanche Maligna, extracted from a letter written by Mr. James Stephens, Surgeon in St. Christopher's, to Dr. Thomas Cochrane, physician in Edinburgh," *Medical Commentaries for the Year M,DCC,LXXXVII* 2 [1788]: 378).
37. Samuel Martin, *Essay on Plantership* (London: T. Smith, 1750), 30.
38. Edmund S. Morgan and Marie Morgan, "Jefferson's Concubine," *New York Review of Books* 55 (October 9, 2008): 15–17.
39. Ralph V. Anderson and Robert E. Gallman, "Slaves as Fixed Capital: Slave Labor and Southern Economic Development," *Journal of American History* 64 (1997): 24–46.
40. Londa Schiebinger, "Naming and Knowing: The Global Politics of Eighteenth-Century Botanical Nomenclatures," in *Making Knowledge in Early Modern Europe: Practices, Objects, and Texts, 1400–1800*, ed. Pamela H. Smith and Benjamin Schmidt (Chicago: University of Chicago Press, 2007), 91.
41. On patients' narratives and their disappearance, see Foucault, *The Birth of the Clinic*; N. D. Jewson, "The Disappearance of the Sick-Man from Medical Cosmology, 1770–1870," *Sociology* 10 (1976): 225–44; N. D. Jewson,

"Medical Knowledge and the Patronage System in Eighteenth Century England," *Sociology* 8 (1974): 369–85; Mary E. Fissell, *Patients, Power, and the Poor in Eighteenth-Century Bristol* (Cambridge: Cambridge University Press, 1991); Roy Porter, "The Patient's View: Doing Medical History from Below," *Theory and Society* 14 (1985): 175–98; and Roy Porter and Dorothy Porter, *In Sickness and in Health: The British Experience, 1650–1850* (New York: Blackwell, 1988).

42. Thomas Dancer, *The Medical Assistant* (1801), 293.
43. Edward Long, *The History of Jamaica*, 2 (1774), 582.
44. The scholarship on the amelioration movement is extensive. It covers both the eighteenth and nineteenth centuries and includes discussions not only of medicine but of efforts to increase sustenance, ease work, and reduce the severity of punishments. For studies that discuss (and criticize) medical care explicitly, see Kenneth F. Kiple, *The Biological Slave*, 137, 142, 151; Richard Sheridan, *Doctors and Slaves*, 268–342; Anya Jabour, "Slave Health and Health Care in the British Caribbean: Profits, Racism, and the Failure of Amelioration," *Journal of Caribbean History* 28 (1994): 1–26; Higman, *Slave Populations of the British Caribbean, 1807–1834*, 261–72; and Michael Crayton, *Searching for the Invisible Man*, 119, 131.
45. "The work regimen" of sugar estates, the anthropologist Sidney Mintz writes, "made slaves into anonymous units of labour—alienated, expendable, and interchangeable—as if they lacked individuality or any personal past" (Mintz, *Three Ancient Cultures: Caribbean Themes and Variations* [Cambridge, MA: Harvard University Press, 2010], 11). Mintz also describes enslaved people as being treated as "interchangeable units" in *Sweetness and Power*, 51. In a recent set of essays, scholars build on Mintz's insights to make a convincing case that plantations generated their enormous profits and levels of productivity by rendering "slaves into new and essentially modern people" (Trevor Burnard, "Introduction: The Management of Enslaved People on Anglo-American Plantations, 1700–1860," *Journal of Global Slavery* 6 [2021]: 1–9, quote on 2).
46. For this definition of technology, see Justin Roberts, "Sugar in the Atlantic World," *Oxford Bibliographies*, last accessed March 5, 2024; and Richard B. Sheridan, "Changing Sugar Technology and the Labour Nexus in the British Caribbean, 1750–1900, with Special Reference to Barbados and Jamaica," *New West Indian Guide* 63 (1989): 59–93. On gang labor, see Roberts, *Slavery and the Enlightenment*; and Burnard and Garrigus, *The Plantation Machine*.
47. Nicholas Radburn and Justin Roberts, "Gold versus Life: Jobbing Gangs and British Caribbean Slavery."
48. Rosenthal, *Accounting for Slavery*.
49. Higman, *Plantation Jamaica*.

50. Catherine Hall, *Lucky Valley: Edward Long and the History of Racial Capitalism* (Cambridge: Cambridge University Press, 2024), 26; Jennifer Morgan, *Laboring Women: Reproduction and Gender in New World Slavery* (Philadelphia: University of Pennsylvania Press, 2004); Morgan, *Reckoning with Slavery*.
51. Childbirth (a natural process) became medicalized as managers forced women to relocate from their own quarters to lying-in houses where managers and doctors supervised how enslaved women gave birth (Turner, *Contested Bodies*; Paugh, *The Politics of Reproduction*).
52. On racial capitalism in eighteenth-century Jamaica, see Catherine Hall, *Lucky Valley*, 24–29. On its Atlantic dimensions, see C. L. R. James, *The Black Jacobins: Toussaint L'Ouverture and the San Domingo Revolution* (1938; New York: Vintage, 1963); and Eric Williams, *Capitalism and Slavery* (Chapel Hill: University of North Carolina Press, 1944).
53. For medicine and race in the Caribbean, see Rana Hogarth, *Medicalizing Blackness: Making Racial Difference in the Atlantic World, 1780–1840* (Chapel Hill: University of North Carolina Press, 2017); William Max Nelson, "Making Men: Enlightenment Ideas of Racial Difference," *American Historical Review* 115 (2010): 1364–94; Suman Seth, *Difference and Disease: Medicine, Race, and the Eighteenth-Century British Empire* (Cambridge: Cambridge University Press, 2018); Kevin Siena, *Rotten Bodies: Class and Contagion in Eighteenth-Century Britain* (New Haven, CT: Yale University Press, 2019), esp. 228–52.
54. Browne, *Surviving Slavery in the British Caribbean*, 4.

1. Catastrophe's Threshold

1. John Cumming, *Daily Advertiser*, June 21, 1790.
2. John Cumming, *Daily Advertiser*, July 15, 1790.
3. John Cumming, *Daily Advertiser*, June 21, 1790.
4. The details of the conflict, including transcriptions of the notices that Cumming and Kelly posted in the Stoney-Hill tavern, appeared in the *Daily Advertiser*, June 19, June 21, July 8, and July 15, 1790.
5. Justin Roberts, *Slavery and the Enlightenment in the British Atlantic, 1750–1807* (Cambridge: Cambridge University Press, 2013), 163–67.
6. On the turn to manufactured medicines, see Zachary Dorner, *Merchants of Medicines: The Commerce and Coercion of Health in Britain's Long Eighteenth Century* (Chicago: University of Chicago Press, 2020).
7. Carolyn Roberts explains that captives taken from the coast of Biafra conceived of their existence through their position within a larger "web of familial, social, environmental, and cosmic relations, that, when imbalanced

or fractured, cause illness, suffering, and misfortune" (Roberts, "Pharmaceutical Captivity, Epistemological Rupture, and the Business Archive of the British Slave Trade," *Business History Review* 97 [2023]: 300). Analogues of this belief existed throughout the plantation Caribbean, where enslaved people understood themselves as moving through a sacralized or spiritual world peopled by ancestral spirits, nature spirits, and malevolent entities. These entities offered protection and resided in particular places (see John Garrigus, *A Secret among the Blacks: Slave Resistance before the Haitian Revolution* [Cambridge, MA: Harvard University Press, 2023]; Pablo F. Gómez, *The Experiential Caribbean: Creating Knowledge and Healing in the Early Modern Atlantic* [Chapel Hill: University of North Carolina Press, 2017]). On enslaved peoples' predicament, see Vincent Brown, "Social Death and Political Life in the Study of Slavery," *American Historical Review* 114, no. 5 (December 2009): 1231–49.

8. Michel Foucault, *The Birth of the Clinic: An Archaeology of Medical Perception*, trans. A. M. Sheridan Smith (New York: Pantheon, 1975); Nicholas Jewson, "The Disappearance of the Sick-Man from Medical Cosmology, 1770–1870," *Sociology* 10 (1976): 225–44.
9. Mary E. Fissell, "The Disappearance of the Patient's Narrative and the Invention of Hospital Medicine," in *British Medicine in an Age of Reform*, ed. Roger French and Andrew Wear (London: Routledge, 1991), 92–109; Mary E. Fissell, *Patients, Power, and the Poor in Eighteenth-Century Bristol* (Cambridge: Cambridge University Press, 1991).
10. Miles Ogborn, *The Freedom of Speech: Talk and Slavery in the Anglo-Caribbean World* (Chicago: University of Chicago Press, 2020), 113–14.
11. An examination of enslaved people's interactions with hospitals—including the managerial staff who manned them—helps to counter what Pablo F. Gómez characterizes as the "artificial muting" of enslaved people's "words and worlds" (Gómez, "[Un]Muffled Histories: Translating Bodily Practices in the Early Modern Caribbean," *Osiris* 37 [2022]: 233–50, quote on 234).
12. Ogborn, *The Freedom of Speech*, 120–21.
13. John Cumming, *Daily Advertiser*, July 15, 1790.
14. B. W. Higman, *Jamaica Surveyed: Plantation Maps and Plans of the Eighteenth and Nineteenth Centuries* (Kingston: Institute of Jamaica Publications, 1998), 82.
15. B. W. Higman, *Plantation Jamaica, 1750–1850: Capital and Control in a Colonial Economy* (Kingston: University of the West Indies Press, 2005), 192.
16. Higman, *Jamaica Surveyed*, 81.
17. Higman, *Jamaica Surveyed*, 81.
18. Higman, *Jamaica Surveyed*, 81–82.
19. See, for instance, Greenwich plantation, Gray's Inn, and Virgin Valley, as documented in Higman, *Jamaica Surveyed*, 131, 136, 129.

20. John Johnson, "Reports Relating to Mr. Gordon's Estates in the West Indies, pt 2," M526a, no page number, image located between pages 22 and 23, Burke Library, Hamilton and Kirkland Colleges, Clinton, NY (hereafter cited as John Johnson Report).
21. John Johnson Report, 7.
22. Roberts, *Slavery and the Enlightenment*, 27; Trevor Burnard and John Garrigus, *The Plantation Machine: Atlantic Capitalism in French Saint-Domingue and British Jamaica* (Philadelphia: University of Pennsylvania Press, 2016), 1–8; Caitlin Rosenthal, *Accounting for Slavery: Masters and Management* (Cambridge, MA: Harvard University Press, 2018), 16–23.
23. [David Collins], *Practical Rules for the Management and Medical Treatment of Negro Slaves in the Sugar Colonies* (London, 1803), 259.
24. Poisons that did not have a human but, rather, an environmental origin were known as miasmas (Caroline Hannaway, "Environment and Miasma," in *Companion Encyclopedia of the History of Medicine*, vol. 1, ed. W. F. Bynum and Roy Porter [London: Routledge, 1993], 292–308).
25. Mark Harrison, *Medicine in an Age of Commerce and Empire: Britain and Its Tropical Colonies, 1660–1830* (Cambridge: Cambridge University Press, 2010), 121–72.
26. Kevin Siena explains putrefaction in *Rotten Bodies: Class and Contagion in Eighteenth-Century Britain* (New Haven, CT: Yale University Press, 2019), 21.
27. Erica Charters, *Disease, War, and the Imperial State* (Chicago: University of Chicago Press, 2014), 95–96.
28. Kevin Siena, "On Courtroom Dramas and Plot Twists: Typhus in Eighteenth-Century London," *Bulletin of the History of Medicine* 94, no. 4 (2020): 590–601, quote on 596.
29. The concerns that plantation managers expressed about space constraints in plantation sick-houses reference this body of thought, although not in precisely the same language. At the Mesopotamia plantation in Jamaica, for instance, John Graham anticipated the possibility that the hospital could not safely accommodate the many people who materialized there during the rainy season. At one point, the number of people crammed therein swelled to between sixty and eighty patients. "Our hothouse is still crowded tho none dangerous," Barham's attorney reassured the absentee (J. Graham to Joseph Foster Barham September 5, 1791, MS. Clar. dep. c. 357, Barham Papers, Bodleian Special Collections, Weston Library, Oxford University [hereafter cited as Barham Papers]).
30. Thomas Roughley advised readers to avoid building the hospital "too near the overseer's house" (*The Jamaica Planter's Guide* [Longman, Hurst, Rees, Orme, and Brown, 1823], 185–86).
31. WHO Yaws Fact Sheet, last consulted June 20, 2022. Both yaws and syphilis share the same genus, *Treponema*. Syphilis is caused by the bacteria

Treponema palladium. Early moderns believed that these two diseases were related (Katherine Paugh, "Yaws, Syphilis, Sexuality, and the Circulation of Medical Knowledge in the British Caribbean and the Atlantic World," *Bulletin of the History of Medicine* 88 [Summer 2014]: 225–52). On syphilis more generally, see Claude Quétel, *The History of Syphilis*, trans. Judith Braddock and Brian Pike (Oxford: Basil Blackwell, 1990).

32. Places for the recovery of the sick, the Jamaican plantation surgeon William Chamberlaine explained, "ought to be as cool, airy, and clean in those hot climates as possible" (Chamberlaine, *A Practical Treatise on the Efficacy and Safety of Stizolobium, or Cowhage*, 4th ed. [1787], 8n). In advocating changes to the built environment, plantation advice writers followed the lead of British medical thought, which had begun to tackle the problem of foul air through the modification of physical space (see James C. Riley, *The Eighteenth-Century Campaign to Avoid Disease* [Basingstoke, UK: Macmillan, 1987]; and Jan Golinski, *British Weather and the Climate of Enlightenment* [Chicago: University of Chicago Press, 2007], 139, 160).

33. James Grainger, *An Essay on the More Common West-India Diseases*, 2nd ed. (1802), 71.

34. [Collins], *Practical Rules for the Management and Medical Treatment of Negro Slaves in the Sugar Colonies*, 255–57.

35. Roberts, *Slavery and the Enlightenment*, 166.

36. [Simon Taylor Testimony], *Minutes of Evidence* (1792), 135; Taylor to Arcedeckne, Kingston, January 17, 1791, box 2, bundle 17, Vanneck Papers, Cambridge University Library (hereafter cited as Vanneck Papers), as quoted in Betty Wood and T. R. Clayton, "Slave Birth, Death, and Disease on Golden Grove Plantation, Jamaica, 1765–1810," *Slavery and Abolition* 6, no. 2 (September 1985): 114. There was already a hospital at Golden Grove that its doctor, John Hayward, designed in 1770. I have been unable to determine whether Taylor enlarged or replaced it (Higman, *Plantation Jamaica*, 193).

37. John Johnson Report, 2.

38. Sarah M. S. Pearsall, "'The Late Flagrant Instance of Depravity in My Family': The Story of an Anglo-Jamaican Cuckhold," *William and Mary Quarterly* 60 (2003): 549–82.

39. On John's and Ann's holdings and the number of enslaved people on each estate, see Pearsall, "'The Late Flagrant Instance of Depravity in My Family,'" 555n18, 557n28.

40. Pearsall, "'The Late Flagrant Instance of Depravity in My Family.'"

41. Richard B. Sheridan, *Doctors and Slaves: A Medical and Demographic History of Slavery in the British West Indies, 1680–1834* (Cambridge: Cambridge University Press, 1985), 274.

42. "Buildings to be Erected, Repairs and Observations Viz: Flamstead Estate," box 1, folder 2, MS. 180.1, Family Correspondence 1757–86, Flamstead

Estate, Crooked Spring & The Pen, Charles Vaughan Papers, Bowdoin College Special Collections, Brunswick, ME (hereafter cited as Vaughan Papers).

43. In 1784, the hospital on the Phillipsfield plantation had higher valuation than the overseer's house. Compare, for example, the "Framed hothouse on a stone wall and shingles £200" against the "Overseers House £50," in "Lands belonging to Nathaniel Phillips ESQ in St. Thomas in the East, May 10, 1784," ref. 11524, Slebech Estate Records, 1780–1812, Llyfrgell Genedlaethol Cymru/National Library of Wales (hereafter cited as Slebech). During his visit to Sanderson, Johnson described a formerly adequate building that had been allowed to fall into a state of disrepair. Its window shutters "were much decayed and admitted wind; many of the beds were wanting repair; and contrary to my expectations I observed the rooms were not swept every morning and were by no means clean." At the next plantation he visited, Johnson reported that the hospital's corners were covered with a "shameful accumulation of cobwebs which hung from the roof within the reach of hand" (John Johnson Report, pt. 2, pp. 6–9, 22–23).

44. On internal exchanges between estates, see B. W. Higman, "Patterns of Exchange within a Plantation Economy: Jamaica at the Time of Emancipation," in *West Indies Accounts: Essays on the History of the British Caribbean and the Atlantic Economy in Honour of Richard Sheridan*, ed. Roderick A. McDonald (Kingston: University of the West Indies Press, 1996), 211–31.

45. For the number of enslaved people at Golden Grove and Holland, see Higman, *Plantation Jamaica*, 172, 140.

46. [Simon Taylor Testimony], *Minutes of Evidence* (1792), 135; Taylor to Arcedeckne, Kingston, January 17, 1791, box 2, bundle 17, Vanneck Papers, as quoted in Betty Wood and T. R. Clayton, "Slave Birth, Death, and Disease on Golden Grove Plantation, Jamaica, 1765–1810," *Slavery and Abolition* 6, no. 2 (September 1985): 114.

47. April 4, June 16, 1757, Series I: Diaries, 1748–1786, OSB MSS 176, Thistlewood MSS.

48. *Further Papers Relating to the Treatment of Slaves in the Colonies (St. Christopher's)*, 3 (House of Commons, 1818), 8.

49. "Inventory of Pleasant Hill," "Inventory of Phillipsfield," Slebech, ref. 11523.

50. Case Eighty-Nine, in Trevor Burnard, ed., *Hearing Slaves Speak* (Caribbean Press for the Government of Guyana, 2010), 186–87 (original citation: C.O. 116/148-123-130, National Archives, Kew, Britain).

51. Chamberlaine, *A Practical Treatise on the Efficacy and Safety of Stizolobium, or Cowhage* (1784), 8.

52. [Collins], *Practical Rules for the Management and Medical Treatment of Negro Slaves in the Sugar Colonies*, 255.

53. Roughley, *The Jamaica Planter's Guide*, 187.

54. [Collins], *Practical Rules for the Management and Medical Treatment of Negro Slaves in the Sugar Colonies*, 255; Hogarth, *Medicalizing Blackness*, 153–55.
55. Burnard, *Hearing Slaves Speak*, 186–87.
56. Collins explained that the hot-house's door needed to be "directly in view, so that nothing of consequence can be transacted there, without its being heard by the proprietor or the manager" ([Collins], *Practical Rules for the Management and Medical Treatment of Negro Slaves in the Sugar Colonies*, 253). See, as well, James Grainger's advice that the sick-house "should be built near the dwelling house, but to the leeward of it" (Grainger, *An Essay on the More Common West-India Diseases; and the Remedies which that Country Itself Produces* [London, 1764], 71).
57. Thomas Plummer to Joseph Foster Barham II, St. Elizabeth's Jamaica, March 16, 1803, Barham Papers.
58. Family Correspondence 1757–86, Flamstead Estate, Crooked Spring & The Pen, box 1, folder 2, MS. 180.1, Vaughan Papers.
59. *Minutes of Evidence Taken before a Committee of the House of Commons* (London, 1790), 89.
60. "Instructions for Running a Sugar Plantation," Samuel Cary Papers, Ms. N-1997, Massachusetts Historical Society, Boston (hereafter cited as Cary Papers).
61. John Williamson lamented "the confused manner [that] is adopted in that country for providing sick negro suitably in a hot-house, or hospital" (Williamson, *Medical and Miscellaneous Observations, Relative to the West India Islands*, 2 vols. [Edinburgh, 1817], 1:54, 57).
62. My thinking on this has been informed by Stephanie Smallwood's writing on slave traders' calculations on the bare minimum of sustenance that would keep enslaved captives alive (Smallwood, *Saltwater Slavery: A Middle Passage from Africa to American Diaspora* [Cambridge, MA: Harvard University Press, 2007], 35–36).
63. [Collins], *Practical Rules for the Management and Medical Treatment of Negro Slaves in the Sugar Colonies*, 268.
64. John Van Heilen to Joseph Foster Barham, July 24, 1787, Barham Papers.
65. Simon Taylor to Chaloner Arcedeckne, November 1, 1789, Vanneck-ARC/3A/1789/27, Vanneck Papers. Thank you to Nicholas Radburn for sharing this source with me.
66. J. Worth Estes, *Dictionary of Protopharmacology: Therapeutic Practices, 1700–1850* (Canton, MA: Science History Publications, 1990), s.v. "Diet," 65–68.
67. [Collins], *Practical Rules for the Management and Medical Treatment of Negro Slaves in the Sugar Colonies*, 298.
68. Burnard, *Jamaica in the Age of Revolution*, 73; Nicholas Crawford, "Calamity's Empire: Slavery, Scarcity, and the Political Economy of Provisioning in the British Caribbean, 1775–1834" (PhD diss., Harvard University, 2016).

69. Samuel Cary to Charles Spooner and Joseph Sill Esq., June 12, 1771; Letterbook for the Simon Plantation, St. Kitts, Special and Area Studies Collections Library, George A. Smathers Libraries, University of Florida, Gainesville (hereafter cited as Simon Plantation Letterbook).
70. Nicholas Crawford, "'In the Wreck of a Master's Fortune': Slave Provisioning and Planter Debt in the British Caribbean," *Slavery and Abolition* 37 (2016): 1–22.
71. Samuel Cary to Charles Spooner and Joseph Sill Esq., June 12, 1771, Simon Plantation Letterbook.
72. Dorner, *Merchants of Medicines*, 89–104.
73. September 6, 1789, Journal of Jonathan Troup, MS 3027, Special Collections, University of Aberdeen (hereafter cited as Journal of Jonathan Troup).
74. Alexander Anderson to Benjamin Rush, St. Vincent, August 24, 1792, Benjamin Rush Correspondence, vol. 1, Rush Family Papers, 1748–1876, Library Company of Philadelphia (hereafter cited as Rush Family Papers).
75. John Johnson Report, pt. 2, p. 6.
76. John Van Heilen to Joseph Foster Barham I, November 6, 1782, Barham Papers.
77. [Collins], *Practical Rules for the Management and Medical Treatment of Negro Slaves in the Sugar Colonies*, 285.
78. Burnard, *Jamaica in the Age of Revolution*, 79.
79. Justin Roberts, "The 'Better Sort' and the 'Poorer Sort': Wealth Inequalities, Family Formation and the Economy of Energy on British Caribbean Sugar Plantations," *Slavery and Abolition* 35 (2014): 458–73.
80. Collins wrote that, in contrast to white people, all "negroes" had a greater tolerance for emetics and that more medicines were necessary to cure Black people's ailments. Collins ascribed enslaved people's insensitivity to pain to their diminished intellectual capacities, which rendered them less sensate ([Collins], *Practical Rules for the Management and Medical Treatment of Negro Slaves in the Sugar Colonies*, 233–34). On enslaved women characterized as animals by slaveholders, see Sasha Turner, *Contested Bodies: Pregnancy, Childrearing, and Slavery in Jamaica* (Philadelphia: University of Pennsylvania Press, 2017), 136.
81. James Adair, "Article 2. A Few Hints on Particular Articles of the Materia Medica, communicated in a letter to Dr. Duncan, from Antigua, by Dr. James Adair, now Physician at Bath," *English Review, or An Abstract of English and Foreign Literature* 7 (1786): 437–39, quote on 437.
82. Adair, "Article 2. A Few Hints on Particular Articles of the Materia Medica," 437.
83. Burnard, *Jamaica in the Age of Revolution*, 84.

84. *Further Papers Relating to the Treatment of Slaves in the Colonies* (St. Christopher's) (House of Commons, 1818), 7.
85. Roughley, *The Jamaica Planter's Guide*, 95.
86. February 21, 1790, Journal of Jonathan Troup.
87. The absentee slaveholder Matthew Lewis described how the enslaved healer, Miss Cook, accused some of the Eboe women on the Cornwall plantation of feigning illness (Lewis, *Journal of a West-Indian Proprietor* [1836], 190).
88. Testimony of Robert Jackson, M.D., *Minutes of Evidence Taken before a Committee of the House of Commons* (London, 1791), 61.
89. The attorney John Johnson also stipulated the importance of the estate's medical man attending the hospital alongside the overseer so that each "may become better acquainted with the *character* and *physical disposition* of the patients" (John Johnson Report, 8, underlining in original).
90. [Collins], *Practical Rules for the Management and Medical Treatment of Negro Slaves in the Sugar Colonies*, 261.
91. [Collins], *Practical Rules for the Management and Medical Treatment of Negro Slaves in the Sugar Colonies*, 277, 291.
92. March 18, 1790, Journal of Jonathan Troup.
93. March 19, 1790, Journal of Jonathan Troup.
94. [Collins], *Practical Rules for the Management and Medical Treatment of Negro Slaves in the Sugar Colonies*, 277, 288.
95. February 22, 1790, Journal of Jonathan Troup.
96. September 15, 1789, Journal of Jonathan Troup; Roberts, "Pharmaceutical Captivity," 303–4.
97. August 24, 1789, Journal of Jonathan Troup.
98. Christopher Hamlin, *More Than Hot: A Short History of Fever* (Baltimore, MD: Johns Hopkins University Press, 2014), ix, 6–7; Randall M. Packard, "The Fielding H. Garrison Lecture: Break-Bone Fever in Philadelphia, 1780: Reflections in the History of Disease," *Bulletin of the History of Medicine* 90 (Summer 2016): 193–221.
99. Charters, *Disease, War, and the Imperial State*.
100. Harrison, *Medicine in an Age of Commerce and Empire: Britain and Its Tropical Colonies, 1660–1830*.
101. Rana Hogarth, *Medicalizing Blackness: Making Racial Difference in the Atlantic World, 1780–1840* (Chapel Hill: University of North Carolina Press, 2017), 17–77.
102. [Collins], *Practical Rules for the Management and Medical Treatment of Negro Slaves in the Sugar Colonies*, 263.
103. "Every day they wash three times, after which they anoint themselves with tallow or palm oil, which is an excellent medicine and is yellow, looking

beautiful as saffron," Andreas Josua Ulsheimer observed during his time at Cape Coast Castle (Adam Jones, ed., *German Sources for West African History, 1599–1669* [Stuttgart: Steiner, 1983], 133).
104. *Further Papers Relating to the Treatment of Slaves in the Colonies (St. Christopher's)* (House of Commons, 1818), 7.
105. Testimony of Alexander Campbell, *Minutes of the Evidence Taken before a Committee of the House of Commons, Being a Select Committee* (London, 1790), 146.
106. *Further Papers Relating to the Treatment of Slaves in the Colonies (St. Christopher's)* (House of Commons, 1818), 9.
107. Sienna, *Rotten Bodies*, 41–42.
108. February 4, 5, 6, 1790, Journal of Jonathan Troup.
109. David Grant, *An Essay on the Yellow Fever of Jamaica* (Bath: Printed by R. Crutwell, 1801), xii. Thomas Roughley also focused on sores in his discussion of feigned illness (Roughley, *The Jamaica Planter's Guide*, 95).
110. Clement Caines, *Letters on the Cultivation of the Otaheite Cane: The Manufacture of Sugar and Rum; the Saving of Melasses; the Care and Preservation of Stock: with the Attention and Anxiety Which Is Due to Negroes* (London, 1801), 161.
111. Roberts, *Slavery and the Enlightenment in the British Atlantic*, 82–89.
112. Simon Taylor to Chaloner Arcedeckne, July 23, 1770, Vanneck-ARC, 3A/1770/8, Vanneck Papers, as quoted in Brown, *The Reaper's Garden*, 53.
113. Nicholas Radburn and Justin Roberts, "Gold versus Life: Jobbing Gangs and British Caribbean Slavery," *William and Mary Quarterly* 76 (2019): 223–56.
114. Lewis, *Journal of a West-Indian Proprietor*, 204–5.
115. Nicole Eustace, *Passion Is the Gale: Emotion, Power, and the Coming of the American Revolution* (Chapel Hill: University of North Carolina Press, 2008).
116. Turner, *Contested Bodies*, 120–21, 135–57.
117. Hector McNeil, *Observations on the Treatment of the Negroes in the Island of Jamaica* (London, 1788), 34–35.
118. Simon Taylor to Chaloner Arcedeckne, Kingston, July 5, 1789, Vanneck-ARC, 3A/1770/19, Vanneck Papers. For other discussions of the concealment of venereal disease, see *Memoires of the Late William Wright, M.D. Fellow of the Royal Societies of London and Edinburgh* (Edinburgh, 1828), 215; and Williamson, *Medical and Miscellaneous Observations*, 1:58–59.
119. February 7, 1790, Journal of Jonathan Troup.
120. On healing, illness, and community formation, see James Sweet, *Domingo Álvares, African Healing, and the Intellectual History of the Atlantic World* (Chapel Hill: University of North Carolina Press, 2011), 123–27; and Turner, *Contested Bodies*, 113, 120–21.

121. John Johnson Report, pt. 2, p. 7.
122. Ras Michael Brown, *African-Atlantic Cultures and the South Carolina Lowcountry* (Cambridge: Cambridge University Press, 2013), 22.
123. Michael A. Gomez, *Exchanging Our Country Marks* (Chapel Hill: University of North Carolina Press, 1998), 43–44, 77, 88, 99–100; Diana Patton, "Punishment, Crime, and the Bodies of Slaves in Eighteenth-Century Jamaica," *Journal of Social History* 34 (2001): 923–54; Elise A. Mitchell, "Across the Atlantic: Morbidity, Geography, and the Eighteenth-Century French Atlantic Slave Trade," *Atlantic Studies* 21 (2024): 90–114.
124. Brown, *The Reaper's Garden*, 41.
125. Robert Dirks, *The Black Saturnalia: Conflict and Its Ritual Expression on British West Indian Slave Plantations* (Gainesville: University of Florida Press, 1987), 153–57; Jerome S. Handler and Kenneth M. Bilby, "Obeah: Healing and Protection in West Indian Slave Life," *Journal of Caribbean History* 38, no. 2 (2004): 153–83.
126. Robert Thomas, *Medical Advice to the Inhabitants of Warm Climates* (London, 1790), x.
127. The warm water was not plain heated water but a specific medicinal drink that enslaved people and colonists used to cure afflictions. Grainger observed that what enslaved people called "hot-water" was the equivalent to what colonists referred to as "warm water gruel," a mixture of ingredients that had been boiled in hot water (Grainger, *An Essay on the More Common West-India Diseases*, 36).
128. September 28, 1789, Journal of Jonathan Troup.
129. Alexander X. Byrd, *Captives and Voyagers: Black Migrants across the Eighteenth-Century British Atlantic World* (Baton Rouge: Louisiana State University Press, 2008), 86–119.
130. Dirks, *The Black Saturnalia*, 53, 70.
131. John Racker Webb, St. Elizabeth's Jamaica to Joseph Foster Barham, August 28, 1805, Barham Papers.
132. McNeil, *Observations on the Treatment of the Negroes in the Island of Jamaica*, 8–9; Dirks, *The Black Saturnalia*, 54.
133. [Collins], *Practical Rules for the Management and Medical Treatment of Negro Slaves in the Sugar Colonies*, 264.
134. Caines, *Letters on the Cultivation of the Otaheite Cane*, 153.
135. Caines, *Letters on the Cultivation of the Otaheite Cane*, 268, 311.
136. Roberts, "Pharmaceutical Captivity," 303.
137. May 18, 1789, Journal of Jonathan Troup.
138. September 15, 1789, Journal of Jonathan Troup.
139. See John Lightfoot's advertisement for his yaws and venereal disease hospital (advertisement, *Jamaica Mercury and Kingston Weekly Advertiser*, March 11, 1780).

140. William Mann, *Kingston Journal and Jamaica Universal Museum*, October 10, 1776.
141. Quotations from the 1815 Jamaica Assembly Report in William Sells, *Remarks on the Condition of the Slaves in the Island of Jamaica* (London, 1823), 14.
142. Roy Porter, "The Gift Relation: Philanthropy and Provincial Hospitals in Eighteenth-Century England," in *The Hospital in History*, ed. Lindsay Granshaw and Porter (London: Routledge, 1989), 149–78.
143. Sampson Wood as quoted in Roberts, *Slavery and the Enlightenment*, 163–64.

2. The New Business of Plantation Medicine

1. Roy Porter, *Health for Sale: Quackery in England, 1660–1850* (Manchester, UK: Manchester University Press, 1989), 2.
2. John Luffman, *A Brief Account of the Island of Antigua* (1789), 95–96 ("young doctors"); Charles Leslie, *A New History of Jamaica, from the Earliest Accounts to the Taking of Porto Bello* (1740), 50 ("raw inexperienced youths"); J. B. Moreton, *West India Customs and Manners* (London, 1793), 21 ("apothecaries' boys," "smattering of Latin"); John Williamson, *Medical and Miscellaneous Observations, Relative to the West India Islands*, 2 vols. (Edinburgh, 1817), 1:189 ("apothecary's boy"); William Vassall to John Wedderburn, January 9, 1777, in *William Vassall Letterbooks, 1769–1800* (Wakefield, UK: Micro Methods, 1963) ("apprentice boy") (hereafter cited as *Vassall Letterbooks*); *Daily Advertiser* (Kingston) April 29, 1790 ("young and transient practitioners in the army and navy"); John Stewart, *An Account of Jamaica and Its Inhabitants by a Gentleman Long Resident in the West Indies* (Kingston, 1808), 145 ("perhaps a voyage or two on board of an African trader"). Thank you to Nicholas Radburn for sharing the Vassall letters with me.
3. Edward Long, *The History of Jamaica*, 3 vols. (1774), 2:583–85. Among slaveholders, Long's Apozem was an enduring satire. It was cited by Joshua Steele and William Dickson in *The Mitigation of Slavery, in Two Parts* (London, 1814), xiii.
4. On the passage of laws mandating that each estate contract with a doctor for the care of the sick, see Elsa Goveia, *Slave Society in the British Leeward Islands at the End of the Eighteenth Century* (New Haven: Yale University Press, 1965), 191–92. In Jamaica, this law was passed in 1781. The Consolidated Act of 1781 (1782) mandated that each estate employ a doctor who would maintain a list of the estate's decrease of slaves and the cause of death. See its wording in full in "XXXI," in *The New Act of Assembly of the Island of Jamaica* (London, 1789), 9.
5. Neil Cantlie, *A History of the Army Medical Department*, 2 vols. (London, 1974), 1:167.

6. Roger Norman Buckley, *The British Army in the West Indies: Society and the Military in the Revolutionary Age* (Gainesville: University Press of Florida, 1998), 65.
7. Vincent Brown, *Tacky's Revolt: The Story of an Atlantic Slave War* (Cambridge, MA: Harvard University Press, 2020), 63, 65. On the regulars and the independent companies, see Stephen Brumwell, *Redcoats: The British Soldier and War in the Americas, 1755–1763* (Cambridge: Cambridge University Press, 2002), 13, 155.
8. Buckley, *The British Army in the West Indies*, 51, 85–86. On the outsized role played by the Royal Navy, see N. A. M. Rodger, *The Wooden World: An Anatomy of the Georgian Navy* (New York: Norton, 1996); Michael Duffy, *Soldiers, Sugar and Seapower: The British Expeditions to the West Indies and the War against Revolutionary France* (Oxford: Oxford University Press, 1987).
9. William Wright, *Memoirs of the Late William Wright, M.D.* (Edinburgh, 1828), 12.
10. Wright, *Memoirs of the Late William Wright, M.D.*, 12, 15, 19, 22.
11. For an example of recruiting within a Scottish ethnic network, see Douglas Hamilton's discussion of Alexander Johnston in *Scotland, the Caribbean and the Atlantic World, 1750–1820* (Manchester, UK: Manchester University Press, 2010), 116. For the mobilization of a family network, see Eliza Farley, the niece of the University of Edinburgh professor and eminent nosologist William Cullen, who beseeched her uncle to ask the absentee slaveholder Mr. Millar to appoint her husband as the joint plantation doctor and attorney for his Antigua estates (Eliza Farley to William Cullen, St. Johns Antigua, March 10, 1787, CUL 1/3/181, Royal College of Physicians of Edinburgh). The Mr. Millar that Eliza referenced in her letter is possibly Dr. William Millar of Antigua, a friend of Cullen. See the identification of Millar in Dr. Alexander Stevenson to Dr. William Cullen, January 14, 1780, in CUL/1/2/884.
12. William Chamberlaine, *A Practical Treatise on the Efficacy and Safety of Stizolobium, or Cowhage*, 4th ed. (1787), 6.
13. For examples of Scottish ethnic networks, see Hamilton, *Scotland, the Caribbean and the Atlantic World*, 112–16. On the necessity of letters of recommendation to gain entry to plantation medical practice, see, for example, Eliza Farley to William Cullen, St. Johns Antigua, March 10, 1787, CUL 1/3/181, Royal College of Physicians of Edinburgh; John Tennent, "Letter from John Tennent to Sir Hans Sloane," *William and Mary Quarterly* 3 (1923): 211 (original citation: John Tennent to Sir Hans Sloane, London, April 1, 1740, in Sloane 4056, folio 217, British Library).
14. http://www.slavevoyages.org/estimates/94jQNzFC; https://www.slavevoyages.org/assessment/estimates.

15. Increases in the price of sugar and slaves are derived from David Eltis, Frank D. Lewis, and David Richardson, "Slave Prices, the African Slave Trade, and Productivity in the Caribbean, 1674–1807," *Economic History Review* 58, no. 4 (November 2005): 672–700; and Ahmed Reid, "Sugar, Slavery and Productivity in Jamaica, 1750–1807," *Slavery and Abolition* 37, no. 1 (March 2016): 159–82, esp. 163. Based on his analysis of shipping costs and the effects of runaway inflation in the 1790s and 1800s, David Beck Ryden argues that planters saw a long-run decline in prices during the eighteenth century, particularly during the years following the Haitian Revolution, regardless of increases in productivity (Ryden, "Does Decline Make Sense? The West Indian Economy and the Abolition of the Slave Trade," *Journal of Interdisciplinary History* 31, no. 3 [Winter 2001]: 347–74). On abolitionist concerns in combination with price increases as drivers of surgeons' employment, see Richard Sheridan, *Doctors and Slaves: A Medical and Demographic History* (Cambridge: Cambridge University Press, 1985), 43–45. The historian of amelioration J. R. Ward reached the same conclusion: "Near the end of the eighteenth century medical services to slaves were extended under the twin pressures of rising slave prices and humanitarian and political agitation to prohibit the Atlantic slave trade" (Ward, *British West Indian Slavery, 1750–1834: The Process of Amelioration* [Oxford: Oxford University Press, 1988]). On surgeons being hired to supplant enslaved midwives and encourage fertility, see Sasha Turner, *Contested Bodies: Pregnancy, Childrearing, and Slavery in Jamaica* (Philadelphia: University of Pennsylvania Press, 2017); and Katherine Paugh, *The Politics of Reproduction: Race, Medicine, and Fertility in the Age of Abolition* (Oxford: Oxford University Press, 2017).

16. Philip D. Morgan, J. R. McNeil, Matthew Mulcahy, and Stuart B. Schwarts, eds., *Sea and Land: An Environmental History of the Caribbean* (New York: Oxford University Press, 2022), 20.

17. On the notoriety of the Caribbean as a white man's grave among Royal Naval sailors, see Nicholas Rodgers, "Archipelagic Encounters: War, Race, and Labor in American-Caribbean Waters," in *The Global Eighteenth Century*, ed. Felicity Nussbaum, 212–25 (Baltimore, MD: Johns Hopkins University Press, 2003).

18. Benjamin Moseley, *A Treatise on Tropical Diseases and on the Climate of the West Indies* (1803), 86. On geophysical disasters, see Matthew Mulcahy, *Hurricanes and Society in the British Greater Caribbean, 1624–1783* (Baltimore, MD: Johns Hopkins University Press, 2006). On the Caribbean disease environment and white mortality, see Trevor Burnard, "The Country Continues Sickly: White Mortality in Jamaica, 1655–1780," *Social History of Medicine* 12 (April 1999): 45–72; and J. R. McNeill, *Mosquito Empires: Ecology and War in the Greater Caribbean, 1420–1914* (New York: Cambridge University Press, 2010).

19. Burnard and Geggus, *The Plantation Machine*, 7.
20. Stephanie Smallwood, "The Politics of the Archive and History's Accountability to the Enslaved," *History of the Present* 6, no. 2 (2016): 118.
21. Brown, *Tacky's Revolt*, 46.
22. July 30, 1789, Journal of Jonathan Troup, MS 2070.
23. Brown, *Tacky's Revolt*, 1–10.
24. Trevor Burnard, *Mastery, Tyranny, and Desire: Thomas Thistlewood and His Slaves in the Anglo-Jamaican World* (Chapel Hill: University of North Carolina Press, 2004), 7, 42, 53, 78.
25. Mark Harrison, *Medicine in an Age of Commerce and Empire: Britain and Its Tropical Colonies, 1660–1830* (Oxford: Oxford University Press, 2010), 64–88.
26. One of his patients, Lord Mulgrave, helped to secure him the post of chief physician to the Royal Military Hospital, Chelsea (Harrison, *Medicine in an Age of Commerce and Empire*, 80). On Moseley's position with the foot, see Moseley, *Observations on the Dysentery of the West Indies* (1781), 24; and Deborah Brunton, "Moseley, James (1742–1819)," in *Dictionary of National Biography* (*DNB*). A more modest example can be found in the itinerary of the surgeon William Lemprière, who came to Jamaica around 1790 as the surgeon to the Jamaica regiment of light dragoons (situated in the barracks at Fort Augusta, now Jamaica's women's prison). Lemprière remained on the island for five years before he returned to Isle of Wight, published *Practical Observations on the Diseases of the Army in Jamaica* (1799), and retired with the rank of deputy inspector-general of hospitals. Prior to Jamaica, Lemprière was stationed at the garrison in Gibraltar (see G. P. Moriarty, "William Lemprière," in *DNB*).
27. Moseley's network likely included John Dalling, acting governor of Jamaica from 1772 to 1774 and governor from 1777 to 1781. In the preface, Moseley dedicated his *Observations on the Dysentery of the West Indies* (1781) to Dalling.
28. The data from *The Medical Register* is limited in a number of ways that go far beyond the editors' exclusion of free and enslaved healers working in Jamaica from its pages. It is only available for two years (1780 and 1783), and though its editors listed practitioners from across the British Caribbean, only under the Jamaica subheading can one find where the practitioners lived (see *The Medical Register for the Year 1780* [London, 1780], 221–23; and *The Medical Register for the Year 1783* [London, 1783], 170–73).
29. Steven Shapin, "Trusting George Cheyne: Scientific Expertise, Common Sense, and Moral Authority in Early Eighteenth-Century Dietetic Medicine," *Bulletin of the History of Medicine* 77, no. 2 (2003): 270.
30. August 26, 1789, Journal of Jonathan Troup.
31. The career of Francis Rigby Brodbelt, a physician (M.D., Edinburgh, 1767) who resided in Spanish Town, is illustrative of this trend. In his screed on

doctors in the Caribbean, the author J. B. Moreton cited Brodbelt and David Grant as the exceptions to his disdain, declaring that "Real physicians are rarely to be met with, indeed; I never heard of any there, save only Messrs Grant and Broadbelt (Brodbelt), the former of Kingston, and the latter of Spanish-Town, whom you will find to be skilled and worthy characters; they have protracted the days of thousands" (Moreton, *West India Customs and Manners* [London, 1793], 19). On Brodbelt's residence in Spanish Town and title as a physician, see, additionally, "Broadbelt," in *Medical Register for the Year 1783* (1784). Brodbelt was also a public figure. When, in 1777, the Jamaican Colonial Assembly considered funding the construction of a hospital for invalids adjacent to a natural spring in Port Henderson, it appointed Brodbelt to a committee to inspect the mineral qualities of the spring. On Brodbelt's appointment, see Dancer, *A Brief Account of the New Settlement and Bath* (St. Jago De La Vega: Printed by Robert Sherlock, 1777), 16. He was also paid by the same body to attend prisoners at the Kingston jail (see *Votes of the Honourable House of the Assembly of Jamaica* [St. Jago de La Vega: Alexander Aikman, 1797], 141). On the growth of Royal Naval hospitals in Caribbean seaports, see Nicholas Rodgers, "Archipelagic Encounters: War, Race, and Labor in American-Caribbean Waters," in *The Global Eighteenth Century*, ed. Felicity Nussbaum, 212–25 (Baltimore, MD: Johns Hopkins University Press, 2003), 214.

32. Elizabeth Lichtenstein Johnston, *Recollections of a Georgia Loyalist* (New York: Mansfield, 1901), 82.
33. Alexander Anderson to Benjamin Rush, July 16, 1791, Benjamin Rush Correspondence, vol. 1, Rush Family Papers.
34. Benjamin Turney to Chaloner Arcedeckne, Golden Grove, March 29, 1790, Vanneck-Arc/3A/1790/3, Vanneck Papers, as cited in "Letters from Jamaica," https://freepages.rootsweb.com/~sedgebrook/history/page20.htm.
35. Benjamin Turney to Chaloner Arcedeckne, Golden Grove, July, 21, 1790, Vanneck-Arc/3A/1790/24, Vanneck Papers, as cited in "Letters from Jamaica," https://freepages.rootsweb.com/~sedgebrook/history/page20.htm.
36. Charles Leslie, *A New History of Jamaica* (1740), 50.
37. The military physician Thomas Dancer, for example, pestered the Kingston physician David Grant for Grant's clientele once Grant left Jamaica, a request Grant refused. For a summary of this request and the ensuing reputational attacks that played out in a pamphlet war, see David Grant, *An Exposition of the Conduct and Character of Thomas Dancer, M.D.* (Jamaica, 1805), 2–3.
38. Williamson, *Medical and Miscellaneous Observations*, 1:251.
39. Colin McLarty, Port Morant, Jamaica, July 23, 1787, to Elizabeth McLarty, Bowden, Scotland; Cunningham Letters, ACC 7285, National Library of Scotland, Edinburgh.

40. Simon Taylor to Chaloner Arcedeckne, Kingston, November 19, 1774, Vanneck-Arc/3A/1774/8, Vanneck Papers, as cited in *Travel, Trade and Power in the Atlantic, 1765–1884*, ed. Betty Wood and Martin Lynn (Cambridge: Cambridge University Press, 2002), 136.
41. Wm. Rodgers to Joseph Foster Barham, Westmoreland, Jamaica, July 5, 1802, MS. Clar. dep. c. 357, Barham Papers.
42. Thomas Clarke to Henry Cullen, Portmorant, Jamaica, September 12, 1783, CUL 1/2/1374, Royal College of Physicians of Edinburgh.
43. Burnard, *Mastery, Tyranny, and Desire*, 47.
44. Clarke received his first official appointment as island botanist from the Colonial Assembly in 1775 (see John Hope to Sir Joseph Banks, September 4, 1775, Banks Letters, vol. 1, folio 52, Kew Gardens Special Collections and Archives). Thank you to Kathleen Murphy for sharing this source with me. In preparing a second edition of the *History of Jamaica* around 1775, Edward Long wrote in the margins of the text that "there is now a botanist, Dr. Clark at £420 per annum" (Long Papers, *History of Jamaica*, vol. 2, Add MS 12416, p. 136, British Library). The Jamaican overseer, planter, and amateur naturalist Thomas Thistlewood recorded in 1777 a "Mr. Clarke, the botanist, in a continual state of ill health since his arrival" (Thomas Thistlewood to Edward Long, June 17, 1777, Add. MS 18725a. f. 128–29, British Library). For a period of time, Clarke maintained himself from his post as surgeon to the island ordnance (see "List of the Arms in Jamaica," in *Douglas and Aikman's Almanack and Register for the Island of Jamaica, calculated for the Year of our Lord 1781* [Kingston, 1781], n.p.). Clarke resumed the position of island botanist and superintendent to the botanical garden in 1785, as was briefly mentioned by Mathew Wallen in his letter, May 6, 1785, to Sir Joseph Banks, Add. Mss 33978, f. 11–12, British Library.
45. Mathew Wallen to Sir Joseph Banks, September 23, 1784, Add. Mss 33977, f. 267, British Library.
46. I am calculating the length of his country business based on Clarke's letter to Henry Cullen, Portmorant, Jamaica, September 12, 1783, CUL 1/2/1374, Royal College of Physicians of Edinburgh, in which he described as being engaged in a "large negro practice." And in his subsequent letter, in 1788, to Henry Cullen, Kingston, Jamaica, April 20, 1788, CUL 1/3/192, Royal College of Physicians of Edinburgh, Clarke mentions that he had quit this arrangement and taken up drug retailing in Kingston.
47. Williamson, *Medical and Miscellaneous Observations*, 1:76.
48. In 1759, for example, the mother of the absentee Thomas Hall speculated that if Thomas, then in London, "could meet with a doctor, one that has some experience and well used to the hospitals you would do well to get one for your estates" (Mary Barclay to Thomas Hall, August 23, 1759, in

Hall Family MSS, FB225–32, box 1, ff 50, Special Collections and Archives University of California, San Diego).

49. William Vassall to John Wedderburn, 9 January, 1777, in *Vassall Letterbooks, 1769–1800.*

50. In nineteenth-century America, this was called "contract practice" (Paul Starr, "Medicine, Economy and Society in Nineteenth-Century America," *Journal of Social History* 10 [Summer 1977]: 588–607, [contract practice], 590).

51. Williamson, *Medical and Miscellaneous Observations*, 2:178.

52. Hamilton, *Scotland, the Caribbean and the Atlantic World*, 125.

53. Alan Karras, "The World of Alexander Johnston: The Creolization of Ambition," *Historical Journal* 30 (1987): 69.

54. July 30, 1789, Journal of Jonathan Troup.

55. Nicholas Radburn and Justin Roberts state that in 1793 "a medium-sized sugar plantation in Jamaica with 250 slaves cost £29, 629 sterling" (Radburn and Roberts, "Gold versus Life: Jobbing Gangs and British Caribbean Slavery," *William and Mary Quarterly* 76 [2019]: 223–56, quote on 241).

56. Nicholas Crawford, "'In the Wreck of a Master's Fortune': Slave Provisioning and Planter Debt in the British Caribbean," *Slavery and Abolition* 37, no. 2 (2016): 1–22.

57. [David Collins], *Practical Rules for the Management and Medical Treatment of Negro Slaves in the Sugar Colonies* (London, 1803), 245–46.

58. John Luffman, of Antigua, specified it was "six shillings currency, equal to three shillings and nine pence sterling, per head" (Luffman, *A Brief Account of the Island of Antigua* [1789], 96). Speaking of his time as a plantation owner in St. Vincent, Sir Ashton Warner Byam stated that "the surgeon was allowed ten shillings per head for each negro per annum." Alexander Campbell, a slaveholder in Grenada, testified it was seven shillings, six pence per person. John Castles, surgeon in Grenada also stated it was this amount, with additional compensation for surgical operations (see Byam, Campbell, and Castles in *Minutes of the Evidence Taken before a Committee of the House of Commons, Being a Select Committee* [London, 1790], 108, 146, 220).

59. Numerous manuscript sources substantiate the consistency of the five-shilling-per-head rate in Jamaica from 1770 to at least 1800. In 1773, for example, that was the rate that Alexander Johnston of St. Ann's, Jamaica, was paid for attendance on the estate of George Gallimore (see Alexander Johnston Papers, 1582/29B, box 1, Journal 1773, Powel Family Papers, Historical Society of Pennsylvania [hereafter cited as Powel Family Papers]). J. B. Moreton also described the rate as five shillings per head in *West India Customs and Manners* (London, 1793), 26. This was also the rate stipulated by the absentee slaveholder James Chisholme in 1801 (see

Chisholme Papers, MSS. 5484, National Library of Scotland, Edinburgh [hereafter cited as Chisholme Papers]).

60. James Tobin, *Minutes of the Evidence Taken before a Committee of the House of Commons, Being a Select Committee* (London, 1790), 280.

61. In 1782, for example, the Jamaican doctor Urquhart Gillespie charged the slaveholder Charles Gordon £2.10 for a visit in which he dressed Gordon's wounds, in addition to the annual charge for attendance on 193 enslaved people from 1 July 1787 to 1 July last £48.5 (Accounts Current [1788] with Francis Grant, Gordon Papers, MS 1160, University of Aberdeen). In residential arrangements, the practitioners were expected to perform these services as part of the annual salary. To be sure, some procedures, such as midwifery, fell outside their wheelhouse. Enslaved women usually performed that work.

62. A surgeon's assistance in childbirth cost anywhere from £5 to £15 local currency. "I allow the doctors to charge five pounds for every leg or arm they cut off and five pounds for every woman they actually deliver with their own hands ... but no other charges besides the five shillings a head on any pretense whatever," the Jamaican absentee James Chisholme instructed his attorneys (Chisholme Papers). In Nevis and in St. Christopher, as the surgeon Robert Thomas testified, the fee for delivery in cases of breached deliveries or caesarean sections was £15 pounds local currency, or £9 pounds sterling (Robert Thomas, *Minutes of the Evidence Taken before a Committee of the House of Commons, Being a Select Committee* [London, 1790], 249).

63. Chisholme stipulated he would pay five shillings per inoculation (Chisholme Papers). The Jamaican John Quier stated that he charged five shillings for each inoculation (D. Munro, *Letters and Essays on the Small-Pox of the West Indies by Different Practitioners* [London, 1778], xxxi).

64. "Twenty shillings moreover for each negro inoculated," Sir Ashton Warner Byam, a former St. Vincent plantation owner testified (*Minutes of the Evidence Taken before a Committee of the House of Commons, Being a Select Committee* [London, 1790], 108). In the same Parliamentary hearings, Alexander Campbell, a slaveholder in Grenada, also testified that the going rate for inoculation was twenty shillings per head (ibid., 146).

65. John Quier estimated that he inoculated between six hundred and seven hundred enslaved patients per year. At the Jamaican rate of five shillings each, Quier's inoculations would have brought in £175, in addition to his other fees (Munro, *Letters and Essays on the Small-Pox of the West Indies by Different Practitioners*, xxxi).

66. There was very little inflation (approximately 12 percent) in the West Indies in the fifteen years between 1775 and 1790. But inflation was very high (20 percent) in the last five years of the 1790s, and it rose by another 21 percent from 1800 to 1804. Inflation rates have been calculated by using the

difference between the current and real value of sugar in any given period. The real value of sugar is calculated using 1700 prices in pounds sterling as an index. These numbers are enumerated in table 2, "Slave Prices and Sugar Prices in the Caribbean 1674–1807," in David Eltis, Frank D. Lewis, and David Richardson, "Slave Prices, the African Slave Trade, and Productivity in the Caribbean, 1674–1807," *Economic History Review* 58, no. 4 (2005): 679.
67. Williamson, *Medical and Miscellaneous Observations*, 1:225.
68. Munro, *Letters and Essays on the Small-Pox of the West Indies by Different Practitioners*, 107–8.
69. Williamson, *Medical and Miscellaneous Observations*, 1:65.
70. The Jamaican John Stewart estimated that most doctors had "ten or fifteen estates," under contract (Stewart, *An Account of Jamaica and Its Inhabitants by a Gentleman Long Resident in the West Indies* [Kingston, 1809], 105). I have estimated the Jamaica ratio on the basis that Jamaican plantations confined, on average, between 150 and 400 enslaved people during the last quarter of the eighteenth century. This number grew significantly during the nineteenth century. B. W. Higman estimates that at the time of emancipation, sugar estates in Jamaica contained, on average, 223 enslaved people, but this number could range as high as 600 people (see Higman, *Slave Population and Economy in Jamaica*, 13, 68–71). In late eighteenth-century Nevis, the ratio of doctors to slaves was similar to that in Jamaica during the same period. There, the Nevis surgeon Robert Thomas stated that he had between 4,000 and 5,000 enslaved people under his attention each year (Robert Thomas's testimony, *Minutes of the Evidence Taken before a Committee of the House of Commons, Being a Select Committee* [London, 1790], 246). These are island-specific estimates. Across the British Caribbean, sugar estates held, on average, a little more than 100 people in bondage during the eighteenth century. That meant that generally a doctor working in the British Caribbean could have between 1,000 and 1,500 individuals under their responsibility annually. For the average size of a sugar plantation, see Philip D. Morgan, "Slavery in the British Caribbean," in *Cambridge History of World Slavery*, ed. David Eltis, Stanley L. Engerman, K. R. Bradley, Paul Cartledge, Craig Perry, David Richardson, and Seymour Drescher, vol. 3: *A.D. 1420–A.D. 1804* (Cambridge: Cambridge University Press, 2011), 378–406, estimate on 386.
71. B. W. Higman, *Slave Populations of the British Caribbean, 1807–1834* (Kingston: University of the West Indies Press, 1995), 88–90; David Watts, *The West Indies: Patterns of Development, Culture, and Environmental Change since 1942* (Cambridge: Cambridge University Press, 1990), 315–16.
72. John Castles, *Minutes of the Evidence Taken before a Committee of the House of Commons, Being a Select Committee* (London, 1790), 207.

73. For this estimate, see W. F. Bynum, "Physicians, Hospitals, and Career Structures in Eighteenth-Century London," in *William Hunter and the Eighteenth-Century Medical World*, ed. Bynum and Roy Porter, 105–28 (Cambridge: Cambridge University Press, 1985), 106.
74. One public hospital in Kingston, known as the Asylum for Deserted Negroes, could admit as many as thirty patients at a time (see *Daily Advertiser* [Kingston], June 6, 1790).
75. Lawrence, *Charitable Knowledge*, table 2.1, p. 39. The Bristol Infirmary held 180 beds (Mary E. Fissell, "The Disappearance of the Patient's Narrative and the Invention of Hospital Medicine," in *British Medicine in an Age of Reform*, ed. Rodger French and Andrew Wear [London: Routledge, 1991], 92–109, Bristol Infirmary size on 104).
76. Lawrence, *Charitable Knowledge*, appendix 1.B, "Number of Positions for Staff Physicians and Surgeons at the General Hospitals, c. 1700–1825," 351.
77. Watts, *The West Indies*, 345. In the years between 1760 and 1809, sugar plantations in Jamaica occupied, on average, approximately 1,000 acres (see table 1 in B. W. Higman, "The Spatial Economy of Jamaican Sugar Plantations: Cartographic Evidence from the Eighteenth and Nineteenth Centuries," *Journal of Historical Geography* 13 [1987]: 26).
78. Long, *The History of Jamaica*, 1:46–53; Michael Craton, "Jamaican Slave Mortality: Fresh Light from Worthy Park, Longville, and the Tharp Estates," *Journal of Caribbean History* 3 (November 1971): 20.
79. Sheila Lambert, ed., *House of Commons Sessional Papers of the Eighteenth Century*, vol. 82 (Wilmington, DE: Scholarly Resources, 1975), 54.
80. September 16, 1789, Journal of Jonathan Troup.
81. Williamson, *Medical and Miscellaneous Observations*, 1:251.
82. December 16, 1789, Journal of Jonathan Troup.
83. James Stewart estimated that locally bred horses in Jamaica fetched between £35 and £70, smaller horses from Cuba, £20 and £35, and stallions from North America and England, between £100 and £200. See this range discussed in David Lambert, "Master-Horse-Slave: Mobility, Race, and Power in the British West Indies, c. 1780–1838," *Slavery and Abolition* 36 (2015): 623. In 1806, the British Army officer Richard Augustus Wyvill purchased a mare from the St. Anne's barracks in Barbados for 60 Joes (Jerome S. Handler, "Memoirs of an Old Army Officer: Richard A. Wyvill's Visits to Barbados in 1796 and 1806–7," *Journal of the Barbados Museum and Historical Society* 35 [1975]: 21–30).
84. Williamson, *Medical and Miscellaneous Observations*, 1:252.
85. Lambert, "Master-Horse-Slave."
86. Lewis Gordon, Kingston, Jamaica, June 9, 1760, to Richard Gordon, Gordon Letters, LA II 498, University of Edinburgh Special Collections.

87. James Knight, *The Natural, Moral, and Political History of Jamaica, and the Territories thereon Depending, from the First Discovery of the Island by Christopher Columbus to the Year 1746*, ed. Jack P. Greene (Charlottesville: University of Virginia Press, 2021), 457.
88. Knight, *The Natural, Moral and Political History of Jamaica and the Territories*, 590.
89. Charlotte Carrington-Farmer, "The Rise and Fall of the Narragansett Pacer," *Rhode Island History* 76, no. 1 (Winter/Spring 2018): 1–38.
90. Knight, *The Natural, Moral and Political History of Jamaica and the Territories*, 590.
91. December 27, 1790, Journal of Jonathan Troup.
92. Knight, *The Natural, Moral and Political History of Jamaica and the Territories*, 590.
93. February 13, 1790, Journal of Jonathan Troup.
94. James Grainger to Thomas Percy, in *Illustrations of the Literary History of the Eighteenth Century*, ed. John Nichols, vol. 2 (London, 1817), 278.
95. Knight, *The Natural, Moral and Political History of Jamaica and the Territories*, 590–91.
96. Long, *The History of Jamaica*, 2:583–85.
97. Stephen Fuller, *Notes on the Two Reports from the Committee of the Honourable House of Assembly of Jamaica Appointed to Examine into, and to Report to the House, the Allegations and Charges Contained in the several Petitions which have been Presented to the British House of Commons, on the Subject of the Slave Trade, and the Treatment of Negroes* (London, 1789), 59–60.
98. Knight, *The Natural, Moral and Political History of Jamaica and the Territories*, 387; Burnard and Garrigus, *The Plantation Machine*, 13.
99. Knight, *The Natural, Moral and Political History of Jamaica and the Territories*, 408. This remained the case into the nineteenth century as well. When Eliza Chadwick Roberts embarked on a tour of the different parts of the island, she noted in her diary that "the most Common way of traveling is on horse back, as there is many places difficult for a Cariage to assend; and some places two Cariages Could not pass on the mountains [*sic*]" (Roberts as quoted in Susan E. Klepp and Roderick A. McDonald, "Eliza Chadwick Roberts: A Voyage to Jamaica, 1805," *William and Mary Quarterly* 58, no. 3 [July 2001]: 667).
100. Knight, *The Natural, Moral and Political History of Jamaica and the Territories*, 457.
101. Lennox Honychurch, *In the Forests of Freedom: The Fighting Maroons of Dominica* (London: Papillote, 2017), 1.
102. Robert Brown, *A Diary of the Defence of the Island of Dominica, against the Invasion of the French Republicans, & the Revolt of the Dominicans of the Quarter of Colyhaut, in June 1795* (Roseau, 1795), 6.

103. December 29, 1789, Journal of Jonathan Troup.
104. December 30, 1789; January 28, 1790, February 17, 1790; March 15, 1790; April 4, 1790, Journal of Jonathan Troup.
105. February 18, 1790, Journal of Jonathan Troup.
106. March 15, 1790, Journal of Jonathan Troup.
107. Alexander Johnston, Memorandum, Monday, December 13, 1767, no. 1582, series 12, vol. 334, Powel Family Papers. Karras dates Johnston's arrival in Jamaica to 1763 (Karras, "The World of Alexander Johnston," 54).
108. "How Far Can You Travel by Horseback in a Day," *Equestrian Boots and Bridles*, https://equestrianbootsandbridles.com/how-far-can-you-travel-by-horseback-in-a-day-things-you-need-to-know/.
109. Philip D. Morgan, "Slaves and Livestock in Eighteenth-Century Jamaica: Vineyard Pen, 1750–1751," *William and Mary Quarterly* 52 (January 1995): 47–76; Verene Shepherd, *Livestock, Sugar and Slavery*; Verene Shepherd and Kathleen Monteith, "Pen-Keepers and Coffee Farmers in a Sugar-Plantation Society," in *Slavery without Sugar: Diversity in Caribbean Economy and Society since the Seventeenth Century*, ed. Shepherd, 82–101 (Gainesville: University Press of Florida, 2002).
110. Joshua Steele and William Dickson, *The Mitigation of Slavery, in Two Parts* (London, 1814), 165.
111. John Luffman, *A Brief Account of the Island of Antigua* (1789), 97.
112. January 26, 1790, Journal of Jonathan Troup.
113. January 26, 1790, Journal of Jonathan Troup.
114. March 16, 1790, Journal of Jonathan Troup.
115. Karras, "The World of Alexander Johnston," 58; A. Johnston, "Memorandum," September 1766, p. 3, A. Johnston Papers, business papers, folio 1, Powel Family Papers.
116. See, for example, *The Medical Register for the Year 1780* (1781), Thomas Cockburn, William and John Reid (St. Mary's), Simpson and Chisholm (Vere), 222, 223; and *The Medical Register for the Year 1783* (1784), George Robertson and Stewart (Hanover), John Watt and John Smith (Trelawny), Gardener and Thompson (Westmoreland), 172.
117. William Bremner, "Bremner Memoires," 39, National Library of Scotland, Edinburgh.
118. Williamson, *Medical and Miscellaneous Observations*, 1:60.
119. Testimony of Robert Thomas, *Minutes of the Evidence Taken before a Committee of the House of Commons, Being a Select Committee* (London, 1790), 258.
120. On his move to Kingston, see Thomas Clarke to Henry Cullen, Kingston, Jamaica, April 20, 1788, CUL 1/3/192, Royal College of Physicians of Edinburgh. I am inferring that Clarke's previous medical practice in Jamaica's hinterlands was primarily organized around attendance to estates on the basis of his description of himself as a medical practitioner engaged "in a

very extensive negro practice" (Thomas Clarke to Henry Cullen, Portmorant, Jamaica, September 12, 1783, CUL 1/2/1374, Royal College of Physicians of Edinburgh).
121. Thomas Dancer, *The Medical Assistant* (1801), 253.
122. Williamson, *Medical and Miscellaneous Observations*, 1:128.
123. For discussion of hiring an assistant, see Testimony of Robert Thomas, *Minutes of the Evidence Taken before a Committee of the House of Commons, Being a Select Committee* (London, 1790), 256.
124. He was one of two assistants employed by the firm; the other was a man named John Carson (Douglass Hamilton, *Scotland, the Caribbean and the Atlantic World, 1750–1820* [Manchester, UK: Manchester University Press, 2010], 120).
125. Hamilton, *Scotland, the Caribbean and the Atlantic World*, 120.
126. Karen Ordahl Kupperman, "Fear of Hot Climates in the Anglo-American Colonial Experience," *William and Mary Quarterly* 41 no. 2 (1984): 213–15. Troup arrived mid-May 1789 but was not dispatched to an estate until mid-June 1789 (June 1, 1789, Journal of Jonathan Troup).
127. June 1, 1789, Journal of Jonathan Troup.
128. August 5, 1789, Journal of Jonathan Troup.
129. April 4, 1790, Journal of Jonathan Troup.
130. January 28, February 5, 1790, Journal of Jonathan Troup.
131. An older practitioner, in the words of one slaveholder, "by . . . extensive practice in the country has acquired a thorough knowledge of the diseases incident to the climate, and the most successful mode of treating them" (John Stewart *An Account of Jamaica and Its Inhabitants by a Gentleman Long Resident in the West Indies* [Kingston, 1809], 106).
132. Stewart, *An Account of Jamaica and Its Inhabitants by a Gentleman Long Resident in the West Indies*, 105. The agricultural advice author James Grainger stipulated that "every estate ought to be visited once a week by some physical person; and oftner, if occasion require" (Grainger, *An Essay on the More Common West-India Diseases; and the Remedies which that Country Itself Produces* [London, 1764], 73).
133. "Minutes of the Evidence Taken before a Committee of the House of Commons, Being a Select Committee, Appointed to Take the Examination of Witnesses Respecting the African Trade," in *House of Commons Sessional Papers of the Eighteenth Century*, ed. Sheila Lambert, vol. 82 (Wilmington, DE: Scholarly Resources, 1975), (1791), 221–22. As the plantation surgeon John Williamson explained, "medical attendance in the interior, or plantation practice, seldom admits of" frequent visits (Williamson, *Medical and Miscellaneous Observations*, 1:145).
134. Harold J. Cook, "Practical Medicine and the British Armed Forces after the 'Glorious Revolution,'" *Medical History* 34 (1990): 2.

135. Christopher Hamlin, "Predisposing Causes and Public Health in Nineteenth-Century Medical Thought," *Social History of Medicine* 5 (April 1992): 43. On the persistence of individuated conceptions of the body into the nineteenth century, see Charles Rosenberg, "The Therapeutic Revolution: Medicine, Meaning, and Social Change in Nineteenth-Century America," in *The Therapeutic Revolution: Essays in the Social History of American Medicine*, ed. M. J. Vogel and Rosenberg (Philadelphia: University of Pennsylvania Press, 1979), 3–25. On predisposition as determining how a body responded to epidemic disease, such as fever, see Kevin Siena, *Rotten Bodies: Class and Contagion in Eighteenth-Century Britain* (New Haven, CT: Yale University Press, 2019), 24–27.

136. Sara Stidstone Gronim, "Imagining Inoculation: Smallpox, the Body, and Social Relations of Healing in the Eighteenth Century," *Bulletin of the History of Medicine* 80, no. 2 (2006): 254. The writing on the role of quotidian habits (or the non-naturals) in shaping the idiosyncratic body is extensive. A good overview is P. Niebyl, "The Non-Naturals," *Bulletin of the History of Medicine* 13 (1971): 486–92. For a recent analysis of the persistence of this concept in medical thinking, see Steven Shapin, "Why Was 'Custom a Second Nature' in Early Modern Medicine?," *Bulletin of the History of Medicine* 93 (2019): 1–26.

137. Zachary Dorner writes of "bulk medicines" and a "take-this-for-that approach" in *Merchants of Medicines: The Commerce and Coercion of Health in Britain's Long Eighteenth Century* (Chicago: University of Chicago Press, 2020), 6, 7.

138. Dorner, *Merchants of Medicines*, 7.

139. Susan C. Lawrence, *Charitable Knowledge: Hospital Pupils and Practitioners in Eighteenth-Century London* (Cambridge: Cambridge University Press, 1996), 150–53.

140. "Westmoreland April 10, 1754. Mr. Richard Beckford's Instructions," box 11, folder 18, Thistlewood MSS.

141. Justin Roberts, *Slavery and the Enlightenment in the British Atlantic, 1750–1807* (Cambridge: University of Cambridge Press, 2013), 27–79; Caitlin Rosenthal, *Accounting for Slavery: Masters and Management* (Cambridge, MA: Harvard University Press, 2018).

142. "List of the Sick" and "In the hot-house," 1788, 1789, 1790, MS 8487–8492, Slebech.

143. John Baillie as quoted in Sheridan, *Doctors and Slaves*, 294 (original citation: *Accounts and Papers [Parliamentary Papers]* 305, no. 127, pt. 2 [1832]: 63).

144. Dorner, *Merchants of Medicines*, 7.

145. Rana Hogarth, *Medicalizing Blackness: Making Racial Difference in the Atlantic World, 1780–1840* (Chapel Hill: University of North Carolina Press, 2017); Suman Seth, *Difference and Disease: Medicine, Race, and the*

Eighteenth-Century British Empire (Cambridge: Cambridge University Press, 2018).

146. James McKittrick-Adair, "Observations on Regimen and Preparation under Inoculation, and on the Treatment of the Natural Small Pox, in the West Indies," *Medical Commentaries for the Years 1781–82* 8 (1783): 213.

147. Munro, *Letters and Essays on the Small-Pox of the West Indies by Different Practitioners*, 65; Elise Mitchell, "Slavery and Inoculation: Kinship, Childhood, and Smallpox Inoculation in the Atlantic World," Omohundro Institute Conference, June 14, 2016.

148. On Ivey's role as a cooper, see "List of Negroes upon Trouthall Estate Taken January 1801," MS 5465; on his death, see Letterbooks of James Chisholme, MS 5476, Chisholme Papers. *Dictionary of Protopharmacology: Therapeutic Practices, 1700–1850* (Canton, MA: Science History Publications, 1990), s.v. "Antimonium Tartarisatum."

149. September 9, 1789, Journal of Jonathan Troup.

150. In his 1803 agricultural advice text, for example, the absentee planter and doctor David Collins wrote that in contrast to white people, all "negroes" had a greater tolerance for emetics and that more medicines were necessary to cure Black people's ailments. Collins ascribed their insensitivity to pain to enslaved people's diminished intellectual capacities, which rendered them less sensate ([Collins], *Practical Rules for the Management and Medical Treatment of Negro Slaves in the Sugar Colonies* [London, 1803], 233–34). On complaints about the abuse of mercury, see Sheridan, *Doctors and Slaves*, 28, 70, 292, 300, 311, 331, 335; and Turner, *Contested Bodies*, 129, 136, 145.

151. On Dancer's appointment to the Eighty-First Regiment, see Thomas Dancer, *A Brief history of the late Expedition against Fort San Juan, so far as it relates to the diseases of the troops* (Kingston, 1781); on the appointment at Bath, see Thomas Dancer, *A Brief Account of the New Settlement and Bath, at Port Henderson, to Which is Added, A short Essay on Cold Bathing* (Kingston, 1777); physician to the elite, David Grant, *An Exposition of the Conduct and Character of Thomas Dancer, M.D.* (Kingston, 1805), 3–5; on his connections with so-called "country practitioners," see David Grant, "Article V: Observations on the Contagiousness and Importation of Yellow Fever, in the Island of Jamaica," *The Medical Repository of Original Essays and Intelligence: Relative to Physic, Surgery, Chemistry* (November 1803–January 1804): 247–54.

152. Thomas Dancer, *The Medical Assistant* (1801), 293.

153. Williamson, *Medical and Miscellaneous Observations*, 1:57.

154. Dancer, *The Medical Assistant* (1801), 293.

155. William Vassall to James Wedderburn, August 19, 1772, in *Vassall Letterbooks*.

156. William Vassall to John Wedderburn, August 2, 1777, in *Vassall Letterbooks*.

157. James Chisholme to James Cragg, March 1, 1803, MSS 5476, Chisholme Papers.

158. B. W. Higman, *Plantation Jamaica, 1750–1850: Capital and Control in a Colonial Economy* (Kingston: University of the West Indies Press, 2005), 184.
159. Simon Taylor to Chaloner Arcedeckne, May 4, 1794, Vanneck-Arc. 3A/1794/8, Vanneck Papers.
160. William Vassall to John Wedderburn, January 9, 1777, in *Vassall Letterbooks*.
161. On Taylor's wealth, see Christer Petely, *White Fury: A Jamaican Slaveholder in the Age of Revolution* (New York: Oxford University Press, 2018), 31, 213. On Taylor as a slaveholder and attorney who thought and managed with a longer time-horizon than other sugar barons in Jamaica, see Trevor Burnard, *Jamaica in the Age of Revolution* (Philadelphia: University of Pennsylvania Press, 2020), 101–2.
162. Simon Taylor to Chaloner Arcedeckne, Kingston, November 19, 1774, Vanneck-Arc. 3A/1774/8, in *Travel, Trade and Power in the Atlantic, 1765–1884*, 136.
163. Higman, *Plantation Jamaica*, 170–71.
164. Robert Pinkney to Joseph Foster Barham, May 16, 1766, MS. Clar. dep. c. 357, Barham Papers.
165. Benjamin Turney to Chaloner Arcedeckne, Golden Grove May 14, 1782, as transcribed by Elizabeth Hampson, http://freepages.rootsweb.com/~sedgebrook/history/page20.htm (original citation: Ad MS 33977-143-144, British Library, London).
166. Dorner, *Merchants of Medicines*, 6.
167. Saturation of the semi-skilled labor market and depression of wages also occurred in Boston as a consequence of the expansion of its military garrison, which began in 1768 (see Jeremy Land and Vincent Geloso, "Colonial Military Garrisons as Labor Market Shocks," *Social Science Quarterly* 101, no. 4 [2020]: 1326–44).

3. "All Lesser Matters Related to the Sick"

1. The working and life biographies of the enslaved healers on Mesopotamia have been reconstructed from Mesopotamia Inventories, MS. Clar. dep. c. 36/2, Barham Papers. Parthenia was described as the hot-house doctress between 1771 and 1781. On Kickery as the "hot-house woman," see the inventories for 1784 to 1786. The inventories for 1782 and 1783 are missing. I have described Parthenia, in her fifties, as in "advanced old age" because enslaved people who lived into their forties were considered elderly (Randy M. Browne, *Surviving Slavery in the British Caribbean* [Philadelphia: University of Pennsylvania Press, 2017], 3).
2. Richard S. Dunn, *A Tale of Two Plantations: Slave Life and Labor in Jamaica and Virginia* (Cambridge, MA: Harvard University Press, 2014), 92.

3. "Doctress" is a term that several plantation management guides used to describe the enslaved woman responsible for healing in the plantation's hospital (see John Williamson, *Medical and Miscellaneous Observations, Relative to the West India Islands*, 2 vols. [Edinburgh, 1817], 1:139; and Thomas Roughley, *The Jamaica Planter's Guide* [London: Longman, Hurst, Rees, Orme, and Brown, 1823], 91). Amanda Thornton also quotes Thomas Thistlewood using this term in his diary (Thornton, "Coerced to Care: Thomas Thistlewood's Account of Medical Practice on Enslaved Populations in Colonial Jamaica, 1751–1786," *Slavery and Abolition* 32 [2011]: 541).
4. In contrast to the antebellum United States, where enslaved healers generally attended in the homes of the sick (Sharla M. Fett, *Working Cures: Healing, Health, and Power on Southern Slave Plantations* [Chapel Hill: University of North Carolina Press, 2002], 125–30).
5. Randy Browne's analysis of and questions about enslaved drivers have very much influenced my thinking about healers' position (see Randy M. Browne, *Surviving Slavery in the British Caribbean* [Philadelphia: University of Pennsylvania Press, 2017], 72–101; and *The Driver's Story: Labor and Power in the World of Atlantic Slavery* [Philadelphia: University of Pennsylvania Press, 2024]).
6. Justin Roberts, *Slavery and the Enlightenment in the British Atlantic, 1750–1807* (Cambridge: Cambridge University Press, 2013), 58–59.
7. On West Indian proprietors' recruitment of young male adolescents as bookkeepers, see Richard Pares, "A London West-India Merchant House," in *Essays Presented to Sir Lewis Namier*, ed. Pares and A. J. P. Taylor (London: Macmillan, 1956), 75–107, esp. 91–92. Bookkeepers' activities in medicine are depicted in *Marly; or, A Planter's Life in Jamaica* (Glasgow: Richard Griffith 1828), 49, 54.
8. Sheila Lambert, ed., *House of Commons Sessional Papers of the Eighteenth Century*, vol. 82 (Wilmington, DE: Scholarly Resources, 1975), 221.
9. [David Collins], *Practical Rules for the Management and Medical Treatment of Negro Slaves in the Sugar Colonies* (London, 1803), 237.
10. Tinde van Andel, "The Reinvention of Household Medicine by Enslaved Africans in Suriname," *Social History of Medicine* 29 (2015): 676–94; Robert Voeks, "The Spiritual Flora of Brazil's African Diaspora: Ethnobotanical Conversations in the Black Atlantic World," *Journal for the Study of Religion, Nature, and Culture* 6 (2012): 501–22; Judith Carney, "African Traditional Plant Knowledge in the Circum-Caribbean Region," *Journal of Ethnobiology* 23 (2003): 167–85.
11. Londa Schiebinger, *Secret Cures of Slaves: People, Plants, and Medicine in the Eighteenth-Century Atlantic World* (Stanford, CA: Stanford University Press, 2017).

12. Pablo F. Gómez, *The Experiential Caribbean: Creating Knowledge and Healing in the Early Modern Atlantic* (Chapel Hill: University of North Carolina Press, 2017), 76–94.
13. For a summary of the transactions in the late eighteenth-century Atlantic that tended to involve go-betweens, see Miles Ogborn, "'It's Not What You Know . . .': Encounters, Go-Betweens, and the Geography of Knowledge," *Modern Intellectual History* 10 (April 2013): 163–75, esp. 170; and Sanjay Subrahmanyam, "Between a Rock and a Hard Place: Some Afterthoughts," in *The Brokered World: Go-Betweens and Global Intelligence, 1770–1820*, ed. Simon Schaffer, Lissa Roberts, Kapil Raj, and James Delbourgo (Sagamore Beach, MA: Science History Publications, 2009), 429–40.
14. On colonists' reliance on enslaved and Indigenous healers for their survival in the Caribbean, see Gómez, *The Experiential Caribbean*, 70–94. On Europeans' reliance upon Africans' knowledge on the coast, see Kalle Kananoja, *Healing Knowledge in Atlantic Africa: Medical Encounters, 1500–1850* (Cambridge: Cambridge University Press, 2021). On enslaved people's extensive botanical know-how, see Karol K. Weaver, *Medical Revolutionaries: The Enslaved Healers of Eighteenth-Century Saint Domingue* (Urbana: University of Illinois Press, 2006); Judith Carney and Richard Rosomoff, *In the Shadow of Slavery: Africa's Botanical Legacy in the Atlantic World* (Berkeley: University of California Press, 2009); Natalie Zemon Davis, "Physicians, Healers, and Their Remedies in Colonial Suriname," *Canadian Bulletin of Medical History* 33 (2016): 3–34; and Londa Schiebinger, *Plants and Empire: Colonial Bioprospecting in the Atlantic World* (Cambridge, MA: Harvard University Press, 2004), 75–99.
15. Susan Scott Parrish, *American Curiosity: Cultures of Natural History in the Colonial British Atlantic World* (Chapel Hill: University of North Carolina Press, 2006), 257–62.
16. This list is derived from Catherine Hall's analysis of the commission system in Catherine Hall, *Lucky Valley: Edward Long and the History of Racial Capitalism* (Cambridge: Cambridge University Press, 2024), 160–61. See also Pares, "A London West-India Merchant House, 1740–1769," 75–107.
17. Zachary Dorner, *Merchants of Medicines: The Commerce and Coercion of Health in Britain's Long Eighteenth Century* (Chicago: University of Chicago Press, 2020), 11.
18. Dorner, *Merchants of Medicines*, 89–106.
19. Mark S. R. Jenner and Patrick Wallis, "The Medical Marketplace," in *Medicine and the Market in England and Its Colonies, c. 1450–c. 1850*, ed. Jenner and Wallis (London: Palgrave Macmillan, 2007), 2.
20. John Tennant, *Every Man his Own Doctor: or, The Poor Planter's Physician* (Williamsburg: William Parks, 1734).

21. "Getting and spending," from chapter 5 in Roy Porter, *English Society in the Eighteenth Century* (New York: Penguin, 1991).
22. Mary E. Fissell, "The Marketplace of Print," in *Medicine and the Market in England and Its Colonies, c. 1450–c. 1850*, 110.
23. Dorner, *Merchants of Medicines*, 100.
24. Scholars of plantation management have not typically positioned plantation advice-guides as medical consumer items. This oversight is understandable as guides from the seventeenth and early eighteenth centuries addressed health (and not sickness) and did so indirectly. One of the most widely cited authors in the plantation improvement movement, Samuel Martin, spent much of his guide encouraging readers to adopt manuring on the grounds that this would diminish enslaved people's toil and improve their health (Martin, *An Essay on Plantership* [Antigua: Printed by T. Smith, 1750]). When authors did address illness, they advised that adequate nourishment and homemade medicinal soups and drinks were better remedies than manufactured medicines. "The Kitchen being more useful in the recovering and raysing [sic] of negroes than the appothycaries shopp [sic]," the Barbadian plantation owner Henry Drax proclaimed (Peter Thompson, "Sources and Interpretations: Henry Drax's Instructions on the Management of a Seventeenth-Century Barbadian Sugar Plantation," *William and Mary Quarterly* 66 [2009]: 565–604, quote on 583). The enslaver (and attorney) Samuel Cary argued that "good nourishment and care perform two thirds of the cure" (Cary, "Plantation Instructions for running a sugar plantation," MS. N-1997, Cary Papers). But they left the details up to readers and probably operated on the expectation that enslaved people would select and make medicines on their own.
25. To cite one example: Robert Shannon's book, *Observations on the Operations and Effects of Certain Medicines in the Prevention and Cure of Diseases to which Europeans are Subject to in Hot Climates* (1794) lifted from the more influential West Indian writers John Hunter, Edward Long, Benjamin Mosely, and James Grainger. Shannon copied his discussion of dirt-eating directly from John Hunter's *Observations on the Diseases of the Army in Jamaica* (1788), 248–50.
26. Katherine Paugh, *The Politics of Reproduction: Race, Medicine, and Fertility in the Age of Abolition* (Oxford: Oxford University Press, 2017), 92.
27. Henry Barham, *Hortus Americanus: Containing an Account of the Trees, Shrubs, and other Vegetable Productions, of South-America and the West-India Islands, and Particularly of the Island of Jamaica* (London, 1794), 248–49.
28. James Knight, *The Natural, Moral, and Political History of Jamaica*, ed. Jack P. Greene (Charlottesville: University of Virginia Press, 2021), 495–96.
29. A. J. Alexander to Joseph Black, April 21, 1773, Coll-16/1/58–63, Correspondence of Joseph Black I, 1754–1783, Papers of Joseph Black and Family (Coll-16), University of Edinburgh Library.

30. Paugh, *The Politics of Reproduction*, 115–16.
31. [David Collins], *Practical Rules for the Management and Medical Treatment of Negro Slaves in the Sugar Colonies* (London, 1803), 415.
32. March 27, April 4, 1758, box 2, folder 9, Series 1: Diaries, Diaries of Thomas Thistlewood, OSB MSS 176, Thistlewood MSS.
33. Paugh, *The Politics of Reproduction*, 108–10.
34. On Old Sharper belonging to the Salt River plantation, see entry for October 18, 1756, box 2, folder 7, Series 1, Thistlewood MSS. In that entry, Thistlewood records that Salt River's manager, Samuel Mordiner, had come to the Egypt plantation with all of Mordiner's people (enslaved people) except Old Sharper and Dorset, implying that Old Sharper belonged to Mordiner and lived on Salt River.
35. William Wright, *Memoires of the Late William Wright, M.D. Fellow of the Royal Societies of London and Edinburgh* (Edinburgh, 1828), 411.
36. March 31, 1756, box 2, folder 7, Series 1, Thistlewood MSS.
37. October 19, 1755, box 2, folder 6, Series 1, Thistlewood MSS.
38. Dunn, *A Tale of Two Plantations*, 91.
39. Some argued that both yaws and venereal disease originated in Africa (Paugh, *The Politics of Reproduction*, 108–10).
40. Andrew Wear, *Knowledge and Practice in English Medicine* (Cambridge: Cambridge University Press, 2000), 154–209.
41. This summary of putrefaction comes from Kevin Siena, *Rotten Bodies: Class and Contagion in Eighteenth-Century Britain* (New Haven, CT: Yale University Press, 2019), 21.
42. On the shift to an inflammatory to a putrefactive model of fevers, see Mark Harrison, *Medicine in an Age of Commerce and Empire: Britain and Its Tropical Colonies, 1660–1830* (Cambridge: Cambridge University Press, 2010), 172–211.
43. William Wright, *Memoirs of the Late William Wright, M.D. Fellow of the Royal Societies of London and Edinburgh* (Edinburgh, 1828), 409.
44. On pox as a putrid disorder that vented its poisons on the skin, see Siena, *Rotten Bodies: Class and Contagion in Eighteenth-Century Britain*, 41.
45. October 15, November 11, 1770, box 4, folder 21, Series 1, Thistlewood MSS.
46. Medical Casebook of David Skeene, MS 4761/182, Special Collections Library, University of Aberdeen.
47. J. Worth Estes, *Dictionary of Protopharmacology: Therapeutic Practices, 1700–1850* (Canton, MA: Science History Publications, 1990), s.v. "Guaic," 92.
48. Estes, *Dictionary of Protopharmacology*, s.v. "Senna," 176.
49. March 27, 1758, box 2, folder 9, Series 1, Thistlewood MSS.
50. Estes, *Dictionary of Protopharmacology*, s.v. "Sulphur," 186.
51. March 27, 1758, box 2, folder 9, Series 1, Thistlewood MSS.

52. Kathleen Murphy, "Translating the Vernacular: Indigenous and African Knowledge in the Eighteenth-Century British Atlantic," *Atlantic Studies* 8 (2011): 29–48.
53. Thistlewood subjected Abigail to Wheatley's remedy on March 16, 1756, box 2, folder 7, Series 1, Thistlewood MSS.
54. June 1, 1756, box 2, folder 7, Series 1, Thistlewood MSS.
55. Sir Hans Sloane, *A Voyage to the Islands Madera, Barbadoes, Nieves, St. Christophers, and Jamaica*, vol. 2 (1725), 127. The attorney and enslaver Simon Taylor also identified "plumtree bark" as a remedy enslaved people used to treat venereal disease (Simon Taylor to Chaloner Arcedeckne, Kingston, 5/7/1789/20, Vanneck-Arc, Vanneck Papers).
56. See, for instance, Thistlewood's discussion of a cure for crab yaws that he received from Col. [Alexander] Barclay (January 5, 1752, box 1, folder 3, Series 1, Thistlewood MSS).
57. March 1, 1756, box 2, folder 7, Series 1, Thistlewood MSS.
58. Dorner, *Merchants of Medicines*, 52–53.
59. Dorner, *Merchants of Medicines*, 5–6.
60. Thomas Plummer to Joseph Henry Barham, St. Elizabeth's Jamaica, September 8, 1801, MS. Clar. dep. c. 357, Barham Papers.
61. John Van Heilen to Joseph Foster Barham, 26 December, 1786, MS. Clar. dep. c. 357, Barham Papers.
62. Malcolm Laing to Phillip Perrin, May 31, 1766, FitzHerbert of Tissington, D239/M/E/16664, Derbyshire Record Office, Derbyshire, England. Thank you to Nicholas Radburn for sharing this source with me.
63. Notebooks of James Chisholme, f.17, MS 5484, Chisholme Papers.
64. James Chisholme to William Anderson, 2 November, 1808, MS 5476, Chisholme Papers.
65. Receipt Book, MS 5466, Chisholme Papers.
66. James Chisholme to William Anderson, November 29, 1802, MS 5476, Chisholme Papers.
67. William Anderson to James Chisholme, no date, MS 5466, Chisholme Papers.
68. Practitioner-druggists, the Jamaican John Stewart observed, "have a monstrous profit upon their drugs, which may be said to be charged *ad libitum*" (Stewart, *An Account of Jamaica and Its Inhabitants by a Gentleman Long Resident in the West Indies* [Kingston, 1809], 106).
69. Alexander Johnston Medical Record, p. 20, series 12, vol. 342, Powel Family Papers.
70. Collins, *Practical Rules for the Management and Medical Treatment of Negro Slaves in the Sugar Colonies*, 248.
71. January 10, 11, February 26, April 19, August 16, October 15, 1770, box 4, folder 21, Series 1, Thistlewood MSS.

72. Alexander Johnston Medical Record, pp. 16, 20, 155, 179, series 12, vol. 342, Powel Family Papers.
73. Alexander Johnston Medical Record, p. 179, series 12, vol. 342, Powel Family Papers.
74. Sloane, *A Voyage to the Islands Madera, Barbadoes, Nieves, St. Christophers, and Jamaica*, vol. 1 (1707), vii.
75. March 17, 27, 31, 1755, box 2, folder 6, Series 1, Thistlewood MSS.
76. Philip Morgan, "Slaves and Livestock in Eighteenth-Century Jamaica: Vineyard Pen, 1750–1751," *William and Mary Quarterly* 52, no. 1 (January 1995): 47–76.
77. Vincent Brown, *The Reaper's Garden* (Cambridge, MA: Harvard University Press, 2008), 41.
78. Hugo Huber, S.V.D., *The Krobo: Traditional Social and Religious Life of a West African People* (St. Augustin: Anthropos Institute, 1963), 76, 221, 279.
79. John D. Garrigus, *A Secret among the Blacks: Slave Resistance before the Haitian Revolution* (Cambridge, MA: Harvard University Press, 2023); Gómez, *The Experiential Caribbean: Creating Knowledge and Healing in the Early Modern Atlantic*, quote on 37, 67; James Sweet, *Domingo Álvares, African Healing, and the Intellectual History of the Atlantic World* (Chapel Hill: University of North Carolina Press, 2011). In the British Caribbean, ritualists known as Obeah men and women conjured and manipulated this sacralized natural world. Their work identified the social, spiritual, and physical causes of illness. Rituals brought together past histories and mediated broken social relations among the living and between the living and the dead. In 1760, Obeah diviners encouraged enslaved men and women to take up organized revolt against slavery in an enslaved insurrection known as Tacky's Revolt. In the aftermath, colonial authorities banned the practice of Obeah. Operating under the threat of transportation and death, Obeah men and women kept their activities out of sight, which makes it difficult for historians to determine whether the people in hospitals and yaws houses were part of this world of divination. See Vincent Brown, *Tacky's Revolt: The Story of an Atlantic Slave War* (Harvard: 2020), 105–7, 111, 138, 213.
80. Pablo F. Gómez, "Transatlantic Meanings: African Rituals and Material Culture from the Early Modern Spanish Caribbean," in *Materialities of Ritual in the Black Atlantic*, ed. Akinwumi Ogundiran and Paula Sanders (Bloomington: Indiana University Press, 2014), 125–42; Pablo F. Gómez, *The Experiential Caribbean: Creating Knowledge and Healing in the Early Modern Atlantic* (Chapel Hill: University of North Carolina Press, 2017), 36, 159–61, 179–84.
81. "Medical news," *Medical and Philosophical Commentaries by a Society in Edinburgh* 2, no. 1 (1784): 96; Gómez, *The Experiential Caribbean*, 96–117.
82. Thomas M. Safley and Leonard Rosenband, introduction to *The Workplace before the Factory: Artisans and Proletarians, 1500–1800*, ed. Safley and

Rosenband (Ithaca, NY: Cornell University Press, 1993), 4; Justin Roberts, *Slavery and the Enlightenment in the British Atlantic, 1750–1807* (Cambridge: Cambridge University Press, 2013), 230.

83. Sweet, *Domingo Álvares, African Healing, and the Intellectual History of the Atlantic World*, 124.
84. July 28, 1789, Journal of Jonathan Troup.
85. Sweet, *Domingo Álvares, African Healing, and the Intellectual History of the Atlantic World*, 123–27.
86. It is unclear whether Thistlewood paid Old Sharper for a "cure" or for a specific quantity of diet drink (March 13, 1755, March 14, 1755, box 2, folder 6, Series 1, Thistlewood MSS).
87. Collins, *Practical Rules for the Management and Medical Treatment of Negro Slaves in the Sugar Colonies*, 238–39.
88. Dorner, *Merchants of Medicines*, 52–53.
89. "An Inventory of Phillipsfield Estate, January 1789," ref. 11523, Slebech.
90. James Chisholme Esq. to William Frye, London October 19, 1804, MS 5465, Chisholme Papers.
91. Peter Dugid, "Art XV: The anthelmintic Virtue of the Bark of the wild Cabbage or Bulge-water Tree; by the late Mr. Peter Duguid, late Surgeon in Jamaica, in a letter to Alexander Monro, senior, M.D. & P.A.," in *Essays and Observations, Physical and Literary Read before a Society in Edinburgh* 2 (1756): 264–65, quote on 265.
92. Collins, *Practical Rules for the Management and Medical Treatment of Negro Slaves in the Sugar Colonies*, 239.
93. Roughley, *The Jamaica Planter's Guide*, 91.
94. "An Inventory and Valuation of Pleasant Hill Estate in the Parish of St. Thomas in the East Belonging to Nathaniel Phillips, esq. January 1789," ref. 11523, Slebech.
95. See, for instance, "List of the Sick," ref. 8487, 8489, Slebech. These dates are approximate—the lists themselves do not have a date, but the worklogs with which they were bundled are dated June 1789 and March 1790.
96. On Hampton as the hot-house doctor, see "List of the Negroes on the Island Estate, 1787," MS. Clar dep. b. 36/1, Barham Papers. On the number of the sick, see John Van Heilen to Joseph Foster Barham, June 26, 1787, MS. Clar. dep c. 357, Barham Papers.
97. Michael Craton, *Searching for the Invisible Man: Slaves and Plantation Life in Jamaica* (Cambridge, MA: Harvard University Press, 1978), 415n15.
98. J. Graham to Joseph Foster Barham II, October 15, 1793, MS. Clar. dep. c. 357, Barham Papers.
99. Randall M. Packard, "The Fielding H. Garrison Lecture: Break-Bone Fever in Philadelphia, 1780: Reflections in the History of Disease," *Bulletin of the History of Medicine* 90, no. 2 (Summer 2016): 210.

100. J. B. Moreton, an observer of Jamaican slavery, visited an estate and looked at its hospital book. It included the names of patients, their afflictions, and instructions provided for their maintenance. According to his example, the enslaved attendant would have had as many of three different things to administer for each (Moreton, *West India Customs and Manners* [London, 1793], 23).
101. Moreton, *West India Customs and Manners* (London, 1793), 21, my italics.
102. William Vassall to John Wedderburn, September 9, 1777, in *Vassall Letterbooks*, my italics.
103. Ogborn, *The Freedom of Speech*, 119–20; Kalle Kananoja, *Healing Knowledge in Atlantic Africa: Medical Encounters, 1500–1850* (Cambridge: Cambridge University Press, 2021), 28, Gómez, *The Experiential Caribbean: Creating Knowledge and Healing in the Early Modern Atlantic*, 101–3.
104. John Johnson Report.
105. John Johnson Report, 8; Gómez, *The Experiential Caribbean*, 15, 37.
106. Kevin Siena, *Venereal Disease, Hospitals, and the Urban Poor: London's "Foul Wards," 1600–1800* (Rochester, NY: University of Rochester Press, 2004), 17. See also Philip K. Wilson, "Exposing the Secret Disease: Recognizing and Treating Syphilis in Daniel Turner's London," in *The Secret Malady: Venereal Disease in Eighteenth-Century Britain and France*, ed. Linda Evi Merians (Lexington: University Press of Kentucky, 1996), 68–84.
107. Porter, *Health for Sale*, 150–56. Siena, *Venereal Disease, Hospitals, and the Urban Poor: London's "Foul Wards," 1600–1800*, 22.
108. Siena, *Venereal Disease, Hospitals, and the Urban Poor*, 23.
109. Siena, *Venereal Disease, Hospitals, and the Urban Poor*, 23.
110. Siena, *Venereal Disease, Hospitals, and the Urban Poor*, 23.
111. November 30, 1770, box 4, folder 21, Series I, Thistlewood MSS.
112. Bynum, "Treating the Wages of Sin," 16; Porter, *Health for Sale*, 153; Siena, *Venereal Disease, Hospitals, and the Urban Poor*, 23.
113. December 9, 1770, box 4, folder 21, Series I, Thistlewood MSS.
114. On Kickery as "pox'd young," see the 1778, 1781, and 1784, MS. Clar. dep. b. 36/2, Barham Papers.
115. See 1786 inventory, MS Clar. dep b. 36/2, Barham Papers. At this point, there were two women named Marina on Mesopotamia. The woman who came from Three Mile River was twenty-three years old, and managers identified her by noting "TMR" next to her name.
116. See 1794 inventory, MS. Clar. dep. b. 36/2, Barham Papers.
117. During the entirety of her time as both midwife and hospital healer, Kickery and Mesopotamia's other midwife, Cretia, facilitated the childbirths of nineteen of Mesopotamia's women—five in 1784, six in 1785, eight in 1786 (see the inventories for those years in MS. Clar. dep. b. 36/2, Barham Papers).

118. See 1795 inventory, where Marina is listed as "learning to be a midwife," and the same inventory for the birth of Sarah, Marina's daughter (MS. Clar. dep. b. 36/2, Barham Papers).
119. November 3, 1789, Journal of Jonathan Troup.
120. May 18, 1789, Journal of Jonathan Troup.
121. November 3, 1789, Journal of Jonathan Troup.
122. [Collins], *Practical Rules for the Management and Medical Treatment of Negro Slaves in the Sugar Colonies*, 418; William Beckford, *Remarks upon the Situation of Negroes in Jamaica* (1788), 31; Williamson, *Medical and Miscellaneous Observations*, 1:65, my italics; John Johnson Report.
123. Samuel Cary, "Plantation Instructions for running a sugar plantation," MS. N-1997, Cary Papers.
124. Mary Fissell, "Introduction: Women, Health, and Healing in Early Modern Europe," *Bulletin of the History of Medicine* 82 (2008): 1–17; Kathleen Brown, *Foul Bodies: Cleanliness in Early America* (New Haven, CT: Yale University Press, 2009), 5.
125. Turner, *Contested Bodies*, 115–21; Brown, *Foul Bodies*.
126. See, for instance, the collection of Countess's menstrual napkin in John Williamson, *Medical and Miscellaneous Observations, Relative to the West India Islands*, 2 vols. (Edinburgh, 1817), 1:139–40.
127. [David Collins], *Practical Rules for the Management and Medical Treatment of Negro Slaves in the Sugar Colonies* (London, 1803), 255–57.
128. [Collins], *Practical Rules for the Management and Medical Treatment of Negro Slaves in the Sugar Colonies*, 290. On the emetic orientation of Afro-Creole materia medica, see B. W. Higman, *Slave Populations of the British Caribbean, 1807–1834* (Kingston: University of the West Indies Press, 1995), 271.
129. Fissell, "Introduction: Women, Health, and Healing in Early Modern Europe," 14.
130. Henry Barham, *Hortus Americanus: Containing an Account of the Trees, Shrubs, and other Vegetable Productions, of South-America and the West-India Islands, and Particularly of the Island of Jamaica*, 57.
131. Fett, *Working Cures*, 120.
132. Turner, *Contested Bodies*, 116–18; Jessica Marie Johnson, *Wicked Flesh: Black Women, Intimacy, and Freedom in the Atlantic World* (Philadelphia: University of Pennsylvania Press, 2020), 176–84.
133. Barham had purchased and displaced forty people from the Three Mile River sugar plantation and another fifteen from a seller located in the Jamaican village Martha Brae. On these purchases, see the Barham Inventories for 1785 and 1786, MS. Clar. dep. b. 36/2, Barham Papers.
134. Case Eighty-Nine, in Trevor Burnard, ed., *Hearing Slaves Speak* (Caribbean Press for the Government of Guyana, 2010), 186–87 (original citation: C.O. 116/148-123-130, National Archives, Kew, Britain).

135. October 28, 1789, Journal of Jonathan Troup.
136. Privilege as defined by B. W. Higman, *Slave Populations of the British Caribbean, 1807–1834* (Kingston: University of the West Indies Press, 1995), 189, 333–36. See also Randy M. Browne's discussion of enslaved drivers in *Surviving Slavery in the British Caribbean*, 72–101.
137. Justin Roberts, *Slavery and the Enlightenment in the British Atlantic, 1750–1807* (Cambridge: Cambridge University Press, 2013), 204–5; Paugh, *The Politics of Reproduction*, 124–46; Justin Roberts, "'The Better Sort' and the 'Poorer Sort': Wealth Inequalities, Family Formation, and the Economy of Energy on British Caribbean Sugar Plantations, 1750–1800," *Slavery and Abolition* 35 (2014): 458–73; Vincent Brown, *The Reaper's Garden* (Cambridge, MA: Harvard University Press, 2008), 120–21.
138. Dunn, *A Tale of Two Plantations*, 78–79, 84; Paugh, *The Politics of Reproduction*, 134–46; Browne, *The Driver's Story*, 68–69.
139. On enslaved women's role in social reproduction in the British plantation Caribbean, see Jennifer Morgan, *Laboring Women: Reproduction and Gender in New World Slavery* (Philadelphia: University of Pennsylvania Press, 2004); Turner, *Contested Bodies: Pregnancy, Childrearing, and Slavery in Jamaica*. The terms and phrases "socially reproductive labor" and "meet basic biological needs" come from Alexandra J. Finley, *An Intimate Economy: Enslaved Women, Work, and America's Domestic Slave Trade* (Chapel Hill: University of North Carolina Press, 2020), 7.
140. "Marginal work" and "marginal jobs" are terms used by Richard Dunn to describe work that did not occur in the field or the Great House and was not skilled work (such as carpentry or boiling) or working with large animals. The people who undertook marginal work were usually enfeebled and weak and had passed their prime working years in the field. These were stations that enslaved people aged into. Dunn includes people who cut grass that fed stock, children's nurses, water-carriers, and cooks. I am surmising based on his examples and my study of the working lives of Mesopotamia's healers that healing was situated as marginal work on that plantation (Dunn, *A Tale of Two Plantations*, 142, 144, 164–65).
141. Browne, *The Driver's Story*, 17.
142. [David Collins], *Practical Rules for the Management and Medical Treatment of Negro Slaves in the Sugar Colonies* (London, 1803), 258.
143. James Grainger, *An Essay on the More Common West-India Diseases; and the Remedies which that Country Itself Produces* (London, 1764), 71.
144. A bedroom ought always to be included in any new hospitals that were constructed for "the comfortable accommodation of such a person, in case his nightly attendance is requisite" (Roughley, *The Jamaica Planter's Guide*, 93–94).
145. Browne, *The Driver's Story*, 23.

146. [David Collins], *Practical Rules for the Management and Medical Treatment of Negro Slaves in the Sugar Colonies* (London, 1803), 258.
147. Warwick was thirty (1762 inventory); Parthenia, forty (1771 inventory); Kickery, thirty-nine (1784 inventory); Quasheba, thirty-eight 38 (1786 inventory); Suckey, fifty-five (1793 inventory); Lydia, forty-two (1796 inventory); and Augustine, thirty-four (1807 inventory) (MS. Clar. dep. b. 36/2, Barham Papers).
148. Regarding Kickery, see Dunn, *A Tale of Two Plantations*, 469n10. Warwick's year of death is approximate, as there is no list for 1779; he would have been around forty-eight. He is not listed in the 1780 inventory. Working backward from the 1762 inventories, which are the first to list ages, I have calculated that Parthenia was approximately nineteen years old in 1751, the year she was listed as an adult in Mesopotamia's 1751 inventory. The 1802 inventory lists three of Quasheba's children, Bob, Bernard, and Claret, as Old Sibby's grandchildren (MS. Clar. dep. b. 36/2, Barham Papers). In his article on Mesopotamia, Richard Dunn describes Quasheba as "the African female doctor," but it is unclear whether his use of the term "African" was to differentiate her from white medical practitioners or to indicate that she was born in Africa (Dunn, "A Tale of Two Plantations: Slave Life at Mesopotamia in Jamaica and Mount Airy in Virginia, 1799 to 1828," *William and Mary Quarterly* 34 [1977]: 32–65, quote on 51).
149. For Augustine's place of origin, see the 1785 inventory (MS. Clar. dep. b. 36/2, Barham Papers). Lydia was African-born (Dunn, *A Tale of Two Plantations*, 91).
150. [No author, no title], *Medical and Philosophical Commentaries by a Society in Edinburgh*, vol. 2, part 1 (1784): 90–92.
151. Thomas Dancer, "Case of a Negro Turning White; Communicated by Mr. T. Dancer, of Kingston, Jamaica," *Medical and Physical Journal* 8 (August 1, 1802): 96–97.
152. "Chamba" here refers to Gur language speakers captured from the middle Niger River delta and ferried to ports in Lower Guinea (Gwendolyn Midlo Hall, *Slavery and African Ethnicities in the Americas: Restoring the Links* [Chapel Hill: University of North Carolina Press, 2005], 107). James Chisholme to James Craggs, July 2, 1793, MSS 5476, Chisholme Papers.
153. Browne, *Surviving Slavery*, 3.
154. On Nanny dressing sores, see December 17, 27, 30, 1770, box 4, folder 21, Series 1, Thistlewood MSS. This affliction was yaws, but colonists claimed it was a subspecies on the basis that, in these cases, yaws sores clustered exclusively on the feet (J. Edward Hutson, "Crab Yaws," in *On the Treatment and Management of the More Common West-India Diseases, 1750–1802*, ed. Hutson [Kingston: University of the West Indies Press, 2005], 160; Henry Barham, *Hortus Americanus: Containing an Account of the Trees, Shrubs, and*

other Vegetable Productions, of South-America and the West-India Islands, and Particularly of the Island of Jamaica [Kingston: Alexander Aikman, 1794], 6; Charles Leslie, *A New and Exact Account of Jamaica* [London, 1739], 329; Thomas Dancer, *The Medical Assistant* [1801], 226).

155. The Kingston-based practitioner David Grant referred to people who addressed ulcers and sores as an "estate dresser." These herbalists managed afflictions of the skin with healing plasters (Grant, *An Essay on the Yellow Fever of Jamaica* [Bath: Printed by R. Crutwell, 1801], xii).

156. Tinde van Andel, "The Reinvention of Household Medicine by Enslaved Africans in Suriname," *Social History of Medicine* 29 (2016): 676–94. Thanks to Jessica Newby for her insights on how enslaved women's affective ties facilitated the development of their medical knowledge.

157. "Awareness," Finch writes, "gestures to a black feminist reading practice that can hear the quiet, excavate the interred and read the unintelligible" (Aisha K. Finch, "Black Feminist Knowledge Production, Archival Recuperation, and Slave Resistance Movements," The Body and the Body Politic Roundtable, *Women and Social Movements in the United States* 23 [2019]: [3]).

158. Case Fourteen in Trevor Burnard, ed., *Hearing Slaves Speak* (Caribbean Press for the Government of Guyana, 2010), 51 (original citation: C.O. 116/138-46-47, National Archives, Kew, Britain).

159. The three-stage model as well as the breakdown of enslaved people's primary work is described in Dunn, *A Tale of Two Plantations*, 140–45.

160. Of the adult workers on Mesopotamia between 1762 and 1833, 63 percent were producing cane during their prime working years (Dunn, *A Tale of Two Plantations*, 143).

161. Finley, *An Intimate Economy*, 4.

162. Kickery's field years: 1762–76 inventory; Quasheba's: 1762–85; Parthenia's known field years: 1762–70 (she may have started as early as 1751, when she was approximately eighteen) (MS. Clar. dep. b. 36/2, Barham Papers).

163. Parthenia's starting year, 1771; Quasheba's, 1786 (MS. Clar. dep. b. 36/2, Barham Papers).

164. There were three head midwives during the period under study—Old Kickery (the mother of Kickery), Kickery, and Elder Phillis—as well as three assistant midwives—Elder Cretia, Marina from Three Mile River, and Tamer. "Old Kickery" was the name given by the attorneys who created Mesopotamia's lists of enslaved people. "Elder Cretia," and "Elder Phillis" are my terms to differentiate these individuals from other, younger women—Phillis and Cretia—who lived on Mesopotamia at the same time. Some women who became midwives, such as Elder Cretia and Tamer, began apprenticing with other midwives while still engaged in field work, in their early to mid-thirties (see Elder Cretia's entry in the 1784 inventory and Tamer's entry in the 1802 inventory). Elder Phillis was in the field until

the fifth decade of her life. Most midwives exited the field in their thirties. Because of gaps in the information tracked in Mesopotamia's inventories, it is impossible to reconstruct Old Kickery's prime working years. She had been on Mesopotamia since 1751 (MS. Clar. dep. b. 36/2, Barham Papers).

165. Parthenia was described as infirm in 1771, the year she entered the hothouse. Starting in 1778 and through 1784, attorneys described Kickery as "pox'd," or "pox'd" young (MS. Clar. dep. b. 36/2, Barham Papers).

166. Lydia from 1784 until 1794; Suckey from 1762 until 1780. Augustine was the exception; she was in the field from 1786 until 1800, but left when she was approximately thirty (MS. Clar. dep. b. 36/2, Barham Papers).

167. For Lydia's age, see the 1796 inventory; for Suckey's, the 1795 inventory; and for Augustine's, the 1807 inventory (MS. Clar. dep. b. 36/2, Barham Papers).

168. Lydia died there at the age of forty-eight. Suckey was so ill that she remained only a year. She spent the next decade infirm. Whether Augustine remained after 1811 remains unknown. Lydia's death at the age of forty-eight was deemed a "sudden visitation by god" (1802 inventory, MS. Clar. dep. b. 36/2, Barham Papers).

169. Scholarship on the efficiencies of scale realized by specialization in Caribbean plantations has mainly focused on the enslaved men who worked as coopers, masons, carpenters, boilers, and distillers (Trevor Burnard and John Garrigus, *The Plantation Machine: Atlantic Capitalism in French Saint-Domingue and British Jamaica* [Philadelphia: University of Pennsylvania Press, 2016], 5; Roberts, *Slavery and the Enlightenment in the British Atlantic, 1750–1807*, 207–12; Michael Craton, *Searching for the Invisible Man: Slaves and Plantation Life in Jamaica* [Cambridge: Cambridge University Press, 1978], 223). Yet in her study of the lower Mississippi valley, Liana DeMarco has shown that plantation owners also tried to extract value from elderly enslaved women's medical labor, carework, and socialization of younger generations (DeMarco, "Managing 'Old Mammy,' Making 'Mother Wit': Older Enslaved Women, Efficiency, and Survival on the Plantation," *Slavery and Abolition* 44 [2023]: 317–33).

170. Studies of labor specialization have shown that the people who held these positions were often Creole (Trevor Burnard, *Jamaica in the Age of Revolution* [Philadelphia: University of Pennsylvania Press, 2020], 94–95; David Beck Ryden, *West Indian Slavery and British Abolition, 1783–1807* [Cambridge: Cambridge University Press, 2009], 139–49; Dunn, *A Tale of Two Plantations*, 142). Among skilled workers, boilers and distillers tended to be African-born (Justin Roberts, *Slavery and the Enlightenment in the British Atlantic, 1750–1807* [Cambridge: Cambridge University Press, 2013], 230–33).

171. Burnard estimates that after midcentury in Jamaica, some 25 percent of men were not in the field and engaged in some form of trade work, whereas

approximately 90 percent of enslaved women were in the field (Burnard, "'Impatient of Subordination' and 'Liable to Sudden Transports of Anger': White Masculinity and Homosocial Relations with Black Men in Eighteenth-Century Jamaica," in *New Men: Manliness in Early America*, ed. Thomas A. Foster [New York: New York University Press, 2011], 137; Burnard, "Evaluating Gender in Early Jamaica, 1674–1784," *History of the Family* 12 [2007]: 81–91).

172. On the uneven apportion of the costs of field work on women compared to men, see Burnard, *Jamaica in the Age of Revolution*, 93–94; Ryden, *West Indian Slavery and British Abolition, 1783–1807*, 147–49; and Dunn, *A Tale of Two Plantations*, 143.

173. Robert Dirks, *The Black Saturnalia: Conflict and Its Ritual Expression on British West Indian Slave Plantations* (Gainesville: University of Florida Press, 1987), 84–86.

174. Dunn, *A Tale of Two Plantations*, 27.

175. Hector received three pints per week, approximately one pint more than the people in Quasheba's group. Besides Camilla, two men—Ochre, a driver of the jobbers, and Dorset, a blacksmith—received one pint (1802 inventory, MS. Clar. dep. b. 36/2, Barham Papers).

176. Historians refer to these categories of enslaved people as "confidentials" (Ryden, *West Indian Slavery and British Abolition*, 133–34; Mary Turner, introduction to *From Chattel Slaves to Wage Slaves: The Dynamics of Labour Bargaining in the Americas*, ed. Turner [Bloomington: Indiana University Press, 1995], 4–7; John Campbell, "Reassessing the Consciousness of Labour and the Role of the 'Confidential' in Slave Society: Jamaica 1750–1834," *Jamaican Historical Review* 21 [2001]: 23–32).

177. The highest amount was given to Phebe, who received ninety plantains per week to maintain herself and children (1802 Barham Lists).

178. Parthenia's working years: 1751–96; Kickery's: 1762–1811; Quasheba's: 1762–1811 (MS. Clar. dep. b. 36/2, Barham Papers).

179. See 1781 inventory.

180. See 1795 inventory.

181. Quasheba's working biography as an adolescent and adult is reconstructed from the 1762–1811 inventories.

182. For Kickery's death year, see 1811 inventory.

183. He likely died in 1779, a year for which there is not an extent inventory. He is listed in the 1778 inventory and not in the 1780 inventory.

184. Dunn, *A Tale of Two Plantations*, 432, (appendix 16, "The Occupation, Health, and Longevity of Mesopotamia Adult Slaves, 1763–1833").

185. Kickery was approximately twenty when Robert Pinkney was Mesopotamia's doctor (see Robert Pinkney to Joseph Foster Barham, April 27, 1765, MS. Clar. dep. c. 357, Barham Papers).

186. 1786 inventory.
187. Fett, *Working Cures*, 125–30.
188. The origins of these substances are discussed in William Lewis, *An Experimental History of the Materia Medica* (London, 1784), sulfur, 625; lignum vitae, 586; senna, 600; Barbadoes Tar, 627.
189. "Vanglo, Wongala, oil-plant," Edward Long, *The History of Jamaica*, vol. 2 (1774), 809–10; "Wolongo, whangra," Matthew Lewis, *Journal of a West-Indian Proprietor* (1836), 135; "Wangla," Williamson, *Medical and Miscellaneous Observations*, 1:172.
190. John Lunan, *Hortus Jamaicensis*, vol. 2 (1814), 252.
191. Sloane, *A Voyage to the Islands Madera, Barbadoes, Nieves, St. Christophers, and Jamaica*, vol. 1 (1707), 161.
192. Lewis, *Journal of a West-Indian Proprietor*, 135–37.
193. Williamson, *Medical and Miscellaneous Observations*, 1:172.

4. Uncontrolled Experiments

1. John Hunter, *Observations on the Diseases of the Army in Jamaica*, 1st ed. (1788), 244.
2. Alexander Anderson to Benjamin Rush, August 24, 1792, Benjamin Rush Correspondence, vol. 1, Rush Family Papers.
3. [David Collins], *Practical Rules for the Management and Medical Treatment of Negro Slaves in the Sugar Colonies* (London, 1803), 231.
4. [Collins], *Practical Rules for the Management and Medical Treatment of Negro Slaves in the Sugar Colonies*, 231.
5. To be sure, a handful of botanists who also practiced on plantations, including James Grainger, Sir Hans Sloane, and Patrick Browne, were recognized for their contributions to the natural history of the islands (and the attendant botanical therapeutics located therein). Grainger was most well-known in his day for "The Sugar Cane," a Georgic poem that listed the various natural remedies produced in the region. But to historians of medicine and Anglo-American slavery he is perhaps more famous for his seventy-five-page domestic medical advice book *An Essay on the More Common West-India Diseases* (1764).
6. Over the course of the eighteenth century, military and Royal Naval practitioners stationed in the tropical theaters of the British Empire systematically studied the diseases that harassed regiments and squadrons, producing what Mark Harrison has described as a "distinctive literature of warm climates" (Harrison, *Medicine in an Age of Commerce and Empire* [Cambridge: Cambridge University Press, 2010], 2).

7. Erica Charters, *Disease, War, and the Imperial State* (Chicago: University of Chicago Press, 2014).
8. Many historians of medicine in Europe have studied hospitals in university cities, such as Paris and Edinburgh, where universities monopolized the instruction of the medical elite. This literature has focused on the role of hospitals as teaching institutions adjacent to universities and medical colleges. See, for example, Guenter B. Risse, *Hospital Life in Enlightenment Scotland: Care and Teaching at the Royal Infirmary of Edinburgh* (Cambridge: Cambridge University Press, 1986); Lisa Rosner, *Medical Education in an Age of Improvement* (Edinburgh: Edinburgh University Press, 1991); Laurence Brockliss, "Medical Teaching at the University of Paris," *Annals of Science* 35 (1978): 221–51; and Erna Lesky, "The Development of Bedside Teaching at the Vienna Medical School from Scholastic Times to Special Clinics," in *The History of Medical Education*, ed. Charles D. O'Malley (Berkeley: University of California Press, 1970), 217–34. Other scholars have highlighted voluntary hospitals in major seaports as sites of teaching and experiment (see, for example, Mary Fissell, *Patients, Power, and the Poor in Eighteenth-Century Bristol* [Cambridge: Cambridge University Press, 1991]; Susan C. Lawrence, *Charitable Knowledge: Hospital Pupils and Practitioners in Eighteenth-Century London* [Cambridge: Cambridge University Press, 1996]; J. H. Woodward, *"To Do the Sick No Harm": A Study of the British Voluntary Hospital System to 1875* [London: Routledge & Kegan Paul, 1974]).
9. Michel Foucault, *The Birth of the Clinic: An Archaeology of Medical Perception*, trans. A. M. Sheridan Smith (New York: Pantheon, 1975); W. F. Bynum, "Physicians, Hospitals, and Career Structures in Eighteenth-Century London," in *William Hunter and the Eighteenth-Century Medical World*, ed. Bynum and Roy Porter (Cambridge: Cambridge University Press, 1985), 105–28; Othmar Keel, "The Politics of Health and the Institutionalization of Clinical Practices in Europe in the Second Half of the Eighteenth Century," ibid., 207–58; Joan Lane, *A Social History of Medicine: Health, Healing and Disease in England, 1750–1950* (London: Routledge, 2001), chap. 5; Malcolm Nicolson, "The Introduction Percussion and Stethoscopy to Early Nineteenth-Century Edinburgh," in *Medicine and the Five Senses*, ed. William Bynum and Roy Porter (Cambridge: Cambridge University Press, 1993), 134–35.
10. Volker T. Hess and J. Andrew Mendelsohn, "Case and Series: Medical Knowledge and Paper Technology, 1600–1900," *History of Science* 58 (2010); Volker T. Hess and Sophie Ledebur, "Taking and Keeping: A Note on the Emergence and Function of Hospital Patient Records," *Journal of the Society of Archivists* 32, no. 1 (2011): 21–33; J. Andrew Mendelsohn, "The

World on a Page: Making a General Observation in the Eighteenth Century," in *Histories of Scientific Observation*, ed. Lorraine Daston and Elizabeth Lunbeck (Chicago: University of Chicago Press, 2011), 396–420; Anke te Heesen, "The Notebook: A Paper Technology," in *Making Things Public: Atmospheres of Democracy*, ed. Bruno Latour and Peter Weibel (Cambridge, MA: MIT Press, 2005), 582–89.

11. On geographies of containment, see Stephanie Camp, *Closer to Freedom: Enslaved Women and Everyday Resistance in the Plantation South* (Chapel Hill: University of North Carolina Press, 2004), 6, 12–34.

12. On the use of enslaved people as experimental subjects, see Londa Schiebinger, *Secret Cures of Slaves: People, Plants, and Medicine in the Eighteenth-Century Atlantic World* (Stanford, CA: Stanford University Press, 2017), 4–14, 65–112.

13. Scholarship on the history of the medical case is almost as large as that on the clinic. A few introductory texts on their function include Gianna Pomata, "Sharing Cases: The Observationes in Early Modern Medicine," *Early Science and Medicine* 15, no. 3 (2010): 193–236; Gianna Pomata, "Observation Rising: Birth of an Epistemic Genre, 1500–1650," in *Histories of Scientific Observation*, ed. Lorraine Daston and Elizabeth Lunbeck (Chicago: University of Chicago Press, 2011), 45–80; and J. Andrew Mendelsohn, "Empiricism in the Library: Medicine's Case Histories," in *Science in the Archives: Pasts, Presents, Futures*, ed. Lorraine Daston (Chicago: University of Chicago Press, 2017), 85–112.

14. On the spiritual resonances of Black Carábenos' and enslaved people's botanical knowledge, see Pablo F. Gómez, *The Experiential Caribbean: Creating Knowledge and Healing in the Early Modern Atlantic* (Chapel Hill: University of North Carolina Press, 2017).

15. Hunter, *Observations on the Diseases of the Army in Jamaica*, 1st ed. (1788), 244.

16. Hogarth, *Medicalizing Blackness*, 81–103; Suman Seth, *Difference and Disease: Medicine, Race, and the Eighteenth-Century British Empire* (Cambridge: Cambridge University Press, 2018), 168.

17. Steven Shapin and Simon Schaffer, *The Leviathan and the Air-Pump: Hobbes, Boyle, and the Experimental Life* (Princeton, NJ: Princeton University Press, 1985).

18. This insight about case histories as currency and gifts is adapted from Elaine Leong and Sara Pennell's discussion of recipes' similar social function (see "Recipe Collections and the Currency of Medical Knowledge in the Early Modern 'Medical Marketplace,'" in *Medicine and the Market in England and Its Colonies, c. 1450–c. 1850*, ed. Mark S. R. Jenner and Patrick Wallis [London: Palgrave Macmillan, 2007], 133–52).

19. For a comparative example of the ways that scientific gift exchange solidified networks of patrons and clients, see Paula Findlen, "The Economy of Scientific Exchange in Early Modern Italy," in *Patronage and Institutions*, ed. Bruce T. Moran (Woodbridge, Suffolk: Boydell, 1991), 5–25.
20. On norms of civility, see Simon Shapin, *A Social History of Truth: Civility and Science in Seventeenth-Century England* (Chicago: University of Chicago Press, 1994).
21. On Troup's Scottish networks and his position within them, see Douglas J. Hamilton, *Scotland, the Caribbean and the Atlantic World, 1750–1820* (Manchester, UK: Manchester University Press, 2007), 117.
22. Sasha Turner, *Contested Bodies: Pregnancy, Childrearing, and Slavery in Jamaica* (Philadelphia: University of Pennsylvania Press, 2017).
23. Katherine Park, *Secrets of Women: Gender, Generation, and the Origins of Human Dissection* (Brooklyn, NY: Zone, 2006); Laura Gowing, *Common Bodies: Women, Touch, and Power in Seventeenth-Century England* (New Haven, CT: Yale University Press, 2003); Mary Fissell, *Vernacular Bodies: The Politics of Reproduction in Early Modern England* (Oxford: Oxford University Press, 2007); Adrian Wilson, *The Making of Man-Midwifery: Childbirth in England, 1660–1770* (Cambridge, MA: Harvard University Press, 1995); Lisa Forman Cody, *Birthing the Nation: Sex, Science, and the Conception of Eighteenth-Century Britons* (Oxford: Oxford University Press, 2005).
24. July 18, 1789, Journal of Jonathan Troup.
25. July 18, 1789, Journal of Jonathan Troup.
26. Turner, *Contested Bodies*, 119–21.
27. July 16, 1789, Journal of Jonathan Troup.
28. Turner, *Contested Bodies*, 99–101.
29. July 16, 1789, Journal of Jonathan Troup.
30. July 17, 1789, Journal of Jonathan Troup.
31. July 21, 1789, Journal of Jonathan Troup.
32. July 27, 1789, Journal of Jonathan Troup.
33. July 30, 1789, Journal of Jonathan Troup.
34. August 1, 1789, Journal of Jonathan Troup.
35. August 21, 1789, Journal of Jonathan Troup.
36. Jim Downs, *Maladies of Empire: How Colonialism, Slavery, and War Transformed Medicine* (Cambridge, MA: Harvard University Press, 2021), 68–87.
37. Edward Long, *The History of Jamaica*, vol. 2 (1774), 582.
38. John Williamson, *Medical and Miscellaneous Observations, Relative to the West India Islands,* (Edinburgh, 1817), 1:viii.
39. The reception of the texts authored by plantation practitioners is murky. Few were cited in the texts composed by the prominent fever writers of their day, and none of the texts written by plantation practitioners, save

for that of James Grainger, were published as a second edition. Some, such Robert Thomas's *Medical Advice to the Inhabitants of Warm Climates* (1790) as well as Robert Shannon's *Practical Observations on the Effects of Certain Medicines in the Prevention and Cure of Diseases to which Europeans are subject in Hot Climates* (1794) were composite—their authors cut-and-paste wholesale from the more famous Caribbean writers on tropical fevers and the natural world of the West Indies. Both Shannon and Thomas lifted from Edward Long and the military physician John Hunter.

40. Only four of the nearly one hundred plantation practitioners identified in the course of researching this book—James Grainger, William Wright, David Collins, and John Williamson—transformed their notes into books and memoirs with original material that described the diseases they treated.
41. These entries had two functions. They served as an aide-mémoire that helped Troup judge the medicines' effects on subsequent visits. And in cases where the medicines were supplied from Fillian's pharmacy, they probably assisted in drawing up an itemized bill for the estate.
42. Lawrence, *Charitable Knowledge*, 14.
43. Lawrence, *Charitable Knowledge*, 150–53.
44. Lawrence, *Charitable Knowledge*, 150–53.
45. The Jamaican slaveholder John Baillie stated that it was customary for the overseers on his estate to visit the hospital at least once per day, where they examined the sick and noted their condition in the hot-house book (Baillie as quoted in Sheridan, *Doctors and Slaves*, 294 [original citation *Accounts and Papers (Parliamentary Papers)* 305, no. 127, pt. 2 (1832), 63]).
46. Elaine Leong and Alisha Rankin, "Testing Drugs and Trying Cures: Experiment and Medicine in Medieval and Early Modern Europe," *Bulletin of the History of Medicine* 91, no. 2 (Summer 2017): 157–82, esp. 158–60.
47. On five shillings per patient, see John Quier, *Letters and Essays on the Small-Pox of the West Indies by Different Practitioners* (London, 1778), xxxi.
48. For analogous informal experiments in Europe, see Andreas-Holger Maehle, *Drugs on Trial: Experimental Pharmacology and Therapeutic Innovation in the Eighteenth Century* (Amsterdam: Rodopi, 1999).
49. Writers on smallpox, for example, maintained that it was far more inflammatory among people who had a "full" or "phletoric" constitution.
50. On colonists' shifting attitudes toward smallpox inoculations and the role of individuation in securing colonists' approval, see Sara Stidstone Gronim, "Imagining Inoculation: Smallpox, the Body, and Social Relations of Healing in the Eighteenth Century," *Bulletin of the History of Medicine* 80, no. 2 (2006): 247–68.
51. James Kirkpatrick, *An Essay on Inoculation* (1741), 15.

52. On the African origins of smallpox inoculation, see Margo Minardi, "The Boston Inoculation Controversy of 1721–1722: An Incident in the History of Race," *William and Mary Quarterly* 61, no. 1 (2004): 47–76.
53. Elise A. Mitchell, "How Far Back Were Africans Inoculating Against Smallpox? Really Far Back," *Slate*, September 4, 2023.
54. On dietary antiphlogistic methods, see Chamberlaine, *A Practical Treatise on the Efficacy and Safety of Stizolobium, or Cowhage*, 2nd ed. (1784), 19. On the importance of mercurial medicines in preparation for smallpox inoculation, see, for example, Thomas Dimsdale, *The Present Method for Inoculating the Small-Pox* (London, 1767), 18–20.
55. Edward Long's explanation of how yaws ought to be cured exemplifies how many colonists imagined the disease process and explains why they turned to mercury as the remedy: "Experience proves that, when left to nature, and the use of flour of brimstone, to keep the humor in a constant elimination towards the skin," yaws, "gradually wears off in about three years" (Long, *The History of Jamaica*, 3 vols. [1774], 2:433).
56. Dr. D. Monro, ed., *Letters and Essays on the Small-Pox of the West Indies by Different Practitioners* (London 1778), 22.
57. Maurice M. Iwu, *Handbook of African Medicinal Plants*, 2nd ed. (Boca Raton, FL: CRC, 2014), 311, 265.
58. Chamberlaine, *A Practical Treatise on the Efficacy and Safety of Stizolobium, or Cowhage* (1784), 19.
59. Chamberlaine, *A Practical Treatise on the Efficacy and Safety of Stizolobium, or Cowhage* (1784), 21.
60. Alexander Anderson to Benjamin Rush, August 24, 1792, in Benjamin Rush Correspondence, vol. 1, Rush Family Papers.
61. Patrick Browne, *The Civil and Natural History of Jamaica in Three Parts* (1756), 336.
62. [No title, no author], *Medical and Philosophical Commentaries by a Society in Edinburgh*, vol. 2, pt. 1, 2nd ed. corrected (London, 1784), 96–98, quote on 96.
63. Evidence that information about cowhage's properties moved between managers abounds in writing about the plant. Thomas Cochrane, a surgeon in Nevis, invoked "planters" who "give it to the negroes with great success," in Thomas Cochrane, "Extract of a Letter from Mr. Thomas Cochrane, Surgeon at Nevis, to Mr. John Balfour, Surgeon at Edinburgh," *Medical Commentaries*, vol. 2, pt. 1, no. 4, p. 82. In the *Natural History of Guiana*, Edward Bancroft described scraping the hair off of cowhage as the "empirical practice of planters" (Bancroft, *Essay on the Natural History of Guiana* [London, 1769], 391). Chamberlaine learned of cowhage's attributes from Cochrane's essay and his contemporary Neil Stewart, who had informed

Chamberlaine about the remedy many times "*vive voce.*" Stewart also gifted to the surgeon an epistolary account of his method of preparation. For citation of Cochrane's article, see Chamberlaine, *A Practical Treatise on the Efficacy and Safety of Stizolobium, or Cowhage* (1784), 32. On Stewart's account and gift, see ibid., 43.

64. Chamberlaine, *A Practical Treatise on the Efficacy and Safety of Stizolobium, or Cowhage* (1784), 25–26.
65. Michael Hemmersam's description of the Gold Coast, 1639–45, in *German Sources for West African History, 1599–1669*, ed. Adam Jones (Wiesbaden: Franz Steiner Verlag, 1983), 121.
66. Williamson, *Medical and Miscellaneous Observations*, 1:57.
67. Chamberlaine, *A Practical Treatise on the Efficacy and Safety of Stizolobium, or Cowhage* (1784), 22.
68. Chamberlaine, *A Practical Treatise on the Efficacy and Safety of Stizolobium, or Cowhage* (1784), 21.
69. Chamberlaine, *A Practical Treatise on the Efficacy and Safety of Stizolobium, or Cowhage* (1784), 22.
70. William Wright, "The Use of Cold-Bathing in the Locked Jaw &c.," *Medical Observations and Enquiries by a Society in London* 6 (1784): 143–62, 152.
71. Chamberlaine, *A Practical Treatise on the Efficacy and Safety of Stizolobium, or Cowhage* (1784), 22.
72. Chamberlaine, *A Practical Treatise on the Efficacy and Safety of Stizolobium, or Cowhage* (1784), 21.
73. William Bowie to William Cullen, May 1783, CUL 1/3/90, Royal College of Physicians Edinburgh.
74. Turner, *Contested Bodies*, 126, 129.
75. William Bowie to William Cullen, May 1783, CUL 1/3/90, Royal College of Physicians Edinburgh.
76. Randall M. Packard, "The Fielding H. Garrison Lecture: Break-Bone Fever in Philadelphia, 1780: Reflections in the History of Disease," *Bulletin of the History of Medicine* 90, no. 2 (Summer 2016): 193–221.
77. William Wright, *Memoirs of the Late William Wright, M.D.* (Edinburgh, 1828), 72n.
78. James Grainger, *An Essay on the More Common West-India Diseases; and the Remedies which that Country Itself Produces* (London, 1764), 410.
79. Clement Caines, *Letters on the Cultivation of the Otaheite Cane: The Manufacture of Sugar and Rum; the Saving of Melasses; the Care and Preservation of Stock: with the Attention and Anxiety Which Is Due to Negroes* (London, 1801), 145–46.
80. Benjamin Turney to Chaloner Arcedeckne, Kingston, July 24, 1791, Vanneck-ARC 7/21/91/15 Vanneck Papers, as quoted in Betty Wood and T. R. Clayton, "Slave Birth, Death, and Disease on Golden Grove

Plantation, Jamaica, 1765–1810," *Slavery and Abolition* 6, no. 2 (September 1985): 99–121, quote on 112.

81. Williamson, however, did not single out enslaved healers for their carelessness. Instead, possibly drawing on his experience as a surgeon in the British Army, he imagined that all practitioners working in clinical settings contended with noncompliance from below (Williamson, *Medical and Miscellaneous Observations*, 1:120, 117).

82. Chamberlaine, *A Practical Treatise on the Efficacy and Safety of Stizolobium, or Cowhage* (1784), 20.

83. William Wright, "The Use of Cold-Bathing in the Locked Jaw &c.," *Medical Observations and Enquiries by a Society in London* 6 (1784): 143–62, quotes on 150–52.

84. Mary Lindemann, *Medicine and Society in Early Modern Europe* (Cambridge: Cambridge University Press, 2010), 17.

85. Jessica Marie Johnson, *Wicked Flesh: Black Women, Intimacy, and Freedom in the Atlantic World* (Philadelphia: University of Pennsylvania Press, 2020), 177–79.

86. James Knight, *The Natural, Moral, and Political History of Jamaica, and the Territories thereon Depending, from the First Discovery of the Island by Christopher Columbus to the Year 1746*, ed. Jack P. Greene (Charlottesville: University of Virginia Press, 2021), 497.

87. August, 4, 1789, Journal of Jonathan Troup.

88. Williamson, *Medical and Miscellaneous Observations, Relative to the West India Islands* (Edinburgh, 1817), 2:82.

89. Suman Seth, *Difference and Disease: Medicine, Race, and the Eighteenth-Century British Empire* (Cambridge: Cambridge University Press, 2018), 168. Many of the Atlantic World's elite medical writers, as Rana Hogarth has shown, collapsed the distinctions that colonists made between different ethnic groups, recently arrived captives from Africa, seasoned slaves, and what scholars have described as "Creoles" (people born in the Caribbean). Instead, they invoked the perceived invulnerability of "negroes" to tropical fevers, thereby giving Blackness meaning in diagnosis and treatment (Hogarth, *Medicalizing Blackness*, 17–77).

90. The slaveholder and slave factor Simon Taylor stated that it was because of the abuse of mercury by doctors that enslaved people had "their blood broke down" (Simon Taylor to Chaloner Arcedeckne, July 5, 1789, Vanneck-Arc/3A/1789/20, Vanneck Papers, quoted in http://freepages.rootsweb.com/~sedgebrook/history/page20.htm). Michael Craton, "Death, Disease, and Medicine on Jamaican Slave Plantations: The Example of Worthy Park, 1767–1838," *Histoire Sociale—Social History* 2, no. 18 (November 1976).

91. William Chamberlaine, *A Practical Treatise on the Efficacy and Safety of Stizolobium, or Cowhage* (1784), 7.

92. His signature remedy involved immersing yaws patients in casks of heated water mixed with woods, described as "Bois Royale" and "Bois Fer," and rubbing an ointment composed of iron rust and lime juice upon their sores (*Medical and Philosophical Commentaries by a Society in Edinburgh*, 2, pt. 1, 2nd ed. [London, 1784], 90–92, quote on 92).
93. On omissions, silences, and biases in the archives of slavery, see Marisa J. Fuentes, *Dispossessed Lives: Enslaved Women, Violence, and the Archive* (Philadelphia: University of Pennsylvania Press, 2016), 4.
94. On different definitions and classifications of cocobay, see William Hillary, *Observations on the Changes of the Air and the Concomitant Epidemical Diseases in the Island of Barbados and Other West India Islands* (London, 1759), 335; Hector R. McNeil, *Observations on the Treatment of the Negroes in the Island of Jamaica* (London, 1788), 35; and Thomas Dancer, *The Medical Assistant* (1801), 230.
95. William Wright, "The Use of Cold-Bathing in the Locked Jaw &c.," *Medical Observations and Enquiries by a Society in London* 6 (1784): 143–62, quote on 158.
96. William Wright, "The Use of Cold-Bathing in the Locked Jaw &c.," *Medical Observations and Enquiries by a Society in London* 6 (1784): 143–62, quote on 160.
97. By conducting trials of comparative diets, James Lind, for example, concluded that scurvy was caused by dietary deficiency and remedied by citrus fruits (Peter Mathias, "Swords and Ploughshares: The Armed Forces, Medicine, and Public Health in the Late Eighteenth Century," in *The Transformation of England: Essays in the Economic and Social History of England in the Eighteenth Century*, ed. Mathias [London: Methuen, 1979], 265–85. quote on 269). Flanks of nurses could control the diets consumed by patients. See, for example, Richard Brocklesby's dietary recommendations based on his attendance to hospitals in Flanders in *Oeconomical and Medical Observations in Two Parts* (1764), 136, 309, as discussed in Charters, *Disease, War, and the Imperial State*, 99.
98. Paul N. Edwards, Lisa Gitelman, Gabrielle Hecht et al., "AHR Conversation: Historical Perspectives on the Circulation of Information," *American Historical Review* 116, no. 5 (2011): 1404–35.

Conclusion

1. John Collins, "Two Letters from John Collins, Esq. of the Island of St. Vincent, addressed to Benjamin Vaughan, Esq., of London, on the Subject of a Species of Angina Maligna, and the use of Capsicum in that and Several Other Diseases," *Medical Communications* 2 (1790): 363–85; William Wright, M.D. "The Antiseptic Virtues of Vegetable Acid and Marine Salt

Combined, in Various Disorders, Accompanied with Putridity, Communicated in a Letter to John Morgan, M.D.F.R.S.," *Medical Commentaries for the Year M,DCC,LXXXVI*, vol. 1 (1787): 189–95, mention of putrid sore throat in Jamaica as having made "considerable havock, both among children and adults," 193; James Stephens, "An Account of the Use of the Pepper Medicine of the West Indies in the Cynanche Maligna, extracted from a letter written by Mr. James Stephens, Surgeon in St. Christopher's, to Dr. Thomas Cochrane, physician in Edinburgh," *Medical Commentaries for the Year M,DCC,LXXXVII*, vol. 2 (1788): 375–78, "many children and not a few adults were attacked with the cynanche maligna [putrid sore throat]," 375.

2. Collins, "Two Letters from John Collins, Esq.," "Experiments," 371, 373, "Trial," 375.
3. Collins referred to this building alternately as a hospital and a sick-house. ("Two Letters from John Collins, Esq.," Sick-house 369, hospital, 370). His enslaved test subjects' confinement is implied—he spoke of one child being "admitted," and another as having "came into the hospital" (369, 370). On the dosage of his remedy, see 373.
4. Collins, "Two Letters from John Collins, Esq.," 365.
5. See, for example, the map of Lavington's plantation in John Johnson, "Reports Relating to Mr. Gordon's Estates in the West Indies, pt 2," M526a, image located between pages 22 and 23, Burke Library, Hamilton and Kirkland Colleges, Clinton, NY.
6. The diagnosis of illness and the administration of medicine and care in a ritual context were central to the ways that Afro-Diasporic people forged bonds of affinity and mediated conflict. For many scholars, the use of ritual to enact a relational view of illness represents the retention of African medical culture (see James H. Sweet, *Recreating Africa: Culture, Kinship, and Religion in the African-Portuguese World, 1441–1770* [Chapel Hill: University of North Carolina Press, 2003], 139–91; James H. Sweet, *Domingo Álvares, African Healing, and the Intellectual History of the Atlantic World* [Chapel Hill: University of North Carolina Press, 2011]; and Robert Voeks, "The Spiritual Flora of Brazil's African Diaspora: Ethnobotanical Conversations in the Black Atlantic World," *Journal for the Study of Religion, Nature, and Culture* 6 [2012]: 501–22).
7. Zachary Dorner, *Merchants of Medicines: The Commerce and Coercion of Health in Britain's Long Eighteenth Century* (Chicago: University of Chicago Press, 2020), 5; Harold J. Cook, "Practical Medicine and the British Armed Forces after the 'Glorious Revolution,'" *Medical History* 34 (1990): 1–26.
8. Dorner, *Merchants of Medicines*, 7.
9. Erica Charters, *Disease, War, and the Imperial State: The Welfare of the British Armed Forces during the Seven Years' War* (Chicago: University of Chicago Press, 2014).

10. For "country practitioners," see D. Munro, ed., *Letters and Essays on the Small-Pox of the West Indies by Different Practitioners* (1778), 65; and Thomas Dancer, "Observations on the Contagiousness and Importation of the Yellow Fever. By Thomas Dancer, M.D. of Kingston, in the Island of Jamaica. Addressed to the Editors of the Medical Repository," *Medical Repository of Original Essays and Intelligence* 1 (November 1803–January 1804): 247–54, "country practitioners," 254n. William Lemprière described learning about tetanus from "some medical gentlemen of the country," in *Practical Observations on the Diseases of the Army in Jamaica*, vol. 1 (1799), 47. For "country practice," see William Wright, "An Account of a remarkable fact relative to the Small Pox," *London Medical Journal* 7 (1786): 63–66, quote on 63; and John Williamson, *Medical and Miscellaneous Observations, Relative to the West India Islands*, 2 vols. (1817), 1:251; "Plantation practice," 224, 248. The Jamaican doctor Thomas Clarke used "country business" interchangeably with "negroe practice." For Clarke, these terms were synonymous. In his letters, they primarily marked the geography and ambit of this particular type of medical business. In a letter to Henry Cullen, for instance, Clarke described his "large negro practice" (see Clarke to Cullen, Portmorant, Jamaica, Sept 12, 1783, CUL 1/2/1374, Royal College of Physicians Edinburgh). In a later letter, he described abandoning his "large country business" (see Thomas Clarke to Henry Cullen, Kingston, Jamaica, April 20, 1788, CUL 1/3/192, ibid.). Alexander Johnston of Jamaica also described his erstwhile medical business as "negroe practice" (see Alexander Johnston to James Johnston, January 20, 1784, 1582/29B, box 2, folder 3, Powel Family Papers; original quote in Douglass Hamilton, *Scotland, the Caribbean and the Atlantic World, 1750–1820* [Manchester, UK: Manchester University Press, 2010], 125).

11. Rana Hogarth has discussed the role of many Caribbean practitioners, mostly working in the nineteenth century, in formulating and promulgating notions of racial difference on the basis of perceived differential responses to epidemic disease (Hogarth, *Medicalizing Blackness* [Chapel Hill: University of North Carolina Press, 2017]).

12. Christopher Willoughby, *Masters of Health: Racial Science and Slavery in U.S. Medical Schools* (Chapel Hill: University of North Carolina Press, 2022).

13. David Reich, *Who We Are and How We Got Here: Ancient DNA and the New Science of the Ancient Past* (New York: Pantheon, 2018).

14. Julia T. Caldwell, Chandra L. Ford, Steven P. Wallace, May C. Wang, and Lois M. Takahashi, "Racial and Ethnic Residential Segregation and Access to Health Care in Rural Areas," *Health and Place* 43 (2017): 104–12.

15. William P. Qiao; Emilie S. Powell; Mark P. Witte, and Martin R. Zelder, "Relationship between Racial Disparities in ED Wait Times and Illness Severity," *American Journal of Emergency Medicine* 34 (2016): 10–15.

16. Andrew T. Simpson, *The Medical Metropolis: Health Care and Economic Transformation in Pittsburgh and Houston* (Philadelphia: University of Pennsylvania Press, 2019).
17. Shawn F. Johnson, Ayotomiwa Ojo, and Haiden J. Warraich, "Academic Medical Centers' Antiracism Strategies Must Extend to Their Business Practices," *Annals of Medicine* 174 (2020): 254.
18. W. E. B. Du Bois, *The Souls of Black Folk*, Oxford's World Classics (Oxford: Oxford University Press, 2007), 8.
19. Linda Cummings, *Listening to Black Californians: How the Health Care System Undermines Their Pursuit of Good Health*, California Healthcare Foundation Report, October 2022, https://www.chcf.org/publication/listening-black-californians-how-the-health-care-system-undermines-their-pursuit-good-health/.

INDEX

Page numbers in italics indicate figures.

academic medical centers (AMCs), 190
Adair, James, 44
advice writers, 33, 37, 42, 173
agricultural improvement movement, 8, 18
Alexander, A. J., 109
amelioration laws, 64
American War of Independence, 66, 67, 70, 74, 77, 79, 86
Anderson, Alexander, 42, 73, 152, 169
Anderson, William, 117
Anglo-Maroon conflict, 64, 67, 100
Arcedeckne, Chaloner, 33, 36, 41, 52, 73–75, 98, 99, 100, 116
assistants, 87–88, 126, 219n62
attrition rates, 7, 198n22
awareness, 141, 239n157

Baillie, John, 91, 246n45
Banks, Joseph, 161
Barham, Henry, 108, 133, 236n133
Barham, Joseph Foster, 57, 98–99, 126, 139
Barnjum, Daniel, 146
Beckford, William, 131
bedside medicine, 26
bedstocks, 37–38, *38*
Bell, David, 83
Biafrans, 55, 58
bilious fevers, 111
blood (enslaved people), 177
bodies, 60; discharges and excretions, 128, 133; fungible, 11, 13, 186, 188; idiosyncratic, 90; interchangeable, 11, 20; internal examination, 50–51; management, 3–5, 9, 13, 103, 105, 186, 187;
predisposition, 189; putrefaction, 32, 33, 111, 112; slavery effects, 177; universal, 90
bodywork, 132
bookkeepers, 1, 4, 69, 91, 103
Bowie, William, 173–74
Bremner, William, 87
British/Britain, 59–60, 93, 111; Anglo-Maroon conflict, 64, 67, 100; hospital medicine, 163–64; imperial project, 66; industrial capitalism, 18; institutions, 89; integrated plantations, 6–7, 18; medical theory, 50; merchant-apothecaries, 106; practitioners, 90; voluntary hospitals, 12, 60, 80, 90, 100, 188; war machine, 76, 153
Brodbelt, Francis Rigby, 215n31
Brown, Ras Michael, 55
Browne, Patrick, 169, 242n5
building design, 35; Lavington's plantation, 29, *30*; movement minimization, 28–29; multichambered, 37, *38*; single-room, 32, 37
Burnard, Trevor, 69, 240n171
Byam, Ashton Warner, 218n58

cabbage-bark remedy: Chamberlaine's experiment, 168, 169, 171, *172*; healers' imprecision, 123; worm treatment, 120–21
Caines, Clement, 51, 58, 107, 174
calabashes (gourds), 119–22
Campbell, Alexander, 50, 219n64
Canefield plantation (Dominica), 134–36
carelessness, 173–74, 249n81

255

Cary, Samuel, 40–42, 131, 230n24
case histories, 156–62, 177
Castles, John, 80, 218n58
Chamberlaine, William, 67, 205n32; bedstocks, 37; cabbage-bark, 168, 169, 171, 172; communication barrier, 171–72; cost issues, 171; cowhage, 168–70, 175, 247n63; hot-house book instructions, 2; interactions with recipients, 172–73; jalap, 168, 171; limitations, 171–75; limited communications, 2, 14; presence on estates, 10; role of, 1; rum, 172, 185–86; smallpox inoculations, 168
charity hospitals, 164, 176, 179, 196n12
childbirth, 53, 68, 103, 158–60, 164, 185, 202n51, 235n117; cost, 79, 219n62
Chisholme, James, 97, 116, 117, 123
Chisholme, William, 117
cinchona remedy, 111, 172
circuit surgeons, 80–89
Clark, James, 158
Clarke, Thomas, 74–76, 87, 217n44
clinical medicine, 26, 90, 163
cognitive dissonance, 95
cold-bathing remedy, 172, 175, 178, 179
Collins, David, 31, 33, 38, 41, 43, 47, 49, 58, 79, 104, 109, 118, 122, 131, 133, 137, 138, 152, 154, 189, 207n56, 208n80, 226n150
Collins, John, 183–84, 251n3
commercial pharmaceuticals, 11, 12, 20, 148
communication, 172–73; barrier, 172; about illness, 47–49; sick-houses, 15, 37, 55
Congo Jack, 45, 49
copartnerships, 86–87
Cope, John, 112–13, 119, 148
Cornwall plantation (Jamaica), 53
corrosive sublimate, 116, 119, 131
cost(s), 218n59; childbirth, 79, 219n62; diet, 40–41; inoculation, 79, 165, 166, 219n65; issue, 171; transport animals, 82; transportation, 86
Cowell, Benjamin, 116

cowhage, 198n26; Chamberlaine's experiment with, 168–70, 175, 247n63; worm medicine, 9, 15, 168, 169
crowding, 31–33, 36
Cullen, William, 173
Cumming, John, 23–25, 27–28, 31, 49

Dalling, John, 215n27
Dancer, Thomas, 17, 95, 139, 156, 216n37
debt-priority legislation, 79
decision-making, 10; healers, 46, 108, 186; incapacity, 46
diets (sick people), 5, 6; costs of, 40–41; dysentery, 41; full, 41; low, 41, 43; managers' experiments with, 40, 44; roasted yams, 58; salt-heavy, 95; soups, 41–42, 133–34; stimulant, 41
dissections, 176
doctress, 103, 126, 140, 147, 186, 228n3
Dorner, Zachary, 106, 115
Dovehall plantation, 149–50
Dracunculiasis, 170
drivers, 135, 136, 144, 146
drugs. *See* medicines/medication
Drummond, John, 118, 178–79
Duckenfield plantation (Jamaica), 97, 98
Dugid, Peter, 123
Duncan, Andrew, 41
Dunn, Richard, 237n140, 238n148
dysentery, 144; diet for, 41; management, 150; signs of, 47–48

Edmonds, John: cowhage remedy, 9, 15; entries in hot-house book, 1–2, 9; responsibilities, 1–2
effluvia, 32
Essay on the More Common West-India Diseases, An (Grainger), 107
experiments (trials), 180; Bowie's, 173; carelessness, 173–74; Chamberlaine's, 168–71; Collins's, 183–84; communication barrier, 171–72; dissections, 176; Drummond's, 178–79; inoculations, 164–68; limitations, 171–75; managers,

40, 44; reliance on family members, 175–76

Fett, Sharla, 133
fever, 47, 49; bilious, 111; infectious, 152, 153; Prancer's plight, 23–24; tropical, 49, 68; yellow, 153
Fillian, Andrew, 42, 69, 81, 87–88, 158, 162, 163
Finch, Aisha K., 141, 239n157
Fissell, Mary, 133
Fitzmaurice, William, 89
Flamstead plantation (Jamaica), 36, 39
food: expression of care, 58; homeland and, 57; rations, 41–43, 58, 144–45. *See also* diets (sick people)
forced medication, 42–43
foul air, 32, 39, 205n32
Franckyn, Gilbert, 39
Fraser, Thomas, 80
full diet, 41
Fuller, Stephen, 83
Fuller, Thomas, 139
Fullerton, Alexander, 86

Gallimore, Alexander, 34
gang-labor, 18
Gillespie, Urquhart, 219n61
Golden Grove plantation (Jamaica), 52, 73, 98, 174; Duckenfield and, 97; hospital at, 33–34, 36
Gómez, Pablo F., 127, 203n11
Good Hope's hospital, 34–36, 35
Gordon, Lewis, 82
Gordon, Mary, 38
gourds, 119–22
Graham, J., 102, 204n29
Grainger, John, 33, 138, 173, 211n127, 242n5; *An Essay on the More Common West-India Diseases*, 107; "The Sugar Cane," 83, 242n5
Grant, David, 51, 216n37, 239n155
Green River plantation (Jamaica), 96–97
Guinea worm, 170
gum guaiacum, 119, 148

Haitian Revolution, 66–68, 75
Harrison, Mark, 242n6
healers, 1, 16–17, 71; access imported medicines, 117; age and experience, 138–40, 146, 149; botanical knowledge, 140; carework, 132–33; competition, 106, 123–24; creativity, 104; critical position, 104; decision-making, 46, 108, 186; demotion, 141; Edmonds's instructions, 2; incapacity decisions, 46; ingenuity, 104, 105, 125, 127; institutional memory, 105, 147, 151; intermediaries, 10, 105; knowledge, 108–9, 121, 132; longevity, 145–46; long-standing ties, 139; medication error, 123; mobility, 109, 118, 119; physical strength, 134, 136, 137; place of origin, 139; power, 10, 103, 105, 120, 125, 136, 151, 187; rations, 144–45; respect, 137; role of, 103–4, 124–25, 137, 186; selection of, 138; social connections, 140, 141, 146; therapeutic memory, 150; workload, 125–26; yaws, 109–11, 113
healers' drug administration: haptic techniques, 127; imprecision, 123; refusal, 127–32; verbal exchanges, 126–27
Hemmersam, Michael, 170
Higman, B. W., 28, 29, 220n70
History of Jamaica (Long), 63
Hockin, H. E., 38
Hogarth, Rana, 249n89, 252n11
hog plum tree: bark and leaves, 108; root, 6, 114, 129
horses, 221n83; cost of, 82; feed, 85–86; imports, 82, 83; practitioners' occupational identity, 84; threats, 84; Troup's sketch, 83, 84
Horsley, John, 102, 146
hospital admission, 44; demand for, 61; denial of, 23–24, 44; incapacity and, 27; petition for, 46
hospitals (hot-houses), 24; bedroom, 237n144; bedstocks, 37–38, 38; confinement, 38, 40, 155, 251n3; "different tale," 60; dislocation, 36–37; door, 207n56; goal of, 25; Good Hope's hospital, 34–36;

hospitals (hot-houses) (*continued*)
  improvements, 33–34; isolation, 15, 37, 54–57; knowledge-making, 40, 154; location of, 29, 31; overcrowding, 31–32, 36; proprietors' view of, 31; punishments, 37, 38, 125, 133; teaching institutions, 243n8; visits, 59
hot-house books, 187; Chamberlaine's instructions, 1, 2; Edmonds's entries in, 1–2, 9; limited communications, 2, 14, 15; notes on patients, 164; one-word symptom descriptions, 91; recordkeeping devices, 91; uses of, 2, 9, 14
Hunter, John, 152, 157
Hutchinson plantation, 37, 45, 49

idiosyncratic constitution, 11, 90
imported pharmaceuticals, 4, 5, 10, 11, 108, 117
incapacity/incapacitated, 39, 44, 58; assessment, 27, 31; decisions, 46; internal examination, 50–51; punishments, 45
infectious diseases, 152–53, 156
inflation rates, 80, 219n66
inoculations, 168; cost of, 79, 165, 166, 219n65; Quier's, 219n65; smallpox, 93–94, 164–67; yaws, 109
integrated plantations, 6–7, 18
intercropping, 8
Island sugar plantation (Jamaica), 39, 43, 57, 126
isolation (of the sick), 11, 15, 25, 37, 42, 43, 54–57, 132, 144, 154, 168, 185

Jack, Congo, 45, 49
Jackson, Robert, 81
jalap remedy, 168, 171
jobbing gangs, 18, 52
Johnson, Jessica Marie, 175
Johnson, John, 29, 34, 42, 127, 131, 206n43, 209n89
Johnston, Alexander, 78, 85, 86, 117–19
Johnston, Elizabeth Lichtenstein, 72

Kelly, Dominic, 24
Kelly, John, 98

Kendall plantation (Jamaica), 37
Kirkpatrick, James, 166
Knight, James, 82–84, 109, 176

labor diversification, 143
Laing, Malcolm, 116, 148
language of affliction/illness, 15–16, 46–48
laudanum, 173
Lavington's plantation (Antigua), 29, 30
Lawrence, Susan, 163
Lemprière, William, 215n26
Leong, Elaine, 165
leprosy, 107
Leslie, Charles, 74
Letters on the Cultivation of the Otaheite Cane (Caines), 107
Lewis, Matthew, 53
life expectancy, 145–46
lignum vitae wood chips, 119
Lind, James, 70, 250n97
Linnaean nomenclature, 157, 184
local networks of recipe exchange, 115
local provisions merchants, 41–42
Long, Edward, 17, 63–64, 81, 83, 162, 247n55
low (antiphlogistic) diet, 41, 43
Luffman, John, 218n58

machine metaphor, 12–13
managers (plantation): brutality, 3; correspondence, 60; diets for the sick, 5, 11, 43; efforts to impose medicines, 42, 127–32, 137; expediency, 15, 17; experiments, 40, 44; hospital arrangement, 89; hospital books, 9, 15; meddling, 105–24; racial capitalism, 19; role of, 2–3; rooms, 29; use of hospitals, 25, 37, 40, 133; warnings, 56
Mann, William, 59
manufactured medicines, 10, 96, 106, 107, 115, 126, 187
manuring, 8, 230n24
marginal work, 136, 137, 146, 237n140
Martin, Samuel, 13, 230n24
McClarty, Colin, 74–75

McKittrick-Adair, James, 94
measles, 144
measuring tools, 122–23
Medical and Miscellaneous Observations, Relative to the West India Islands (Williamson), 163
medical charlatan. *See* quack
Medical Observations and Enquiries, 73–74
medical periodicals, 73, 156, 157, 159
medical racism, 190–91
Medical Register, The, 71, 86, 215n28
medical vocabulary, 48
medicines/medication, 25, 118, 127–32, 154, 175, 185; antimonial, 111; bedside, 26; botanical, 113; clinical, 26, 90, 163; dangerous/enfeebling, 127–32; doses, 94; expensive, 77; expulsive, 133; forced, 42–43; manufactured, 10, 96, 106, 107, 115, 126, 187; measuring tools, 122–23; medical advice texts, 107; modern, 5–6, 26, 165; practitioners' trials, 171; smallpox inoculation, 79, 93–94; social, 120; standardization, 6; "take-this-for-that" approach, 90, 187; testing, 165; theft, 117; verification, 12. *See also* healers' drug administration
mercury: abuse, 249n90; in inoculators' preparatory regimens, 167; side effects, 128, 168, 177–78; venereal disease, 128, 167–68; yaws management, 131, 167–68, 177–78
Mesopotamia: healers, 102, 128, 138–39, 141–47; midwives, 138, 239n164–240; slavery, 195n8; sugar plantation, 102
microclimates, 96–97
military hospitals, 91, 154, 163, 164
Mintz, Sidney, 198n25, 201n45
Mitchell, Elise A., 166
modern medicine, 5–6, 26, 132, 165
Monro, Alexander, 161
morbidity, 7, 17, 60, 64, 154
Moreton, J. B., 126, 216n31, 218n59, 235n100
Morgan, Edmund, 13
Morgan, Marie, 13

mortality, 3, 7, 17, 45, 59, 60, 64, 154
Moseley, Benjamin, 68, 70–71, 215n27
movement minimization, 28–29
Mukharji, Projit, 198n26
mules, 83, 84

nature spirits, 55
negroe practice, 188, 252n10
Newton plantation (Barbados), 60
nourishment, 40–42. *See also* diets (sick people)
nurses, 104; in Bowie's experiment, 173–74; mixed-race, 135, 136; position, 136; yaws house, 108, 125

Obeah/Obi, 55–56, 233n79
Observations on the Dysentery of the West Indies (Moseley), 70
Ogborn, Miles, 26
overcrowding, 31–33, 36

pacers (animal), 83
Packard, Randall, 126
pain: denials of, 190; insensitivity to, 44, 208n80, 226n150; yamming, 48
patient neglect, 90, 93
Paugh, Katherine, 107, 109
Pearsall, Sarah, 34
Perrin, Philip, 116
Petley, Christer, 195n10
Phillipsfield plantation (Jamaica), 91, 92, 123, 125, 206n43
Pinkney, Robert, 98–99, 146
plantation management guides, 107–8, 122
Plummer, Thomas, 39
poisons, 32, 111, 112, 128, 204n24
positions of privilege, 135–36
postmortem, 176
practitioners, 11; attentiveness, 96–101; caseloads, 89, 93; circuit surgeons, 80–89; compensation, 77, 79, 99; competition, 79, 100, 106, 123–24; country, 188; enslaved-to-practitioner ratio, 80; expectations of, 96; expediency, 15, 17, 20, 94, 101; extensive travel, 82

practitioners (*continued*)
(*see also* transport animals); failure to investigate infectious ailments, 152–53; fee-per-head, 77, 79; fee-per-service, 76; greedy, 78; indifference, 93–94; knowledge, 97; loss of income, 75–76, 80; migration to Caribbean, 50, 66, 67; older, 224n131; paltry pay, 14, 101; racial capitalism, 19; rejection of local practitioners, 98; resident, 77, 99; seaport, 72, 156; smallpox inoculation, 165; "take-this-for-that" approach, 90, 187; transportation cost, 86; veteran, 78, 88; working conditions, 62, 65; workload, 155. *See also* experiments (trials)
Pringle, John, 70
productivity, 8, 18, 129; quotas, 13–14
protests, 11, 24
provision grounds, 57–58, 106, 134
punishments, 25, 37, 38, 45, 125, 130, 133, 141, 185
putrid effluvia, 32, 50
putrid sore throat, 47, 183, 187, 200n36

quack, 63–64
Quier, John, 94, 168, 219n65

race/racism, 96, 176–77; arithmetic of racial violence, 69; imperviousness, 157, 176; medical, 93, 190–91; mixed-race, 135, 136
racial capitalism, 19–20
racial difference, 188–89, 208n80, 226n150
Rankin, Alisha, 165
rationalization, 8, 19
rations (food), 41–43, 58, 144–45
Rawlins, William, 45
recipe: Cope's, 112–13; exchange networks, 114–15, 127
Rediker, Marcus, 198n25
red-pepper plant, 183, 184, 200n36
regimental surgeon, 66
reproduction, 6, 18–19, 159. *See also* childbirth; women (enslaved)
resident practitioners, 77, 99
rest (denial of), 27, 43, 45, 46, 53, 61, 147

Roberts, Carolyn, 55, 58, 202n7
Roberts, Eliza Chadwick, 222n99
Roughley, Thomas, 33, 123–24
Rule, John, 51
rum: Chamberlaine's experiments, 172, 185–86; rations for healers, 144–45
Rush, Benjamin, 42, 73–74

Sanderson sugar plantation (Antigua), 34, 131
sarsaparilla, 116, 148
Schaffer, Simon, 157
scurvy, 250n97
seaport medical work, 71–74
Seawell sugar plantation (Barbados), 33
sensory epistemology, 121, 124, 127
sesame seeds, 149
Seven Years' War, 8, 68, 70, 77, 116
Shapin, Steven, 157
Siena, Kevin, 32, 127
silence, 28, 53, 54
Simon plantation (St. Kitts), 41
single-room buildings, 32, 37
skin health, 49–50
slaveholdings: size of, 7, 106; booming increase in, 67–68; Tharp family's, 36
slave ship, 5, 65, 198n25
slave-trade abolitionism, 6, 34, 68
Sloane, Hans, 149, 242n5
smallpox, 47, 144
smallpox inoculation, 79, 93–94, 164–67
Smallwood, Stephanie, 69, 207n62
social (remedies) relations, 25–26, 54–58, 133–34, 140, 141, 146
sores, 50–51, 96–97, 107, 112
specifics, 11, 26
speech, 26–28, 53–54, 60, 127
spirits, 55, 120
Stephens, James, 200n36
Stewart, John, 89, 220n70, 221n83
Stewart, Neil, 247–48n63
stimulant diet, 41
Stirling, James, 67
St. Vincent hospital, 34
"Sugar Cane, The" (Grainger), 83, 242n5

surgeons: case histories, 156; circuit, 80–89; consequence of war-making, 64, 66–67; entries in hospital books, 91; income, 79; inoculations, 167; seaport work, 74; supervision, 68; yaws management, 110
surgeon's mates, 66, 67, 74
syphilis, 32, 204n31

Tacky's Revolt, 233n79
Taylor, Simon, 33, 36, 41, 52, 54, 75, 97–99, 174, 249n90
tetanus, 42, 172, 173, 175, 185
Tharp, John: construction of Good Hope's hospital, 34–36, 35; marriage to Gallimore, 34; slaveholding, 36
Thistlewood, Thomas, 37, 69, 70, 75, 111, 118, 217n44; exchanging recipes, 114; mercury pills, 128; Old Sharper's gourd, 120–22; yaws poisons, 112; yaws remedy, 110, 113
Thomas, Robert, 56, 87, 220n70
transport animals, 81, 84; copartnerships, 86–87; costs of, 82; feed, 85–86; horses, 81–86, 221n83; Jamaica's topography and, 84, 85; maintenance, 85–86, 88; mules, 83; pacers, 83; threats, 84–85
Treatise on Tropical Diseases and on the Climate of the West Indies, A (Moseley), 70
Treponema pertenue (bacterium), 32
Troup, Jonathan, 42, 46–48, 51, 57, 59, 69, 72, 78, 94, 121, 176; as assistant, 87–88; Canefield nurse's actions, 134, 135; case history, 158–62; diary, 83–84, 84, 86, 130, 161, 163; horse-keeping, 81–86
tuberculosis, 144
Turner, Sasha, 132, 160
Turney, Benjamin, 73–74, 99–100, 99

ulcers, 50, 51, 95–96, 112
uniformity, 12, 19, 40
urban hospitals, 163
U.S. health care system, 190–91

Van Heilen, John, 40, 43
Vassall, William, 77, 96–98, 126

Vaughan, Benjamin, 183
Vaughan, Samuel, 39
venereal disease, 33, 34, 37, 54, 111, 114; corrosive sublimate, 116; managers' remedies for, 127–31; mercurial remedies, 128, 167–68; poisons, 112; syphilis, 32, 204n31
ventilation, 33, 39
vocabulary of affliction, 47

wangla, 149, 150
Ward, J. R., 214n15
war-making, 64, 66–67, 75
warm baths, 173
Washington, George, 83
Wedderburn, John, 96–97
West Indian Garrison, 66
white homosociability, 88
Williams, Eric, 18
Williamson, John, 40, 74, 77, 78, 80–82, 87, 149, 150, 162–63, 170–71, 176, 189, 249n81
wine glasses, 123
women (enslaved), 18, 142; labor diversification, 143; mixed-race identity, 135; post-delivery rituals, 160. *See also* childbirth
Wood, Sampson, 60–61
worklogs, 18, 31, 91, 92, 187
worms, 176; cabbage-bark remedy, 120–21; cowhage, 9, 15, 168, 169; Guinea, 170
Wright, William, 67, 110, 172, 173, 175, 186

yawey ingredients, 118–19, 122
yaws, 4, 47, 58, 204n31, 247n55; Caines's text, 107; careful nursing, 173–74; Cope's recipe, 112–13, 119; crab, 140; first phase of, 112; herbal baths, 109; hog plum tree root, 6, 114; inoculation, 109; management, 110; managers' remedies for, 127–31; mercurial remedies, 131, 167–68, 177–78; poisons, 112; remedies, 109–16, 119, 128, 131; symptoms, 111–12; untreated, 32–33
yaws houses, 31, 59, 103, 111
young medical men, 63, 65, 68–70

Early American Histories

Matoaka, Pocahontas, Rebecca: Her Atlantic Identities and Afterlives
Kathryn N. Gray and Amy M. E. Morris, editors

To Organize the Sovereign People: Political Mobilization in Revolutionary Pennsylvania
David W. Houpt

Plain Paths and Dividing Lines: Navigating Native Land and Water in the Seventeenth-Century Chesapeake
Jessica Lauren Taylor

The Travels of Richard Traunter: Two Journeys through the Native Southeast in 1698 and 1699
Edited by Sandra L. Dahlberg

Making the Early Modern Metropolis: Culture and Power in Pre-Revolutionary Philadelphia
Daniel P. Johnson

The Permanent Resident: Excavations and Explorations of George Washington's Life
Philip Levy

From Independence to the U.S. Constitution: Reconsidering the Critical Period of American History
Douglas Bradburn and Christopher R. Pearl, editors

Washington's Government: Charting the Origins of the Federal Administration
Max M. Edling and Peter J. Kastor, editors

The Natural, Moral, and Political History of Jamaica, and the Territories thereon Depending, from the First Discovery of the Island by Christopher Columbus to the Year 1746
James Knight, edited by Jack P. Greene

Statute Law in Colonial Virginia: Governors, Assemblymen, and the Revisals That Forged the Old Dominion
Warren M. Billings

Against Popery: Britain, Empire, and Anti-Catholicism
Evan Haefeli, editor

Conceived in Crisis: The Revolutionary Creation of an American State
Christopher R. Pearl

Redemption from Tyranny: Herman Husband's American Revolution
Bruce E. Stewart

Experiencing Empire: Power, People, and Revolution in Early America
Patrick Griffin, editor

Citizens of Convenience: The Imperial Origins of American Nationhood on the U.S.-Canadian Border
Lawrence B. A. Hatter

"Esteemed Bookes of Lawe" and the Legal Culture of Early Virginia
Warren M. Billings and Brent Tarter, editors

Settler Jamaica in the 1750s: A Social Portrait
Jack P. Greene

Loyal Protestants and Dangerous Papists: Maryland and the Politics of Religion in the English Atlantic, 1630–1690
Antoinette Sutto

The Road to Black Ned's Forge: A Story of Race, Sex, and Trade on the Colonial American Frontier
Turk McCleskey

Dunmore's New World: The Extraordinary Life of a Royal Governor in Revolutionary America—with Jacobites, Counterfeiters, Land Schemes, Shipwrecks, Scalping, Indian Politics, Runaway Slaves, and Two Illegal Royal Weddings
James Corbett David

Creating the British Atlantic: Essays on Transplantation, Adaptation, and Continuity
Jack P. Greene

www.ingramcontent.com/pod-product-compliance
Lightning Source LLC
Chambersburg PA
CBHW030612230426
43661CB00053B/1955